W9-CON-536

Soldier Girls

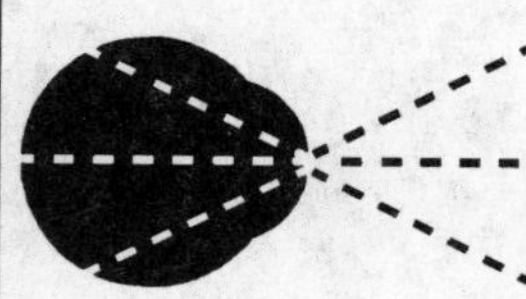

This Large Print Book carries the Seal of Approval of N.A.V.H.

Soldier Girls

THE BATTLES OF THREE WOMEN AT HOME AND AT WAR

Helen Thorpe

THORNDIKE PRESS
A part of Gale, Cengage Learning

GALE
CENGAGE Learning®

Farmington Hills, Mich • San Francisco • New York • Waterville, Maine
Meriden, Conn • Mason, Ohio • Chicago

Thorndike Press, a part of Gale, Cengage Learning.

Thorndike Press® Large Print Popular and Narrative Nonfiction.
The text of this Large Print edition is unabridged.
Other aspects of the book may vary from the original edition.
Set in 16 pt. Plantin.

LIBRARY OF CONGRESS CATALOGING-IN-PUBLICATION DATA

Thorpe, Helen, 1965-
Soldier girls : the battles of three women at home and at war / by Helen Thorpe. — Large print edition.
pages cm. — (Thorndike Press large print popular and narrative nonfiction)
ISBN 978-1-4104-7865-8 (hardcover) — ISBN 1-4104-7865-3 (hardcover)
1. United States. Army—Women—Biography. 2. Women soldiers—United States—Biography. 3. Afghan War, 2001—Women—United States—Biography. 4. Iraq War, 2003-2011—Women—United States—Biography. 5. Indiana. National Guard—Biography. 6. Afghan War, 2001—Campaigns. 7. Iraq War, 2003-2011—Campaigns. 8. Women veterans—United States—Biography. 9. Single mothers—United States—Biography. 10. Large print books. I. Title.
UB418.W65T56 2014b
956.7044'342092520973—dc23 2014049813

Published in 2015 by arrangement with Scribner, a division of Simon & Schuster, Inc.

Printed in Mexico
1 2 3 4 5 6 7 19 18 17 16 15

for John
with thanks

The Army National Guard, which has fallen short of recruiting goals during the prolonged fighting in Iraq, is trying new marketing beyond the traditional enticement of college tuition aid. New ploys include free hunting and fishing licenses, passes to state parks, more chances to get signing bonuses, and pink T-shirts bearing the words "Soldier Girl."

— from a compilation of news headlines
published in the *Wrench Daily News,* a
newsletter serving the 113th Support
Battalion, 76th Infantry Brigade

CONTENTS

AUTHOR'S NOTE

This book is a work of nonfiction. To report it, I spent four years interviewing the three main characters, as well as many other individuals. I supplemented those interviews with information from emails, letters, diaries, Facebook posts, Facebook messages, notebooks that the soldiers kept with notes about their missions, yearbooks that the soldiers brought home from their deployments, photographs, newspaper articles, court documents, medical records, therapists' notes, and a newsletter distributed to soldiers who belonged to the Indiana Army National Guard's Bravo Company, 113th Support Battalion, 76th Infantry Brigade.

Two of the main characters wished to use their real names in this book, and one did not. I refer to her by a pseudonym throughout the work, and also changed the names of her family members and friends. Other soldiers and family members whom I was fortunate enough to have a chance to speak with were offered the choice of whether to use real names or pseudonyms. When I did not have the chance to interview a particular soldier, I generally chose to use a pseudonym. The translator the soldiers worked with in Afghanistan, who presently works at a prison where many members of the Taliban are incarcerated, was afraid that using his real name would bring danger, and I have used a pseudonym for him as well.

Much of the dialogue is reconstructed, which is to say that it is accurate as far as the people who said those words or heard those words could recall when they spoke to me. Otherwise, all details are factual to the best of my knowledge.

I
Indiana, 2001–2003

1
Hooah!

Michelle Fischer had not yet reached twenty but she already knew how to find the National Guard Armory, a low-slung, modern-looking building made of red bricks with a green metal roof. It commanded a prominent seat beside the Lloyd Expressway, the main east–west thoroughfare that split the heart of Evansville, Indiana. People used the building as a landmark when they gave directions — other places along the Lloyd Expressway could be described as east of the armory or west of the armory. The recruiters who worked there had established many ways of meeting young people, and Michelle had swayed to pop music inside the vast blue gymnasium there at both her junior and her senior prom. She did not have the nerve to return and talk to the recruiters on her own, however, which was why she had badgered her boyfriend of six months into accompanying her. It was March 2001, and Michelle was eighteen years old. From her vantage point, the Indiana Army National Guard looked like the answer to a dilemma, which was that she found her circumstances dreary.

Michelle had thrust through a childhood full of neglect, making her both headstrong and vulnerable, and it was no accident that she had dreamed up the idea to enlist but required Noah Jarvis's steadying company to execute it. That was Michelle — audacious, needy, a little bit self-absorbed. Michelle was quite certain she knew what the Guard would ask of them in return: one weekend a month, two weeks every summer. Maybe they would also be asked to hem a swollen river with sandbags, or gather up the pieces of a town shattered by a tornado. She thought that was a price she might be willing to pay, in exchange for the prospect of leaving home.

Michelle did not look like a soldier. On the short side, buxom, a face framed by masses of long, curly, blond hair, with big brown eyes and a button nose, she brimmed with cherubic innocence, which made her mischievousness a constant surprise. She looked angelic but through her sluiced a prodigious appetite for naughty things such as boys and pot and punk rock music. Life rendered itself to her in contradictory ways, brackish and clear, bitter and honeyed; she had formed the habit of looking for what was funny in sad moments, and she had a laugh like a bell, loud and clear and ringing.

Michelle had spent her entire childhood in southern Indiana, mostly in and around Evansville, an industrial city tucked into a bend in the Ohio River. The rest of the Midwest had forgotten about Evansville so long ago it might as well have been southern, and the pace of life was slow. Vast barges heaped with black coal sank low onto the river, crawling past casino boats where people went to hazard their earnings. Michelle's father lived on the opposite shore, buried deep in the woods of Kentucky, in an air-conditioned trailer where he hoarded mementos and told unlikely stories. Everybody Michelle knew seemed bled of hope. She had grown up watching businesses shutter and jobs disappear and her mother slip into poverty and her siblings enthrall themselves with drugs. Ten months earlier, in the spring of 2000, when she had graduated from Evansville's Central High School, the theme of her commencement had been "Oh, the Places You'll Go!" So far, however, she had gone nowhere, and the year since she had finished high school had been dispiriting.

Thanks to her extraordinary intelligence, Michelle had excelled at school. In the mandatory journal that she kept for her psychology class, she had written that she had set her sights on going to Indiana University, one of the most prestigious colleges in the state. It had a beautiful tree-lined campus up in Bloomington, and demanding professors who had gotten their degrees from the Ivy League. For a while it had looked as though she might achieve that dream, for she had earned the right marks, and when she had taken the ACT she had scored 34 out of 36, which put her in the 98th percentile. Nobody else in her family had ever been to college, however, and Michelle did not know how to find the path that led to a fancy campus. Her mother lost factory jobs as often as she found them, and her father alternately drove a truck or got himself locked up in jail, and neither of her parents had set aside any money for college.

In the fall of 2000, Michelle had enrolled instead at the University of Southern Indiana, a commuter college that squatted beside another part of the Lloyd Expressway, to the west of the armory. She had borrowed the maximum possible amount in student loans, as she was paying her entire tuition bill by herself. As she began her college career, Michelle was sharing a one-bedroom apartment with her mother, working as a waitress at a steakhouse called the Golden Corral, and driving back and forth to classes in the Tank. That's what she named her 1994 silver Ford Tempo. It had been a gift from her father. A burly wreck of a man, he loved Michelle dearly, but he had never stuck with any of his four wives, nor had he safeguarded the economic well-being of his children. He had bought the car used for $2,000, and had given it to Michelle in lieu of paying the $40,000 in child support that he owed to her mother. Michelle's mother eked out a thin existence with occasional welfare checks, irregular jobs, regular packs of Marlboro Lights 100s, and a steady supply of Double Cola. After he bought the car for Michelle, her father had made her mother sign a letter saying she wouldn't sue him for the money that he owed, and then he had handed Michelle the keys. She liked to joke that she drove a $40,000 beater. The joke encapsulated everything about her childhood — what she had been given, what her parents had failed to provide, and the spark that let her laugh about it all, especially the parts that were not really funny.

Michelle had spent the winter of 2000 in the Tank, driving to and from her classes, her job at the chain restaurant, college parties, and the one-bedroom apartment she shared with her mom. Michelle smoked too much pot, went to too many keg parties, started dropping acid. In the spring of 2001, she learned that her standing in the University of Southern Indiana honors program had been thrown into jeopardy because she had been failing to show up for an algebra class that was held at nine o'clock in the morning. Somehow, she had taken a wrong turn. She knew where this road led, because she had watched various older siblings take it: you started off drinking too much and then you wound up battling a lifetime of addiction. Michelle wanted to leave all this behind. She wanted to stride across a pretty campus, she wanted to be assigned a room in a dormitory, and she wanted to take classes that were challenging. Yet she could not calculate out how to pay for her aspirations until she remembered the military recruiters who had visited the economics class she had taken during her senior year at Central High. They had handed out fake dog tags and spoken of true heroism. One recruiter had said the National Guard would send students to *any college in the state, free of charge.* With more than sixty armories, Indiana had one of the most robust National Guards in the country, and many of Michelle's fellow students had accepted the offer, which struck them as low risk. The country had been at peace for more than a decade, and the only serious conflict that had occurred in their lifetimes was the Persian Gulf War, which had been wrapped up in months. Plus, everybody in southern Indiana knew that the Guard did not go to war — if you wanted to see combat, you joined the regular army.

Michelle had not pursued the matter because she did not see herself as the military type. She thought of herself as a music-loving, pot-smoking, left-leaning hippie — not a soldier. By the spring of 2001, however, after almost a full school year of driving the Tank back and forth to the bleak campus of her commuter college, she found herself recalling the pitch made by the recruiters. She told her boyfriend Noah that she was thinking about signing up for the Guard and hinted that he should enlist, too. Noah was older than Michelle, albeit more adrift. After dropping out of college, he had slouched through a series of dead-end jobs — for a while he had driven an ice cream truck, and at another point he had sold doughnuts. Often he drank so much that when he woke up he could not remember what had happened the night before. Noah had gotten stuck in a side eddy, and the main current of life was passing him by. When Michelle suggested that he join the Guard, however, Noah confessed that he found the idea intimidating — he wasn't in very good shape, he said, and he wasn't sure if he would measure up as a soldier. But Noah was besotted with Michelle, and thought it would not be chivalrous to send his girlfriend off to talk to the recruiters alone.

It had been a grim and frigid spring. On a gray day with the temperature stuck down in the thirties, Michelle and Noah drove over to the armory in Noah's gray Chevy Astro van. They japed their way past the immense howitzer guarding the entrance to the building, pushed through the armory's double glass front doors, and turned right down the wide main hallway. Inside the recruiter's office, a height and weight chart hung on the wall, and posters urged BE ALL YOU CAN BE. There were two desks. Behind one sat a middle-age black man in a uniform. He was a sergeant first class and his name was Wilber A. Granderson. Michelle sat down in one of the two chairs facing him, and Noah sat down in the other. Michelle announced that they might enlist, but first they had some questions. Was it really true the Guard could give them a free ride to college?

Granderson had a generous smile. He confirmed that the Guard would pay 100 percent of their college tuition at any institution in the state if they signed up for six years of regular Guard duty, plus two years in the Individual Ready Reserve. While in the reserves they would no longer go to drill, but they could be called upon in an emergency. That was it, he said. An eight-year commitment. In return, he could offer: full college tuition, a housing allowance of $220 per month, and a kicker bonus of an additional $200 for each month they spent in school. Plus, he would throw in a onetime enlistment bonus of $8,000. And the Guard would pay off any existing student loans.

It was a lot of money. Michelle wanted to

make sure she understood the whole deal. What if she failed to make it to drill one weekend? She could make the time up, Granderson told her. What if she wanted to study abroad? Not a problem. She could simply add on an extra semester of drill time after she got back. The recruiter turned to Noah. What was on his mind? Noah wanted to know if a misdemeanor charge for possession of marijuana would be an issue. He could still sign up, Granderson replied, but first a specified amount of time had to elapse. While Noah could do the preliminary paperwork along with Michelle, he would have to wait several months before he could actually join the military.

That was the extent of their questions. Granderson told them to return with their birth certificates, and gave them a form to fill out that required all kinds of information about their backgrounds. That would take a while to pull together, Michelle thought — her family being so convoluted. After they left the armory, Michelle tallied up all the benefits Granderson was offering. Signing up for the National Guard would allow her to pay off her existing debt, realize her dream of transferring to Indiana University, quit her waitressing job, and move onto campus. She could be a real college student, living in a dorm, at a famous university. For that she would gladly surrender one weekend a month. Remembering the buff soldiers displayed in the posters on Granderson's walls, Michelle fantasized that joining the Guard could also help her lose weight — she could go to a great school and get in better shape at the same time.

Michelle and Noah returned to the armory to take a multiple-choice exam called the Armed Services Vocational Aptitude Battery. In a room filled with other potential soldiers, they sat down at neighboring desks, Michelle jazzed because she loved triumphing on standardized tests, Noah a wreck because he hated flubbing them. Afterward, Granderson phoned Michelle to discuss her marks. She had been two answers shy of a perfect score, he told her, and he rarely saw such good results. Granderson said she was leadership material, she could become an officer. He explained that joining the National Guard would give her limited options because of her gender. Over the preceding two decades, the percentage of the total army that was female had inched upward from 9.8 percent to 12.5 percent (and would grow to 15.7 percent in the decade to come). However, women were still banned from certain occupations. Specialties judged most likely to see direct combat — such as infantry and field artillery — remained restricted to male soldiers. And the main Guard unit that drilled in Evansville was field artillery. The only positions open to women in Evansville were slots in a small detachment that did support work. Michelle's choices would be limited to driving a truck, fixing a truck, or repairing broken weapons. Granderson saw a more rosy future ahead if Michelle would pledge herself to the military full-time. She was really smart, she could do military intelligence, as long as she joined the regular army, Granderson told her. Michelle enjoyed the flattery, but understood herself to be a nonconformist — taking orders would not come easily. She stuck with her plan to join the Guard.

Over the next several weeks, Michelle filled out various documents, including a form in which she swore that she had never been fired from a job nor ever been court-martialed. Noah promised to enlist as soon as he could. Michelle felt less alone after she dropped by the armory one day to learn how to march and bumped into Angela Peterson — Angela's younger brother had been in Michelle's class at Central High, and when they had been underage Angela used to buy them beer. Angela was a pretty girl with a heart-shaped face and a pixie haircut. She had signed up that spring, too.

Granderson told Michelle to report back at the end of the month, ready to take a trip to the closest military entrance processing station, down in Louisville, Kentucky, an hour and a half south of Evansville. When Granderson put her into a military vehicle bound for Kentucky, she found Angela Peterson already inside. The two of them shared a hotel room in Louisville, where they spent a lot of time doing push-ups. Every female recruit had to be able to do three regular push-ups, no knees touching the floor. When she had first shown up at the armory, Michelle could not do any, but she hated being bad at something, so she and Angela practiced every night.

At the military entrance processing facility, medical staff took Michelle's blood, asked her to pee into a cup, prodded her lymph nodes, and administered tests of her vision, hearing, and depth perception. She did her push-ups, as well as the requisite number of sit-ups, and then she performed a duck-walk in her underwear, so that the doctors could check for flat feet. On March 26, 2001, after she had passed all of the entrance requirements, a drill sergeant put a document in front of her. This was her formal contract, and after she signed her name, her commitment to the military would become binding. They told her to read the document out loud. "I, Michelle Fischer, do solemnly swear or affirm that I will support and defend the Constitution of the United States and the state of Indiana against all enemies, foreign and domestic; that I will bear true faith and allegiance to the same; and that I will obey the orders of the president of the United States and the governor of Indiana and the orders of the officers appointed over me, according to law and regulations," Michelle recited. "So help me God." That's pretty much all the document said. Michelle trusted that it meant what Granderson had suggested — twelve weekends a year, plus two weeks of annual training. She signed.

Michelle had a particularly close relationship with her mother, and when she thought about basic training, which she was slated to start in June 2001, she thought about it as their first separation. Yet Michelle had also been parenting herself for a long time. Her mother, Irene, battled crippling anxiety, the legacy of a childhood trauma. One day, when Irene was nine years old, her parents had been burning trash in the yard, and Irene had picked up a stick and begun playing with the fire. Her dress had ignited. She spent almost an entire year in the hospital, and the extensive burns left white ripples fanning across her back and arms. Irene grew into a fearful woman.

Michelle's father possessed the opposite sort of temperament. His given name was Wilfred, though he always went by Fred. He was a bluff, colorful ne'er-do-well whose storied life included many hard-to-believe moments, such as the time he shot his own stepson or the time he volunteered to grapple a declawed grizzly bear inside a wrestling arena. "My dad's the guy who sticks his hand up, and he's like, 'I'll wrestle it,' " said Michelle. "You know?" Before Irene had married Fred, she had been married to one of his cousins, and they had two children, Michelle's half siblings Tammy and Donovan. Meanwhile, Michelle's father had been married a total of six times to four different women: Twice he had married one woman, twice he had married Michelle's mom, and then he also married two other women one time apiece. It was by one of the other wives that Michelle's three other half siblings, Daniel, Ray, and Cindy, were conceived. After Michelle's parents had divorced for the second time, they had lived together for a third stint before they split for good. This last iteration of their relationship — the only one that Michelle can really remember — had ended one night while Michelle was in first grade, after her father had gotten drunk and belligerent, and her mother had called the police. Michelle had been sent to her aunt's house, and what she remembered most vividly about that evening was the brusque police officer who came to her aunt's door and asked if she could draw a picture of where her father kept his guns.

Michelle was the youngest child, and the only one her parents had had together. Like her half brother Ray, Michelle strongly resembled her father in physical appearance — she inherited his button nose and his laughing brown eyes — while the other children looked more like their mothers. All of them were heirs to a family history in which many men had served in the military: Michelle's paternal grandfather had driven tanks across France in World War II, and Michelle's father, one of her uncles, and her mother's first husband had all served during Vietnam. Only Michelle's uncle and stepfather actually saw combat, however; her father had spent those years locked up in various military prisons for repeatedly going AWOL, according to Michelle.

After he had left the military, Michelle's father had held a steady job for about a decade at a company called Swanson Electric. They manufactured motors. She remembered going to visit him once and being awed as she watched him lower an immense engine into a vat of varnish. After ninety years in operation, however, that company had closed abruptly, and Fred Fischer never again found such steady work. Meanwhile, Irene had worked as a bookkeeper for twenty-five years at an industrial recycling company called General Waste, but lost that job when General Waste also closed. Irene had started doing factory work instead, and in the process her earnings greatly diminished. Michelle attended four different elementary schools and three different middle schools, as they moved almost every year. They became visibly poor, and onetime friends shunned Michelle because she did not own the right sort of clothes. After Irene began working in a factory where she made rubber seals for car doors, she and her daughter moved into a particularly rundown trailer.

Irene was working the first shift, which meant that by the time Michelle woke up, her mother had already left. One day, while Michelle was in the middle of taking a shower, the water quit working, and she was stuck in the shower with no water and unrinsed shampoo in her hair. Michelle was eleven years old. She didn't know how to fix the water, or whom to call, so she just stayed home from school. At times, Michelle and her mother relied upon food banks — beef stew out of a can, dried mashed potatoes. Michelle's favorite movie was *Return to Oz.* Darker than the original, the movie depicts Dorothy unable to sleep, while the farm is about to fall into foreclosure. Dorothy is in trouble, and none of the adults around her can help — she is on her own. No matter how many times Michelle and her mother changed residences, Michelle rented that movie over and over again, and she found the act of repeatedly watching Dorothy endure her harrowing plights and come out all right in the end to be soothing.

Michelle harbored complicated feelings toward her father. She knew her precarious economic situation stemmed from his inability to provide support to her mother. She glowed when he bestowed his oft-wandering attention, but disliked the way he grew unpredictable after five or six drinks. She also became embarrassed by his garishness. One night, when she was invited to an awards ceremony at one of her middle schools, she felt excited about the prospect of bringing both of her parents to the dinner, as she rarely got to be with the two of them at the same time. Then her dad showed up at their trailer wearing short sleeves, and Michelle could clearly see the tattoo on his forearm, an image of a naked Indian squaw with particularly generous breasts. White trash, that's what the other students would think. Michelle announced that she felt sick, and they skipped the awards ceremony.

Beginning when Michelle was about fourteen, she and her mother started sharing various homes with a series of relatives. First they lived with one of Michelle's half sisters, and later they moved in with Michelle's half brother Donovan. Michelle had looked forward to sharing a home with Donovan — they had been close when she was small, back before he had joined the navy. While they were living with Donovan, however, Michelle's mother began working the night shift, and after Irene went to work, Michelle often watched Donovan do meth with a friend. The house Donovan had rented was an old, rambling place, and Michelle grew afraid of being alone there, since it creaked so much and had so many inscrutable corners. At the beginning of her sophomore year of high school, Michelle spent all of her school clothes money on a black Lab puppy that she named Potato. She threw tantrums when Donovan did meth around the dog, because she thought the stinky fumes would harm Potato.

After she got to Central High, Michelle announced that she was done with being the new girl — her mother could move again (and did), but Michelle would stay at Central. For the first time in her life, Michelle formed enduring friendships. In her freshman year, she hewed to a girl named Veronica. Like Michelle, Veronica had grown up poor, yet was smart and ambitious. Veronica was also wickedly funny, and Michelle admired her boldness. She thought it was cool when Veronica introduced her to pot. During her sophomore year of high school, Michelle and her mother began sharing a home with Michelle's maternal grandmother. In that house, Michelle was not allowed to use the microwave, not allowed to use the back door, not allowed to use the telephone. If she wanted to use the bathroom, she had to ask permission. And her grandmother made Michelle take Potato to the pound. Michelle figured that her grandmother, a strict Catholic, must have hated Michelle's father because he had divorced her mother not once but twice, and therefore hated Michelle, who so closely resembled him.

Partway through sophomore year of high school, Michelle and Veronica had a falling out. Michelle, now fifteen, attached herself fiercely to a boyfriend named Joe Hill, who lived less than a mile away from her maternal grandmother. Joe Hill wore black clothes and smoked Marlboro reds and looked like Sid Vicious. Despite his dangerous looks, Michelle found Joe Hill waiting for her faithfully in his gray Oldsmobile Cutlass Ciera in the parking lot at Central High School every single day when the bell rang. She could set her watch by Joe Hill. Together they discovered grunge, then punk rock, blasting the Ramones and the Sex Pistols. To memorialize their union, Michelle and Joe went to a photography studio and took a formal portrait: Joe spiked his black hair skyward and donned a Ramones T-shirt and a necklace of heavy chain links, while Michelle wore a choker made of ball bearings and a T-shirt that said PORN STAR. She looked like a lost angel, blown off course. Michelle's father proudly hung it up on the wall of his trailer.

During her high school years, Michelle

tried asking her father to wear long sleeves because the sight of his tattoos caused her mortification, but he just laughed. Eventually Michelle learned to laugh, too, even about his six marriages and the stints in jail, though she considered her family a dark kind of comedy. The one bright thread running through the otherwise gloomy tapestry was the bond she forged with her paternal grandparents, who lived in one home for the entirety of Michelle's childhood, and cherished her all their lives. Michelle spent many magic nights and weekends there, particularly after her mother started working at the factory. In the evenings, she could count on her grandfather to take out his banjo or guitar or violin — he played each of those instruments with equal virtuosity — and fill the house with music. Meanwhile, her strict, Bible-reading grandmother fed Michelle a proper meal and put her to bed at a set hour. Her grandparents provided all the safety she had ever known.

During senior year of high school, Michelle broke up with Joe Hill, although they remained friends. By this point, Michelle and her mother had moved into an apartment building called Maple Manor. The once-grand house, a ramshackle old redbrick mansion with a wraparound porch, had been divided into six apartments. Michelle and her mother shared a one-bedroom on the second floor, which featured fading fleur-de-lis wallpaper. Michelle's mother was still working nights and Michelle secretly dated a cocaine addict for a while but she started having bad panic attacks, which ceased only after she ditched the cokehead. She and Veronica made up and Michelle spent the rest of senior year partying with her best friend.

The following year, Joe Hill introduced Michelle to his friend Noah Jarvis — a fellow guitar player — and Michelle started dating Noah during the fall semester of her first year at the University of Southern Indiana. Noah was a lanky, six-three stoner with olive skin, dreamy brown eyes, brown hair, and a goatee. He played guitar in a local punk rock band named Crank Case. Methamphetamine, or crank, was ubiquitous in southern Indiana, and by this point, half of Michelle's siblings were hooked on it, but it wasn't something she wanted to sample. She and Noah mostly just got high. They hung out with Veronica and Veronica's other best friend, Colleen, who had both gone to Central High and were now both enrolled at the University of Southern Indiana, too. During their first year of college, Veronica and Colleen threw frequent parties in a raucous apartment they had furnished with old couches and band posters. Noah and Michelle listened to Pink Floyd a lot and talked about how much they hated the status quo. In November 2000, Michelle cast her first vote in a presidential election for Ralph Nader. In the tumultuous weeks that followed, as lawyers for Al Gore and George W. Bush debated hanging chads in Florida, some of Michelle's ardently Democratic friends castigated her for giving her vote to a third-party candidate. Michelle replied that she could see little difference between the two big party candidates. Politically, she tended to cataclysmic scenarios of redemption. In a strange sort of way, four months later, the same kind of thinking impelled Michelle to enlist. The two acts appeared to be at odds — until Noah Jarvis joined her unit, Michelle often wondered if there was one single other Nader fan serving in the entire Indiana National Guard — but in both cases, she had been trying to flee from what scared her most: abject hopelessness. She had voted for Nader because she wanted to upend the political universe, and she had signed up for the Guard because she wanted to upend her life. She wanted to run away from her lousy job and the easy classes and all the meaninglessness she found up and down the Lloyd Expressway. She wanted to escape her father's ruinous life and her mother's sad dysfunction. She wanted to get out of this forgotten place where good jobs evaporated and bad jobs drained the life out of people. She wanted to leave behind the booze and the pot and the meth. She wanted not to end up like her older siblings, with blurry tattoos and raging addictions. That's what she thought she was signing up for when she told Granderson that she would enlist: the opposite of what she knew, a way out.

Right before Michelle left for basic training, her half sister Tammy threw her a going-away party. Tamara, known as Tammy, held the party in her front yard. Noah showed up in a pair of blue jeans and a short-sleeved button-down shirt worn over a long-sleeved T-shirt. He slouched down low in a lawn chair, holding a beer in one hand and a cigarette in the other. Michelle's friends Veronica and Colleen dropped by on their way to another party. Most of her complicated family came, including her father, who drove up from Sebree, Kentucky, with his latest wife, a woman named Kathy. To celebrate Michelle's decision to enlist, Fred Fischer had gotten a new tattoo on his other forearm — a naked soldier girl. He showed it off proudly. She wore only boots and a helmet, but she carried a big gun. Michelle got falling-down drunk on Mike's Hard Lemonade and threw up in front of her church-loving grandmother. For years afterward, shame seared her at the thought of her grandmother watching her get so sloppy.

Michelle shipped off to basic training on June 4, 2001. Her mother drove her to the armory, and Noah came along to say good-bye. Michelle's mother broke down in tears, triggering Michelle to follow suit, and even Noah misted up. Then Michelle clambered into the van that would take her to the airport, where she boarded an airplane for the first time in her life and flew to South Carolina. She had dressed in her most beloved clothes: a faded pair of Paris Blues jeans, an orange Roxy surf hoodie, and a light pink athletic T-shirt that had once belonged to Noah. As soon as she arrived at Fort Jackson, however, she was told to put her civilian clothes away.

VICTORY STARTS HERE, the post's motto trumpeted. Fort Jackson was the army's busiest point of entry, where half the country's soldiers got their introductory training. It was hot and startlingly humid. Drill sergeants started yelling at the new recruits as soon as they got off the bus — Michelle had to drop and do push-ups right there in the parking lot — and quickly she became just another soldier in green, brown, and tan camo. She was issued four sets of battle dress uniforms, or BDUs, as well as a field jacket, and gray and black army workout clothes. She had to give up wearing her contact lenses — during basic, soldiers with bad eyesight were given identical brown plastic glasses. The glasses were so ugly that everyone called them birth control glasses, or BCGs, the idea being that nobody would have sex with you if you were wearing a pair.

Michelle had to wear her long hair pulled back into a bun or a braid; she was not allowed to tie it back in a ponytail. She was not allowed to use lacy scrunchies, fancy bows, barrettes with butterflies or sparkles or fake gems; she was not allowed to wear jewelry unless it was of a religious nature; she was not allowed to wear brightly colored eye shadow or visible lipstick. There was no time to put on makeup anyway. Suddenly there were acronyms for everything, and Michelle looked exactly like everyone else. In her BDUs and her BCGs, Michelle felt as though she had surrendered her entire identity. She found herself bitterly homesick and pined for home in the letters that she faithfully wrote to each of her parents. Michelle's mother lost every letter that her daughter sent, but Michelle's wayward father hung on to each one. He numbered the letters and kept them inside a red, three-ringed binder, along with the Valentine's Day cards she had drawn for him when she was a little girl. "I love you and making you proud is really important to me," Michelle wrote on June 17, 2001. Then she wished him a happy Father's Day.

At the point when Michelle mailed that letter, she was in the middle of the first three weeks of basic, known as the red phase, when the drill sergeants were introducing the idea of total control. The recruits had to make their beds perfectly, with sharp corners and no wrinkles. They had to keep their personal areas immaculate. They had to wake up in pairs in the middle of the night for CQ duty, which basically meant standing guard. The fundamental idea was to get new soldiers into the habit of following orders, no questions asked. There was an ice cream machine in the chow hall, but Michelle was not allowed to go near it. She was not allowed to talk during a meal. At one point, Michelle's mother mailed her photographs of the party at Tammy's house, and Michelle wrote to her father, "Mom sent me some pictures of my going away party, so I have a picture of me, you & Kathy together. But I'm not allowed to hang it up because you & I have beer in our hands! I'm not allowed to hang up pictures w/alcohol in them. So that eliminates just about every picture from that day. But I showed them to my friends and they all say we look so much alike it looks like I was 'picked out of your ass'! Go figure."

Basic training proved to be an astonishing fitness program, and Michelle shrank in size as fat turned to muscle. The army had different standards for soldiers depending on gender and age. Before she could graduate, Michelle had to be able to perform thirteen push-ups and forty-seven sit-ups, and she had to be able to run two miles in at least nineteen minutes and forty-two seconds. (By comparison, a young man her age had to do thirty-five push-ups, forty-seven sit-ups, and two miles in sixteen minutes and thirty-six seconds.) As the days went by she kept shaving time off her clocked runs. "I just finished my physical strength test," she wrote in her next letter to her father. "I missed my run time by thirty-five seconds . . . I am so mad at myself! I could have sucked it up and pushed myself a little harder. But I passed my push-ups and sit-ups."

She learned how to read a topographical map, use a compass, administer basic first aid, rappel, and four different ways to choke a person into unconsciousness. She learned how to do the low crawl and the high crawl. One night, while she was hustling across a field of sand on her knees and elbows, under a snarled maze of barbed wire, with fake bullets flying overhead, she realized she had outdistanced the rest of her peers. For a moment she flipped over and lay on her back, looking up through the barbed wire at the orange tracer rounds glowing across the black sky. She found the sight unexpectedly beautiful. Afterward, she discovered that so much sand had gotten down into the sleeves of her BDUs that her elbows were rubbed raw and bleeding.

The temperature climbed into the nineties, and the humidity hit 100 percent. They put on their uniforms and all their gear, and donned rucksacks that weighed thirty pounds, and marched for miles through swampy, furnace-like afternoons. "Beat the heat cause their ain't no heat like the Carolina heat 'cause the Carolina heat is hot! Hooah!" the soldiers had to chant before they were allowed to take a drink of water. Michelle was astonished at how profusely she sweat. Her dog tags left green stains on her breasts, and constantly snarled in her bra. Each of them had been assigned a "battle buddy," and they were told to look out for each other. Michelle was paired with a Haitian immigrant who almost never spoke. Instead Michelle grew close to other members of her platoon. She formed strong ties with three young women, Carson, Shea, and Lawlor, as well as two young men, Davidson and McDonough. It was always last names; that was how they knew each other. McDonough grew infatuated with Michelle, but Michelle remained faithful to Noah. To Michelle's surprise, the platoon chose her to represent them in a formal ceremony. "I was so flattered I almost cried," she wrote to her father. "Everyone in my platoon means a lot to me. We're still rough around the edges, but we're starting to act as a team."

On the first day of the white phase of basic training, drill sergeants herded Michelle and other trainees into a gas chamber. After they put on their masks, they were doused with tear gas. Then the drill sergeants ordered them to take off their masks, breathe in the tear gas, spell their names, and say their Social Security numbers. After the deliberate exposure, Michelle walked around outside in a big circle flapping her arms, with her eyes and nose streaming. They spent the next three weeks focusing on their M16 assault rifles. Until she entered the white phase of basic training, also known as the gunfighter phase, Michelle had only fired a weapon once. Back in elementary school, in an attempt to seek a greater closeness with her father, she had begged for permission to fire his shotgun. He had taken her outside of her grandparents' home, rested the gun on top of a cooler, and stood behind her to help catch the recoil. Now Michelle slept with her gun, did push-ups with it lying across her hands so that her lips kissed it when she bent toward the ground, used it as a weight during PT, and carefully took it apart and cleaned it and put it back together every night. She also spent hours and hours firing it. Unexpectedly, Michelle fell in love with shooting. Her experience of time became suspended, and half a day would slip by unnoticed.

Targets popped up, then disappeared, and she had only a few seconds to hit each one. They all carried instructions for how to unjam their rifles on pieces of paper tucked into the band of their helmets, and when the omnipresent sand fouled Michelle's rifle, one of the other soldiers would read the instructions to her out loud, so that she could get her rifle working again. Gradually, she grew familiar with the factors that affected her accuracy: whether she pulled or squeezed the trigger, how loosely or firmly she held her weapon, if her body was relaxed or tense. She decided that shooting was all about breath, for her shots varied wildly until she began relaxing her body and squeezing the trigger gently at the very bottom of her exhale. Then she qualified as a marksman.

Michelle learned how to operate a machine gun, how to dismantle a land mine, how to fire a grenade launcher, and how to throw a hand grenade. The real grenades felt unexpectedly heavy. Her drill sergeant told her she would blow herself up if she made a mistake, which made her clumsy with terror, but as she leaned against a wall clutching two grenades against her chest, a trainer standing beside her asked where she was from, and when she said Indiana, he brought up Bobby Knight. So then they chatted about college basketball while she pulled out the pins and threw the grenades over the wall, and she lobbed them far enough to survive. After that, the drill sergeants let the trainees have a rare day of freedom, when a band performed a rock concert. The afternoon ended badly when a soldier tossed a full plastic bottle in the air, causing a long silver arc of water to splash over the crowd. The drill sergeants made the entire crowd kneel down for the rest of the concert.

One week later, it was time for the last phase of basic, the blue phase: night ops and MREs. In the second week of August, Michelle and the rest of her platoon began the final test, a seventy-two-hour war simulation exercise. They rucked out in all their gear, hiked six miles, then started digging foxholes. The temperature climbed to a high of 99 degrees, although with 97 percent humidity, the sweat-drenched soldiers experienced a heat index of 107 degrees. That night, while Michelle was helping to unload MREs off a truck, lightning flared, and she finished the job wrapped in sheets of rain. Michelle slept in a leaky tent, curled up in a cloth sleeping bag, lying in a puddle. Sometime after the rain ceased, drill sergeants threw tear gas into her tent, and then at dawn, they hustled everybody into the foxholes. They were supposed to watch for an attack, but instead Michelle rested the edge of her Kevlar helmet on a post, closed her eyes, and slid into a lucid dream in which a drill sergeant leaped into the foxhole to berate her.

The following day, when the heat index hit 102 degrees, the merciless drill sergeants took them home by a more circuitous way, so that the foot march lasted nine miles instead of six. They finished by trudging through an enormous expanse of sand, where Michelle's calves began to burn and her hip began to ache and she fell farther and farther behind. She had developed a stress fracture in her hip due to the training exercises, although she did not know this yet; all she knew was that she could not keep up. Her friends Davidson and McDonough dropped back to make sure she finished the exercise, and toward the end of the hike, the two young men took her by the elbows and half carried Michelle across the sand. When they neared the barracks, they heard Survivor's "Eye of the Tiger" blaring over the intercom. "Had the guts, got the glory," reverberated across the post. "Went the distance, now I'm not gonna stop." Not her kind of music, but it meant the ordeal was over. As they lined up in formation, she saw that half of the newly minted soldiers around her were crying.

On August 16, 2001, Michelle put on her dress greens and marched to her graduation ceremony. She felt bold, able, ready for action. Her body had grown lean and she knew the name and function of every single part of her assault rifle. She had also proved to herself that she could survive nine weeks of separation from her mother, who drove all the way to Fort Jackson for Michelle's graduation. In the years since she had lost her bookkeeping job, Irene had grown antisocial, to the point where she rarely left the house except to go to work. Yet she had made the marathon drive — ten hours in a car with Donovan and Noah. Thrown by the unfamiliar surroundings of the busy military base, Michelle's mother appeared uncomfortable, wilting in her baggy shorts and T-shirt. She complained about the humidity, which was her way of voicing that she felt off-center, but Michelle was so happy to see her that she didn't care.

Noah arrived wearing black Doc Martens, black jeans, and a T-shirt that said DR. FUSION'S FUNK BAND. Michelle's mother snapped a photograph of the pair of them standing together — Michelle in her crisp dress greens, Noah in his grunge attire. The difference in their clothes spoke of how far Michelle had traveled from her old self in only two and a half months. She had called Noah every single week, but when she first saw him in person, she could not stop giving him hugs. Donovan wore a sleeveless orange shirt with gaping armholes that let him sweat unimpeded through the blazing day. He had been the first of their generation to put on a uniform: Michelle had been five or six years old when he had joined the navy. She had missed him terribly when he left. He had sent back dashing pictures of himself in his dress blues, but after he was discharged Donovan had come home aimless, lacking a clear future, and then came the losing battle with meth. Michelle knew it had to be hard for Donovan to set foot on an active duty post and loved that he had come to celebrate her accomplishment.

The following day, Michelle had to report to Aberdeen Proving Ground, on Chesapeake Bay in Maryland, for the second half of her training. She was going to spend the next thirteen weeks at Aberdeen, studying to become a weapons mechanic. Noah had volunteered to drive her there. On August 17, 2001, they loaded Michelle's belongings into his rental car: her civilian identity folded up inside her backpack (Roxy hoodie, Paris Blues jeans, Noah's old pink T-shirt, flip-flops), and her military self packed into a dark green duffel bag (two pairs of shining black boots, black wool socks, BDUs, PT clothes, white athletic socks, sneakers, underwear, sports bras). Nobody else she knew from Fort Jackson was coming with her to Aberdeen, and Michelle said goodbye to all of the people she had just grown close to. Then she said goodbye to her mother and her brother. She and Noah headed north on I-95.

Nine hours away, Aberdeen Proving Ground was where the army and the marine corps trained their weapons mechanics. Michelle had elected to become a small-weapons mechanic — a 45B, in military shorthand, which everybody pronounced as "forty-five Bravo" — because it seemed better than becoming a truck driver or a truck mechanic, which were the only other job specialties open to her at the armory in Evansville. She would spend the next thirteen weeks learning how to take apart and put back together every small weapon used by the army. Noah dropped Michelle, her backpack, and her duffel bag off at the building that housed the post's command. He teared up as they said good-bye, and hating to see the pain she was causing him, Michelle cut their farewell short. She ducked inside the building, then caught sight of Noah through a window; as he drove off, she saw him execute a sad salute in her direction.

When Michelle checked in at the post's command, a drill sergeant introduced her to a short, heavyset white girl wearing black glasses. He told the girl to show Michelle to the barracks. The other young woman had already completed most of her time at Aberdeen. She explained to Michelle that the female barracks were under construction, and for the time being women were being housed in a restricted hallway in an otherwise all-male barracks. There were not very many women there. At Fort Jackson, Michelle had belonged to a company that had included roughly equal numbers of men and women, but at Aberdeen there were about one hundred soldiers in Alpha Company, 16th Ordnance Battalion, 61st Ordnance Brigade, and on the day she arrived, Michelle became the company's fourth female. As they walked to the barracks, the other woman looked Michelle over, noticed her curvy figure, long blond hair, face still shining with innocence. "They are just going to love you," she announced drily.

The female soldier escorted Michelle down a hallway of white cinder block and white linoleum to the small room that she would now share with Julieta Mendoza, a Latina soldier from New Mexico. Mendoza would become Michelle's closest friend at Aberdeen. Everybody went by their last names, and Michelle never learned the first names of the other women who lived on their hallway: Jackson, an African American soldier from Florida, and later Nguyen and Cordero, who were Vietnamese American and Native American, respectively. Soldiers arrived and departed from Aberdeen at staggered intervals, and over the thirteen weeks that Michelle spent there, the number of women in the company would rise to ten, but women would always remain a scarce commodity.

The drill sergeants were vigilant and fearsome. They inspected rooms at all hours, and Michelle and Mendoza learned to keep theirs spotless. The most alarming drill sergeant was a woman who could veer with astonishing swiftness from likable into what Michelle called "bitch mode." She ripped their rooms apart, even tossing the ceiling tiles to check for contraband cigarettes. The female soldiers took turns cleaning the bathroom and the hallway. Once a week, one of them would sweep and mop the white linoleum floor, and then polish the floor with an enormous buffing machine. When it was her turn, Michelle put on headphones and cranked up Incubus, her favorite band. At night, when they did CQ duty, sometimes Michelle could not resist putting her head down on her arms and closing her eyes, even though she knew she would pay a penalty if the drill sergeants caught her napping. There was a square white telephone on the desk that was only supposed to be used in an emergency, but bored soldiers often used the phone to order Chinese food or pizza, or to sneak phone calls to friends. Michelle had not reported her hip injury until she arrived at Aberdeen because she had feared being "recycled," or having to start basic all over again. The drill sergeants at Aberdeen hassled her about being unfit, saying she shouldn't be there at all, but they sent her to physical therapy and let her continue.

The rest of the female soldiers in her company were studying welding or maintenance of military vehicles, and when her weapons classes began Michelle discovered that she was the only woman in the room.

The other students were National Guard, regular army, marines — but all men. The instructors handed out manuals with yellow paper covers and mimeographed sheets. They began with the fundamentals, then worked their way through each one of the guns jointly used by the army and the marines. They started by studying the M16 assault rifle that Michelle had just learned to shoot, followed by the .50-caliber machine gun, and an automatic grenade launcher. Michelle memorized the parts of each gun and soon became fluent with the workings of trigger mechanisms and firing pins. She excelled on tests, which infuriated a highly competitive army soldier from Illinois who vied ferociously with her for top marks. Michelle often outscored the gung-ho soldier, but when it came time for the class elections, the other students voted him their leader. Michelle got it. She wasn't part of the club — you had to be male to belong.

In the classroom, Michelle could not earn full respect from the male soldiers, but outside of the classroom, she could not escape their attention. Even when she slouched around the barracks wearing a pair of baggy sweatpants and a gray T-shirt that said ARMY in block letters, male soldiers fell over each other to compete for her favor. Soldiers were expected to look sharp, and at first Michelle stayed up late wearing a headlamp, struggling to press the wrinkles out of her uniform, but then two different male soldiers declared they really liked ironing and volunteered to press her uniform for her. The help allowed Michelle to focus on her boots. In the common room where everybody gathered in the evenings to watch television, other soldiers vied to teach her how to use a heat gun to open up the pores in the leather to get that glassy shine.

Of her many suitors, the most assiduous was Alfred Turner, a handsome, sweet-talking soldier from North Carolina. Alfred was nineteen years old, African American, with mahogany skin, a muscular body, dark brown eyes set wide apart, full lips, a pencil mustache, and a radiant smile. He had signed up to serve in the army reserves, and was studying the maintenance of Bradleys. Alfred had a sentimental nature, and sought opportunities to prove his devotion. Where the women's hallway intersected with the rest of the building, a large sign announced in red letters FEMALE SOLDIERS ONLY. Failure to comply would result in disciplinary action according to the Uniform Code of Military Justice, warned the sign. This did not stop Alfred from sprinting down the hall to slip love notes decorated with hand-drawn flowers underneath Michelle's pillow. He called the sprints "night missions," and conducted them while other soldiers gathered in the common room.

As the weeks slipped by, Michelle slowly warmed to the sweet-talking soldier from North Carolina. She intended to remain faithful to Noah, but as Alfred waged his fervent pursuit, she began to question how long she would be able to hold out. Alfred was spectacularly handsome — "he was easy on the eyes," Michelle would say later — as well as persuasive. During study breaks, they began sitting together in a small wooden gazebo, where Alfred crooned to her, singing amorous lyrics from R&B songs while listening to the originals on his Discman. One day, Alfred presented Michelle with a tiny silver key, possibly taken from his luggage, upon which he had scratched a homemade engraving of a valentine. It was the key to his heart, he said. Alfred's attention caused Michelle's self-esteem to soar and made her longing for Noah dwindle. Realizing that she was not going to be able to honor her commitment, Michelle broke up with Noah in a letter, then stole secret moments with Alfred. They secluded themselves in the laundry room, one of the few places on the base where they could achieve any sort of privacy, and held trysts while washing their clothes. Michelle took a ridiculous photograph of Alfred with a French fry stuck up his nose and hung it inside her wall locker.

In the middle of their nascent romance, Alfred told Michelle that he was going to leave the reserves and join the regular army. He loved the military, he said, he had found his calling; he wanted to serve in the army full-time. He made the change while they were at Aberdeen. Alfred had arrived there before Michelle, and he finished his training at about the time Michelle reached the midway point of her thirteen weeks. Alfred was ordered to leave for a US Army base in Germany, but first he went home to see his family in North Carolina. He called Michelle frequently on the CQ phone, once causing a ruckus when a drill sergeant answered. On September 7, 2001, Alfred wrote Michelle a steamy letter. He used a stamp that said LOVE with a red rose where the O should have been, drew roses twining up and down the borders of the letter, and told her that he saw her face every time he closed his eyes. He described listening to a voice mail Michelle had left for him over and over again, and apologized for getting her in trouble by calling on the CQ phone. He also enclosed a calling card so that they could spend more time on the pay phone. Mentioning a memorable interlude in the laundry room, he wrote: "Hooah!" He promised to visit Aberdeen at some point, although coyly he refused to say when.

Alfred's letter arrived during the week when Michelle was tackling her fourth gun. She had already mastered the rifle, the machine gun, and the automatic grenade launcher. Now she had begun studying the M9 semi-automatic. On a carefree, Indian summer kind of day, Michelle had all the pieces of a 9mm laid out across her desk when a drill sergeant named Mark Reed burst into the classroom. Reed was a thirty-six-year-old noncommissioned officer (NCO) in the marine corps, with olive skin and chiseled features. One week earlier, he had taught the class how to operate the .50-caliber. Now Reed appeared jangled. A plane had just crashed into the World Trade Center, he announced. Other planes had been hijacked, too, and one was in the air somewhere over Pennsylvania. The base represented a potential target. Reed told the students that if they heard anything unusual, they should jump out of the window and lie down close to the building. Then he left.

Michelle looked down at the pieces of the 9mm strewn across her desk. Should she reassemble the gun? But the training models were held together with wire and pins, and she had no bullets. The absurdity of her situation struck Michelle: she was a trained soldier on a military base studying weapons, and yet she did not have a gun that would fire. Why did Reed want her to jump out of the window and lie down next to the building? That seemed like a dumb thing to do. Michelle felt unarmed, defenseless. When the instructor released them for their midmorning break, the students spilled out of the room. Many of them rushed to the bank of pay phones over by the vending machines. Michelle stood in line waiting to call her mother, but the base command turned off the pay phones before she got her chance. They had decided that it might be a security risk to let anyone call out. This left Michelle rattled. So did the increased security measures — drill sergeants organized night patrols and had everyone sign in and out at the entrance to each building.

That evening, a crowd gathered in the common room to watch the impossible images — the passenger planes flying too low, the shuddering collapse of the towers. The room filled with noise as the soldiers hollered army chants and thundered, "HOOAH!" The weird energy in the room disturbed Michelle as much as the unbelievable images on the television screen. All that billowing dust met by this angry glee. Why were her classmates cheering? She felt so afraid that she didn't even know she was afraid and instead had the unsettling sense that the scene around her had become surreal. Michelle felt cut off from the other people in the room, as if they were walled off behind glass. Money for college, a viable future — that's all she had meant to sign up for. But as she watched the first tower fall and then the second one, and saw smoke pouring out of a hole in the Pentagon, she saw that she was also watching the collapse of her pretty expectations. The notions she had cherished in the spring, when she had brought Noah along to talk to the recruiters — the idea that they would upgrade their lives while also getting in better shape and risking nothing essential — now appeared vain and foolish. Her future seemed dim and freighted and hard to discern, but she could see already that it would be nothing like what she had imagined.

2
Don't Worry About Being a Female

Debbie Helton regarded herself a daddy's girl, and her father had been a drill sergeant in the US Army. Seeking to emulate him, she had joined the Army National Guard when she was thirty-four years old, and by the fall of 2001, at age forty-nine, she had become one of the longest-serving women in the Indiana National Guard's 113th Support Battalion, based in Bedford, Indiana, where she was a weapons specialist — 41C ("forty-one Charlie"), fire control. Debbie could make the big guns on a tank shoot straight. She could also make grown men shrink with her smuttiness, and she had no problem drinking beer in the morning. She had been one of the pioneers who had integrated the unit, back when women were first allowed to join, and she had always gotten along seamlessly with the men who surrounded her — she was not the type to mutter if a guy started talking about anatomy.

Over the years, Debbie came to play a

maternal figure to most of the men in the unit, and to the growing number of women who served alongside them. Debbie was benevolent, chatty, kind. She had ivory skin covered in faint freckles; prominent cheekbones set high in a square face; short, curly dark brown hair that she often pinned back with barrettes; and a tall, spare frame. People called her Olive Oyl. She was a softball fanatic, a perennial volunteer, cheerful, buoyant. She took care of everybody else. Debbie liked to talk, though she rarely said anything personally revealing, perhaps because she did not consider her interior world important, and she had a way of constantly bestowing affirmation on others. She called other people "honey" or "dear" or "sweet pea." If the 113th Support Battalion had a den mother, it was Debbie Helton. And being in the National Guard gave Debbie what some people found at church — a community, a way to connect to a larger circle, a means of submerging herself in a group that she held in high esteem.

That was Debbie on drill weekends. In her civilian life, she managed a beauty salon inside a department store at one end of a shopping mall. The department store was called L. S. Ayres. Debbie lived in Bloomington, Indiana, where she had grown up and was now raising her daughter. In addition to managing the salon, she also saw clients for waxing or electrolysis. Once a month, she drove up to Indianapolis to confer with her boss, who lived and worked out of Fort Wayne, Indiana — they would each drive to the L. S. Ayres store in Indy, meeting halfway.

On the morning of September 11, 2001, Debbie left her house around nine, as the drive to Indy took roughly an hour. At about 9:15 a.m. she was heading northeast on Highway 37 in the gold 1990 Cavalier she had bought used after she had enlisted in the Guard, and could finally afford a vehicle, listening to the *Bob & Tom Show.* A person had to have a sick sense of humor to enjoy the syndicated comedy show, but it was Debbie's main source of news. That morning the hosts ripped into the idiot who had accidentally flown his plane into an iconic part of the New York City skyline. The hosts were still apologizing for their misreading of the terrorist attack when she got to Indy. Her boss asked if she needed to leave. "No, I didn't get a phone call," Debbie replied. "I have a feeling we will have some type of involvement going forward, but I don't know what or when."

Debbie was mesmerized by the idea of firefighters running up all those stairs. She also wore a uniform, she also strove to rescue. She wondered if she would find a call from the Guard on her home answering machine, but when she got back to Bloomington, no call had come. That was disappointing to her — she would have liked to be needed. Her regular monthly drill weekend fell four days later. When she arrived at the armory in Bedford, she found the 113th Support Battalion's Bravo Company in a tumult. People were milling around, tasks abandoned. She heard a fellow Guardsman say that maybe the active duty troops would go, maybe the Guard would assume responsibility for security in the United States. They talked about the fact that Bill Clinton had just finished closing bases. If there was a war, the regular army would be stretched thin. The uncertainty assailed the unit in disparate ways — emotionally, they were splintering. Some of the younger guys feared being left out of the action. "Let's join the marines," Debbie heard one urge another. More settled members of the Guard worried about being sundered from spouses and children, while others expressed anxiety about the danger of a deployment. Debbie herself did not chafe. She thought she would find whatever sacrifices might lie ahead infinitely more satisfying than her job at the beauty salon.

Debbie had acquired ideas about devotion and selflessness from her parents. She idolized her father, a warm and attentive man who worked construction and had allowed her to follow him around on job sites, making mortar, carrying hod, toting bricks. She always spoke kindly of her mother, but without the same degree of adoration, suggesting a hidden rift. Debbie's mother battled anorexia and addiction to prescription pills, and Debbie found her father a more reliable source of emotional support. When she had declared that she wanted to learn how to shoot a gun, back when she was a teenager, he encouraged her to take a formal class at the rifle range at Indiana University, and then he gave her a .22. She spent most afternoons at the quarry, dropping plastic containers into the deep, cold water, and perforating them until they tilted from view. Most of her friends were boys, but she was the best shot of them all.

Debbie graduated from high school in 1971, and one year later she married her high school sweetheart. Her husband persuaded Debbie they should have children, then started an affair while Debbie was pregnant, according to Debbie. After Debbie gave birth to their daughter, Ellen Ann, she and her husband divorced. He married the other woman, had another daughter, and got another divorce. Debbie would shoulder the cost of rearing their child alone. In 1975, when Ellen Ann was one, Debbie looked up the nearest military recruiting station in the phone book, imagined offering herself to the army. She was twenty-three. The recruiter, a uniformed soldier in his forties, rejected her as soon as he heard about Ellen Ann. Really and truly, he said, the military does not recruit single parents. Debbie had imagined that the military would receive her gladly, and left staggered.

A practical person, Debbie scouted for another way to support herself and her child. Growing up, Debbie had cut hair for all the boys in the neighborhood — it had started when her best friend, Jim, came to her and said he wanted to keep the money that his father had given him to pay for a haircut. Debbie's grandmother worked as a cosmetologist at Redken Laboratories, making color mixes for hair dye. She suggested that studying electrolysis would provide a guaranteed income, and it would take only one year. "That sounds like fun," Debbie responded. "I like working with my hands, I like working with people." Good-humored, stoic, practical — that was Debbie. If she experienced anguish at being asked to trim her dreams, that was never articulated.

Debbie finished her cosmetology degree in 1976. She found a job working for a woman who ran an electrolysis business, then started her own. She lived frugally. Debbie and her daughter shared a two-bedroom efficiency apartment, and Debbie got around town by walking or by bus. She supplemented her income by waitressing at a local bar called Time Out. A coworker recruited her to join a local softball team, and the two of them played together in the outfield. One evening, her coach's brother dropped by to watch the game. How cute is that guy, Debbie thought. To her surprise, Tony sought her out after the game. He was suave and good-looking — "kind of like a Greek god," Debbie told friends — and mentioned that he was serving in the army. Later he stopped by the bar where she worked a few times, and flirted with her some more. Tony's charm bamboozled Debbie, leaving her starstruck. One evening, Tony seemed loath to part from such a rapt audience.

"Are you going my way?" he asked.

"I wish!" Debbie replied.

So Tony asked her out on a date. He was five years younger, and Debbie assumed the relationship might be brief, but he never broke it off. After Ellen Ann turned three, Tony and Debbie married, and two years later, Tony legally adopted Ellen Ann. By then, Tony had left the army and had started working at the sheriff's department. When Tony lost that job, however, he did not seem in a hurry to find another. He loved material things, and while unemployed — during which time Debbie supported all three members of the family — he bought aquariums, rare fish, fancy cologne, gold jewelry, according to Debbie. After several years of this, Debbie confronted her second husband.

"You've either got to work or you've got to go," she said. "Because you're expensive."

Tony moved out when Ellen Ann was eight, although they stayed in touch. Looking for a more consistent income, Debbie landed the job at the salon at L. S. Ayres. She earned $110 a week. Debbie's best friend, T.J., was also a single mother. Often Debbie went to the bar where T.J. worked — it was called Shipwrecked Jimmy's, and T.J. had to wear a ruffled top and tight shorts with an anchor on her bottom. One evening, T.J. introduced Debbie to a friend named Jim May, a member of the National Guard. "Oh, I wanted to do that," Debbie said. "I tried to sign up for the army, but they told me I couldn't. They won't take single moms."

The National Guard would take her, Jim May said. But she had to be under thirty-five. From that point forward, when Debbie ran into Jim, he asked if she had signed up. On July 11, 1986, Debbie turned thirty-four. She steeled herself for another rejection and returned to the same recruitment office she had visited a decade before (which recruited for the Army National Guard as well as the regular army). A recruiter explained that if she gave up custody of Ellen Ann, then she could enlist in the Guard, as May had suggested. Training would force a separation from her daughter of anywhere from six months to a year, depending on her job specialty, but then all she had to do was show up for drill one weekend a month and two weeks in the summer.

Ellen Ann was thirteen going on fourteen and when her mother raised the possibility of living with her grandparents, she responded with enthusiasm. Ellen Ann seemed to think the new arrangement would involve the suspension of parental authority. Her grandparents lived close by, and Ellen Ann would not have to change schools. Debbie made certain to underscore that she didn't really want to give her daughter away. "This is a legality," Debbie told Ellen Ann. "You've still got Mommy." Tony opposed the idea, saying he didn't think Debbie could make it through boot camp. "You're too old!" he told her. Debbie's mother said, "Well, if you really want to . . ." But her father encouraged her. "You've wanted to do this for so many years," he said. "You should sign up." The thought infused Debbie with a renewed sense of purpose. The extra income would help, too — and she craved travel. Sometimes mechanics from the 113th Support Battalion flew to Germany to maintain vehicles for the regular army. She wanted to fly to Germany. She had never flown anywhere overseas.

Debbie started running to get in shape. Right after the July Fourth holiday — one week before her birthday — she went to the closest processing station, in downtown

Indianapolis, and said she was ready to sign up. A nurse took down her vital statistics. "You don't weigh enough," the nurse pronounced. The scale said that Debbie had dropped to 110 pounds. At five feet eight inches she was supposed to weigh at least 113 pounds, according to the height and weight chart. The nurse said to come back after she gained some weight. "I have to sign up before July eleventh or they won't let me in!" cried Debbie. The nurse mentioned an old army trick: go home and eat bananas. Debbie returned the following week and stepped back onto the scales.

"Tell me it's a hundred and thirteen," she begged.

"It's a hundred and thirteen," the nurse said.

Debbie borrowed her parents' car to visit the National Guard armory in Bedford, Indiana. She learned that the jobs that were open to women in the 113th were office work, cooking, or fire control. She chose fire control, because she had always liked guns. In the fall of 1987, after Ellen Ann had started eighth grade, Debbie shipped off to Fort Jackson, South Carolina, where her father had done his basic training. There were forty women in her dorm, and she was the oldest. A few were as young as eighteen or nineteen; most were in their twenties. Debbie fell into the category expected to perform the fewest exercises; to graduate, she only had to complete nine push-ups and thirty-four sit-ups, and run two miles in twenty-three minutes and six seconds. But she kept up with the others out of pride. And when it came to shooting, nobody could touch Debbie. "I can see you've done this before," one of the instructors said after her first day on the range. She had to get twenty-three out of forty to pass; she had scored in the high thirties. The instructor said he thought she still had room to improve and taught her how to coordinate her shooting and her breath. Then Debbie got a perfect score, forty out of forty. She was the only woman to make "expert"; the rest were ranked "marksman" or "sharpshooter." When the drill sergeants couldn't find fault with Debbie's performance, they hazed her about her age. "What's wrong with you?!" a drill sergeant yelled at a young woman who could not keep up with Debbie. "You're nineteen years old, you're going to let her pass you? She's thirty-five! She's a granny here!" After that, they called her Granny Helton.

Back in school, the other kids had called her Two-by-Four, Rail, Olive Oyl. Well, I am skinny, she had told herself. Now she said, Well, I am old. Debbie found basic training harsh physically but not mentally. She never crossed the drill sergeants; it only resulted in extra push-ups. Instead she tried to fit herself seamlessly into the whole. Debbie watched the younger recruits squander energy in rebellion; she found the time went easier when she aligned herself with the commander's overarching goals. When punishments befell Debbie, it was generally for wrongs enacted by her bunkmate, Kathy, a perpetually disorganized young woman who jumbled her tasks and could not figure out how to reassemble her weapon. Kathy made her bed sloppily, and both of their beds got ripped up. The girl eventually confessed to Debbie that she came from a home that had involved battering. She may have had a learning disability, Debbie thought; Debbie showed Kathy how to make a bed with tight corners, how to organize the parts of her weapon as she broke it down. "Get yourself a pattern," Debbie coached. "Don't scatter the pieces; you're more likely to make a mistake. Lay it out in a certain order."

Halfway through basic training, Ellen Ann wrote to say that her grandparents were mean. Debbie phoned home. It seemed that once Debbie's parents had assumed full responsibility, they had forbidden Ellen Ann to go to parties, or to go out with a boy, or to go to movies.

"I told her, 'Mom always let me do that!' " said Ellen Ann. "When are you coming home?"

Debbie could only stay on the telephone

for three minutes. She asked Ellen Ann to put her grandmother on the phone.

"It's okay for her to go to the movies, Mom," Debbie said. "And I don't mind if she goes to parties with her friends."

"Well, I just wasn't sure," said Debbie's mom. "Your father and I just weren't certain."

Debbie figured that of all the things that could go wrong, this was not the worst — her daughter would survive a little overprotection. Years later, however, Ellen Ann revealed that while her mother was gone she had snuck out of her bedroom window and had run wild, getting into the kind of trouble a mother would have wanted to shield her fourteen-year-old from experiencing. But Debbie knew nothing of this, and envisioned Ellen Ann leading an especially quiet life. When Debbie returned home for Christmas, her father told her, "I am so proud of you. I knew you could do it the whole time." Even Tony seemed impressed. Ellen Ann looked taller and curvier and more mature; the difference caught Debbie by surprise.

In January, Debbie reported to Aberdeen Proving Ground, in Maryland, to study the army's big guns. At Aberdeen, Debbie learned the mechanics of scopes, gun tubes, and what to do about parallax. She worked on howitzers, mortars, and the large guns up in the rotating turrets of tanks. Debbie found the big guns romantic. Leveling a howitzer made her feel important in a way that she had never felt at the beauty salon.

Back in Indiana, Debbie resumed parenting Ellen Ann full-time, and joined the 113th Support Battalion's Bravo Company, which drilled in Bedford. The previously all-male unit had just opened to women. At various times in US history, women had taken up positions on the battlefield — during the Revolutionary War, Mary Hays McCauley famously picked up the rifle of her fallen husband at Monmouth and began firing at the British. Generally speaking, however, the armed forces had operated on the principle that women could serve their country but only men should be asked to experience combat. During World War I, World War II, the Korean War, and the Vietnam War, every branch had restricted the types of jobs that women could hold in battle zones with the aim of preventing women from seeing war firsthand in any role other than that of nurse. After Vietnam, however, the military's attitude had shifted. The women's rights movement had transformed ideas about the roles of women generally, and Vietnam had made the idea of conscription intensely unpopular. The US government declared it would now field an all-volunteer military, and began recruiting women for jobs that had previously been reserved for men. The army continued to prohibit women from certain jobs that were considered to be at the very heart of combat, but opened up many jobs on its periphery.

Four years before Debbie had enlisted, the US Army had adopted the Direct Combat Probability Coding System, specifically to address this question. “Each position is then coded on a scale of P1 to P7, based on the probability of engaging in direct combat,” wrote Victoria Shaw in *Women in the Military.* “P1 represents the highest probability and P7 the lowest. Women are excluded from positions that are coded P1.” The army coded the job of infantry soldier as P1, because during a war the infantry soldier was the most likely person of all to experience combat. As it happened, most soldiers of the Indiana Army National Guard belonged to the 38th Infantry Division, but infantry soldiers needed other people to cook their meals, do their laundry, order their supplies, drive their trucks, fix their guns, and bury their dead. Around the time that Debbie enlisted, many of those support positions had just opened up to women for the first time. Commanders found the transition from all-male to mixed-gender units to be bumpy. The 113th Support Battalion had tried admitting women previously but had run into difficulties and reverted to an all-male status. Bravo Company reopened to women in 1987 — the year in which Debbie enlisted.

In the spring of 1988, when Debbie began drilling with the 110 soldiers who composed the Bedford unit, she became the fifth woman to join the company. Soon after, they were joined by a sixth. Military men referred to the newcomers as "females" instead of women; Debbie adopted that language, too. She prided herself on doing the tasks she had been assigned without asking for help. She figured that was how you won over the guys — by carrying your own rucksack, no matter how heavy. In the years that followed, some women left the unit and others took their place, but the total number remained relatively constant for ten years. This meant that for about a decade Debbie found herself operating in an extremely male-oriented culture. She loved it. Once she walked into a late-night game of cards where a bunch of guys who had been discussing the merits of various pairs of tits were suddenly confronted by an individual bearing tits herself and were thrown into a state of confusion. Debbie resolved the awkwardness by saying she considered a certain man to be especially well hung. "They looked like they were about to drop their teeth!" she would recall later. Debbie did not have trouble discerning which men would prove accepting. Some of them didn't want "females." Some of them only wanted to talk to her for one reason. Others made a point to come up and shake her hand.

"Welcome aboard," one of these men told her. "You're going to do just fine. Don't worry about being a female."

When they went out to the range, Debbie shot forty out of forty, a perfect score. She did not even miss any of the three-hundred-yard targets — the ones that other soldiers would sometimes sacrifice. The guys had figured she would do all right, because she had made it through basic training, but they never imagined she would outshoot them all. "Did you see Helton's score?" she heard one of the guys ask another with wonder in his voice. "She hit every single target!"

In those days, people viewed annual training as mostly an excuse to drink beer. "It was pretty much all party time," Debbie said about her early years in the Guard. Debbie joined the crowd that went to Shorty's Den, a local dive bar — it was an older crowd, mostly male, people who had been in the Guard for years. Open conflict divided the group on the subject of gender after a couple of women objected to hearing what they interpreted as derogatory comments. Debbie sided with the men. "I wondered how you could be that easily offended and come into the military," she said later. "Are you really that delicate that other people can't say anything in front of you?" The battalion's leaders promulgated a series of rules about sexual harassment, including a prohibition on vulgar language. Confusion ensued in Bravo Company. Exactly what was vulgar? Since when had speech turned into the equivalent of a weapon? Men interrupted themselves while telling dirty jokes or avoided women entirely. "It was much more natural and relaxed before the big to-do about how to behave toward women," said Debbie. It was not that she did not believe in equality, she simply prized belonging more highly. During the particularly fraught years, a few of the men told Debbie explicitly that they considered her "one of the guys." Debbie treasured the compliment.

During the same time frame, Debbie discovered that much of her knowledge about howitzers and mortars was becoming obsolete. The howitzer had been designed for static warfare, when grunts dug trenches and created opposing front lines and called the space in between a no-man's-land. Once you set a howitzer up, it could launch a shell over a mile, but you weren't going anywhere in a hurry. War rarely called for howitzers anymore, and the Bedford unit did not even have any tanks. A few times, during annual training, Debbie went to Camp Grayling in Michigan, and then she did get to work on the instruments inside of tanks — once, after she finished leveling the main gun in the rotating turret, a sergeant even allowed her to drive the tank out into a remote area and shoot the main gun to see if it was actually working properly. After they returned, exhilarated, he admonished, "You didn't shoot that, right?" That was as close as Debbie ever got to actual tank warfare.

And then the army overhauled its fire control systems. The new tanks came equipped with digital instruments — laser range finders, thermal tank sights, computerized ballistic systems. After Debbie had been in the Guard for about a decade, her job literally vanished. One day, her superior informed Debbie that the slot of 41C no longer existed, and she was now a 45G ("forty-five Golf") — she had been reclassified as a person who did "systems repair" on the digital tools. In truth, however, Debbie never received additional training and did not know how to repair the computerized systems. For reasons that never became clear to Debbie, but might have involved her gender, she was also passed over for promotions. She remained an E4, the lowest rank of specialist, even as she got the responsibilities of an acting E5. It rankled, doing a job that should have earned her more pay, without actually being given the money.

When other members of Bravo Company's retention team approached her about joining, after one of the team's members retired, Debbie decided to make the switch. Nothing was going to change over in armament, she figured, and she was already friendly with

Gretchen Flood, another member of the retention team; later, Debbie's good friend Will Hargreaves would join the team as well. When it was time for somebody to reenlist, the retention team discussed the decision with the soldier. "Since I knew everybody in the unit, a lot of those guys felt comfortable talking to me, and they could say anything they wanted," Debbie said later. "If they had issues with somebody in their section, they could tell me, and know it was not going to travel somewhere else. Or if it was something that I could see that I could fix, then I would talk to the proper person. And some of them wanted out, they didn't want to extend — and of course the purpose of retention was obviously to retain the soldier. So I just felt the need was greater there." Because her time in armament had proved disappointing, she figured what the heck. "I thought, you know, I've only got a few years left. I think that's the perfect place to ride out my time."

What Debbie really did was run the hot dog wagon. That's what everybody called the PX truck, out of which she sold pop, Gatorade, French fries, nachos, baked potatoes, and hot dogs every summer, during their two weeks of annual training. During the rest of the year, on drill weekends, she sold a more limited fare — pop, water, Gatorade, chips, candy bars. From the outside, the hot dog wagon looked just like any other army truck

— camouflage paint job — but through big double doors at the back people could step inside and order food. Shelves lined the interior of the trailer, and on the counters stood Crock-Pots, a microwave, and a freezer. The hot dog wagon doubled as the place where the retention team met with every member of the unit on an annual basis, to discuss how to keep them in the military, but after retention expanded the offerings, it became a favored hangout, too. Debbie and her colleagues chatted with every single person who came by, turning the retention center into a hub of social activity. Soon the hot dog wagon actually started making money, to the consternation of the brass. Previously the retention center had always operated at a loss, and profits perplexed the company's leadership. Supervisors argued about whether to require the hot dog wagon to stop making money or whether to give the extra money back to the state of Indiana. Debbie solved the dilemma by starting a fund for members of their Guard unit: If somebody had trouble paying their bills, they got assistance, or if a family member died, the unit sent flowers. She made the math work so that the hot dog trailer neither made nor lost any money, which pleased her superiors.

After she worked there for a few years, Debbie earned a certain degree of fame, and whenever she walked into a veterans' organization, people who had once been or were still in the 113th Support Battalion would come up to her and say, Oh, it's the hot dog lady! But her bosses found the hot dog wagon unmanly and were slow to appreciate the way in which the food truck was boosting morale. Then one of the main skeptics, a man named Captain Hoskins, was promoted to company commander. After he observed firsthand the emotional lift that his soldiers received from chatting with Debbie, he became a convert. In May 2000, when the 113th Support Battalion prepared to go to Louisiana for a joint readiness training exercise — a practice battle in which the soldiers mimicked the roles they would perform if they actually went to war — the commander of Bravo Company made sure the hot dog wagon went, too. Soldiers loaded all of the cooking equipment into the truck. But they could not put the potatoes on the truck without violating weight requirements. Hoskins did not want to try to pull off a field training exercise without Debbie's baked potatoes, but he couldn't exceed the weight restrictions, because the trucks were going to be loaded onto barges and floated down the Mississippi. Hoskins ordered every soldier in the company to put five pounds of potatoes into their rucksacks. That was when Debbie knew that she had become beloved.

Over the previous decade, Debbie had seen a steady influx of young women join the unit after the passage of the Montgomery GI Bill. The original GI Bill, of 1944, had provided a range of benefits, including college tuition, to soldiers who were returning home from World War II. By contrast, the Montgomery GI Bill offered tuition benefits as an inducement to enlist. Because the United States had moved to an all-volunteer force, the military was constantly looking for ways to entice young people to sign up, and tuition benefits were being used alongside cash bonuses. The ratio of men to women in the roughly one-hundred-person group that drilled in Bedford had shifted to about three to one, meaning there were now about twenty-five female soldiers. Debbie adopted them all. They turned to her for guidance in every arena — life, love, the military. And yet, running a hot dog wagon was not exactly what she had envisioned, years earlier, when she had signed up to join the National Guard. Where was the glory in making baked potatoes? Somehow her dreams had shrunk. She took fulfillment in her work, but she had envisioned more. She had thought she might stem a flood, secure power, go overseas. But the 113th Support Battalion had stopped sending mechanics to Germany, and during emergencies Debbie was not needed. On March 12, 1991, a freak storm sheathed vast swaths of northern Indiana in several inches of solid ice, and then sent high winds gusting through the frozen, glittering landscape. Tree branches that had started to leaf out cracked down across roads and power lines. Miles of utility poles toppled over, and half a million people lost electrical power. National Guard soldiers rushed to get communities functioning — but only those soldiers who had experience with generators were needed. Other people from her unit received calls to assist in nearby towns that had been hit by tornadoes, but the twisters never touched down close to where Debbie lived. During the entirety of Debbie's service in the National Guard, the state of Indiana experienced no emergencies that called for expertise in fire control. More than sixty thousand members of the Army National Guard were sent overseas during Operation Desert Storm, but the United States had troops on the ground for only a short time, and the Guard soldiers primarily assisted with tasks such as laundry services and field sanitation. Once again, Debbie's skills were not required.

Debbie had not voted for George H. W. Bush — and she would not vote for his son, either — but that was just because Debbie did not vote. It was a secret, and one of which she felt ashamed, but she had never voted in an election in her entire life. Wasn't even registered. The problem was she never felt certain that she knew enough to make a solid choice. There was just one man in public life

Debbie could imagine taking the trouble to cast a vote for, should he ever run, and that was Colin Powell. During the Persian Gulf War, Colin Powell won Debbie over with his cool unflappability and his direct manner. He was a military man, a straight shooter, she decided. Debbie had absolute faith in Powell. Otherwise she remained entirely skeptical of politics.

By this point she had grown skeptical of romance as well. One night at Shorty's, Debbie met an auto mechanic named Bill, and they dated for a few years. At one point Bill suggested that they marry, but Debbie said, "Bill, it's not going to happen. I enjoy your company, I like being with you, but as far as getting married again, that just isn't in the books for me." Instead, they fell into a regular arrangement, where they saw each other most Saturday nights. Usually Bill would drive up to Bloomington and spend the night with Debbie. Or if it was a drill weekend, she might spend the night with him in Bedford. Bill was comforting but not central. It was the crowd at Shorty's that filled her life. The crowd at Shorty's, and her beloved dog Maxx. That's all she needed; no more husbands.

In Bloomington, Debbie often went to the local Moose Lodge on Friday nights. Both of her parents had belonged to the organization, and Debbie herself was a member of Women of the Moose. She and T.J. got in the habit of dropping by on Friday nights, when their friend Diane worked as a waitress. In 1997, Debbie attended a Moose convention, along with T.J. and Diane. Diane's husband, Jerry, who managed the maintenance shop at E-Z-GO, a company that serviced electronic golf carts, brought his coworker, Jeff Deckard. T.J. and Debbie were out on the dance floor, acting silly.

Jeff said, "Who are those two girls?"

Jerry explained, "Oh, they're friends of ours from the Moose."

"You need to ask T.J. out," Diane told Jeff. "She's single."

"What about that other girl?" Jeff asked.

"Oh, you don't want to go out with her," Diane said. "She's dating somebody."

Jeff was a road mechanic with E-Z-GO. He drove all over Indiana, working on golf carts. He was forty years old, and had been divorced for about five years. A steady, old-fashioned man, he had been raised by a Pentecostal woman, and he would never approach another man's girlfriend. One evening at the Moose Lodge, Diane came over with some drinks and told Debbie and T.J., "These are from Jeff."

She added, "T.J., he said to tell you hi and that he hoped you were doing okay."

"Well, what's he saying hi for?" grumbled

T.J. She liked men who looked like Mr. America, and objected that Jeff's hair was thinning.

"He's a really nice guy," counseled Diane. "You'd like him once you talked to him."

"Diane, I'm not interested," said T.J.

One night, Debbie showed up at the Moose alone and saw Jeff drinking at the bar.

"You care if I sit next to you?" she asked.

"Oh, no," said Jeff. "Go right ahead."

They talked for two hours, and learned that they both liked guns. Jeff mentioned that he had served in the navy.

"Well, can I ask you a question?" Jeff said.

"Of course," Debbie said, figuring he wanted tips on how to approach T.J.

"I understand that you're dating somebody," Jeff said.

"What? No. Have you ever seen me in here with somebody?"

"Well, no, but Diane says that you have a boyfriend."

"Really," said Debbie. "I don't have a boyfriend — I have an acquaintance. If you say boyfriend, that means commitment. And I don't have commitments."

Jeff looked quizzical.

"Why are you asking anyway?" Debbie wanted to know.

"Well," said Jeff, "I've wanted to ask you out for a really long time. I kept trying to tell Diane, I want to meet the other girl. But I really don't want to ask somebody out that's already in a situation — I don't believe in that."

"Well, let me tell you," said Debbie. "First, I don't have a serious boyfriend. Second, I don't want a serious boyfriend. And third, T.J.'s not interested in you. You don't have enough hair for her. I'm sorry to say that, but you just don't."

"Yeah, I already figured that out," said Jeff. "I'm not interested in her. I never have been. But if I like somebody, I only like to see them one-on-one. I don't like to see multiple people at the same time."

"Well, suit yourself," said Debbie.

They chatted a little longer and then decided to leave. Right before they departed, however, Jeff had a change of heart. "You know what?" he said. "I think I am going to ask you out. Would you be willing to go?"

"Yeah," said Debbie. "I'm not making you no promises, but I'll go with you."

Debbie never dated another man again. Jeff kept his home spotless. He washed the dishes, made the bed, and scrubbed the shower stall before he left for work. Mr. Clean, she called him. Debbie worried that Jeff would reject her as soon as he saw that she was a bad housekeeper. After her refrigerator had broken, Debbie had taken to living out of a cooler, which she kept full of beer and ice; she had stopped buying food, and just picked up meals when she was out. Jeff asked if she was ever going to invite him over, and she said no, because she was not a Suzy Homemaker. Then Jeff's landlord sold the home that he had been renting, and Jeff moved in with his mother. One night Debbie and Jeff had sex in the basement with the heating vents wide open. Jeff's mother announced that Debbie was no longer welcome to spend the night.

"My God, I'm forty years old," said Jeff. "And my mother's not letting me have a sleepover!"

"Honey, she's Pentecostal," said Debbie.

Jeff spent the following night at Debbie's house. The next morning, he gave her one of his looks.

"You have no food in the fridge," he observed.

"Why would I have food in the fridge?" Debbie asked. "It's just me."

"I guess you don't have to have food," said Jeff.

He moved in that year. He offered to help pay the bills, but Debbie declined, saying she would feel obligated. Debbie remained entirely faithful to Jeff, but she still logged many hours at Shorty's. Debbie rarely acted drunk, but in the diary that she kept on an intermittent basis, she carefully noted what sort of alcohol she consumed and what effect it had upon her. When Debbie and Jeff took a trip to Belize, after Debbie was named "manager of the year" by the company that ran her salon, Debbie wrote in her diary that they ordered shots of Baileys with their coffee at breakfast. Debbie explained to the waitress that this was their "get up and go" drink. In the afternoon, they drank multiple piña coladas, and afterward, Debbie noted, with obvious regret, "Can't get a buzz." There was nothing unusual about her behavior, Debbie felt — everybody she hung around with in the Guard consumed large amounts of alcohol. And she was never late for drill. Debbie was proud of her ability to put away a lot of liquor and still make it to wherever she needed to be. She jokingly called herself a lush, but what she meant by that term was that while she depended on alcohol, she could still function.

By the time she reported to the armory in Bedford, four days after the two hijacked airplanes hit the Twin Towers, Debbie had clocked fourteen years with the National Guard — fourteen years of drill, fourteen years of being overlooked, fourteen years of drinking. When Bravo Company divided in response to the tremendous uncertainty around what the future might hold, her greatest concern was not if they would go to war, but whether she would be included. Maybe she would finally get to participate in a meaningful cause, maybe her life's path would head in a more fulfilling direction. Debbie hungered to join with a purpose larger than herself. She wanted to see the rest of the world — what lay beyond the blinking fireflies and plentiful cornfields of Indiana.

At drill, Bravo Company's first sergeant called the clamorous group to order. Chattering ceased and the part-time soldiers gathered into formation, lining up in rows in the battle dress uniforms they put on once a month. The first sergeant kept his remarks short. "We don't know anything," he said. "Expect changes in your training in the future."

3
Drill

At Aberdeen Proving Ground, jittery soldiers on high alert reported a rash of false alarms. There was a van on the post. Two strangers were spotted lurking behind a building. As ordered, Michelle Fischer rolled underneath military vehicles to look for anything suspicious. She had no idea what to deem suspicious, though — everything down there looked pretty strange. For weeks she had been looking forward to changing back into her Roxy hoodie and her Paris Blues jeans, which she was supposed to be able to do during her fifth week of training, but such privileges were abruptly rescinded — it was easier to spot an intruder if everybody else wore a uniform — and that was when Michelle began to apprehend that she might not get her civilian identity back again. How had she misplaced something so vital? The soldiers in training assumed they might be sent somewhere soon, but they could get no hard information. In this fashion, Michelle came to appreciate the enormousness of the commitment she had made to the military.

Three days after the attacks, Congress passed a bill called the Authorization for Use of Military Force, giving George W. Bush broad powers of response. "The President is authorized to use all necessary and appropriate force against those nations, organizations, or persons he determines planned, authorized, committed, or aided the terrorist attacks that occurred on September 11, 2001, or harbored such organizations or persons, in order to prevent any future acts of international terrorism against the United States by such nations, organizations, or persons," the bill declared. Everybody at Aberdeen seemed to think the bill was a good idea; apparently Michelle was the only person there who did not want to give Bush such leeway. Michelle had been temporarily categorized as "active duty" while in training, and now she heard a rumor that all active duty soldiers were going to remain on active status indefinitely, even if they had only signed up for a part-time role. Michelle got into fierce arguments over whether this was even legally possible. She was stunned to learn that the contract she had signed would allow the military to do pretty much anything if she was put on active duty. She was a GI now — it stood for "government issue" — and could be moved around as if she were a Humvee.

One lone elected official had opposed the Authorization for Use of Military Force. Barbara Lee, a black woman who represented the Ninth Congressional District in the state of California, had cast the only vote against the bill in either house of Congress. It intrigued Michelle to learn that Lee had grown up in a military family. Michelle tracked down a videotape of Lee's speech on the floor of Congress and decided that she agreed with the reasons Lee gave for her opposition: Lee said the bill granted an authority that was too sweeping, and cautioned against "an open-ended war with neither an exit strategy nor a focused target." Lee called the bill "a blank check to the president," pointing out that it allowed him to attack "anyone . . . anywhere, in any country . . . and without time limit." Michelle marveled at the fortitude it must have taken for Lee to stand up to all her peers, a black woman in a place dominated by white men. Opposing the war was lonely. On September 20, 2001, Bush delivered a historic speech to a joint session of Congress, and the soldiers at Aberdeen crowded into the common room; they applauded when Bush called for a "war on terror." Michelle could feel in a tangible way how solitary she was in being troubled by that phrase. She lionized Barbara Lee in secret.

One day led into another, and no additional

attacks occurred. The officers kept some of the ramped-up security measures (people still had to sign in and out of buildings) but revoked others (Michelle did get to change into her civilian clothes and leave the post on a pass). Alfred Turner returned at the end of September — he surprised Michelle by showing up in time to celebrate her nineteenth birthday, which fell on a cool, drizzly Thursday. Alfred took her away for a romantic weekend in Baltimore, Maryland, an hour's drive to the south. They stayed in a bed and breakfast, a rambling Victorian with odd, pleasing nooks. Michelle confessed how grim she found the possibility of war. Alfred responded by saying they should get married, they should have children. Michelle seriously entertained the idea of saying yes, but nineteen seemed too young. College. She wanted to go to college.

After Alfred left for Germany, Michelle struggled to make sense of the news. Bush's top advisers were split over how to respond to the attacks: One faction supported the idea of going after Al-Qaeda by attacking their strongholds in Afghanistan, but another faction was lobbying for the invasion of Iraq as well. Nobody held Saddam Hussein responsible for the recent attacks, yet the hawkish faction thought the American public would rally around the idea of ridding the country of one of its archenemies. What preoccupied

Michelle was the idea of war itself, rather than the question of where it might be waged. On October 7, Bush authorized air strikes in Afghanistan; he said the bombs were falling on the terrorist camps of Al-Qaeda. Great Britain allied itself with the United States and joined in the attacks. Another spate of rumors flooded the base at Aberdeen. One soldier told Michelle that a woman from Pennsylvania who had recently graduated from their job training program had just been deployed, even though she had joined the National Guard. Was it true? Nobody could say.

Strangely, the weather remained glorious. In the mornings and the evenings Michelle's face pinked in the cold air, but the afternoons stayed bright and temperate, out of step with the tidings. Finally it grew so cold that Michelle realized she needed sweaters, and she asked her mother to put some in the mail. A box arrived, and even before she cut through the tape, Michelle could smell the stale cigarette smoke. Her mother flew through a pack a day, and they had always lived in close quarters. Michelle had never noticed before how her clothes held on to the stench. She had been away from home for six months.

New suitors dogged Michelle. She was young and naive and had never been away from her mother for so long, and she found the attention gratifying. Mark Reed, the chiseled marine drill sergeant who had rushed into her classroom, invited her to watch him play soccer. Thirsting to be singled out, Michelle made certain to attend his practices as well as his games. When he handed her an envelope fat with photographs of himself, which happened to have his cell phone number scrawled on the outside, and told her that she might enjoy looking at the photographs in the bathroom, she did as he bid. Then she called him up, enamored. He was thirty-six, she was nineteen. Only after the drill sergeant seduced her did Michelle finally catch sight of his essential indifference, and then she caught Reed lavishing the same scrutiny upon another young woman. She gathered scraps of gossip about the drill sergeant and deduced that he was a predatory being. The recognition left her soiled, queasy. What scared her most was her own blindness. During the thirteen weeks of training that she spent at Aberdeen Proving Ground, perhaps the most valuable lesson she took away, as painful as it was, was that in the military she needed to watch out for men like Reed. Maybe someday she might want to know how to throw a grenade or how to replace a broken trigger mechanism, but she was certain to work alongside men like Reed. For someone with her level of neediness, such men could pose an even greater danger than any foreign enemy. It was another kind of friendly fire.

During the second half of her time at Aberdeen, Michelle was permitted to leave the post regularly, and young men jockeyed to invite her to parties thrown in rented hotel rooms in the nearby town of White Marsh. Not one but two different marines begged her to accompany them to the Marine Ball that was held at Aberdeen, and she said yes to both. Michelle and her two escorts attended the ball together, Michelle dressed in an iridescent purple gown that she had chanced upon in Baltimore. At one of the debauched hotel parties over in White Marsh, she put on girlish attire, only to wind up in a wrestling match with a male soldier. Later another partygoer gave Michelle a photograph he had taken of her pinning the male soldier in a hold, straddling him in her finery. The guys loved when she did that sort of thing — proved she was one of them and not one of them at the same time.

Michelle would later refer to this period as a "thirteen-week spiral into inappropriate behavior." It culminated with a spectacular infatuation with James Cooper, a witty, athletic soldier from Cassadaga, New York, a small town near the shores of Lake Erie. She and Cooper were the same age; he was a 44B ("forty-four Bravo") — a welder. She got to know him one night in the common room, while another soldier was hitting on Michelle relentlessly as the three of them played a game of pool. Michelle found herself drawn to Cooper's cool, witty sarcasm, and the way he never tried too hard; he had a magnetic self-confidence, a wiry body, and a face with angular features. Before the pool game ended, Michelle was smitten. She worked to seize Cooper's full attention, which she never quite obtained. She did manage to sleep with him, during one of the hotel parties in White Marsh. Even after they spent the weekend together, however, Cooper remained aloof. Michelle found it seductive.

Soon Cooper could prevail upon her to do most anything he wanted, and they executed a series of crazy pranks. They bought the sound track to the movie *Top Gun,* which was full of sappy songs they both hated, slipped the sound track into the stereo at the gym, then doubled over as the tough-looking soldiers wilted upon hearing "Take My Breath Away." Cooper was always pulling pranks — they had overlapped at Fort Jackson, South Carolina, as it turned out, and he confessed that he had been the guy who had thrown a water bottle in the air during the rock concert. Cooper persuaded Michelle and another female soldier to climb up the fire escape to the male-only part of the barracks to meet him and a friend for a double siege. The two couples stole inside two unoccupied rooms, with a lookout posted nearby, the surreptitious intimacy twice as exciting thanks to the fear that a drill sergeant might discover them in a state of undress. "You're adorable," Cooper told Michelle, then retreated into his self-sufficient solitude.

Even as he remained elusive, Cooper kept Michelle's anxieties at bay. She was a creature of thought, but he was a person of action — he did not ruminate the way she did. He made her laugh, made her lighten. It helped, even though they did not join up well philosophically. Cooper hewed to black-and-white beliefs, and he was gung ho about the possibility of war. When Congress passed the Patriot Act, greatly expanding the power of the federal government to gather intelligence, oversee financial transactions, and detain individuals suspected of terrorism, Michelle found the very name of the act frightening, yet she said nothing about her dismay to Cooper because she feared he would turn away. It chilled Michelle to watch her country surrender its liberties so easily, but nobody else she knew of at Aberdeen seemed worried.

In the classroom, Michelle continued to excel. She proved handy with mechanical tasks, and the art of repairing weapons came easily. Toward the end of her stay at Aberdeen, after eleven weeks of studying the same weapons, the marines broke off to study their own sniper rifle, while the army and the Army

National Guard soldiers worked on howitzers. The big gun was massive — the breech weighed more than Michelle — although everybody considered them obsolete. Michelle wasn't sure exactly what kind of war Bush had in mind, but she doubted the soldiers were going to be using howitzers. "I mean, what kind of a situation would I be in where I would have to fix a broken howitzer?" she would ask. She did not believe that the members of Al-Qaeda were going to dig trenches and line up to be shelled.

And then she was finished. James Cooper had gone already; he had finished his welding courses before her and gone home to New York. When Michelle graduated from Aberdeen toward the end of November, nobody came to celebrate. Michelle packed up her things shortly before Thanksgiving. At the Baltimore airport, she ran into the newly heightened security measures involving airline travel for the first time. At the ticket counter, an airline staff person told Michelle she could not board the airplane while wearing her uniform. If there was a terrorist incident, said the woman, Michelle's uniform was likely to make her a target. She was told to go to the bathroom and change her clothes. The country was awash in fear, Michelle realized. She had stepped outside of the civilian world for just half a year, but in that time it had been transformed.

Back in Evansville, Michelle found six people living in the one-bedroom apartment that she had been sharing with her mother. Her aunt had moved in after losing her job; her brother had moved in after finding a job at a nearby McDonald's and stayed even after he got fired; her sister had moved in, along with her two children, after her husband had abandoned them. Nobody living in the apartment was working except for her mother. Michelle had given her mother access to her bank account while she was gone, and her mother had plundered it to pay for rent and groceries. Donovan had commandeered the Tank, and after somebody smashed one of the windows he had neglected to repair the glass. It had rained, and the car stank of mildew. Donovan had also run up a bill of more than $1,000 on her cell phone. Michelle had earned thousands of dollars in active duty pay during her six months away, and all of that money was gone. Once Michelle might have slumped into this, but she had been through basic training — she knew how to choke somebody until they passed out, she knew how to fire an M16. "I don't have to take this shit anymore," she told her family. Then she packed up her things and left.

Michelle moved in with Veronica and Colleen. They were sharing a two-bedroom apartment, and Michelle slept on the couch. She had fallen out of step with her friends, however; Veronica and Colleen were now sophomores at the University of Southern Indiana, while Michelle had returned home in the middle of the fall semester and could not resume taking classes until the spring. She still hoped to apply to Indiana University, but she planned to take another year of courses at USI while she waited to hear if she was accepted. She found a job at Target, working third shift. Veronica and Colleen threw Michelle a welcome-back party, and Noah Jarvis brought his guitar and stood outside and played "Wish You Were Here," which he had taught himself while Michelle had been gone. They started dating again, but Michelle did not feel the same way, and the relationship did not cohere. Moody, bored, she got into a fight with her roommates over their failure to clean the kitchen. Veronica and Colleen were slobs, she said. She got her mother to kick everybody else out and moved back home.

Once a month, Michelle reported for drill at the armory on the Lloyd Expressway. She showed up wearing shiny boots and a pressed uniform, as she had been trained to do. The rest of her unit looked like slouches, dusty boots and wrinkled uniforms straight out of the dryer. Her colleagues had a hybrid ethos, a combination of the strict military culture she had encountered at Aberdeen and the more relaxed standards of everyday life in

Evansville. "It's a bunch of people who are [practically] back in civilian mode, which you will get to, but you have a hard time with that," Michelle said. "It's hard to go back and forth between the two modes. Guardsmen have a unique way of straddling both, in their own neglectful way."

At the armory, Michelle recognized half a dozen people. She knew Lucy Schneider and Agnes Harmon from middle school, for example, and she knew Angela Peterson and Bridget Palmer from high school. All of the women belonged to a small detachment of the 113th Support Battalion. The main part of the 113th drilled in Bedford, several hours away, but the detachment had been formed so that women could drill in Evansville, as the principal unit operating out of the armory at Evansville remained male-only, because it was field artillery. Michelle belonged to the 113th's Bravo Company, primarily a maintenance unit. The women whom Michelle recognized from her school days were all 88Ms ("eighty-eight Mikes"), or truck drivers, and they belonged to the 113th's Alpha Company, which drove the trucks that Bravo maintained. Sergeant Joe Haverty told Michelle that she was the first person they had gotten who was authorized to work on a howitzer — the archaic big guns still composed the bulk of the field artillery unit's inventory, and at first Michelle thought her skills would make her important. But actually the howitzers were kept in storage, and Haverty assigned her to a maintenance team that worked on trucks.

The rest of the maintenance team were 63Ws ("sixty-three Whiskeys"), or truck mechanics, and in the armory's vast, chilly garage, which smelled of motor oil and solvents, they taught her how to work on vehicles. She changed tires, changed radiator fluid, and once even changed the head gasket on a five-ton truck. The team consisted of her superiors Sergeant Haverty and Corporal Ezra Schmidt, as well as a young woman named Amber Macdonald, who had spiky blond hair, large breasts, and a bubbly personality. Macdonald enjoyed flirting and giggled a lot. Macdonald was not Michelle's intellectual equal, but she served as a reliable ally. One weekend, Macdonald called Michelle to warn her that everybody who showed up for drill was being subjected to drug testing, and Michelle, who had recently smoked pot, called in sick. Another weekend, Michelle showed up still drunk from the night before, and Macdonald walked her up and down the halls of the armory until she was sober enough to stand in formation. Their superior Corporal Schmidt hit on Michelle or Amber indiscriminately and often. After a while, Noah Jarvis joined the team, too. He had become a diesel mechanic ("sixty-three Bravo"), and Michelle started working alongside him on drill weekends, sometimes lying beneath trucks, sometimes bending under their hoods together.

That winter, when Michelle watched the news on the small combination television set and DVD player that her mother owned, she found it hard to keep track of the cities in Afghanistan that the United States and its allies were capturing. It looked as though it would be a swift war; major parts of Kabul, Kandahar, and Herat had been hit with bombs and cruise missiles, and the United States and its allies had taken the Taliban-controlled districts of Zari, Keshendeh, and Aq-Kupruk. Then they captured the important city of Mazar-i-Sharif, the capital city of Kabul, and finally the Taliban stronghold of Kunduz. Michelle had never heard of these strange-sounding places; she did not know where to find the cities on a map. It was hard to follow the war's narrative. She took away only the gist of the story: American generals said the war was going well. And indeed, the war in Afghanistan got off to the kind of start that military historians would later call spectacular. US special operations teams and CIA forces worked with Afghan fighters who were loyal to their cause to topple the Taliban regime in less than three months, with only a dozen US fatalities. Michelle assured her mother there was no way anybody would send her to Afghanistan, and as the military alliance announced its string of victories, she began to believe that might actually be true.

Yet as the weeks slid by, the reports grew more confusing. Fighters aligned with the Taliban somehow smuggled weapons into a prison in Mazar-i-Sharif. Forty Northern Alliance fighters died, as well as an American CIA agent, Johnny Micheal Spann. Just before Christmas came dramatic news: supposedly bin Laden was holed up in an elaborate cave complex in the mountains on the country's eastern border, close to the legendary Khyber Pass. News reports said the caves of Tora Bora might be bin Laden's headquarters; it might be a vast hideout capable of sheltering more than a thousand people. Al-Qaeda might have stockpiled ammunition there, or maybe its fighters. All that could be said for certain was that the caves were in one of the least accessible areas in a country full of impassable mountains. For days, US and British special forces negotiated the brutally rugged terrain, first bombing the cave complex and eventually breaching the caves themselves (which turned out to be smaller and less impressive than suggested). They searched the redoubt, but like a specter bin Laden had vanished.

In the months since they had trained together at Aberdeen Proving Ground, James Cooper had not reached out to Michelle, so that winter she got in touch with him. Michelle found his home number in the telephone directory and sweet-talked his parents into providing updated information. After she tracked Cooper down, they started talking on the phone. He was unmoored, and she felt the same way. In search of the assurance Cooper had provided, Michelle went to visit him for a week. He took her to Niagara Falls and kissed her while the water thundered around them, and she thought it was one of the most romantic moments of her life. With scant encouragement, she then moved to Fort Wayne, Indiana, so they could be geographically closer. In the spring of 2002, instead of returning to the University of Southern Indiana, she enrolled at the campus jointly operated by Indiana University and Purdue University in Fort Wayne. Located in the far northeastern corner of Indiana, Fort Wayne was a six-hour drive from Evansville, where she had to go to drill, and a six-hour drive from western New York, where James Cooper lived. It was as close as Michelle could get to the object of her desire while still serving in the Indiana National Guard. Before the trip, Michelle had taken out her first loan and bought a red 1999 Mercury Cougar with a growly V6 engine for $10,000. She hoped the fast car would allow her to secure the new relationship while still obtaining a college degree.

Thanks to her membership in the National Guard, Michelle qualified for 100 percent of her tuition, just as Sergeant Granderson had promised. Unexpectedly, however, she had to wait ninety days for the credit to show up in the system, and during those three months she could not obtain her housing allowance or her kicker bonus. This threw her into a cash crunch. Meanwhile, she had rented a studio apartment for several hundred dollars per month, and now she also had to make car payments. Michelle got a job at the Golden Corral in Fort Wayne and started working full-time to make ends meet.

Finding herself back at the Golden Corral, after she had made so many sacrifices, proved disheartening. She knew nobody in Fort Wayne, and Cooper drifted away. Desperate for affirmation, Michelle zeroed in on a handsome classmate, but he proved unattainable. She spent her time worrying about boys and lost the ability to focus on her studies. Then Noah decided to move to Fort Wayne, which Michelle allowed to happen. Noah drove up in his gray Astro van and got a job at a bong shop. She found his familiar presence comforting even as she wondered whether their relationship should continue. They both became devoted fans of the left-leaning television show *Democracy Now!* That spring the Bush administration began arguing more consistently that the United States should take action against Iraq because it possessed "weapons of mass destruction." Vice President Dick Cheney toured eleven Arab nations to build support for the Bush team's policies in the region. *Democracy Now!* hosts Amy Goodman and Juan González ran a series of stories ripping into the Bush team for its eagerness to attack Iraq. The reports painted a sinister picture of Cheney's motivations, interpreting his actions through the prism of his ties to the massive oil field services company Halliburton. "Why is the United States going after Iraq, when in Saudi Arabia, for example, you have a government that has not cooperated with the investigations of the hijackers?" Amy Goodman asked. "Fifteen of them were Saudi." The answer, according to *Democracy Now!*, had to do with the close relationship between the Bush family and the Saudi royal family, and the fact that Iraq possessed upward of 143 billion barrels of oil, making its oil reserves the third-largest in the world.

Michelle and Noah shared Goodman's antiauthoritarian leanings, and they figured the whole "weapons of mass destruction" argument was a scripted hoax. Michelle thought she might as well have been watching theater; the actors already knew they would go to war with Iraq, they just needed to scare the audience into going along. It was jarring to listen to Amy Goodman and then report for drill, but Goodman served as a stiff antidote to the military mentality. Michelle cleaved to Noah as the only other person who could understand both why she was in the Guard and why she would need such a countermeasure. Once Noah moved to Fort Wayne, however, Michelle stopped going to classes regularly and ceased turning in her homework. She could have aced her courses but she simply lost the will; she gave up on herself and on school. At the end of that dismal semester, she had earned a total of only six credits. She had obtained an F in political science and a D in early developmental psychology; those credits would not transfer. That summer, she moved back to Evansville and signed up to return to USI in the fall, although she continued to stay in touch with Cooper by phone. She was right back where she had started before she had signed up for the Guard — living in Evansville, partying too much — except now she was almost a year behind her peers in terms of college credits.

Once she got back home, Michelle decided to make up for what had happened by focusing intently on her courses at USI, so that she could succeed in transferring to Indiana University. But she did not need Noah as badly as she had in Fort Wayne, and they parted ways again. She still saw him regularly, of course, because they drilled together every month. It was awkward at first, but eventually the awkwardness got familiar. That summer, Michelle attended her first annual training. She rode in a truck for three hours with her superiors Haverty and Schmidt, heading north to central Indiana. Their destination was Camp Atterbury, a sprawling army base that served as the main training hub for the Indiana Army National Guard, as well as the main point of departure for thousands of regular army, reserve soldiers, and marines who were shipping off to Afghanistan. When they arrived, Michelle saw a sea of identical low cinder-block buildings, all painted lemon yellow, with brown shingled roofs, stretching away in all directions. The chapel; prison; Laundromat; Subway; and the NCO Club, where the noncommissioned officers went to drink — each of those establishments was also made out of cinder block and also painted lemon yellow. The astonishing conformity of the buildings and the troops, all wearing nearly identical uniforms, left Michelle disoriented. She could not find her way around, as the identical buildings left her no way to get her bearings. They stayed in the barracks for a few days and then it was time to head into the woods, so they could pretend they were also at war. Instead of fixing trucks, Michelle was assigned to the armament team, again under the direction of Haverty and Schmidt. There were no broken weapons to fix, however, so they just participated in the group exercises, setting up a perimeter, digging foxholes, unrolling concertina wire, and keeping guard.

During the two weeks they spent at Camp Atterbury, the small detachment of soldiers from Evansville trained alongside the rest of the soldiers in the 113th Support Battalion. This meant that the other soldiers from Bravo Company who drilled up in Bedford were getting their first look at Michelle Fischer and Amber Macdonald. The arrival of the two young women caused an intense commotion. Young men hounded them, old men, too. One night, a noncommissioned officer named Frank Garrison, who was twice Michelle's age, climbed into a foxhole with her, although he had not been assigned overnight guard duty. Garrison offered to take Michelle to a rock concert because he knew she loved music, and when she declined, he continued to seek out opportunities to spend time with her. Technically he outranked her, and she did not know how to keep him at bay. Several nights later, Michelle woke in the dark to discover that Garrison had put his cot right next to hers, and was sleeping with his face only inches away. She started calling him Nose Hairs.

In response to all of the ruckus, Haverty and Schmidt sequestered Fischer and Macdonald inside their truck and forbade them to step outside of the vehicle without permission. Eventually they put up camo netting next to the truck, which slightly expanded the terrain claimed by the armament team. When they did step outside of the camo netting, Haverty instructed the two young women not to walk around in their T-shirts. Instead he ordered them to wear their tops, the camouflage shirt that matched their camouflage pants. Most days, the temperature was more than ninety degrees, and none of the men were wearing their tops over their T-shirts, but Michelle and Amber did as they were told.

Haverty's attempts to sequester Michelle and Amber away from the rest of the unit backfired, however, when Michelle and Amber discovered that just on the other side of their camo netting were four young men who had been assigned to the company's missile repair section — Patrick Miller, Ben Sawyer, Timothy Reeves, and Frank Perez. Within days Michelle had become friends with the guys in missile. She could flirt with them through the camo netting as much as she liked without violating the letter of Haverty's prohibitions. She wasn't sure if she wanted to sleep with any of the soldiers from missile, but she liked the fact that missile so clearly wanted to sleep with her. Patrick Miller was cocky, short, high-strung, and married; he had been a marine and thought he knew everything. But it was Ben Sawyer who most successfully attached himself to Michelle. Sawyer was also married. Instead of trying to seduce Michelle, he simply became her friend. Michelle allowed herself to get drawn in, certain that nothing would ever happen between them.

The only place Michelle could socialize without raising Haverty's ire was the hot dog truck. Each day, after their exercises were complete, Michelle followed the crowd over to the camouflaged trailer, where she got in line to buy a Gatorade and a pack of chips. The woman who manned the truck — talkative, bighearted Debbie Helton — chatted to Michelle so effortlessly that right away Michelle felt a great sense of ease in her company. Michelle grew to depend on the reliable warmth she got every day from Debbie Helton, who made her feel welcome and wanted in an environment that was otherwise estranging. Perhaps they did not share the same political views, but on that score Michelle was used to being out of step with her colleagues in the Guard, and mainly she noticed that Debbie was unflaggingly kind.

There was one woman in Bravo Company whom Haverty expressly warned Michelle to avoid. At one point, Michelle's sergeant pointed out a National Guard soldier named Desma Brooks.

"Watch out for her," Haverty warned.

"That's Brooks. You want to stay away from that one."

"Why?" Michelle asked.

"Because she's trouble," Haverty said.

And that sounded intriguing. Michelle had never liked Haverty very much. Perhaps the enemy of her enemy was a potential friend?

4
Three Months of Hell

Desma Brooks observed the commotion that her younger colleague Michelle Fischer caused with amusement, disdain, and a little bit of jealousy. The guys were acting like dogs, lusting after a piece of tail. Perfectly reasonable men whom she had known for years became incapacitated as soon as they got a whiff of Fischer and Macdonald — it was hilarious, the leering stupidity. At the same time, Desma noticed how the blond pair kept to themselves, stayed inside their truck, scrupulously avoiding others. Somebody told her they were college kids. Desma had never made it to college. She could have handled the material, but she had gotten pregnant with her first child at age sixteen. At the point when Fischer showed up at annual training, too good to associate with the likes of her, Desma had three children whom she was raising primarily on her own, and she was holding down three jobs. She had no time to better herself by going to college, and no interest in associating with people who had it easy and then decided they were better than she was. Desma dubbed the new girls the Kitty Cat Club. Soon half the unit was calling Fischer and Macdonald the Kitty Cats. Desma had that knack — she was a shrewd observer, she could name things.

Desma had put on weight since becoming a mother but she remained an attractive, sociable brunette with tan skin, brown eyes, a square face, movie star cheekbones, and naturally ruddy cheeks. She offset her beauty with a habit of dressing in football jerseys and blue jeans, and while she had a gorgeous smile she also smoked cigarettes until they gave her voice a raspy edge. With friends, she was capable of extraordinary loyalty, but she had a hard time with authority figures. She had a lengthy belly laugh that chugged upward through a variety of registers, starting down low and ending up high, and it was infectious. The fact that Desma had enlisted was an accident, as far as she was concerned — something that was true of most pivotal events in her life. Agency she ascribed to others.

Desma had grown up in Spurgeon, Indiana, a town buried deep in the southern part of the state and small enough for her to ride her bike from one end to the other. She had grasped early that her mother could not function. "I call her a manic-depressive, because she never came out of her bedroom," Desma would say later. "But I don't know. Let's just say my mom was crazy. I love her, but she was crazy." Most nights, Desma made dinner and brought food to her mother; her mother drove them both to the grocery store, but Desma did the shopping. Her three older siblings had married and left home before she was born, and by the time she came along her mother had stopped trying. Desma was on her own from a young age.

Desma was extraordinarily bright, and before she finished elementary school, she devoured *The Secret Garden* and *Little Women.* Later she raced through *Oliver Twist* and *The Raven.* The books spirited her away from her surroundings and shielded her from her mother's rage. Her mother vacillated between catatonia and violence, according to Desma; when displeased, she might beat a child, but if Desma was reading, her mother left her alone, Desma said. In seventh grade, both Desma and her younger brother, the last of the five children in their family, were placed into foster care. The notes that would eventually come to be contained in Desma's Veterans Administration file alluded to some kind of abuse, but she did not want to discuss the incident, even years later with her VA therapist. "It's not who I am," Desma said. "It has nothing to do with how I handle my day-to-day. It has nothing to do with how I raise my children. I raise my children in a better atmosphere than I grew up in, that's the only way that affected [me]."

Caseworkers assigned Desma to a foster home in the same county where her mother lived, and she kept attending the same middle school, although she took a different bus. The couple that had agreed to foster her had previously adopted two children and were also fostering two more, making Desma the fifth child they were sheltering in their two-bedroom house. Initially, Desma expected to stay for only a short period, but then her mother was injured in a car wreck, and the weeks stretched into months. Desma began fighting with her foster parents' adopted daughter. Her foster father worked for Whirlpool and had an even temperament, but her foster mother was an evangelical Christian with a fragile personality. Eventually the placement ended after the foster parents said they could not handle Desma. "I know in their hearts they were trying to be good people," Desma said later. "And, you know, he was. She should never have been a mother, but, whatever — that's not my call. Not a very good parent, the house got filled, she got stressed, and I left."

The move occurred abruptly. One day, after Desma had finished school, a caseworker picked her up, suggested that they take a ride in her car, and then dropped Desma off at a group home. Residents were supposed to graduate after five weeks, provided they completed the program. Desma progressed rapidly at first, but then balked after she was ordered to clean an oven in which someone else had exploded a green bean casserole; she thought the person who had made the mess should clean it up, and refused to touch the burned splatter. She got bumped back down to the beginning of the program. Later she stumbled across a group of friends and forgot about the time and missed curfew. Then she got caught smoking. "I spent ten months in a five-week program," said Desma with a long raspy laugh. "I learned how not to get caught smoking, and where to hide your cigarettes — that's what I learned in the group home."

Halfway through eighth grade, a caseworker placed Desma in a second foster home, belonging to a couple named Mike and Diane Lewis. Again, she became the fifth child in a busy household: Mike and Diane had two children of their own and were fostering two boys when Desma arrived. But she soon grew to appreciate Mike and Diane. "They were good people," she said. "They held jobs and they went to work and they took care of the kids. Made sure you hit the appointments you needed to. It was a normal household." Desma would stay in contact with both sets of foster parents for the rest of her life, but she always considered Mike and Diane the two people who had really been there for her when it had mattered most.

Halfway through freshman year of high school, a caseworker announced that it was time for Desma to go back home. Her younger brother had already returned to their mother's care and seemed to be thriving. "Semester break, I went back to — ugh — I went back home," Desma said. Her mother still could not run a household and Desma missed Mike and Diane's orderly routines. The following year, Desma contracted a protracted case of strep throat, which turned into tonsillitis, and then a doctor recommended surgery. By the time she returned to school, she was not able to understand what was going on in her classes. Desma had thought she would get extra help to catch up, but that assistance did not materialize. She went to the principal to complain. "He basically told me that he had better things to do with his time than worry about me," Desma said. "So I told him to piss off. I threw all my books at him and I left. Told him I quit, I'm not coming back. And I didn't."

In the area where she lived there were no jobs for a carless teen, so Desma left home and moved to Jasper, Indiana, where she shared an apartment with friends she met on the streets. "I immediately started looking for work," she said later. "Not much you can do at fifteen. But I turned sixteen the following

January, and then I got a job." Over the next few months, she worked as a cashier at Hardee's, then began making pizzas at Papa John's. "It was a job. I got a paycheck. Paid my rent." After that she found work with a construction company that assembled mobile homes. Before a year had elapsed, however, she learned that she was pregnant. All she ever says about that is the child was born of a not so good situation; her son Joshua was born on March 16, 1993, two months after Desma turned seventeen, and immediately became the central source of love and affection in her life.

Desma moved back in with her mother again, and asked for a birth-control implant to be surgically inserted into her upper arm, to make sure she did not have any more children. Josh had colic and during the night Desma read *Gone With the Wind* while pacing around her bedroom with the fussy baby in her arms. When he was about four months old and finally sleeping, Desma enrolled in a program to get her GED. She obtained her high school equivalency degree a full year before she would have finished high school. When she took the GED exam, she scored in the 90th percentile, compared with the rest of the state. She also wrote an essay that won her an invitation to breakfast at the Governor's Mansion in Indianapolis with Governor Evan Bayh. She had never been to Indianapolis, but studied a map to learn the way. She put on her Sunday best — a pretty brown and white patterned dress, carefully cinched at the waist — and left her house at dawn. She drove her mother's old gray Chevy Citation north on Highway 231 until the engine sputtered and fell silent. She did not make it to the breakfast.

While caring for her infant son, Desma also began babysitting for a man who lived down the street — his name was Keith and he was a single father. After several months, Desma began dating her employer. "It was convenient," she said. "We were already there. He lived right up the street from me." Soon Desma and Josh moved in with Keith. As Josh began to speak, Desma's boyfriend prompted her son to call him Dad, and Josh and his surrogate father developed an enduring relationship, such that Keith essentially became voluntary kin to the boy. After she and Keith broke up, Desma got an apartment of her own, but Josh continued to spend time with Keith. When Desma's first set of foster parents called to ask how she was doing and heard she was living out of a cooler, they took her to the Whirlpool store and bought her a refrigerator. After only six months, it became clear that she could not afford the rent, and she and Josh and the refrigerator moved back into her mother's house.

Desma likes to say she joined the military

on a dare. It's a story she tells often. "A friend of mine showed up at the house," said Desma. "We were neighbors, and she was dating a recruiter from the National Guard. And she says, 'Hey, come with me. Let's go take the ASVAB test.' " It was March 1996, and Josh was three years old. Both Desma's older brother and her new boyfriend, a man named Dennis Brooks, had served in the navy. At the time, she was making office credenzas at Jasper Desk for $8.65 an hour. "I ain't got nothing better going on, and Josh was with Grandma," said Desma. "She was keeping him all night. So I jumped in the car with her and the boyfriend and we went to Evansville and I took the ASVAB and scored really well."

Two weeks later, the same friend showed up again and urged Desma to take the physical exam, too.

"I don't want to join the army," Desma said.

But the following day, her friend showed back up, along with the military recruiter she was dating, and they urged her to join the Army National Guard. It was not such a big commitment, they said — just twelve weekends a year, two weeks in the summer.

"I dare ya," her friend said. "Just go do the physical — I bet you won't make it in."

Desma's friend said she was planning to sign up, too. They drove down to Louisville, Kentucky, together. At the military processing station, Desma made the rounds, culminating with the duckwalk in her underwear. "And they herd you all into this one big room and there's some guy with a big, powerful voice telling you that it's the finest thing to serve your country and the next thing you know, he's like, 'Raise your right hand and repeat after me.' And I couldn't hear a word of the oath he said. All I heard was, blah blah, blah blah blah. So that's what I did, I raised my right hand, and apparently that meant I was in the army [National Guard] now. Completely unintentional." Afterward, Desma found her friend crying in the canteen — she had failed the physical because she had psoriasis. Desma refused to speak to her for months.

The story Desma never tells is the one about the military recruiter who actually processed her enlistment. Her friend's boyfriend had introduced Desma to the recruiter who handled her paperwork. "Turned out to be a real dirtbag," said Desma. He sexually assaulted her after she signed her contract, according to Desma, although she never reported the incident. Desma enlisted for three years and received a $2,500 bonus. She was told to be ready to leave for basic training at the end of the summer. Perhaps because she was about to leave for an extended period, Desma's relationship with Dennis turned serious. In June she accepted his proposal. "I know it was retarded," she would say later. "I don't know why I did it." Dennis was nine years older, and for a while, he had been treating Desma like a princess. They went for long drives, and they walked through coal country, nothing fancy, but he said nice things. The idea of marriage appealed to Desma for a highly practical reason: The military did not allow single parents to enlist, and she had gotten around this by not mentioning that she had a son. She had been planning to solve the problem by giving custody of Josh to her mother, but after Dennis proposed, she decided it would be helpful to get married, too. Then nobody could accuse her of being a single mom.

The wedding took place on July 20, 1996, in the living room of Dennis's parents' home. Desma wore an off-white dress that fell below her knees and had cost $6 at a local thrift store. Dennis wore blue jeans and a dress shirt with sleeves that were too short. Desma had gotten a meat and cheese tray from the supermarket, and half a dozen two-liter bottles of pop. "It was awful," she said later, laughing her belly laugh. "Threw it together in less than a week." According to Desma, on their wedding night, after they had gone to a hotel, Dennis caught her off guard by saying, "It will be over my dead body that you ever leave me." She described him as having a controlling nature, but said that she only came to see this side of his personality fully after basic training. Dennis Brooks would later dispute much of what Desma said about him, and described Desma as someone who slanted stories about their relationship so that she came out in a better light and he came out in a worse light when that was not exactly how it was in real life.

On August 19, 1996, Desma Brooks left for Fort Jackson, South Carolina. She had never held a gun before, and it was the first time she had traveled outside of the state of Indiana. She had a gritty determination that served her well, however, and she responded positively to the structured environment, even as she also proved injury-prone. Halfway through the training, Desma rolled her right ankle while running. She limped back to the barracks. Her company was slated to rappel down a wooden tower that afternoon — and to get to the tower, they were going to road-march three miles. Desma didn't want to complain of an injury, for fear of being forced to restart basic training from the beginning, because she felt she was already spending too much time away from her son. Desma did the road march, crossed three styles of rope bridges, and then rappeled down the wall while a belayed rope passed under one thigh and over the opposite shoulder. The soldier who went before her was supposed to make sure the rope belayed smoothly, but he gave Desma a jerky descent, culminating in an abrupt drop. She landed hard and buckled. A drill sergeant started hollering at the soldier who had done belay, but Desma interrupted.

"I'm all right, I'm all right," she said. "I just need help up."

They marched three miles back. At the barracks, she could not get her boot off. Her battle buddy alerted another drill sergeant.

"What the hell is wrong with you, Private?" he demanded.

"I don't know, Drill Sergeant, I hurt myself."

"Why didn't you say something?"

"Because I didn't want to be recycled."

He took out a Gerber and cut the boot off. Desma's foot was black and blue up to her shin. The drill sergeant said she could try doing kitchen duty for a couple of days and see if the injury healed. She missed the gas chamber and hand-to-hand combat, but rejoined her platoon for the rest of basic training. She injured herself a second time, after she got her foot tangled in the straps of a duffel bag while standing on the tailgate of a truck, and fell, landing on her tailbone, which split in half. But she made it through the final exercises without reporting the second injury.

When Desma made an appointment with a medic to have the Norplant contraceptive removed, thinking she might want to have children with her new husband, the doctor had to dig out six plastic cartridges from her newly muscular bicep. She still could not say why she had joined the military, but she was proud of what she had achieved. "Nobody thought I would make it through basic training," she said afterward. "And just out of spite, I finished it. I hated every minute there, it was the hardest thing I ever did in my life. But at the end, I cried. I had accomplished something. And to somebody out there, it was something meaningful. Maybe not so much to myself, but whatever. You know? I proved them wrong."

Desma went straight from Fort Jackson, South Carolina, to Fort Lee, Virginia. She had chosen to become an automated logistics specialist, or a 92A ("ninety-two Alpha"), because she thought it would give her job skills that would translate into the civilian world. A logistics specialist ran computer programs that allowed battalions to order vehicle parts, guns, night vision goggles, and other equipment. Men and women enrolled in the classes in roughly equal numbers, and at Fort Lee Desma found herself in an environment in which she drew no special attention for her gender. She trained on large desktop computers, using four-inch floppy disks.

When Desma returned home for Christmas, she was shocked to discover that during her five-month absence, Josh had developed a stutter. She had intended for Josh to stay with his surrogate father, Keith — the man for whom Desma used to babysit — but instead Josh had been bounced around, staying alternately with Keith, Desma's new husband, and Desma's mother. Dennis was living with his parents, and Desma moved in there, too. They shared his old bedroom in the upstairs part of his parents' house. "Josh didn't want to stay there — he wanted to stay with Grandma," recalled Desma. "So at night, I would take him down to Grandma's and first thing in the morning I would go get him. He was my sunshine. I would rock him and sing the Barney song and he would go to sleep in my lap."

Desma turned twenty-one on January 28, 1997. Flush with cash for a change, she decided to buy a car. She had never owned one before. She bought a used Chevy Corsica, gray with a red interior. Her older sister had the same car in the opposite color scheme — red with a gray interior. When she showed up for drill for the first time that February, Desma could see her reflection in the toes of her boots. "Oh, a newbie," said a noncommissioned officer, looking her over. "That'll wear off quick." In the months that followed, Desma stopped pressing her uniform but stubbornly continued to shine her boots; she took pride in the fact that she could make a mirrored toe and heel. Her chugging belly laugh and ready smile endeared her to other members of Bravo Company, and she fit easily into the unit. She worked in the section that handled automotive repair and weapons parts. That's what she was *supposed* to do; actually, the National Guard armory in Bedford had few parts. Mostly Desma and her fellow soldiers counted tent poles and camo netting, then played euchre. At annual training, they did the usual required exercises, and played war games in the woods. To burn off their extra ammo, they would hide wearing their MILES gear — it stood for multiple integrated laser engagement system — and shoot blanks at each other. You put the gear on over your uniform, and if you were shot it would beep incessantly, indicating that you were dead, until somebody came and turned it off with a key. Bravo Company and Charlie Company ganged up on Alpha Company; it had become a tradition after the time when Alpha had gotten their trucks tangled up in their own concertina wire. Bravo and Charlie would kill off everyone in Alpha, declare the war over, and then drink a keg of beer. Desma loved the camaraderie.

Of course Desma befriended talkative Debbie Helton. During one annual training, they found themselves stuck in a foxhole together, and Debbie asked, "Want something to drink?" They shared some whiskey. Both women belonged to Bravo, although they worked in different sections and spent time with different friends. When they socialized after their training exercises, Debbie gravitated toward the older crowd, a mostly male group that habitually drank at Shorty's, while Desma ran with a younger crowd that frequented a variety of bars. Of everyone in her company, Desma grew closest to a woman named Stacy Glory — she happened to be the sister of the person who had originally dared Desma to join the Guard, and they lived near each other in Spurgeon. They carpooled to Bedford on drill weekends. Stacy had four children — two boys and two girls — and also was a single mother. She had joined the regular army straight out of high school, and when her term of service ended, she joined the reserves. She had deployed to the Gulf War, shortly after she had given birth to her oldest child. Stacy had found the yearlong separation painful, and later she transferred into the National Guard, because they did not send people overseas for lengthy tours of duty. Stacy had a degree in political science, and she and Desma talked politics in the car; they both listened to National Public Radio, and both followed international news on the BBC. Often they got so caught up in their conversations that they did not notice how late they were until they got to the armory and saw everybody else already standing in formation.

Debbie Helton marveled at Desma's insouciance, the way she and Stacy would casually stroll in late every single drill weekend. It got to be a running joke. The first sergeant would call out, "Brooks!" Invariably there would be no answer. "She's on her way!" soldiers started calling out in response, to rolling laughter. Usually Desma would saunter in before the first sergeant had finished taking the roll, and make a face at the assembled company; this is what you get, she seemed to be saying. "I remember her always being late," recalled Debbie. "Never on time. Really funny, and always late." But Debbie approved of Desma's high spirits and the way she never missed a chance to socialize and always put on something revealing. "And then when she wanted to clean up, she'd clean up. Like if we'd all go out at night, a bunch of us, then she'd be nice and cleavagey," Debbie said. "She would wear the tops to enhance herself. That's our Desma. Not shy — not a bit shy."

The keg parties and the euchre games and the late nights at bars made the experience of belonging to the National Guard a lot more fun than Desma had anticipated. In a few years, she realized that she had grown closer to her fellow soldiers than she had been to friends in school. During one annual training, Desma went out drinking with Peggy Weiss, the administrative NCO of Bravo

Company 113 — basically she made sure that jobs in the unit were filled and that Bravo Company soldiers got their paychecks. They returned to Camp Atterbury at about two in the morning, and by then Peggy had gotten loud and boisterous. They ran into Captain Hoskins in the orderly room. Despite the late hour, he was wearing a crisply pressed uniform, but he was accompanied by a disheveled lieutenant who was covered from head to toe in mud and grass. Peggy turned to Hoskins.

"Sir, are you lazy?" she barked. "Or are you just too stupid to get down in the mud?"

Hoskins just shook his head and walked away.

"I'm going to bed," announced Peggy. "People are pissy."

Desma lived for those moments.

And she had come to depend on the extra paycheck. Desma and Dennis had purchased a stick-built house with yellow siding for $42,000. It had three bedrooms, one bath, a full basement, and a screened-in porch. They had signed up for a variable rate mortgage, however, and over time the interest rate climbed from 6.8 percent up to 23 percent. In the process, their monthly payments tripled, from $325 to almost $900. As the financial stress mounted, Desma's husband began to have problems controlling his anger, according to Desma. Once he shoved her backward into a glass door that broke, and a shard of glass punctured one of her lungs, Desma said. She also remembered that Dennis could only hold on to a given job for a few months at a time. He quit one job while Desma was pregnant. Desma developed preeclampsia, and the baby had to be induced; after their daughter Paige was born early, the hospital sent a bill for $6,000. To help pay off the debt, Desma returned to work at Jasper Desk. When her husband lost his next job, she had to make their monthly house payments by herself for a while, according to Desma.

Dennis remembered everything differently. He said that Desma was the cause of their financial problems, as she kept spending more money than he was earning. She bounced one check after another, according to Dennis — and according to court documents Desma was charged with several counts of check fraud (for amounts ranging from $28 to $38). He was never out of work for more than a few days at a time, Dennis said, and even when he lost one factory job, he still worked part-time as an emergency medical technician in an ambulance. Dennis also recounted an alternate version of the story about the fight where Desma wound up with glass in her back: he did give her a "little shove" that sent her into a glass door, which did break, Dennis conceded, but that's not when the glass went into her back; according to him, the glass went into her back about ten minutes later, when she stepped backward and accidentally bumped into the already broken shards of glass.

Figuring that they had better not have any more children, Desma got another Norplant device; it suppressed her heavy periods, just as the previous device had done, which she considered a blessing. Several months later, however, she began to puzzle over the fact that she could no longer button her favorite jeans. A doctor discovered that she had somehow conceived another child, despite using the birth control device. At this point, her husband was working again, but according to Desma, Dennis lost the job before she gave birth, and once again Desma delivered a child without health insurance. Their daughter Alexis was born in 1999 — Desma opted for a tubal ligation after the birth, to avoid getting pregnant again — and they got another hospital bill, this time for $9,000.

A few weeks after giving birth, Desma found a factory job in Huntingburg, Indiana. She caught baseboards as a router spat them out and stacked them on a skid, and she made $7.50 an hour. Her relationship with her husband continued to fray. Desma felt that Dennis was failing to support their family and in her estimation his temper got worse. At one point, Desma said, he shoved a rifle so far into her mouth that he chipped one of her back teeth. Dennis vehemently denied that this ever happened. Desma's drill weekends turned into a form of escape — a way to get away from the perpetual financial worry and the perpetual conflict. The Guard offered camaraderie, a supplemental income, and an alternative arena in which to prove her competence.

Desma could be brittle, especially around her superiors, but they could see that she was a wizard with gadgets. In the spring of 2000, the battalion was issued a shipment of used SINGCARS radios that had been passed along by active duty army troops. SINGCARS stood for Single Channel Ground and Airborne Radio System, and the new radios employed voice encryption and frequency hopping systems to defy an enemy's ability to listen in — although the frequency hopping system sometimes meant that even friendly soldiers heard only garble. Desma took a class at Atterbury and learned the radios had digital clocks that needed to be synched within three seconds, and painstakingly retimed every radio in Bravo Company so that the soldiers could actually hear one another talk. She spent drill weekend after drill weekend teaching everyone else how to use the radios without accidentally changing the timing.

Later that spring, the 113th Support Battalion traveled to Fort Polk, Louisiana, to spend two weeks in joint readiness training exercises. While most of Bravo Company flew to Louisiana, Desma instead rode in a convoy down to Louisville, Kentucky, where she helped load trucks onto river barges. The barge operators balked at allowing Desma herself to board, as there were no other women in the flotilla, but after a short commotion during which she cursed a lot, she was allowed onto a barge. They floated slowly down the Ohio and then the Mississippi. At Fort Polk, the contingent that had come by water met up with the others who had come by air, carrying Debbie Helton's potatoes in their rucksacks. Hoskins grew frustrated when he discovered that only Bravo Company could use their radios; soldiers in the other companies kept causing the radios to malfunction. And if the soldiers couldn't talk to each other, they couldn't do joint readiness exercises. The whole point of joint readiness was acting in concert, which was only possible if they could communicate.

Hoskins sent Desma around to fix what was wrong. She walked all over Fort Polk, stopping at one truck after another, giving impromptu courses on the radio's digital timing. Desma delivered her lessons in plain language, never made people feel dumb, cracked jokes about the idiocy of the military in giving them this complicated shit, and made the radios work. At one point, Desma realized she had been retiming radios straight through the night and had not slept at all. The Louisiana sun blazed overhead. She crawled under a trailer because the shade looked so inviting. A sergeant major found her napping there.

"Soldier, get out from underneath that truck!" he hollered.

Desma snapped, "Sergeant Major, I've been running my ass off for twenty-three hours out of the last twenty-four. What have you done today? When did you get out of bed?"

He marched off in a huff and she went back to sleep.

When she got all the radios up, Hoskins was so relieved that he gave Desma a medal of commendation. "Specialist Brooks was selected by the joint readiness training center's observer controllers as a unit logistics warrior for the training period," wrote her commanding officer. "Her knowledge of the SINGCARS operation was instrumental in the success of the mission. . . . Specialist Desma D. Brooks devoted attention to all of her many responsibilities with resourcefulness and enthusiasm. Specialist Brooks displays a winning personality coupled with a positive attitude which resulted in her surpassing the standard in setting the example for other soldiers to follow."

Years later, Desma would call that moment

her single greatest achievement. Sometimes Desma seemed compromised in other areas of life, yet when the military put her in front of a piece of technology, she performed like a virtuoso. Her friend Stacy Glory was the unit's most adept user of the complicated military software known as SAMS (Standard Army Maintenance System), and she taught Desma the system's rules and kinks. Soon Desma became known as a whiz on the SAMS system, too. In the summer of 2000, when it came time to renew her contract, Desma did not hesitate to sign up for another three years. "I got friends," she said. "I only have to show up one weekend a month and hang out for two weeks in the summer. Yeah, it's a bitch, but it ain't so bad. It's an extra paycheck, you know? They ain't going to send me anywhere, no big deal." She got another $2,500 bonus for reenlisting.

That fall, Desma voted for George W. Bush for president. She did not consider herself a Republican, necessarily; she voted for the person who struck her as the most real human being, regardless of their place on the political spectrum. She was moved by small, idiosyncratic revelations of character — she followed the news closely, and read current events like a novel, zeroing in on particular moments she found telling. She decided not to vote for Gore after she saw him fail to recognize a marble bust of George Washington, for example. She voted for Bush because she thought he was no bullshit. Also, she had liked his father. Back in the 1990s, Desma had devoured news of the Persian Gulf War. She had been surprised to learn that before the war, the United States had helped to bolster Saddam Hussein's hold on power so as to thwart Iran. Desma thought if you were going to carry a gun, you might as well try to understand the context in which it might be fired.

Initially, she had applauded getting the US troops out of the Gulf quickly, before too many American soldiers lost their lives, but in the years that followed, after she heard about Hussein's alleged atrocities, she came to view the decision to leave him in power as a mistake. Desma was troubled by Hussein's alleged barbarity, such as the killing of thousands of Kurds in what became known as the Halabja massacre. "If you didn't agree with him and you were not of his particular Muslim belief — Sunni, Shiite, whatever — he mustard-gassed them. He drew them into an auditorium, offering land by parcel, first come, first served, shut the doors, and killed four thousand people with mustard gas." She did not believe in allowing despots to remain in power.

Early in 2001, Desma's marriage fell apart. Desma recounted the developments in this way: her husband started a new job and told her he was earning enough to cover their bills, but somehow the mortgage payments did not get paid, and the bank announced it was going to put the house into foreclosure. Dennis moved out, and they began divorce proceedings. Josh started third grade that fall, while Desma was still in the middle of trying to unsnarl the financial tangle. The girls were only two and three years old, and spent their days at home with Desma, or with her cousin Lesley, when Desma had to go to work. One morning that September, Desma put Josh on the bus and turned on *Good Morning America* while she fixed eggs for her daughters. Jury selection had begun in the trial of Andrea Yates, a woman who was accused of drowning her five children. Then the hosts interrupted the show. "There's been some sort of explosion at the World Trade Center in New York City," said Diane Sawyer. "One report said, and we can't confirm any of this, that a plane may have hit one of the two towers of the World Trade Center." Desma stared at a live image of black smoke billowing out of the tower, then she watched as a second airplane plowed into the other tower.

"My God!" cried Diane Sawyer. Her co-host, Charles Gibson, announced, "This looks like some sort of a concerted effort to attack the World Trade Center."

Desma agreed; she knew what she had just seen was not an accident.

A neighbor called. "Are you watching this?" she asked in disbelief.

"Holy shit, what does this *mean*?" Desma said.

"I don't know — I just needed to call somebody," her neighbor replied.

Desma heard from her readiness NCO later in the day, but all he said was, "We're not going anywhere, we're not doing anything right now. Just wait for more instructions."

"Well, if you need me, I'm here," Desma said.

That evening, she kept the television on, hoping for survivors, but every time Josh saw the airplanes fly into the skyscrapers he told his mother that another attack was occurring. "Pick a movie," Desma finally told him. They turned off the news and watched *The Lion King.* That was how 9/11 unfolded for Desma — live TV, phone calls from friends in the Guard, and then a Disney movie. She did not find it incongruous to yaw from conversations with fellow soldiers to caring for her children; these were the various aspects of her life, her incoming and outgoing tides, and they felt to her like an integrated whole. She happened to be both a soldier and a mother, and did not see the two roles as being at odds.

In the days that followed, anti-Muslim sentiment flared across southern Indiana. Desma drove through Petersburg and saw a sign in the window of a family-owned gas station that said, RUN, RAGHEADS, RUN. She and Stacy Glory made bets on who would utter the most racist comments inside the Bedford armory, but neither of them anticipated hearing that kind of talk from one particular leader, a man they had always respected.

"Drop a bomb, kill 'em all," Desma heard him say. "Fuckin' ragheads."

"How can you say that?" she objected. "I can understand you being angry, but Jesus Christ! You can't just wipe out an entire nation of people because of a small group of extremists. Then you're no better than Hitler, or those people in Rwanda!"

But she might as well have been speaking Latin.

Although Desma did not like the blanket hatred that she saw around her, she supported President Bush's "war on terror." He had to take decisive action, she thought, he couldn't just stand by and let it happen; otherwise more people would do the same thing. She took note of the subsequent vote in Congress, and felt scorn for the individual who had cast the lone dissent. How could you vote against a war on terror? The new security measures at the airport should have been adopted long ago as far as she was concerned. At the same time, Desma held part of herself in reserve, waiting for fallout. That was what she did in a crisis — put part of herself away for safekeeping. He has to do something, God help him, Desma thought; I think he's doing the right thing, but I'm going to wait and see.

In the months that followed, Desma tried to track the course of the war in Afghanistan, but she had trouble finding good news coverage. It drove her crazy that the reports were so niggling; only BBC Radio seemed to disburse much information. As casualties began to accrue, she was struck by how few people around her seemed aware that the war was resulting in deaths. The following year, Desma sold her house in lieu of foreclosure, and used the proceeds to pay off the outstanding property taxes and mortgage payments. She made no money on the deal, but succeeded in wiping out their debt. After her divorce became final, Desma got a new job waiting tables at a nearby truck stop. It served food and fuel to the traffic flowing along Interstate 64. A modern-day river of freight, I-64 echoed the course of the nearby Ohio as it cut from east to west across southern Indiana. The truck stop was near the town of Dale, right where the interstate crossed Highway 231, then the longest north-to-south route in Indiana. Desma dropped her children off at her cousin Lesley's house on her way to work; she paid her cousin to care for the two girls while Josh went to school. Sometimes Lesley watched Josh, too; Lesley had two children of her own, one of them a boy close to Josh's age, and the pair of them wrangled like brothers.

At the truck stop, Desma learned how to carry a big tray, and joshed amiably with the regulars. Steel haulers stopped by for dinner, killing time as they waited for their rigs to be loaded at AK Steel's cold mill facility, down beside the Ohio. It produced the widest steel sheet in North America. Other drivers ate lunch while their rigs were loaded with shiny rolls of aluminum over at the Alcoa smelting facility in Warrick. Desma also got to know the truckers who worked for Heartland Express, an Indiana-based trucking company that specialized in short to medium hauls for the automotive, plastic, paper, manufacturing, food, and retail industries, as well as the drivers for Montgomery, an Ohio-based trucking company that specialized in refrigerated goods and dry freight. She knew the drivers by their CB handles. Bone Hauler carried steel; Old Man worked for Heartland Express; Scatterbrain and Outlaw did repo work, confiscating rigs from owner-operators who could not make their payments. The truckers appreciated the outgoing waitress with the saucy manner. You could walk in looking pretty rough and you would not faze Desma. She took home several hundred dollars a week in tips.

Desma met Jimmy on a cold night in

November 2002. He delivered brand-new rigs to truckers all over the states of Indiana, Iowa, Ohio, and Pennsylvania. Jimmy sat down at one of Desma's tables with a group that was telling jokes that got dirtier as the sky darkened. Jimmy grew chagrined after spotting a plastic bracelet on Desma's wrist that said WHAT WOULD JESUS DO? Josh had brought it home from Bible school one Sunday afternoon as a gift for his mother. It wasn't Desma's style but she wore it for his sake.

Jimmy assumed she was church-going and said they better stop telling such bad jokes or they were going to offend their waitress.

"What screws like a tiger and winks?" asked Desma.

"What?" said Jimmy.

"Roar!" said Desma and winked.

The other truckers slapped at the Formica until their plates jumped. Jimmy asked her what she was doing that evening. She had plans, Desma said. It was karaoke night. She was going to make a fool of herself with some of the other waitresses. Jimmy came along and watched. Then he asked if Desma would like to go out to dinner sometime. She said no thanks, because the transmission had just dropped out of her car, and it was in the shop, leaving her stranded.

"I have a Firebird you can drive," said Jimmy.

"I'm not going to drive your car," said Desma.

"Just until you get yours fixed."

"I've got kids," said Desma.

"I understand," said Jimmy.

He drove her back to his place and gave her the keys to his Firebird. It was red, fast, and low to the ground. Jimmy told her not to wreck it. That evening, snow started falling, and did not stop until the following day. While trying to pick up Josh, Desma spun the Firebird into a four-foot bank of plowed snow. The car was not damaged, but she couldn't get it to move. She called Jimmy.

"I got your car stuck," she confessed.

"What the hell!" he said. "You haven't had it for twenty-four hours!"

She laughed that chugging belly laugh. Jimmy and his father came to dig the car out. Jimmy was ten years older than Desma, lean, rough-looking, with dark hair and a long mustache that drooped down either side of his mouth. He had never been in the military and had no enthusiasm for her service, but he liked her and he liked her children. He had some of his own, although they were older. Desma and Jimmy dated for a few months, fell into a routine, and decided to try living together. They found an old concrete garage in Hatfield, Indiana, that had been converted into a living space. It was twelve hundred square feet and prone to flooding. When they got heavy rain, Desma had to walk up and down the street, cleaning out the old leaves and debris from the ditch. Otherwise water came in through her front door. "I'd be out there up to my knees in mud," said Desma. "But you can't have three inches of water in your living room while you're raising children. It doesn't work." Desma and Jimmy split the rent, which was $550 a month.

With the salary she was earning as a waitress and the extra salary she got from the Guard, Desma was making a total of about $9,000 a year (supplemented by the tips she got at the truck stop); she had the wherewithal to feed, clothe, and house herself and her three children, but not much else. Desma saw a newspaper advertisement for a part-time job that paid $8 an hour working as an aide at the Owensboro branch of the Kentucky United Methodist Homes for Children and Youth. It served children who had histories of abuse, neglect, abandonment, or trauma. She applied. Owensboro, Kentucky, was a twenty-minute drive, over on the other side of the Ohio River. Desma started working at the group home two or three days a week, filling in as a substitute. It felt like a calling. Desma learned that she had a knack for getting along with the troubled kids who washed up there flotsam-like. She was tough enough to stand up to them, yet there was no case so hard that she did not feel for the child. She knew they were all paying the price for somebody else's dysfunction. After about a year, the organization hired her part-time. The pay she earned at the youth home boosted her total income to about $17,000.

Throughout the fall of 2002, as they drove to Bedford for drill each month, Desma and Stacy listened to news reports about Hans Blix and the team of UN inspectors who were attempting to determine whether Iraq possessed so-called weapons of mass destruction. Desma had no doubt that Hussein possessed chemical weapons — she had heard convincing news stories about his purchases of chemical and biological agents — but she had no idea whether there was any real crisis, or whether the Bush team was trying to manufacture a sense of outrage so that Bush could finish the task his father had failed to complete. She thought Hussein probably needed to be removed from power, but wanted to be sure it was done for the right reasons.

Desma watched the hearings of the Senate Foreign Relations Committee in which Senator Joe Biden tried to slow the Bush people down. She felt swayed by the argument that it was not a good idea to invade Iraq while there were still soldiers in Afghanistan — fighting two wars at the same time struck her as risky. Did they really have enough soldiers to finish both jobs? Around the country, National Guard units were starting to go overseas for the first time in decades. On drill weekends, her unit began doing exercises with live ammunition. They had never before practiced with live ammo — it was expensive. They were also getting lectures on the Geneva Convention, and what was legally permissible in a war zone. And they had just been told they could earn $1,000 for every new recruit they brought to the armory, and an additional $1,000 if the recruit made it through basic training. All the changes — the live ammo, the lectures, the lure of $2,000 per recruit — she knew what they meant. The regular army was being asked to cover too much ground.

That Christmas, Desma bought her son a Mongoose mountain bike from Walmart. He had outgrown his old bicycle and he rode the new one constantly. Paige and Alexis, now five and three, respectively, had started going to Head Start. At home, they watched a lot of PBS and Disney, especially *Lilo & Stitch.* On Sunday, March 16, 2003, Josh turned ten, and Desma got him a twelve-foot trampoline. Josh rode his Mongoose mountain bike off the roof of the shed onto the trampoline; he said he was being Evel Knievel. Desma took the bike away and turned on *Meet the Press.* Vice President Dick Cheney was speaking about Iraq; the United States had amassed a hundred thousand troops in Kuwait. "I think things have gotten so bad inside Iraq from the standpoint of the Iraqi people, my belief is we will in fact be greeted as liberators," Cheney said on *Meet the Press.* "I think it will go relatively quickly. Weeks, rather than months."

Desma stared at the guy. Was he serious? They still had troops in Afghanistan. Did he really think they would be out of Iraq in weeks?

"If your analysis is not correct, and we're not treated as liberators, but as conquerors," asked Tim Russert, "and the Iraqis begin to resist, particularly in Baghdad, do you think the American people are prepared for a long, costly, and bloody battle with significant American casualties?"

"Well, I don't think it's likely to unfold that way, Tim, because I really do believe that we will be greeted as liberators," Cheney answered. "I've talked with a lot of Iraqis in the last several months myself, had them to the White House. The president and I have met with them, various groups and individuals, people who have devoted their lives from outside to trying to change things inside Iraq. The read we get on the people of Iraq is there is no question but that they want to get rid of Saddam Hussein and they will welcome as liberators the United States when we come to do that."

"Bullshit!" Desma said out loud.

Was Cheney an idiot or was he just lying? Desma hated it when people didn't call things straight. She shrugged off her anger and left the house to pick up the cake she had ordered for Josh's party that afternoon. He had gotten so big — he didn't care about *Toy Story* anymore; now it was motorcycles, motorcycles, motorcycles. Eight fourth-graders came over that afternoon to bounce on the new trampoline and eat motorcycle cake.

Four days later, the United States began intensive bombing of Iraq. The idea was that a display of overwhelming force could destroy an enemy's will to fight; the United States planned to bomb Iraq into submission, in hopes this would render the country easy to invade. Desma was struck by the fact that while "shock and awe" was taking place thousands of miles away, everything seemed completely normal at home — *Lilo & Stitch* and the thrill of the bouncy trampoline. Special forces moved into the oil fields around Basra, while the main part of the invading army started advancing up through southern Iraq.

One factor that the Bush team had not anticipated, however, was the immense difference in the quality of intelligence they were getting out of Iraq, compared with the intelligence they had gotten out of Afghanistan. In Afghanistan, the CIA had a long history of involvement, deep ties, and numerous trustworthy sources; the reports that the CIA had been delivering about that country had proven highly accurate. In Iraq, however, the CIA's work would turn out to be wildly off base. According to *Cobra II: The Inside Story of the Invasion and Occupation of Iraq,* by Michael R. Gordon and General Bernard E. Trainor, the agency told the US military to expect easy surrenders, warm welcomes, and possible parades. Instead soldiers and marines found themselves confronting not only Iraqi military but also armed civilians dressed in black who were fighting back ferociously. All over Iraq, US forces ran into unexpectedly stiff resistance, and at the same time they also encountered a series of thorny logistical problems.

In a town called Nasiriyah, a convoy of the 507th Maintenance Company from Fort Bliss took a wrong turn and drove straight into the city instead of going around it. Located near an important crossing over the Euphrates, Nasiriyah was the site of bitter fighting. Soldiers in the 507th were not supposed to see combat — they were just a maintenance outfit — but they had mistakenly driven right into the fray. Among the soldiers who had gone missing were several women. One of them, Jessica Lynch, a nineteen-year-old supply clerk from West Virginia, had just joined the army to pay for a college education. Also missing in action were Lori Piestewa, the driver of the Humvee that had taken the wrong turn — she was the mother of two children — and an army cook named Shoshana Johnson. On March 27, 2003, seven days after the start of the Iraq War, while Lynch was still missing in action and Johnson was being held captive (Piestewa had died), Desma reported to the Bedford armory. It was a Thursday, and she didn't usually go to the armory during the middle of the week, but she had missed a drill weekend and had to make up the time. She was supposed to arrive at 7:30 a.m., but actually arrived closer to 8:00 a.m.

"I know, I'm late," she announced to Sergeant First Class Andrew Hendrikson.

"You need to come in and have a seat," Hendrikson said.

"I've never sat down for an ass-chewing in my life," said Desma. "Why start now?"

Her drinking buddy Peggy Weiss stood nearby in the hallway. Desma looked over and saw to her surprise that Peggy's face was beet red. Was Peggy crying?

"Desma," Hendrikson said, his voice stony, "you need to go home, you need to pack all your stuff, all your military gear. And you need to be back here on Monday morning, zero-seven-three-oh. You're being mobilized with Alpha Company. You're going to Iraq."

Unable to absorb what Hendrikson was saying, Desma focused on a single detail.

"Alpha Company?" she objected. "Who the fuck thought *that* was a good idea? They die, every year, at AT! I can't go to war with those people!"

Hendrikson said nothing.

"I'm not going," Desma announced.

Then she got her official orders, a piece of paper that said she would serve a "period of active duty not to exceed three hundred and sixty five days," and realized she did not have much of a choice in the matter. She could fail to show up, in which case she would most likely go to jail, or she could plead hardship, saying she wasn't able to find care for her children. But nobody did that. It was not a socially acceptable option. "I'm a single mom, I [could] claim hardship, I can't go," Desma would say later. "There's no dignity in that. Might as well just say, 'Hey, I'm a dirtbag.' " So Desma obeyed her orders, because she could not bear to lose the esteem of her fellow soldiers. She knew what it had cost Josh when she had gone away to basic training; she would never forget returning to his stutter. But every parent in Alpha Company had been asked to leave their children, and she was not going to desert her teammates.

She went home and told her children that she was being sent to Iraq for a year. The girls asked if she was going to die. "I'm not going to die," Desma said. "I stay on the post and work on computers. I just have to go away for a while." She had been given three days to figure out where her children would live. Josh wanted to stay with his surrogate father, her ex-boyfriend Keith. Keith had married and moved half an hour north to Gentryville, Indiana, but he still spent time with Josh on a regular basis, and agreed to keep Josh for the year. Desma figured the girls would feel most at home with her cousin Lesley, who lived nearby in Petersburg. Desma wrote a will, named her cousin and her sister as the executrices, and took out a $400,000 life insurance policy. On Sunday, Desma drove the two girls to her cousin's house, told them not to worry, said listen to Lesley, and that she would call often. Then she drove Josh to his father's. The girls had been hysterical; Josh was silent. She did not say good-bye; she just said, "I'll talk to you soon."

Desma reported to Bedford as instructed on March 31, 2003, along with another dozen members of Bravo Company who were also being deployed with Alpha Company. The soldiers from Bravo picked up their weapons from the arsenal at Bedford and boarded a bus bound for Stout Army Air Field in Indianapolis, where they were going to meet up with their colleagues from Alpha Company. A young woman Desma did not know sat down behind her, looking glazed. Desma spent April 1 in a chaotic crowd of soldiers who were busy debating the merits of the second war; administration officials were now backpedaling, and Bush had observed that a campaign in a country the size of California could be longer and more difficult than predicted. The headline in *USA Today* read, OFFICIALS WHO FORECAST A BRIEF CONFLICT NOW SAY IT'LL BE NEITHER QUICK NOR EASY. Desma started calling the whole predicament (being at Stout Field, all the media hullabaloo) the worst April Fool's joke ever. At the same time, Desma's paycheck from the National Guard increased more than twentyfold: she had been earning $128 per month for drilling with her unit, but now her pay jumped to $3,000 per month. She was suddenly making $36,000 a year as a soldier — double what she had previously been earning from all three of her jobs put together.

Stout Field served as the headquarters of the Indiana National Guard. They were only going to be there for perhaps a week. Before they went to Iraq, they would train for several months at Fort Bragg, in North Carolina. The army called this period of time being in "premob"; later Desma would refer to it as "three months of hell." At Stout Field, Desma and the other soldiers picked up additional gear they would take with them to Iraq — ballistic vests, gas masks, and night vision goggles, among other things. They had to complete a combat driving course in which instructors urged them to drive like they stole it, and showed them how to force other vehicles off the road. And they spent hours in the freight yard, counting tents and tent poles, matching trucks by identification number to those listed on their inventories, packing motor oil and spare parts, weighing everything, and loading it all into large metal shipping containers known as conexes. There were no pay phones at Stout Field, so Desma bought the cheapest cell phone she could find, a flip phone from Verizon. "Please don't cry," she told the girls. "I'll be home as quick as I can." She told Josh, who never said much, "I'll see you when I get a pass."

One evening, Desma walked into the dining hall and glanced around. She did not know as many people in Alpha. Off to one side, Desma spotted a group of happy families having some sort of celebration; the soldiers belonged to a different unit, and apparently their command had given them permission to invite their spouses and children to join them for a meal. Desma sat down in a foul mood. She spotted the young woman who had not spoken on the bus, holding a tray with a blank stare on her face. "Hey," Desma said, and pulled out a chair. The young woman sat down but did not eat. She just froze, still holding the tray with both hands.

"What's your name?" Desma asked.

"Mary Ferren," said the girl.

"How old are you?" Desma asked.

"Eighteen," said Mary.

Oh, holy shit, Desma thought, but she just nodded. Mary said she had only recently finished basic training and she had not been able to say good-bye to her mother. In the middle of shock and awe, she had left a note on the kitchen table. And over there, on the other side of the room, happy soldiers were milling around with their families. Mary was white with anger. Then she broke into tearless convulsions. The two of them became inseparable. Ostensibly, Desma took Mary under her wing, although sometimes it worked the other way around. For Desma, Mary became the one constant in an ever-changing landscape of upheaval as plans for their unit altered almost daily. First there were delays because of ghost records. The commander of Alpha Company had a large number of people on the roster who were not actually in the military anymore. Additional soldiers had to be called up to fill the empty slots. Then there were ghost trucks — they could not find all of the vehicles they were supposed to have.

Eventually their destination changed, too: they were not going to Fort Bragg after all, they were going to Camp Atterbury instead. Supposedly the reversal came about due to all of the media attention being paid to nineteen-year-old Jessica Lynch, who had just been rescued by a team of special forces. Lynch, Johnson, and Piestewa were not supposed to see combat, and yet the three female soldiers had driven right into it. The idea of more female truck drivers being captured by the Iraqi military had spooked the top brass, according to rumors. Alpha 113 was a truck driving company, and it had been open to women for a long time. Of the ninety soldiers in Alpha Company, the group that Desma was being deployed with, one-third were women. Supposedly the generals had decided that sending so many women to Iraq was a bad idea; the new plan was for them to support the infantry from the safety of Kuwait. Because they were going to train at a facility in Indiana, Desma would be able to see her children more often during the months before they mobilized, although each time they met, they would have to separate again, and the thought of having to part from her children repeatedly almost made her not want to see them at all, so painful did she find the act of leave-taking.

At Camp Atterbury, on her first evening, Desma looked up from a meal to see CNN broadcasting live from Baghdad. The sun was just coming up in Iraq, and bombs were dropping with ferocious rapidity. Desma stared at the TV screen, unable to eat. Noticing the pall that had fallen over the room, a master sergeant walked over and turned off the television. As the days slipped by, the invading forces plowed forward into the center of Iraq. By the middle of April, they had taken Baghdad, Kirkuk, and Tikrit. Meanwhile, Desma spent hours at the shooting range, certifying that she was qualified to use her weapon; took mandatory classes on sexual assault, because ever since women had joined the military, there had been ongoing reports of harassment, assault, and rape; took mandatory classes on equal opportunity law, because there had also been allegations of workplace discrimination; attended lectures on the Geneva Conventions, because in a war zone soldiers sometimes did other things that were not legally permissible; and listened to briefings by Operations Security experts who instructed the soldiers not to discuss their mission, their deployment dates, the location of their sleeping quarters, their convoy routes, the names of their colleagues, their equipment, trends in morale, or security procedures. "Don't tell people shit," was how Desma summarized the OpSec lectures.

They also repeated key parts of basic training. One day, they were doing three-to-five-second rushes — the soldiers lay down on the ground, as if they were under fire, and then jumped up and ran for three to five seconds with their weapons pointing forward, and then lay back down on the ground. During the exercise, Desma whacked the top of her rifle into her mouth so hard that she split her top right lateral incisor in two. A medic pulled the broken tooth, leaving her with a black hole in the middle of her grin. It made her look rakish.

Desma and Mary took advantage of every opportunity they had to leave the post. One day, they drove over to Edinburgh, Indiana, because they wanted to pick up some toiletries at Walmart. After that, they were just driving around aimlessly when they stumbled across a tattoo parlor.

"Hey, you want to get a tattoo?" Desma asked.

"Why not?" said Mary. "If I'm old enough to be sent to Iraq, then I guess I'm old enough to get a tattoo."

Desma leafed through albums, studying pictures of tattoos, wondering what image to take with her. Mary knew what she wanted right away: a big heart with wings and her father's name underneath. He had died of a heart attack and she missed him terribly. While the tattoo artist worked on Mary, Desma found a picture of twining vines and orchids, which she decided would look nice spread across her lower back. After about an hour, the tattoo artist finished working on Mary, and told her to sit up.

"Whoa, I think I'm going to be sick," said Mary.

"Hold on a minute," said the tattoo artist.

"No, really. I'm going to be sick," said Mary.

She threw up everywhere. The tattoo artist had to close the shop so that he could clean up properly. Desma returned the following day. The needle hurt so much that she told the tattoo artist to stop after he had completed only the outline, but he said no, he couldn't send her off to Iraq like that. He rubbed lidocaine on her back to make it numb, and then he made the leaves green and the flowers pink.

Desma figured she was ready. But Alpha Company was not. The more the Alpha Company commander tried to get organized, the more disorganized the company revealed itself to be. After he rounded up additional soldiers, the commander had tried to locate the missing trucks and trailers. In a misguided attempt to rectify the situation, a group from Alpha Company allegedly stole a trailer from another location and tried to disguise it as one of their own by painting new numbers on its side. The military began an investigation into the alleged theft, soon dubbed "Trailergate." During the ensuing commotion, the commander of Alpha Company was replaced, and for about a month the executive officer filled in as acting commander.

On May 1, 2003, President George W. Bush put on a flight suit and got into a Lockheed jet that landed on the deck of the hulking gray USS *Abraham Lincoln,* an aircraft carrier that had just returned from combat missions in the Persian Gulf. Bush posed for photos under a red, white, and blue banner that said MISSION ACCOMPLISHED. Then he made a speech in which he declared that major combat operations in Iraq were over. Saddam Hussein had gone into hiding, and Bush suggested all the troops needed to do now was mop up. It made Desma wonder why she was still stuck at Camp Atterbury. The soldiers in premobilization — who were still being told that they were being deployed — gossiped feverishly about their prospects, given Bush's proclamation. If combat operations were over, would they still be sent overseas?

In June, the rest of the 113th Support Battalion arrived for their two weeks of annual training. Desma was walking toward her barracks when a vehicle pulled up alongside her. She looked inside and saw Debbie Helton and a truckload of the older guys whom Debbie liked to socialize with. They said they were on their way to the PX. Everybody got out of the truck to give her a hug. Debbie gave Desma a tight squeeze. "Are you doing okay?" she asked. "Is there anything you need? Just say what it is, and I'll be glad to send it along." It was nice for them to stop,

Desma thought, although seeing everyone who had not been asked to deploy also made her wonder all over again why had she been plucked out of Bravo Company.

Desma was relieved when she learned that a new commander had been selected for Alpha Company. It was a man she had worked with before and trusted completely. He came by to speak with them as soon as the news was announced. "I could hug you!" Desma told him. "Come here," the new commander said, and gave her a bear hug. But the following weekend, he had an accident in a motocross race, hit his head multiple times, and did not regain consciousness. The Alpha soldiers were utterly demoralized. Were they jinxed? A rumor swept through the ranks saying that because they had lost two different commanders, and because major combat operations in Iraq had been declared over, they were now going to be sent to Djibouti, Africa. For months, whenever Alpha Company stood in formation, they had hollered, "Let's roll!" (It was what Todd Beamer had said on board United Airlines flight 93 before he and other passengers had tried to tackle the hijackers.) After their commander's accident, Desma and some other soldiers started yelling, "Demob!" instead. Alpha Company was losing its motivation.

Toward the end of June, Desma loaded thousands of dollars' worth of gear onto a conex bound for the East Coast, including a footlocker filled with personal items such as knee pads, elbow pads, a sleeping bag, a Sony PlayStation, and assorted video games. She was slated to leave any day. Then Alpha Company got word that they were not getting a new commander after all — they were going to demobilize. Desma was not going to Iraq; she was not going to Kuwait or Djibouti. She was going home. Alpha threw a killer party that night, wall-to-wall madness. Halfway through the celebration someone offered Desma some kind of drink that involved a lot of grain alcohol, and several hours later Desma found herself on all fours, throwing up in a ditch, while Mary Ferren stood over her, whooping and hollering with one fist in the air, pretending to ride her like a horse. The following day Desma wearily collected her children and headed back to southern Indiana. That August, when she reported for her monthly drill weekend as usual at the armory in Bedford, she ran into Debbie Helton and stopped to talk, because Debbie had cared enough to ask whether she needed anything, when Desma had thought she was about to be shipped overseas.

As it happened, Desma's time in the Guard was about to expire. She dropped by the hot dog trailer to discuss her future with the retention team, later that weekend. Debbie explained the newly enhanced benefits that she could earn if she reenlisted: Desma would qualify for the GI Bill now, provided that she reenlisted for six years, Debbie said. In exchange for a six-year commitment, Desma would get 100 percent of her college tuition and a $5,000 signing bonus, and if she enrolled in college, she would also receive an extra $200 monthly kicker bonus as well as a $600 monthly allowance to cover the cost of books and other items. Peggy Weiss told Desma she was crazy if she did not accept. Stacy Glory agreed. "You should go to college," Stacy said. "You're really smart, Des. You could make something of yourself. You could become a licensed clinical social worker." Desma thought about how reenlisting would allow her to obtain the college degree she had always coveted. Why did she have to struggle all the time? If she went to school, she could get a better job. It seemed as though the war in Afghanistan might be winding down, and surely the war in Iraq would not drag on much longer. And if not — well, maybe she would get deployed. "I didn't care," she would say afterward. "I wasn't even thinking about it. It wasn't an issue. Yeah, they'll probably come back and get us again. But, you know, by that time you're already in it. And you don't want to send your friends off without you, you know? You don't want to be that guy. Nobody wants to be that guy." She loved the euchre games and the keg parties and the camaraderie, she could not envision a more attractive future. Before the weekend was over, Desma signed up for another six years.

Even though Bush had declared the war in Iraq to be practically finished, many soldiers from the Indiana National Guard continued to serve there, including some whom Desma knew personally. The 293rd Infantry Regiment was over there, and the 152nd, too. While the rest of America seemed to forget about the wars, Desma kept hearing about injuries and fatalities. That fall, one of her high school classmates, Darrell Smith, died after his Humvee rolled off a road and fell into a river. He drowned somewhere near Baghdad, leaving behind a wife and three children. Desma did not know exactly what was happening in Iraq, but she decided Bush's announcement had been a little premature.

It was hard to get a clear sense of the war's trajectory from news reports. The US military had become adept at steering journalists away from its mistakes and toward its victories. That December, the media went into a frenzy when Saddam Hussein was captured outside a farmhouse near Tikrit. Hussein looked half-mad in the humiliating images of him that aired on television, stumbling out of a hole in the ground. Surely the end of the conflict must be near, Desma's colleagues told each other, if they had toppled an enemy like Hussein.

Meanwhile, Desma had enrolled at Ivy Tech Community College, over in Evansville. It was hectic: Desma dropped her children at school in the morning, went to class herself until noon, took a nap in the afternoon, woke up in time to cook dinner, then got her children into bed, and went to work from 10:00 p.m. until 6:00 a.m. She decided to major in human services, hoping that would deepen her ability to help delinquent teens. In the fall of 2003, she aced general psychology, basic algebra, and English composition, but ran into problems in speech class. One day, Desma was giving a required "how to" oral presentation to the class. She had chosen the subject of how to operate a turn signal. Props were required, and she had brought in a hollowed-out steering column complete with a working turn signal, as well as an electronic board that showed how the interior wiring of the steering column worked. Near the end of her talk, however, she noticed that the instructor was apparently texting on his cell phone. "I would kindly thank you to pay attention!" Desma snapped. "If you're going to be grading me, you should be listening!" He gave her an F.

Desma figured she would make up the credits in the spring. She did enroll in courses, but she did not get to complete them. Instead she got a phone call shortly before April 1, 2004 — she liked to call it her second great April Fool's joke — from Greg Addis, her platoon sergeant.

"This is a raging bull message," Addis told her.

"Bullshit," Desma replied.

"Desma, don't you hang up on me," Addis said.

"Raging bull, my ass," said Desma. "I don't know what you think you're talking about. I ain't goin' nowhere."

A raging bull message meant there was a deployment coming. Addis told Desma she was supposed to report to Bedford in two weeks. He did not say where they were going but Desma was pretty sure it was Afghanistan, because several Guard units from Indiana were already in Iraq. She dropped her spring classes (Sociology, Algebra II, American History) before she earned any credits. When she showed up at the armory, George Quintana, a good-looking former marine, asked if she had gotten her burka yet.

"What are you talking about?" Desma said.

"You've got to wear a burka over there," said Quintana.

"How the hell would I carry a weapon inside of a burka?" Desma asked.

"Out of sight, out of mind, woman!" crowed Quintana.

Everybody loved George Quintana, because he made them take things less seriously. They all called him GQ. Desma tried to adopt his casual attitude, and told Stacy Glory the news of her latest deployment in a blasé tone. Stacy said sharply, "This is not a joke, Desma. You have to get ready for this." Stacy had been designated to stay back, and was going to serve as a liaison between the home unit and the group that was being sent overseas. Peggy Weiss was staying back, too. Desma wondered who she would hang out with in Afghanistan. Who would she talk with about politics? Who would carouse with her in the middle of the night?

The previous summer, shortly after she had returned home from her false deployment, the people who worked at the armory had informed Desma that all of her gear had vanished. Everything she had put into the conex at Stout Field was gone, never to be seen again. All the soldiers from Bravo Company who had been through the false deployment had lost their gear, too. When she thought about the fact that all her carefully weighed gear had gone missing, it did not seem like an accident to Desma. War meant pandemonium. It meant ghost records and missing trailers and lost gear. It meant having to obey a commander you did not respect, and losing the commander you did. It meant being told you were going to Fort

Bragg and winding up at Camp Atterbury; being ordered to Iraq and hearing it might be Djibouti; getting ready to live in your uniform and hearing the president say the mission had already been accomplished. It meant acquiring a tattoo you did not really want, because that's all you could control. War meant thinking you might never see the faces of your children again and then being told to go home. It meant getting jerked around in a cosmic fashion. It meant reenlisting for six years because you thought you could go to college, then learning you would not finish your associate's degree as planned. And it meant, in Desma's case, once more having to tell her children that she was leaving them for an extended period.

This time she had two weeks to prepare, which allowed her more time to pack their belongings and also prolonged the agony of the impending separation. Paige was about to finish kindergarten, Alexis was still in preschool. Josh was almost through fifth grade and had started playing the trumpet in band. Desma took the two girls back to her cousin's house once more, and she took Josh back to his surrogate father's. She told the children that she loved them and would talk to them soon and drove away. She would be gone by the time Josh started middle school in the fall. Leaving the three children again, one year after the last time she had left them, made Desma a little unhinged. In years past she had believed in making things work; once she had cared enough to stay up for twenty-three hours in a row, making every SINGCARS radio function. But she did not care anymore. Now she had a bad attitude. That's why, in the summer of 2004, after Desma wound up back at Camp Atterbury, "mobing up" again, she decided to see what would happen if she used her new position as a supply clerk to order a few things the company commander had not actually requested. After Desma started acting out, Michelle Fischer decided she really liked that woman named Brooks, who made her laugh out loud when they were stuck in a place where Michelle thought she might never laugh again.

5
High Altitude

Michelle had just fallen in love. In the fall of 2002, she had moved back in with her mother again, and started taking classes at the University of Southern Indiana once more, but the following year she applied to the University of Indiana in Bloomington and received the heady news that she had been accepted. She was nearly living her dream. When the bombs started raining on Baghdad, in the spring of 2003, Michelle flinched to see that they were the wrong hue; the explosions appeared green on her mother's small television set, because they had been recorded through night vision technology. It disturbed Michelle that the media were reporting everything through a military filter and not showing her the true color of things. She started reading *Adbusters,* which satisfied her in a way the mainstream news did not. Then all of the Alpha girls vanished: every female soldier whom Michelle had known from middle school or high school —

Angela Peterson included — they were all 88Ms ("eighty-eight Mikes"), all truck drivers, all gone. Two years earlier, when she had visited the recruitment office to sign up, that had been the alternate job specialty that Michelle had written down: truck driver. If she had not gotten her first choice, to become a weapons mechanic, then she would have been placed in Alpha Company, too, and she would have been headed for Iraq. She felt that call-up pass her by like a wind on her cheek, it brushed so close.

Reading *Adbusters* and watching *Democracy Now!,* Michelle had a million doubts about the war in Iraq. Yet nobody else around her seemed to question what was taking place. Some of her peers even thought Iraq had something to do with 9/11, and told Michelle she was crazy when she said that was not the case. Political figures such as Rumsfeld and Cheney had begun using the terms "war on terror" and "weapons of mass destruction," and then suddenly the Alpha girls were gone, and almost nobody in Evansville objected to their absence. It was as if the spectral language had justified what was going to unfold. Because the other students felt at no risk of being drafted, the remote conflicts did not touch them personally. They did not see the void that the missing Alpha girls left behind. It was war without the debate that had always accompanied war; war when only the poor had to serve. Without the Alpha girls, Michelle found the armory's big bay more cavernous, more echoing. The guys who belonged to the 163rd still showed up, but most of her detachment was at Atterbury, getting ready to go to war. Michelle's relief at missing the deployment was matched by the guilt she carried because people she had known for years had not been so lucky. It felt random, the question of who among them got sent off to a combat zone, even though there wasn't anything random about the roster; the generals with responsibility for Iraq had asked for truck drivers, and Michelle was a weapons mechanic. It all came down to what you had studied back when you were in training. None of them had known, during those fat and innocent years, that the job specialties they had chosen would carry such life-altering ramifications.

After Bush declared the war in Iraq to be a fait accompli — even as so many women she knew personally were preparing to deploy there — Michelle watched other people shrug off the idea of the wars, as if one or both were really over. Everybody seemed tired of the twin conflicts, and happy to put them out of mind. At USI, the students partied as if it were peacetime. Veronica and Colleen, who were on the verge of completing their sophomore year (by this point they were a full year ahead of Michelle in their schoolwork because of the time she'd lost in basic training and in Fort Wayne), had become the party queens of their peer group. On weekends, students flocked to the gatherings they hosted at their apartment. As much as she opposed the wars, Michelle could not help identifying with the Alpha girls, so it was impossible for her to participate in the collective amnesia. Was she paranoid or simply unusually perceptive in her habit of spying spider-webbed connections between the far-off wars and the humdrum? One day she turned a corner at Walmart and saw boxes of shotgun shells stacked into a pyramid, right beside an aisle full of toys. "Like it was candy or something," Michelle objected. She started photographing the display. A manager threw her out of the store, and then she started boycotting Walmart. It was all interlaced as far as she was concerned: Bush, the weapons industry, the collective amnesia, the vanished Alpha girls.

After she had returned from Fort Wayne, Michelle had lurched through a series of ill-advised flings and then withdrawn from romantic interactions entirely. During the spring of 2003, Michelle had dated nobody during what friends jokingly called her "semester of celibacy." By May, however, as she was slogging through textbooks to prepare for her final exams, Michelle had begun spending time with a friend of Veronica's named Pete Peterson. Pete had gauged ears and nipple rings and smoked pot. He was tall, with sandy hair, light blue eyes, and a gentle merriness. A music fan, he worked at WSWI, known as "the Edge," the college's award-winning radio station. Pete and Michelle quickly discovered their shared passion for music, even though Michelle was now listening to more melodic groups such as the Dave Matthews Band, while Pete liked heavier stuff — Queens of the Stone Age, Disturbed, Godsmack. Pete continued to split an apartment with an ex-girlfriend named Sharon, and had also begun sleeping with Veronica, yet he found himself intrigued by Michelle, a small, curvaceous figure with flowing blond hair in bell-bottom blue jeans who surprisingly put on a uniform to drill with the National Guard. "It was like, '*You* go to the National Guard every other weekend?' " he would say later. "It was like, 'What?' "

One evening, during another party at Veronica and Colleen's apartment, Pete asked Michelle why she had joined the military.

"For school," she said.

"We just invaded Iraq," he observed.

"Yeah, I screwed up," she told him. "That whole September eleventh thing happened after I had already enlisted."

Pete was sympathetic. His mother, his father, and his stepfather had all served in the navy, and Pete had grown up on or near various naval bases in Hawaii, California,

Connecticut, England, and Puerto Rico. After his mother remarried, she and Pete's stepfather had a daughter, Stephanie. Pete's mother left her two children behind with Pete's stepfather for one year when she was assigned to work on an oiler that was refueling ships in the Caribbean and the Mediterranean, and she left the family again when she was stationed for several months at a naval base in Bahrain. That summer, Veronica went on an extended trip to Europe. Pete swore to Michelle that his relationship with Sharon had ended, even though their lease had not, and declared he was not interested in Veronica. He liked Michelle. Michelle let Pete take her to Burdette Park, a vast complex of lakes, tennis courts, waterslides, and playgrounds. Later she would write in a letter to Pete: "I remember the way it felt to kiss you at Burdette, for the first time, surrounded by crazy ducks. I felt like I had waited an eternity for that moment."

Michelle and Pete began meeting on the sly — at his house if his ex-girlfriend was not there, or at Michelle's house if her mother was working. They wanted to keep their romance a secret until they could tell Veronica. One night, however, Pete's ex-girlfriend Sharon walked into the apartment when she was supposed to be visiting her parents. Pete threw a blanket over Michelle, but his ex figured out who was underneath. She grabbed a knife and ran outside and slashed the tires on Michelle's red Cougar. After this, Pete wrote Michelle a lengthy apology — for sleeping with her friend Veronica, for getting her embroiled in the ongoing saga with Sharon — in a steno notepad. Certain he had ruined the chance to have a serious relationship with Michelle, he described his desperate state of mind. "[There is a] black feeling in my chest," wrote Pete. "Sick." Then Pete recounted a painful moment in his childhood that had occurred during his first lengthy separation from his mother. His words made clear, despite the passage of time, how much had been left unresolved for the child whose mother was serving in the military:

> Let me paint this picture. . . . My mom is my world and it hurt to see her go. She left around the springtime of my sixth grade year and would be gone for one year. We coped. My dad cooked and cleaned and I watched Stephanie. This is the way life moved on. . . .
>
> This story takes place around Christmas time. It was after school and my dad was not home so I had the chore of watching Stephanie. The day was overcast and we had nothing but the tree lights on. . . . The phone rings. . . . It's [my friend] Charlie doing a very bad crank call. I know it's him and laugh and hang up. I

make my way to the living room and the phone rings again and again the same. . . .

Time goes by and the phone rings I run to the phone Stephanie trails closely behind. I answer "Ricco's Pizza" there was nothing. Stephanie laughs and I put down the phone. . . . [T]he phone rings again. I run and answer the same "Ricco's ha ha Pizza" I can't contain my laughter.

A small, distant voice says "Pete?" It's my mom standing on the street in Greece on a pay phone with traffic whizzing past her. . . . She tries to talk "Pete?" She was crying now, half the world away, on a busy street, not seeing us in months, using time and money to call us. . . . She was crying the strongest woman I know is crying because of me. I don't know how to handle that I really don't to this day I don't know. . . . My dad took this the wrong way, he had no idea how I suffered and how I suffer to this day. I got beat.

Pete told Michelle that he had gotten "that feeling" again when he worried that she might not want to see him anymore. Pete closed the letter by promising never to hurt Michelle again. "I need you . . . ," he wrote. "I can't let go of the best thing that's ever happened to me."

Michelle wrote a six-page response on the

same steno pad. "Every moment I am with you has become the only time I am allowed to be myself," she told Pete. "You've swept me away into a dreamland. . . . I know you and I are good for each other." Michelle worried that she would have to choose between maintaining her friendship with Veronica or having a relationship with Pete. "Then I remember that ideally I'll be going away to school [in Bloomington] next year. So if we are going to separate . . . is all this anguish worth what will end up as a guaranteed broken heart anyway?" But she told Pete that his actions had not compromised her feelings. If anything, she believed they had grown closer because of the difficulties they had experienced.

> I'm scared for our future together, simply because I want so badly for there to be one. . . . No matter what happens, you have to understand how much you mean to me. . . . I know you look at this and see all the complications you've brought to me. But there is so much more to us than that. Us.

Pete found a new apartment on the ground floor of an old brick building on the west side of Evansville. Veronica and Colleen lived upstairs, and Michelle confessed her involvement with Pete as soon as Veronica returned.

Her friend took the news better than Michelle had expected, and soon Michelle was spending almost every night at Pete's. The apartment had old linoleum floors and Formica countertops and kitchen cabinets that looked like wood but were actually made of metal and clanged when they closed. Pete and Michelle got an old sofa with no legs, and a tiny gray kitten they named Halloween. On the walls they put up a movie poster from *Trainspotting.* They got high and lay on the sofa in each other's arms for hours. If they felt ambitious, they went upstairs to watch *Sex and the City* with Veronica and Colleen.

In the summer of 2003, when Michelle had to report to Camp Atterbury for annual training, she found it excruciating to separate from Pete. Furious about all of the national security measures that had been adopted, Michelle decided to reread George Orwell's classic novel *1984.* She borrowed Pete's copy, wanting to take something of his along with her. Pete could always tell which of his books she had been reading, for he kept his books pristine, whereas his new girlfriend tended to fall asleep on top of them, or to stuff them into her bag. By the creased spines and rumpled covers, Pete could see she had worked her way through his copies of *Zen and the Art of Motorcycle Maintenance* and the *Zombie Survival Guide.* At Camp Atterbury, Michelle immersed herself in Orwell's satire about a society that had willingly surrendered all of its liberties to live in a state of never-ending war, then lifted her head and was confronted by identical rectangular cinder-block buildings that repeated themselves endlessly in all directions. The book allowed her to cope with the daily act of putting on her uniform — it was her way of being subversive, of declaring she did not belong.

One day, Michelle crossed paths with a few of the Alpha girls who were staying in a female barracks nearby. They radiated animosity. Everyone else they knew had just showed up to play pretend war games, while they had been stuck at Atterbury for months, gearing up for the real thing. When her unit set up camp out in the woods, Michelle found the training exercises had gotten more serious, as if the leadership thought they might be next. General Martin Umbarger, who was in charge of the Indiana National Guard, wanted every soldier in the state ready to go to war. As a result, Patrick Miller, the cocky, swaggering ex-marine who had worked in missile repair, now had a new job. He was no longer part of the missile team but had been assigned to investigate whether other soldiers were correctly performing the prescribed war exercises. Miller confided to Michelle that he hated ratting out colleagues, and said he was planning to quit the Guard as a result. Michelle figured he must be confiding in her because he knew she was unorthodox. Miller offered Michelle some dip; sucking the sour tobacco made her nauseated, but Michelle did not want Miller to think her weak. When she finished reading *1984,* she handed it over to his friend Frank Perez, who was still working in missile repair. "Here," she said. "See what you think of this." Perez hardly came out of his tent, he became so enraptured by Orwell's story. And as usual, their colleague Ben Sawyer trailed after Michelle everywhere.

It was fun to flirt with the guys from missile, but Michelle longed for Pete. She purchased a writing tablet at the PX and wrote daily letters to him. "Hey sweetheart," she began. "Day 2, round noon, sitting in the barracks with nothing to do. It's making me miss you even worse than I thought I would. This is horrible, I want to come home, I want you to hold me." In another letter, Michelle bemoaned being woken up from a vivid dream of being in Pete's arms, only to have to report for guard duty. "I was pissed I had to leave my warm sleeping bag and sweet thoughts to go freeze my ass off outside," she wrote. Stuck in a foxhole, bored and cold and tired, Michelle began texting Pete during the predawn hours. He sent messages back and forth with her until her shift ended. She wrote later that she had never loved anybody else as much as she loved him. "I'm on radio check, watch, whatever, the easiest damn job I've ever had," she said. "I just sit and read in a heated trailer. Think of you and decide to pick up my pen. Missing you bad, thinking of all the ways I want to kiss you." The more time they spent apart, the more passionate her letters became.

> It's day 11, only four days left to go and we'll be together again. . . . I can't believe we've been apart for this long. It seriously feels like two months instead of two weeks. . . . When I lie in my sleeping bag and I'm bored and I can't sleep, I think about making love to you and my imagination is so vivid, and my memory can call out the smallest details of the way you look naked, the way it feels to have you inside of me, our rhythm, everything. And it's like I can't stop torturing myself. I can't stop thinking about you. I miss you. It's almost over, it's almost over, it's almost over.

Michelle moved in with Pete as soon as she got home. They both worked long hours at menial jobs, and their schedules did not align. Michelle got a job making $7.62 an hour at Berry Plastics, where she manufactured disposable cups for fast-food restaurants. Pete worked the evening shift at Staples, and the overnight shift at WGBF, a for-profit FM rock station. They left each other domestic updates and love notes on the steno pad and the writing tablet. Michelle wrote to Pete that she had left clothes in the dryer, then added, "You mean everything to me." Pete wrote to Michelle that a mechanic had called about her car and signed off, "I worship you." Michelle thanked him for cleaning the apartment and added, "PS Will you marry me?" And Pete wrote, "Yes!!"

In August 2003, when Michelle reported for drill weekend, she experienced immense relief to see the missing Alpha girls had returned. Their false deployment made Michelle hope that perhaps the war in Iraq might really end without anybody from her battalion being sent there. That same month, NATO took over what was being called "peacekeeping" in Afghanistan, and Michelle let herself imagine that war drawing to a close, too. Perhaps she might be able to realize her dreams after all. Pete and Michelle planned to live apart while she attended college in Bloomington, starting in the fall of 2004, and then they planned to move to Seattle together. They hung a large map of Seattle over their bed so they could get to know their future home.

Michelle's final semester at USI, in the spring of 2004, was grueling: physics, chemistry, calculus, and Spanish. She wanted to get a degree in environmental science, and she was trying to get two of her science requirements out of the way before she switched schools, because she thought the courses would be easier at the University of Southern Indiana. She spent most of her waking hours poring over her textbooks. Right after she started her spring classes, however, Michelle heard that the battalion she belonged to was going to be deployed sometime in the coming year. Supposedly most of the fighting was over, and the nation-building had begun, yet large numbers of soldiers were still required. At the armory, her supervisor instructed everyone to get into better physical shape, because they were going to be stationed at high altitude. Michelle went home and looked up the elevations of the capital cities of Iraq and Afghanistan: Baghdad sprawled across a vast alluvial plain, at an elevation of only 112 feet, while Kabul rested in an alpine valley at 6,000 feet above sea level. Odds were she was headed for Afghanistan.

Michelle hatched various schemes to get out of the coming deployment. She could break her legs, she could get tattoos on her face, she could get pregnant. She settled on the idea of marrying Veronica. Michelle figured that if she clearly violated the military's policy of "don't ask, don't tell," she would get kicked out of the Guard. Michelle told Veronica they could get married in Canada, and said she would pay for the entire trip. She had already been saving money for an apartment in Bloomington by working as a waitress at a restaurant called Hacienda, where she made great money in tips. She could afford to spring for gas and a hotel room. They decided the best time to go would be in May 2004, after finals. Supposedly the deployment would not happen until summer. One day that March, however, Michelle was at home when the telephone rang. It was Ezra Schmidt, her immediate supervisor, who had recently been promoted to sergeant. He had been leading the maintenance team ever since Sergeant Joe Haverty had transferred to another company.

"You've been activated," Schmidt told her. "It's Afghanistan."

He said he was going, too. They had about a month before they went on active duty status. Michelle could hear the effort it took for Schmidt to maintain his composure. When she asked who else was going, Michelle learned that the other members of their five-person maintenance support team — her former boyfriend Noah Jarvis, her ally Amber Macdonald, and a friend of Noah's who had joined the group — were staying back. They were all truck mechanics. Only she and Schmidt, the two weapons mechanics on the team, had been selected for this deployment. At least, Michelle thought, she did not have to watch Noah go to war.

Michelle had been alone when the call

came. She went upstairs and told Veronica and Colleen the news. By the time Pete came home from work, Michelle was sloppy drunk. She accosted him in the kitchen and loosed a river of words, brokenhearted because she was going to miss out on her twenties. Pete let her talk and talk. The whole matter of her impending absence became much more real for him when Michelle brought home a copy of her orders, and he saw the font that the military used, which he knew so well from his childhood. "You are ordered to active duty as a member of your Reserve Component Unit for the period indicated unless sooner released or unless extended," the orders said. "Period of active duty: Not to exceed 545 days. Purpose: 1A MOB #96-3, OPERATION ENDURING FREEDOM (OEF)." So much for the idea that she would only be a soldier one weekend a month and two weeks in the summer. Five hundred and forty-five days, that was eighteen months; unofficially, she was told the deployment should last no more than a year.

Michelle shut down. Inside she was full of a strange, airy nothingness where her feelings might have resided. It was Pete who felt a storm of emotions for them both, and the more he responded, the less inclined Michelle was to feel at all. They talked about eloping but there was no time. Michelle disassembled her life. She quit her job at Hacienda and went to the registrar's office to withdraw from her classes. She earned no credits; all her hours of studying had been for nothing. Pete said he would move to Bloomington with her, after she got home from Afghanistan, so they didn't have to spend so much time apart.

Michelle had saved up $1,300 for an apartment in Bloomington. Instead she ordered kegs of Killian's Irish Red and threw a party, took friends out to dinner, bought her mother a new bed. She also took out a large life insurance policy and wrote a will leaving everything to her mother. Irene was too consumed by anxiety to comfort her daughter, and instead Michelle had to keep telling her mother that she would be all right. Pete's mother took the news in stride. She bought Michelle's red Cougar with the V6 engine, so that Michelle wouldn't have to worry about making her monthly car payments. By the end of April, Michelle's money was gone.

Michelle was told to report for duty on May 1, 2004. She spent her last evening walking back and forth from the bedroom to the kitchen, where she had laid out her two duffel bags. Pete, Veronica, Colleen, and some old friends of Pete's who dropped by at the wrong time sat on the sofa without legs. Nobody spoke to Michelle, who clearly wanted to be left alone. The next morning, Pete drove her to the armory. Later that day, he was supposed to take a final exam; he had asked if the exam could be rescheduled, but the professor had said no. The questions were going to be about international relations — how did the United States get along with this country or that country? In all his life, it was the only exam that Pete would ever fail.

Inside Pete's blue pickup, Michelle put a pillow over his lap and laid her head down. He pulled up at the armory.

"We're here," said Pete.

Michelle lifted up her head and checked the time.

"We're early," she said. "Just keep driving."

Pete headed east on the Lloyd Expressway. A while ago, he had given Michelle a ring he had been wearing, a silver circle with a pressed pattern; it fit her index finger. He liked the idea that she was going to take his keepsake to Afghanistan. She had bought him a copper ring in its place but he had lost it already, and she teased him about that. They returned to the armory, stood around in the parking lot. Most of the other soldiers were male, and most of the people saying goodbye were female. Michelle hugged Pete. "It's just a year," he told her. "It'll be over soon, it's just a year." She lined up in formation and marched over to the bus that would take her to Camp Atterbury. Perhaps she still could have married Veronica, but in the end Michelle had qualms about the scheme. Why was she so special, she had asked herself, that she should skip a deployment when everybody else who had gotten that phone call was going?

6
The Tiki Lounge

Ellen Ann was getting married. The wedding would take place in May 2004, and six weeks before the ceremony Debbie Helton threw her daughter a wedding shower. In the club room of the apartment building where Debbie's parents lived, she hung streamers and blew up balloons. In the middle of the shower, the phone in the club room rang, and somebody said it was Jeff. Debbie knew her boyfriend would not call in the middle of the shower just to chat.

"You got your call," Jeff said. "You're on alert."

Debbie had been told a deployment was likely. She could not wait — she had been wanting to do something like this for ages. The only problem was that the idea of her traveling to a war zone made Ellen Ann hysterical. To shield her daughter, Debbie hid her enthusiasm when she shared the news.

"Mom! You can't go!" cried Ellen Ann. "You'll miss the wedding!"

"No, you know, I've just got to call them back," Debbie said. "I've just got to check in, that's all."

"But you're going, aren't you?" asked Ellen Ann.

"Well, this isn't a definite thing," Debbie hedged. "We'll have to wait and see."

But she could barely contain her elation. "Finally!" she told her friend Will Hargreaves when she saw him at drill the following weekend. "We get to go do something!" Debbie had waited years for a chance to show her worth, a chance to shine in a crisis, a chance to see the world. Since 9/11, Debbie had supported most of the stances taken by the Bush administration: she thought it made sense to invade Afghanistan; the Patriot Act seemed like a necessary precaution. The question of whether to attack Iraq had confounded her at first — Debbie had not known whether to believe the assertions about "weapons of mass destruction" — but then Colin Powell had addressed a plenary session of the UN Security Council and said with certitude the allegations were well founded. "There can be no doubt that Saddam Hussein has biological weapons and the capability to rapidly produce more, many more," Powell had said. That was all Debbie needed to hear. She trusted the man. He would never have pushed for the invasion of Iraq unless a second war was warranted and feasible, she thought.

But it was a relief to be heading instead to Afghanistan. There were supposed to be beautiful mountains, women in burkas, strange spices, and camels. All that concerned Debbie was whether the doctors would find her fit enough. At fifty-one, she was the oldest woman in Bravo Company, and she had to make it through a screening designed to weed out individuals with mental or physical impairments. Other soldiers were hoping to be held back. One member of the unit even claimed that he felt out of control and might start shooting at people randomly. After the medics nixed his orders, the rest of the battalion nicknamed him Weasel, and shunned him so thoroughly that he requested a transfer. But Debbie, to her great joy, was cleared to go.

Then Bravo Company's executive officer — they called him the XO — pulled her aside.

"You aren't going to Afghanistan," he said. "You're a stay-back."

"Why?" asked Debbie.

"We already have enough people on the team," he told her. She was supposed to be joining a four-person team, led by ex-marine Patrick Miller, that would handle armament. That meant fixing broken weapons, for the most part. But the XO said the team might travel off-post, might see combat.

"It's probably going to be an all-male

team," he told her.

"I'd really like to go," Debbie said.

But he did not relent, and Debbie went home crestfallen. The Guard was the center of her life, and now the rest of her colleagues were going to go to Afghanistan, and leave her behind. Maybe the XO had been trying to protect her; or maybe he thought she was past her prime. Jeff had never seen Debbie so disconsolate.

Then Debbie heard that two 45Bs from Evansville were joining the armament team. That had to mean Schmidt and Fischer; they were the only two 45Bs in Evansville. How did Michelle Fischer gain a spot on the supposedly all-male team?

"I'm a little upset," she told the XO the following month. "Didn't you indicate that it was going to be all guys for armament? And the job they were doing — there weren't going to be any females?"

"Yes."

"Well, then, how come Fischer's on it?"

"What makes you think Fischer's on it?"

"I know she's on it. And the last time I checked, she was female. How come she gets to go?"

"I think they are going to take her," the XO conceded. "But I don't know that she's actually going to be doing any traveling off-post."

He said they were only taking 45Bs, and Debbie was a 41C. Debbie reminded the XO that she had been cross-trained as a 45B, but she could not talk him into letting her join the team. She tried a Hail Mary pass. Debbie knew that Patrick Miller's wife was pregnant, and beside herself because her husband was going to miss the birth of their child. Debbie sought Miller out and said she would gladly take his place. Miller shrugged her off — as a former marine, he could not imagine letting a fifty-one-year-old woman serve in his stead. Debbie spent the rest of that drill weekend watching everybody else pack up their gear. People kept telling her they couldn't believe that she wasn't coming; she was the heart of the unit, they said, it wasn't right to leave her behind. Debbie said good-bye to everyone and went home feeling useless. Jeff grew alarmed when he could not cheer her up. In June 2004, however, when the rest of the battalion had been at Camp Atterbury for a month, Debbie got another phone call. A member of the armament team had just collapsed. Supposedly he was overweight, and during a strenuous workout, his knee had given out. They offered her his spot.

Debbie was euphoric. She delivered a crash course on the beauty salon's payroll to the woman who was going to fill in as manager and showed Jeff how to care for her pets. Debbie gave Ellen Ann power of attorney and asked if her daughter could pay her bills. "Mom, I'm trying to get pregnant!" Ellen

Ann objected. "What if I have a baby while you're gone?" Debbie said these things take time and she was sure she would be home before Ellen Ann made her a grandmother. Debbie's mother asked, "What if you get killed?" But Debbie's father said, "She'll be home safe and sound in a year." Debbie ran to Kmart for deodorant, shampoo, toothpaste, Q-tips, and foot powder, but she could not find a footlocker there. Walmart was sold out, too. Indiana was pouring soldiers into the two wars, and even the PX at Atterbury had run out of footlockers. Debbie would have to make do without one until they restocked. When she arrived at the women's barracks, Debbie took the only empty bed in the place, which happened to be next to Michelle Fischer. Fischer was a mess. She was so young, Debbie thought, only twenty-one. Fischer did not have a very good attitude about being sent to Afghanistan, but Debbie decided she was just a kid and forgave her. Guys were following Fischer around like puppy dogs. It had been a long time since anybody had trailed after Debbie like that. "Us older ones were like, look at those young guys, all they want to do is just follow that tail," Debbie would say later. "But she handled the attention pretty well."

Debbie got into the habit of waking Fischer up, because the young woman was drinking heavily and had trouble rousing herself in the mornings. The girl was all drama and self-involvement; she talked endlessly about boys. She was in love with someone named Pete, who wrote her sweet letters, but at night Ben Sawyer from missile repair attached himself relentlessly to her side. Sawyer was married, but not happily. Already some of the married men were not acting very married, after having been prised away from their families; people were looking for ways to unwind. Party time was seven to ten in the evening; ten o'clock was curfew.

And nobody was partying harder than Desma Brooks. One of the first things that Debbie Helton had noticed upon walking into her barracks was that every bed had been made up with the same regulation green wool blanket, except for the bed that belonged to Brooks. The rules stated that everybody had to draw linen from the base, flat white sheets, hospital corners, make it tight, then the green wool blanket. Brooks had not wanted to use the communal sheets, however, so she had gone to Walmart and found a bed in a bag — a full set of sheets and a comforter — in a florid print, bright purple with big pink lips. Bed after bed in army green, then the shocking purple. There was nobody else in the unit quite so defiant. At the foot of her bed Brooks had a cooler full of ice and assorted adult beverages. Brooks said, "Help yourself," and Debbie did. She liked beer. Brooks drank

Smirnoff Ice Triple Black.

Brooks looked good, Debbie thought. She had let her hair grow down to her shoulders and had a new haircut with bangs that emphasized her generous cheekbones. She had streaked her hair blond, too, and her skin had turned golden from all the time they were spending outdoors. One night, when they were allowed to go off-post wearing civilian clothes, Brooks put on frosted lip gloss and a black T-shirt that said in hot pink letters *kiss me quick*! She was only twenty-eight years old, and when she fixed herself up, you would never guess she had three kids. Brooks knew how to lift everyone's spirits. Outside their barracks, she had hung up a string of plug-in party lights shaped like moons and stars. Then she had set up tiki torches in a grassy area right by the door and dubbed it the Tiki Lounge. Sometimes Debbie socialized with the young women over at the Tiki Lounge, but more often she joined the older crowd at the NCO Club, a bar on post favored by the lifers, or she slipped away to supply to see Gary Jernigan, a longtime colleague who kept a hidden stash of booze in his office. In the new diary that she began keeping, Debbie noted with relish that they were consuming at least as much alcohol as they did at annual training. "Everyone seems to be glad I am here," she wrote. "Hugs from everyone, and welcome home. Felt good and right to be with my longtime friends. I know no one understands but I am a happy camper."

War preparations flooded Camp Atterbury. Waves of "rolling stock," military vehicles of all kinds, surged through the post: Humvees, Bradleys, and Armored Security Vehicles came back in need of repair, and soldiers washed the dirty vehicles, changed the oil, changed the tires, replaced fluids, switched out parts. Waves of military personnel poured through Atterbury, too: various National Guard units showed up for training or for a deployment. Meanwhile, marines, regular army, and army reserve units paused here before shipping off to war or paused here on their way home. On the walls of the NCO Club where Debbie went to drink hung the insignias of every unit that had flowed through the post, and the display told a story of constant movement. Atterbury offered soldiers their passage into war and their passage back home. It was therefore a place that evoked in the soldiers who were streaming through it some of the strongest emotions they would ever feel — it made them angry, sad, confused, lonely, fulfilled, bored, excited, and, most of all, afraid. At the same time, there was something about the uniformity of the buildings and the uniformity of the vehicles and the uniformity of the uniforms that sought to contain all those emotions. Atterbury served as a place where individuals marked the significant turns in their journeys. Every outbound soldier who moved through this place was traveling away from an ordinary life, and every inbound veteran returned to this same endless tract of yellow cinder block and brown shingles changed in ways they would only begin to recognize upon washing up against this familiar shore, no longer the same people they had been before.

At Atterbury, Debbie got shots for measles, mumps, rubella, tetanus, hepatitis, meningitis, tuberculosis, and influenza; attended briefings; and stood in line for gear. She picked up an M4 assault rifle (a new version of the old M16), a Kevlar helmet, a flak jacket. The flak jacket, known as an Improved Ballistic Vest, or an IBV, was made with hard ceramic plates and weighed around forty pounds. "Boy this IBV is really heavy it kills my shoulders," Debbie wrote in her diary. "I hope I can make it ok. I will still [be] a happy camper!" Down at the range where the red flags were flying, signifying that soldiers were using live ammunition, she fired the M4 until she qualified. Other soldiers liked the M4 better, because it was lighter and had a shorter butt stock, but Debbie was tall and had long arms and the M16 had fit her big frame more comfortably. Plus, it had become familiar to her, over the years. It was difficult to get used to the new gun, and her eyes were not as sharp as they had once been. She scored in the low thirties. Everyone else considered that acceptable, but Debbie was disappointed not to get a perfect score. She practiced driving in a war zone, which wasn't anything like driving in the civilian world. "Drive like you mean it!" the instructors yelled. "Drive like you stole it!" She redid the chemical warfare training she had done years ago, practicing how to use a gas mask. And she did endless sit-ups, push-ups, sprints, marches, runs. Despite all of the exercise, Debbie found it hard to sleep. The other women had set up huge fans inside the sweltering barracks, and the thrumming noise kept Debbie awake. She tried Tylenol PM but the tablets only helped her wrest a few hours of oblivion. She pined for her dog. "I miss my Maxx!" Debbie declared repeatedly in her diary. "I miss my Maxx!" She missed Jeff, too, though not quite as much. He was feeling the strain of their separation acutely. After several weeks, he told Debbie over the phone that her absence was making him glum, but added that he had cheered himself up by cleaning out their fire pit. Debbie promised to visit as soon as she got a pass.

Nothing deflated Debbie's good spirits. "Had latrine duty!" she wrote cheerfully. She marveled at her pay; Debbie was now earning more than $1,000 every two weeks. Excitement swept the barracks when they learned that in a few days they would get their desert camouflage uniforms, or DCUs. "Can't wait!" Debbie told her diary. The desert camo seemed surprisingly drab to her after the stronger contrasts of their familiar BDUs, but even Fischer posed for photographs in the dusty, washed-out colors of their future. Debbie's one regret about being confined at Atterbury was that she could not leave the base to visit Jim, her closest childhood friend — the boy whose hair she used to cut for free. He now lived in Florida, and he had just learned that he had an inoperable brain tumor. "He has to wait till I get home so I can see him one more time," Debbie wrote in her diary.

Toward the end of June 2004, everybody in the 113th Support Battalion had to pass a test in land navigation. They were given a compass, told to shoot an azimuth, and find three specific points in the woods. Desma Brooks slipped on some wet leaves, rolled down a hill, and hurtled straight into a pond, while wearing all of her gear. She emerged covered in muck, and dubbed her maneuver "rolling thunder." When Debbie's turn came, the needle of her compass kept getting stuck, but after she got a new compass she doggedly found every one of her points — even wading through boggy swampland, up to her knees in water, to do so. Debbie was her own harshest critic. "Getting slower at everything now that I'm older," she wrote.

But she was not the slowest. That was Michelle Fischer. The girl got lost, gave up, was sent back out, and ultimately found her points only with help from another soldier named Jeremy Toppe who tagged along to babysit her on the supposedly solo exercise. Toppe reported to the rest of the unit that Fischer kept stopping to marvel at the cicadas blanketing the fields, and had babbled to him about the plenitude of butterflies, which she said were an indicator species, or a sign of the health of the local ecosystem. She had spent more time looking at the butterflies than she had at her compass, Toppe said; he had nicknamed her "Poison Butterfly," and that's what everyone started calling her. Fischer seemed to like the nickname. She did not aspire to be a good soldier; she did not care whether she could shoot an azimuth. She just wanted to go home.

Debbie mothered her anyway, and as the days went by, she began to admire Fischer's outspokenness. The young woman kept voicing things that were true but that everybody avoided acknowledging. She went around calling one of the battalion's leaders "a womanizing piece of shit," for example; Debbie would never have put it that way, but she couldn't argue with the assessment. They had all heard about how the man was busily hitting on vulnerable young women, despite the fact that he was married, and the female soldiers were reporting to him, which specifically violated military regulations. At one point, he had his eye on Michelle Fischer, according to several members of the battalion, although she rebuffed his advances. Eventually her immediate supervisor, Patrick Miller, decided to speak to the man, who was Miller's superior in the chain of command. Miller saw it as his job to protect the young female soldier who was reporting to him from harm. "I had to tell him, 'You can't have her,' " Miller recalled.

At the moment, Fischer was locked in a battle of wills with her company commander over her habit of wearing a braid of rainbow-colored hemp around her ankle. Captain Nicholas Mueller was a beefy, barrel-chested man with a ruddy face and a dark blond buzz cut. He had spied the anklet during an inspection and demanded that she cut it off. Fischer had complied — and then braided herself a new anklet. Who packed rainbow hemp when heading off to a war zone? But Debbie was impressed with the way Fischer stubbornly made herself a new anklet every night, only to cut it off every morning. Debbie wasn't like that; she did not rebel. The girl had spunk, Debbie decided.

Debbie's crowd, the older guys who had been in the Guard forever, were preoccupied with another drama — the emerging power struggle between Captain Nicholas Mueller and Bravo Company's most experienced soldier, a Vietnam War veteran named John Perkins, who was known to everyone by the nickname John Wayne. To Debbie, Mueller appeared young and green, while she idolized John Wayne. He was tough and grizzled, used an old-fashioned straight razor to shave, and had seen combat. From Debbie's vantage point it looked as though Bravo's commander felt threatened by Perkins's real-world expertise. When they split, she aligned herself firmly with John Wayne, on the side of experience — and when Mueller subsequently rearranged the unit's leadership so that Perkins would not go to Afghanistan, Debbie lost faith in Mueller. "John Wayne came by what a small world always so glad to see him," she wrote in her diary. "Love that man. Mueller is an idiot but oh well his loss . . . we need [Perkins] too bad they have a personality conflict."

At the end of June, the soldiers participated in a three-day simulation of what life would be like inside the compound where they would be living in Kabul. There was no drinking, there were armed guards posted in the towers, and there was a lot of concertina wire. The post was locked down, and they had to show ID to get inside the wire. On the first day of the simulation, Debbie spotted a double rainbow, which she interpreted as a sign of good fortune. On day two, a female soldier from Alpha Company started cutting herself and was put on suicide watch. And then Michelle Fischer decided to go AWOL and attend a Dave Matthews concert. Debbie wondered how that stunt was going to work out — going AWOL constituted a significant offense. As it turned out, Fischer managed to sneak off-post without getting caught, but she missed the concert because she had ordered the tickets online, and the vendor had canceled the order after being unable to verify the transaction. Fischer had shrugged off the disappointment with a weary resignation, as if she had grown accustomed to things not going her way. On the last day of the simulation, Debbie wrote in her diary, "We saw another double rainbow tonight. Two in two days. Amazing it's good luck!!" Brooks said she was not a religious person, but the second double rainbow meant that God still existed, even if she was stuck in this hellhole without her children. Fischer thought it meant she might get to go home.

After the simulation ended, everyone was given a pass for the weekend. Jeff drove up to get Debbie and brought along her dog. "Maxx just whined and cried and whined for 10 to 15 minutes," wrote Debbie in her diary. "Then laid on my lap for twenty minutes of loving." Back at their house, Debbie reveled in the sanctity of her bedroom, where she finally got a good night's sleep. "So nice to wake up no fan!!!!" she wrote the next morning. She watched *The Wizard of Oz* with Maxx glued to her side. Then it was time to return to Atterbury. Back in the barracks, Fischer told her all about the romantic weekend she had spent with her boyfriend Pete at a hotel in nearby Edinburgh; Pete had driven three hours to meet her there, and Fischer was starry-eyed. Meanwhile, Brooks had caught a ride down to southern Indiana with another soldier. Jimmy had picked her up at the truck stop, and she had spent two bittersweet days with her children. Brooks seemed unusually subdued.

The break helped, but by July, the soldiers had grown restless and were chafing at the confinement. Some of them thrived in the regimented environment; Ben Sawyer from missile, for example, shed his hangdog look and acquired a stance with greater purpose. Others wilted from the boredom. Flush with cash and eager for distraction, the soldiers started buying laptops and DVD players. Debbie watched countless episodes of *M*A*S*H* with Will Hargreaves. Later she borrowed Desma Brooks's player to watch *Harry Potter.* "It really was a good idea I didn't think I would like it but I did really enjoy it," she wrote afterward. Then she bought a laptop computer herself — it was amazing to be able to afford such a luxury. Debbie watched *Seabiscuit* on her new laptop and then played a lot of solitaire.

Fischer and Brooks had emerged as Bravo Company's two natural troublemakers, and they were spending increasing amounts of time together. Fischer kept getting drunk with Brooks and then wandering off to sing "I'm a Little Teapot" with Patrick Miller and his friends. Ben Sawyer walked her back to the barracks a lot, and seemed to be trying to act like a gentleman. Once Brooks got so wasted that she slept outside on a picnic table, under a tarp that somebody threw over her, in case it rained. It was often impossible to get Brooks out of bed in time for formation, and a female lieutenant tried to discipline her by rousting her early one morning and ordering her to say the pledge of allegiance, but Brooks brazenly said the pledge while standing naked in the middle of the female barracks, and that was the last time the sergeant woke her up early. Later, Brooks had the crazy idea to buy a kiddie swimming pool and stage a mud-wrestling contest between soldiers who were covered in baby oil. Half the battalion turned out to watch that sloppy debacle.

The parties got wilder and the drinking escalated. When the governor of Indiana arrived to celebrate the sacrifices they were making, they had to stand for hours under the hot sun, and they could smell the rancid alcohol fumes sweating out of each other's bodies. Two women passed out during the ceremony. The soldiers standing next to them caught their limp bodies before they fell to the ground, and passed them toward the back, away from the dignitaries. Illicit affairs sprang up across the post. Sex was one way to blow off steam, Debbie figured, and they had few other distractions. It was almost as if they lived in two coexisting universes; they knew they still had families back home, but in this world it seemed as though they only had each other. Debbie spent all her free time with Will, who also served on the armament team with her and Michelle Fischer, but nothing romantic took place. It was just nice to have a companion; somebody to drink beer with, somebody who asked if you wanted to watch *M*A*S*H.* As a widower, Will relied heavily on Debbie for female company. When Jeff came to visit, he drove the three of them to a nearby lake because Jeff knew that otherwise Will would be on his own.

Debbie turned fifty-two that month. Desma Brooks surprised her with a sheet cake decorated with a picture of Maxx, and Debbie started crying when she saw it. That was just like Brooks, Debbie decided — she had a way of making you feel like you were family. One day later, the first group of soldiers from the 113th Support Battalion left for Afghanistan. The rest of them would follow in staggered bunches. Fischer and Brooks were going next, at the end of July. Will and Debbie were going last, at the beginning of August.

Desma Brooks looked like she was having fun, but actually she was in a slow boil of fury. Finding herself back on the post, separated once more from her children, had left her enraged. Plus, Mueller had stuck her in supply. Desma had been trained to do logistics; supply was a whole different story. She had to spend hours filling out an annoying form called a 2062 *in triplicate,* ordering wrenches, screwdrivers, hoses. They were a company of mechanics, and her job was to fill up the toolboxes. Then the copy machine broke, and she had to fill out the 2062s by hand. The military wanted her to abide by the rules: everybody in uniforms at all times; yellow building after yellow building; "Yes, sir." And she was not in the mood. So she flaunted her purple comforter, she put up the tiki torches, she stepped outside of the barracks in her pajamas to smoke cigarettes. And she started a kick-ass affair with one of the unit's leaders. Desma was notorious for conducting illicit affairs. "Yeah, that was part of my reputation," she would concede later. "It's why I was always in trouble. If you couldn't find me, I was out having sex somewhere." Generally, it was the same guy for a few years. And then he'd move on, and she would move on. She considered the affairs a relatively innocent form of diversion. What happened at Atterbury was supposed to stay at Atterbury. It was like Vegas — a place apart, another world.

But she never imagined she would have the opportunity to sleep with Lieutenant Mark Northrup. He was whip smart, good-looking, kept himself in shape, had a decent job out in the real world. They had begun a flirtation perhaps two years earlier — back before he had become a noncommissioned officer. They had spent an entire day at the same roadside checkpoint collecting for the March of Dimes, and wound up friends. Unlike most of the men in the unit, Northrup could keep up with Desma in a conversation, and she adored his acerbic sense of humor. Then Northrup had gone away to officer training while Desma had endured her false deployment. By the time she had rejoined Bravo Company, he seemed beyond reach. "He was way out of my league," said Desma. "The preppy boy in high school who you don't figure ever notices you."

But that summer, back at Atterbury again, she was assigned to be his driver. It was one of her extra duties, and it meant they saw each other regularly, often just the two of them alone in a vehicle. "We were talking and talking and talking. It was just flirtation. And then all of a sudden it was, oh, God, some of the best sex I've ever had in my life."

Desma told nobody. Her lover was happily married, and probably would never have started sleeping with her if he had not been forcibly separated from his wife. He was also her superior officer, which meant that the affair was prohibited. Plus, Jimmy was waiting for her back at home. The affair had to remain a secret, which added to the excitement, as far as she was concerned. In all of these ways — purple bedding, tiki torches, partying like hell, secretly screwing one of her supervisors — Desma channeled her fury into an angry sort of fun.

After a while she decided to have some fun over at supply, too. The federal government had a national database where you could look up serial numbers for *everything.* One day, she and her friend Mary — who had gotten married and was now Mary Bell — discovered that the federal database had about thirty different serial numbers for condoms: ribbed or regular, lubricated or unlubricated, extra sensation, all sizes. Although, as Desma discovered when she tried to order a batch, condoms were categorized as medical supplies. That meant they belonged to goods in class eight, and class eight didn't fall under her realm. She could only order from classes two, three, six, seven, and nine. Then Desma found the national serial number for hamburger meat, frozen and pattied; another for hot dogs; buns, ketchup, mustard. Food fell under class six, miscellaneous — no problem.

"Hey, Mary," said Desma. "Let's throw a party. We can call it a family day."

"About time!" said Mary.

They ordered three hundred pounds of frozen hamburger meat, three hundred pounds of hot dogs, vast quantities of mustard and ketchup, and ten kegs of beer.

"We need something for morale," Desma told Mary. "It's just not enough to have family day — I want a horse."

Livestock was class ten, technically out of her domain, but she could probably purchase the horse, if the supervisors in Building Three signed off on the 2062. Desma ordered a Clydesdale. She also ordered a bridle, saddle, and blanket. Unfortunately, a scrupulous supervisor spotted the unusual request and sent the 2062 back, along with a note asking for a letter of justification. Desma wrote up a beautiful memorandum; all it needed was the company commander's signature. She stapled the 2062 behind the memo and slipped them both into the middle of a stack of counseling statements for Mueller to sign. He whipped through the counseling statements, signed the letter of justification, and then paused to read the memo. Desma heard him bellow from half a block away.

"Goddamn it!" yelled Mueller. *"Addis!"*

Desma's boss, Gregory Addis, looked

shaken when he came to find Desma.

"You need to get over there," Addis told her.

Desma put on a big smile as she stood at attention.

"Why in the hell did you order a horse?" Mueller demanded.

"Morale and welfare, sir!" said Desma.

"What the hell are you going to do with a damn horse?"

"I'm going to *ride* it, sir! Didn't you notice that there's also a requisition for the saddle, the bridle — all its tack?"

"Get out of my office," Mueller told her. "Don't go back to supply. I don't know what I'm going to do with you, but you can't work there anymore."

Great, Desma figured; no more 2062s. They did not get the Clydesdale, nor the kegs, but they did get the hamburger meat and the hot dogs. The story of Desma trying to order the horse made the rounds and just the idea of the Clydesdale had a galvanizing effect. Michelle Fischer, for example, loved hearing that Brooks had tried to order a horse, and decided afterward that being friends with Desma Brooks was how she would survive Afghanistan. At the end of July, right before they had to board the airplane, they snuck off-post together. It was Desma who coined the idea to go to the Classy Chassy, a strip club with an Indy 500 race car theme, over on the south side of Indianapolis. Their departure was looming and they were desperate for distraction. Desma rounded up people she thought needed to be shown a good time and herded them into her Vista Cruiser, a vast station wagon with paneled siding and a floaty ride. It was the middle of the week and they had no permission to leave post. What the hell, Desma figured, the advance party had already left, and pretty soon they were all going to be in a war zone. It seemed like a good idea to go AWOL now, while they were still surrounded by the forgiving cornfields of Indiana, which lit up every evening with galaxies of fireflies. One last hurrah before they left all this behind. She said that she would be the designated driver.

Mary Bell sat beside Desma in the passenger seat, dressed in a pink tube top and a white tennis skirt. Behind them, on the wagon's middle bench seat, were Michelle Fischer and her perpetual shadow, muscular, tattooed Ben Sawyer. Michelle claimed they were just friends but it looked like more than that to Desma. On the rear-facing backseat sat Suzy Allen and Don Southard. A devout Christian, Suzy had been leading a relatively wholesome life on post, despite the debauchery going on around her, but Desma had grabbed her anyway, figuring she had to be freaked out, too. Sawyer had persuaded Southard to join them on the way to her car;

he was a good-looking married man who was fond of boxing.

"We're going to sneak off to the Classy Chassy," Sawyer had told him. "Want to come?"

"Hell, yeah!" Southard had said.

The Classy Chassy was hopping. Drag cars hung from the ceiling, lit up by red neon, while black lights sucked the color out of everything in the room except the white parts of the strippers' costumes. One stripper was dressed up as a cowgirl, another as Captain America. They saw other soldiers in the audience, but they were the only women. The DJ fanned the crowd into a frenzy when he played "Whip It," and then Michelle requested Def Leppard's "Pour Some Sugar on Me." The chairs had wheels, and Desma and Michelle and Mary rolled from their table over to the area by the stage. The strippers lavished attention on them, delighted to be entertaining women. Desma stuck to her promise and ordered only Diet Cokes, but she harassed the bartender into making stiff drinks for her friends. "Listen, we didn't drive all the way down here to drink juice and water," Desma told him. "If I wanted them to drink juice and water I could've kept them at home."

Over the course of the night, Michelle consumed a total of nine vodka Collinses. They got so rowdy that the manager told them they were going to have to leave unless they settled down. They rolled back to their table and were quiet for a while but then a particularly attractive stripper came over and made purring sounds in their ears. She put her head down between Suzy's legs, and vaulted upward into a headstand so that her tiny white underpants, which glowed under the club's black lights, were nearly touching Suzy's face. "Oh, my goodness!" exclaimed Suzy. The stripper's underpants had tiny red cherries on them.

"I need to get in the car," Mary announced.

Desma told the others that she was going to take Mary outside. They walked around the parking lot until Mary felt better and then Desma got her into the Vista Cruiser and rolled her window down and told her not to puke in the car. A lonely Mexican tried to chat with Mary, so Desma rolled up her window. He came around to Desma's side.

"Does she want to fuck?" he inquired.

"Do you see her? She is knocked-out drunk."

"What about you?"

"Get the hell away from me," Desma told him.

The others finally emerged, and the Mexican vanished. Desma got them onto 465, the highway that looped around Indianapolis.

"I don't feel good," Mary said.

"You need to tell me before you're going to

vomit so that I can pull over," Desma instructed.

"Okay," Mary said.

But the car had that floaty ride. Desma looked into the rearview mirror for a moment and saw that Ben Sawyer had put his arm all the way around Michelle and was holding his hand over her mouth to keep her quiet, while she was shaking with laughter. Behind them, Desma saw two feet, up by the roof of the car. Were those Suzy's feet? Then she heard Mary make a little sound like a meow.

"Did you just puke in my car?" Desma cried.

"No — in my tube top," Mary reported.

"I know you got napkins," said Ben Sawyer. "You're a mom."

They could not clean Mary up sufficiently with the car moving floatily along at sixty miles an hour, so Desma pulled off onto the shoulder of the highway. Mary stumbled out of the car, pulled off her tube top, and flung it into the darkness. Desma and Michelle were mopping her puke-stained breasts when another vehicle pulled up behind them. It was the company commander and the XO. Mueller and his second in command just sat in their van, taking it all in. "Oh, Mary, your boobies!" cried Michelle. She stepped behind Mary and cupped her friend's naked breasts in her hands. They stood like that looking at the two leaders of their unit as Don Southard and Suzy Allen pulled on their clothes and stumbled out of the car. Alcohol-induced stupidity, Suzy Allen would say later, but she wasn't sober yet, and she was looking at her commander.

Desma stepped forward and observed tartly that she believed the company's two leaders were AWOL. "You're not supposed to leave the post," she announced. "So what exactly are you doing out on this highway?"

Mueller sighed. He asked if she was sober enough to drive and told them to go back to Camp Atterbury.

Desma bumped into Mueller the next morning.

"How's everybody feeling?" Mueller asked drily.

"We're feeling just fine," Desma told him. "Where did you go?"

"We went to the Red Door. Where did you go?"

"We went to the Classy Chassy."

"That's why everybody was puking in your car."

"Oh, not everybody was puking," Desma said.

Michelle Fischer was twenty-one years old, and she hadn't gambled on any of this. She hadn't gambled on 9/11, hadn't gambled on Camp Atterbury, hadn't gambled on Afghanistan. She was as scared as she had ever been.

Every night, she drank herself into a stupor, trying to subdue the bone-gnawing anxiety. Mostly she drank Hypnotic, a pale blue mixture of prepackaged vodka, cognac, and fruit juice. She called it "ghetto fabulous." But she put on a brave front when she communicated with her parents, because she did not want to make them worry. At the beginning of May, she wrote her father a short letter in a chipper tone. She told him:

> I am trying to make the most of my time here. Right now I'm trying to organize a recycling program for my company. We drink so much beer in cans, so I'm trying to convince my first sergeant to let me recycle them. I'm having a hard time, but I'm stubborn. (Thanks to you and Mom!) I drink almost every day here. There's not much else to do. I just let myself drink whenever I want to because I know I can't drink at all in Afghanistan so I don't have to worry about coming home with a drinking problem. . . .
>
> I'm not afraid of this experience anymore and I'm not mad about it. All I can do is keep myself positive. . . .
>
> I love you Daddy!

But in a letter to Pete, written on the very same day, she struck a different tone.

This sucks. I really miss my old life, this army shit is for the birds. . . . There is no one here like me, not even close. I have a few close friends but even they don't have much in common with me. Oh well — at least I won't have to worry about anyone wanting to borrow my *Adbusters*. . . .

Kiss Halloween for me. I miss him. When I get home he'll be a cat. Not a kitten.

Michelle's old hip injury flared up after one of their runs, and she asked the medics to look, hoping the stress fracture from basic training had reemerged. They sent her down to Louisville, Kentucky, where the doctors pronounced her fine. Then Michelle was out of excuses. She made a calculated decision not to renew her Indiana driver's license when it expired, however, because driving a truck in a war zone was probably the most dangerous job that the military was assigning to women. And she stubbornly kept wearing her rainbow hemp anklet.

In other respects, however, it was simply easier to conform. The PX carried certain basics, but otherwise everybody went to Walmart. Buses took the soldiers over to Walmart and brought them back to the post. It was the only place the buses would go. So Michelle ended her boycott and resumed shopping at Walmart. The military was vast, and it did not tolerate idiosyncracy. It was exhausting to fight all of the time to maintain her identity. At least she would be rich when she got back, Michelle figured. In the middle of May she got her first active duty paycheck: she was now earning $994.68 every two weeks. Once she got to Afghanistan, she would earn hazard pay, too. And while she was there, she would pay no federal income tax. Her income would skyrocket — and all her meals would be provided, her laundry would be done, and movies would be shown at night for free.

Michelle lost Pete's ring one day in the pool, and she slept with Ben Sawyer shortly afterward. She still loved Pete, but Sawyer was there and Pete was not. She had been shit-faced on Hypnotic when it happened — drunk, lonely, and scared. Most other people would have found her behavior understandable, but she could not forgive herself. She did not tell Pete what had happened because she wanted so badly for it not to have taken place. But when she wrote to him next her words were imbued with an unmistakable tone of regret.

> I love you so much, and I really miss you. I'm sorry that this experience is changing me. I know that you can tell the difference already. . . . I miss my colorful life so much. Some days I am okay, but

only if I am really busy. I can't think too much. But when I do it's always of you, or Halloween. And the little things I miss like *Sex and the City.* Just dumb shit you take for granted every day of your life. Let's take this year to dream, because when I get home I'll have enough money and we can do whatever we want.

The following month, Michelle went with Ben Sawyer to Fort Benjamin Harrison, over in Lawrence, Indiana, to become certified as a combat lifesaver. "It was the most nerve-racking thing, I never, ever thought I could stick a needle in somebody's vein," Michelle wrote in a letter to her father. "But I did it perfectly. I am so squeamish around blood, but now that I've done it once I feel like I could do it a million times." By then she had gotten falling-down drunk once more, and had sex with Sawyer again. She had not intended to repeat her mistake, but she had no self-control when she was plastered.

Michelle wrote one final letter to Pete before she left the country. She found a card with a drawing of a green olive. Inside, the card said, "Olive you!" It was an inside joke. At the radio station on campus, when Pete had been behind the glass, unable to hear anything Michelle was saying to him, she used to pantomime kisses and hold up notes that said "olive juice." She knew he would get the joke. Inside she wrote:

> Dear Pete,
>
> You are the love of my life and I am forever grateful for your love. I know that I could not make it through this experience without your support. You are my <u>only</u> support, you're my family, my partner, my love, and my best friend. Thank you so much for everything you do for me. <u>I'll always love you.</u> Keep your chin up. Think of Europe, Bloomington, Seattle, and all of the dreams that we share. I'll be home soon.
>
> Love always,
> Michelle

She went AWOL and snuck out to the Classy Chassy with Desma right after she mailed the letter. Even the nine drinks she ordered could not obliterate her sense of guilt at having cheated on Pete, nor the terrible fear that was fueling her need for physical reassurance. They left for Afghanistan the following day. Michelle, Desma, and Desma's friend Mary boarded an airplane that left the United States on July 20, 2004. The next time Michelle saw Debbie Helton was in Kabul.

■ ■ ■ ■

II
Afghanistan, 2004–2005

■ ■ ■ ■

1
Off Safety

Michelle's group got stranded in Germany for days, sleeping on cots in an enormous tent on the sprawling Rhein-Main Air Base just outside of Frankfurt. It was run jointly by the US Air Force and NATO and served as the primary way station for American soldiers passing through Europe. The chow hall was all blond wood and bright lights, and reminded Michelle of an IKEA cafeteria. Nobody wanted to leave because they served such good food — huge plates of sausages and immense slabs of cake. When their first two flights out of Germany were canceled for mechanical reasons, Michelle began to imagine being granted a reprieve. One night at dinner, she heard that a group that had left after them had already arrived in theater. Was there a reason they could not get where they were going? The following morning the soldiers lined up to depart again, only to be told that a powerful storm had devastated the airport; the roof of their terminal had collapsed. That evening, Michelle saw another double rainbow. It was a sign, she knew it. The soldiers were told they could go out drinking. Michelle, Desma, and Mary found a bar with a sand volleyball court, and whooped it up for hours, trying different German beers. Michelle got wasted, then called Pete to say she thought there had been some kind of mistake, she would be home soon. She stumbled back to her cot in a beery stupor and passed out. She had been asleep for only a few hours when an officer walked in, flipped on the lights, and said, "It's time to go."

As they boarded the immense green C-17 Globemaster troop transport aircraft, Desma announced that the perfect cocktail for riding in a plane that was going to do a combat landing was one Valium and one Ambien. She handed those two pills to Michelle and to Mary. "One plus one equals you don't feel a thing," Michelle would say afterward. None of them stirred much when the plane stopped to refuel in Turkey; when they neared Kabul, the C-17 plunged downward in a dive so steep that some of the other soldiers felt as though weights had been placed on their bodies, but neither Michelle nor Desma retained clear memories of the landing. "Sank into that cargo webbing like it was my mother's womb, slept the whole way," Desma would say later.

Michelle stumbled off the C-17 in a groggy state of disbelief and for one disorienting moment thought maybe they had landed on the sun. When her eyes adjusted to the glare she noticed there was no sign of the army unit that was supposed to greet them. The empty-bellied C-17 took off anyway, leaving them marooned on the tarmac without any ammunition. Somebody wondered out loud if they might get shot before they left the airport. Mary hunkered down by her hand luggage, onto which she had tied a small pink and orange worm that she had nicknamed Gwormy — many of them had brought mascots, as if the toys could keep them safe. Desma slowly absorbed the fact that barbed wire orbited them, and small red triangular signs posted on the barbed wire warned of mines, and beyond those signs a flock of small children had gathered. They were staring at the soldiers. The children wore mismatched clothes, some too big and some too small, nothing that belonged together, as if they had found the items at Goodwill. The soldiers looked like astronauts ready for a moon landing. They had on desert camo pants, desert camo jackets, bulletproof vests, Kevlar helmets, M4 assault rifles. The gear obscured the question of what shape or what gender they might be underneath, and everything matched perfectly. What unearthly prospect did they present? Desma watched a boy run away from them through the field full of land mines, and only after he had gotten quite far did she perceive that he was following a well-worn path.

The regular army arrived and gave the Army National Guard soldiers ten bullets apiece. "Load up," a sergeant instructed gruffly. "Don't lock. Leave the chamber empty. Take your weapons off safety." Neither Michelle nor Desma had ever taken their weapon off safety before, except when they were aiming at a target. He said they should not trust children and they should watch out for cars approaching at high speed and for roadside bombs. A box, a bag of trash, a pile of dirt. He said there could be Taliban out there. Then the army soldiers herded them into the backs of open-air trucks lined with sandbags. Michelle grabbed a seat next to Desma. As they peered out between the planks, they saw rocky, barren terrain ringed on all sides by mountains so tall they looked blue. Kabul itself appeared bleak: bombed-out buildings, bullet holes, junked cars, debris by the side of the road. But the traffic milling around them was fantastic; they saw wildly painted trucks, people wearing robes, barefoot children, donkeys, goats, and women cloaked from head to toe in blue burkas. And then billowing clouds of dust consumed it all.

At Camp Phoenix, uniformed guards

cleared them through the gate. Their battalion belonged to the 76th Infantry Brigade from Indiana, which was taking over from the National Guard soldiers from Oklahoma, and the turnover had been staggered. For the time being, both sets of soldiers were going to be double-bunked in the same quarters. On their first night, Oklahoma set up a big screen in the middle of the main courtyard and played the movie *Groundhog Day.* Michelle skipped the forced entertainment, but Desma watched Bill Murray wake up over and over again to the exact same reality. It was 5:59, then 6:00. *Put your little hand in mine, there ain't no hill or mountain we can't climb. I got you, babe.* Over and over. Afterward, Oklahoma made sure they got the joke — their days at Phoenix would be so mind-numbingly unchanging as to seem identical. "Yeah, we got it," Desma told them. "We're not dumb."

About those hazy, sleep-deprived first days, living double-bunked in a ten-person tent with twenty other women, Michelle kept only smeared, partial memories. There was no privacy, and Michelle found herself observing other women changing their tampons as well as their clothes. Even Debbie Helton, who got to Camp Phoenix about ten days later, squirmed with self-consciousness due to the communal living arrangements. "I've got gas galore these poor people in my tent,"

Debbie wrote in her diary. "It's really bad." The elevation of 5,869 feet rendered them short of breath, and their bodies required time to adjust to the dry climate, too. Many of the newly arrived soldiers got nosebleeds. The temperature routinely hit one hundred degrees (though later in the year the temperature would drop below freezing), and they had arrived just as the region was staggering through the last phases of a blistering seven-year drought. The wind that constantly scoured the land was literally blowing the ground into the air, and whenever she drew a breath, Michelle felt as though she were inhaling sand. The grit crept into her eyes and ears and undergarments. It stuck to her teeth and it coated her scalp. Her pen no longer rolled smoothly over paper when she wrote letters.

Michelle spent a lot of time smoking cigarettes, mostly with Desma. Oklahoma showed them Camel Rock, a piece of concrete jutting out of the ground that was the designated smoking area, and in the middle of the night when they could not stay inside the stifling tent any longer, they would head over there. They often waited for the dawn together, or just walked around in circles. It was an entirely different night sky than the one Michelle knew; she saw more stars than she had believed existed. Eventually she learned not to point out shooting stars because they flew by so fast that invariably the other person would crane up asking where to look in that immense carpet of light.

Michelle found it hard to sleep because the soldiers had been ordered to take Lariam, a potent antimalarial. The pills were handed out in the chow hall, right next to the silverware. Lariam caused unusually vivid dreams; people also complained of Lariam inducing hallucinations, paranoia, and psychosis. Other soldiers said Lariam caused brain aneurysms, but nobody knew if that was true. Desma announced proudly that Lariam gave her highly realistic sexual dreams, in full color, but Michelle felt as though she had bugs crawling over her skin. Because they had been alerted to watch for insects such as camel spiders, which could grow as long as six inches, Michelle had a hard time ignoring her hallucinations. She grew afraid to thrust her feet down into the bottom of her sleeping bag, then afraid to enter her sleeping bag at all. After a few days, Desma started giving Michelle other pills — muscle relaxants, sleeping pills, antianxiety medication — to help her get some rest. Michelle fell in love with Vicodin, an addictive narcotic that she started taking nightly. After Desma ran out, the medics provided her with a regular supply. "It wasn't hard to get a prescription," Michelle said later. "They were handing that stuff out like candy."

Their new home had originally been constructed as a Soviet air base, and they found it a spare, utilitarian environment. After the Soviets had withdrawn, a local tractor trailer company had used the area as a junkyard; one year before the soldiers from Indiana arrived, NATO had leased the property and turned it back into a military installation. Now a sea of dark green tents spread across two and a half square miles of concrete, interrupted by islands of tan prefabricated buildings. Everything else was made of plywood. "If you think plywood is one-dimensional, then you haven't been to Camp Phoenix," wrote Diana Penner, a reporter for the *Indianapolis Star* who visited during their deployment. "There is nothing, it appears, that plywood can't be used to create. There are desks and bookcases, phone cubicles and computer stations, chests of drawers and armoires, chapel pulpits and a smoking gazebo, signs and entire dwellings." So much plywood meant strict fire codes and weekly inspections. "A base fire station is now under construction," added Penner. "It also is made of plywood."

Eight hundred soldiers from seven different countries were stationed at Phoenix. They spoke a babel of languages and wore camouflage of different patterns but all belonged to the Combined Joint Task Force Phoenix III, an international military organization formed to train and mentor Afghan National Army soldiers.

Ever since the United States and its allies had failed to capture Osama bin Laden at Tora Bora, they had been searching for him in the mountains of Afghanistan, primarily along the country's border with Pakistan. Between Afghanistan and Pakistan rose the formidable peaks of the Hindu Kush mountain range, some reaching more than 25,000 feet high, most shrouded in perpetual snow. The terrain was so harsh that the mountain range had gotten its name — literally, Hindu Kush means "killer of Hindus" — from bloody journeys of the past in which large numbers of captive Hindus had died while crossing over in the hands of slave traders.

The American soldiers had not found bin Laden anywhere, but they had gotten entangled in a series of difficult conflicts with various of his supporters. It was hard to tell how the war was going, exactly — it just kept dragging on, one firefight after another waged across remote and inhospitable mountain valleys. Meanwhile, the Bush administration had become preoccupied with the question of how to secure the rest of Afghanistan and make it a less friendly place for bin Laden's supporters, such as the Taliban. To that end, it was now working with their NATO allies to build up the Afghan National Army.

Every nationality in the coalition had their

own particular specialty. The French soldiers removed land mines, wearing special footwear that everybody called "egg boots," while the Romanians knew the most about Soviet weapons. Their foreign colleagues had notably different habits; Debbie got a kick out of watching the French soldiers do their PT exercises, because the French soldiers were wearing the smallest nylon shorts she had ever seen on a man. "Not a sloppy French guy," Debbie said approvingly afterward. The classes for Afghan soldiers were held at a variety of locations around Kabul, and usually they were led by American instructors. The 113th Support Battalion maintained the vehicles that American soldiers used when they traveled to the training locations, and also repaired or replaced any broken weapons, night vision goggles, and other equipment. All told, the NATO coalition was training and deploying almost ten thousand Afghan National Army soldiers per year. The governing idea was that someday Afghanistan would have a stable democracy and a military capable of warding off threats to stability posed by groups like Al-Qaeda or the Taliban and they could all go home.

Michelle and Desma explored the post together. They found Morale, Welfare, and Recreation, known to everyone as MWR, where soldiers congregated to watch TV or play pool, Ping-Pong, foosball, and video games. There was free water and free microwave popcorn. The post also featured a small library and a Green Beans coffee shop. They found the phones, the Internet computers, and the gym. A large outdoor bazaar took place every other week on Fridays. Michelle saw jewelry set out in red boxes lined with white fabric, cashmere throws, marble tea sets, and ornately patterned wool rugs in rich browns, reds, ochers, and deep midnight blues. She bought a hand-embroidered silk tapestry and a postcard of a man wearing a turban. "I guess I spoke too soon; I left Germany about two hours after I called you," she wrote to Pete. "I am okay, things aren't too bad here. A little boring. The altitude kind of sucks. But the mountains are breathtaking. I have seen so much already that I will never forget. Please try not to worry, I don't think Camp Phoenix is very dangerous. I love you I really do. Write soon."

She received a letter the following day that Pete had put in the mail two weeks earlier. "I got your letter today," she wrote back. "It made me cry. I feel how far away I am now. In time and in distance. I miss you so much. I feel like when I get home everyone will have a new and different life without me in it. . . . I hope we can just pick up where we left off. I am so sad right now." Before she sealed her letter, Michelle thought of all she had forgotten to pack, and added a hasty postscript:

My wish list:
nasal spray
Visine (a shit ton)
lipgloss or chapstick with SPF
really good lotion (Aveeno)
Beach Blonde Wavemaker

She hoped the last product would help her deal with her hair, which had lost its curl in the dry air. It was ridiculous to fret about her appearance while living in a combat zone, she knew, but she had to wear an ugly uniform every day, and there wasn't much left that made her feel feminine. Another woman in her tent was compulsively applying makeup for hours at a time. Later that week, Michelle mailed Pete the silk tapes-try she had found at the bazaar, telling him someday they would hang it up in the house they were going to share in Bloomington. Pete mailed Michelle all of the items on her wish list. He also sent a sand bucket, since she wouldn't stop talking about how sandy it was. Michelle used it as her shower caddy. The women's showers had been constructed inside of a shipping container; everybody called them conexes. The showers did not drain well, and Michelle kept having to clear large clumps of other women's hair. The latrines, which were located elsewhere, flushed with a kick pedal. Then somebody found a viper by the latrines. It was just a small snake, but supposedly that meant they should watch out for the rest of the nest. Over in Debbie Helton's tent, somebody caught a rat — the trap snapped closed loudly in the middle of the night, causing a ruckus. A few days later, Debbie told everybody excitedly that she had just seen her first scorpion. Michelle knew she was supposed to worry about the Taliban, but it was the snakes and bugs that she could not get out of her mind.

The altitude and the sand and the wind and the Lariam and the pills and the lack of sleep transported Michelle to a place of sun-drenched surreality. She showed up for work as instructed and did as ordered, but she could not have said what she was doing. There were hardly any weapons to fix, and Patrick Miller, the ex-marine who was now in charge of armament, grew testy as he struggled to figure out how to keep his crew busy. Michelle used the spare time to write letters. "Hey! How are you doing?" she wrote to her father. "I hope this letter finds you well. I am sitting at the shop where I work with nothing to do. This deployment isn't anything like I imagined. Sometimes I have work to do but I spend most of my time sitting around bored off my ass."

Back in Indiana, the previous summer, Patrick Miller had been friendly to Michelle — sharing his dip, confessing his unhappiness — but after they got to Afghanistan, he became an entirely different person. He himself said that he had been Patrick Miller when they had horsed around, but now he was Sergeant Miller instead. Sergeant Miller seemed frustrated with the state of affairs in general and with Michelle Fischer in particular. Michelle kept showing up late, and when she did arrive, she was sulky. Miller annoyed her with his driven, promilitary attitude. He was a slight man with a buzz cut and an Alabama twang; they were about the same height. "Huge Napoleon complex," Michelle would say later. When she showed up late yet again, Miller threatened to give her a written reprimand. She said insolently, "Go ahead, write me a counseling statement, I really don't care." Miller cursed her out fluently, berating her until she broke down. The rest of the armament team could see both sides: on the one hand, Sergeant Miller was used to the discipline of regular military life; on the other hand, Michelle Fischer had voted for Ralph Nader in 2000 and had not seen 9/11 coming. Even Debbie Helton — who had arrived bubbling over with enthusiasm and kept saying that Afghanistan was the single most exciting thing that had happened in her entire life — could see that from Michelle's point of view the yearlong deployment looked like a raw deal.

Debbie's journey to Afghanistan had been uneventful. Her group had stopped in Ireland, where one commander had told them they could have a pint and then another had nixed the idea, which had disappointed Debbie. Then they had flown to Budapest, and the following day to Kyrgyzstan. "The days are drifting together," Debbie had written. "I've had little sleep." She had strapped herself into a harness inside a green C-130 Hercules headed for Afghanistan, full of exhilaration to be leaving the civilian world behind. Even the steep plunge of the combat landing did not dismay her. "What a wild ride that was," she wrote. "During descent because of pressure your body feels like it's becoming squished down completely."

In the open-air trucks that picked them up, she grabbed a seat next to Will Hargreaves. Everything in close proximity was pale tan. But the mountains — Debbie had never seen anything like those twilight-colored peaks.

"Well, you finally finagled a way to get here," Will teased. "You probably did something to the guy who collapsed to get his spot."

"No I didn't!" she laughingly protested.

"Are you scared?"

"Not really scared, just anxious to see how this fits together. I wish John Wayne was here."

They were the last group to arrive, and they found the rest of the battalion already in full swing. Debbie was grateful to be given two days to acclimate before she had to go to work. At the Green Beans coffee shop, she ordered her first chai tea and, charmed by the taste of cinnamon and nutmeg, soon returned for more. The bazaar captivated her. "Has many great things to buy not too expensive," she wrote. "Cheap like Mexico." She decided to save up and buy all of her Christmas presents there. For a few nights she was assigned temporary quarters in a tent filled with strangers, but then Oklahoma pulled out. On Saturday, August 7, 2004 — three days after Debbie had arrived, and almost two weeks after Michelle and Desma had gotten to Camp Phoenix — Indiana shuffled people around into more permanent berths. Debbie and her friend Gretchen found a spot together in a tent with some medics from Charlie Company and a non-commissioned officer from Alpha. (Gretchen Flood had gotten married right before they left for Afghanistan and had changed her name to Gretchen Pane.) Because their tent was an amalgam of women from different ranks and companies, at first it lacked cohesion. Later Debbie would become grateful for the level of maturity inside her tent, but at the beginning she found the atmosphere slightly strained, as the women did not trust each other entirely.

The American troops at Camp Phoenix were banned from drinking (although the

Europeans were not), and if they wanted to go on a bender, they flew to Qatar. Nevertheless, Debbie had smuggled in miniature bottles of whiskey, hoping to make herself a cocktail. Once she got her permanent housing assignment, however, she realized it would be unsafe to expose herself as a drinker, so she kept the bottles hidden inside a coffee can. At the end of her first day in the new tent, Debbie longed for a drink but did not make one. "Boy a cocktail would be great," she wrote in her diary. "No ice cubes yet I know there has to be some somewhere." The following evening, Debbie did manage to fix herself a drink. "Finally found some ice had a cocktail it was great. Hope I get to take that time to Qatar I'll be at the local bar if needed." While Debbie considered the Afghanistan deployment a privilege, it was hard to sleep in a tent with nine other women, and a drink helped ease anxieties that she kept well hidden. At the same time, she relished her new surroundings. "At night the wind really comes up strong can't hardly sit outside very well too much sand in the air. Go to MWR a lot, great tea. Call when I can. Haven't done the Internet yet. Stars are beautiful because of the altitude."

Michelle moved into a ten-person tent that she had to share with only nine other women, including Desma and Mary. Michelle and Desma had requested that Debbie Helton become the senior person in their new tent, but instead they wound up with Sergeant Karen Shaw. Karen's moods swung in arcs so epic that Michelle wondered if she was chemically unbalanced. Desma started calling her "Shock and Awe Karen Shaw." The other women sharing their tent included a churchgoing soldier named Stella Brown; Jaime Toppe, who was even more devoutly religious than Stella; Caroline Hill; Katie Elkins; Elizabeth Ziegler, known as Ziggy; and Betsy Merrick. Mostly they were mechanics or worked in supply, with the exception of Jaime Toppe, who served as the unit's public affairs representative.

Now that Oklahoma was gone they could use the top bunks for storage. Desma and Mary snagged opposing bunk beds right by the front door, and Michelle got a bed next to Mary. Caroline Hill got the bed next to Desma, across from Michelle. The next two opposing beds were occupied by Karen Shaw and Jaime Toppe, then Stella Brown and Ziggy after that, and finally Betsy and Katie. From the get-go, they had friction. "Catty, catty, catty, catty, catty," Michelle would say later, describing the atmosphere inside the tent. "I mean, we had probably six feet by four feet of personal space." The tent was divided politically, too, with Michelle representing its most liberal occupant, and Jaime Toppe its most conservative. And the women did not agree on what was socially acceptable behavior, either, with Michelle, Desma, and Mary condoning activity such as smoking pot, and Jaime and some of the other women disapproving of that kind of behavior. How they were going to get along for twelve months remained an open question.

Yet Michelle felt elated to be sharing a tent with so many fewer people. She could still hear every cough and rustle, but she got an empty top bunk where she could store her gear, and a shelf with a bar to hang up her uniforms. She unpacked at last, and put photographs of Pete and Halloween next to her bed, where she could look at them every evening. A few days later, when the staff at the chow hall baked a large cake for a birthday party for some of her coworkers, Michelle went to the party and had a decent time. "Everyone is in good spirits about being here, finally," she wrote to Pete. "Of course I still miss you desperately. . . . [I]t's really hard for me when I think of you because I can feel how slow time is. No one else in the world matters."

It was immediately obvious to Michelle that Camp Phoenix was not the kind of place where it would be safe to wander around late at night in an alcoholic stupor, uncertain of the location of her tent. Entire zones of the post belonged to all-male infantry units, and anybody who showed up there in an incapacitated state would be considered fair game. She saw that the brain-numbing partying she had engaged in back at Camp Atterbury would make her vulnerable, and consequently she stopped drinking. Instead she became more and more reliant on the pills she took once she was safely inside her own sleeping bag. But the same pills that helped her lose consciousness at night also left her groggy in the morning, and upon waking she had to fight off the gloom of remembering where she was. And so even as she started to feel more at home, she still kept showing up tardy for work, and Miller kept going ballistic until she broke down crying. It became their daily routine.

Michelle started visiting the gym right after work, where she trod up and down on the StairMaster for an hour at a time, then lifted weights. The furious workouts funneled stress out of her body and made it easier to fall asleep. She decided that her weight was one of the few things she could control, and started tracking it compulsively, determined to shed pounds. Then Miller announced they had some guns to repair. "I got my first broken weapon tonight!" she wrote to Pete. "I was pretty excited, I'll actually get to do my job tomorrow." They were all relieved to have work; even Debbie had begun to worry that the biggest challenge of her deployment might be boredom. She had been distracting herself with a mystery novel by Iris Johansen, but to her astonishment she finished it after only a few days. "Amazing," she had written. "Usually takes me one year to finish." After they got busy, Debbie happily changed the butt stock on a damaged M4 assault rifle and organized toolboxes.

The spurt of broken weapons dried up in the middle of August, and then Sergeant Miller announced that they were going to build a secure weapons room. In a corner of the same building that housed the motor pool, he planned to construct a twelve-foot-square space to house weapons in need of repair. George Quintana helped oversee the project. He and Miller got along well because they were both ex-marines and both devout Republicans; the rest of the team loved GQ because he was unflappable. They cleared away debris, then lugged in tools and lumber. "We started the office today!" Debbie wrote in her diary on August 13, 2004. "Miller + Q are the bosses we are the workers."

For the rest of that month, the armament team sweated through the construction project and grew accustomed to working with each other. Debbie injured her lower back while carrying lumber, and started worrying that she might be too old for the deployment. Three Tylenol and one Aleve did not even touch her pain, and she finally had to get a muscle relaxer called Feldene from a medic.

He ordered her not to bend, twist, or lift anything over twenty-five pounds, which made her feel useless. But Miller found other ways for her to help, and she regained her confidence. At one point, GQ praised George Bush. Michelle announced that she found his stance unfathomable. "How is it that you ended up being Republican, if you're Puerto Rican and from the Bronx?" she asked. GQ told her, "Any man under thirty who is not a liberal has no heart. Any man over thirty who is not a conservative has no brains." She thought he had made it up, only to learn it was Winston Churchill. But it didn't really matter, about his politics. Once, back at Camp Atterbury, Michelle had walked for miles carrying a heavy rucksack, and her feet had sweated inside her combat boots, giving her hot spots. GQ had helped pull off her boots and picked up her red feet in his hands and covered them in soothing Gold Bond foot powder. Even if they disagreed about Bush, she would always think of GQ as an ally.

She no longer felt the same way about Patrick Miller. Their tendency to get crosswise only increased after they started building the secure weapons room, and now he routinely treated her with contempt. Sergeant Miller wanted the team to go at the project full tilt, but Michelle had never done construction work before and could not even hammer a nail properly. Then, while he was trying to determine whether the walls would meet at a right angle, Michelle suggested they use trigonometry. Didn't he know about Pythagoras's Theorem? Miller appeared to think that she considered him stupid. He ripped into her again, cussing ferociously. During one of these frequent displays of temper, affable George Quintana intervened.

"You'll never make a soldier out of that girl," he observed.

"Yes I will!" vowed Miller.

Quintana stuck out his hand and offered to bet that Miller would fail. At the end of the deployment, GQ maintained, Fischer would remain as unsuited to military life as she had been at the beginning. They put money on the question. It helped, naming the power struggle: Miller wanted to remake Michelle over in his own likeness, while she was determined to remain unchanged. No way would she let Sergeant Miller turn her into an automaton. Day after day, she kept showing up late, and Miller kept exploding. He got even more loud and vulgar, as if he could browbeat Michelle into submission. It was hard for the others to watch Miller bully the girl, but she remained implacable. Debbie wondered at Michelle's backbone. Did she herself care too much about making other people happy? That did not seem to be a problem for Michelle.

In a couple of weeks, the armament team finished framing the room, putting up the walls, hanging the door, and laying down the floor. After the secure weapons room was done, Miller took the team on an eye-opening trip to a nearby military base called Pol-i-charkhi. The base was infamous because it was home to a prison where supposedly many atrocities had been committed. It was also one of the locations where NATO had been training Afghan National Army soldiers.

The drive took only twenty minutes but seemed longer because of the state of the road. There were no traffic lights, no stop signs, and no posted street names (the signs had been taken down during the first Soviet occupation), and many streets were rutted with potholes so enormous that traffic lurched from one side of the road to the other to avoid the spine-jolting chasms. If the right side of the road was especially bad, everybody veered to the left, then used their horns to force one another out of the way. The armament team bumped into other cars as they jostled for a spot in the weaving confluence. The soldiers were fascinated by the surrounding traffic. Michelle was charmed by the sight of tiny three-wheeled taxis with cartoon-like stickers on their windshields. They saw a stooped man in a brown robe herding some woolly-looking goats. They saw men riding camels with brightly colored bridles, and other men riding Suzukis. Will Hargreaves kept pointing out the jingle trucks, transport vehicles elaborately painted scarlet, turquoise, yellow, and flaming orange. Some of the jingle trucks had ropes of beads strewn over their windshields, others featured swaying pom-poms, or regal crowns. Noisy metallic fringes below swayed with their movement, making a constant jingling sound; the noise was supposed to ward off evil spirits. Michelle supposed the drivers needed good luck, for their vehicles were piled with stacks of goods so alarmingly high that she kept expecting things to fall off.

Looking out of the dusty windows of her own vehicle, she apprehended that Afghanistan was a country of grinding poverty. They saw a child with only one leg, and others with no shoes. The children were terribly skinny. Afghanistan ranked as one of the poorest nations on earth, and the average life expectancy was forty-four years — lower than that of any neighboring country. Women died in childbirth at sixty times the rate in industrialized nations. Against the backdrop of lofty mountain peaks, they saw people living in mud homes without running water and children who seemed inadequately dressed. Yet the children kept flashing the soldiers the thumbs-up sign, thrusting themselves forward with vivid enthusiasm. "It's worse than Belize as far as Third World," Debbie would write in her diary that evening. "This is real poverty. . . . I hope our time here can only really help the future of these kids."

Inside the gates of Pol-i-charkhi, the armament team beheld a sea of old Soviet tanks, now serving as military vehicles for the Afghan National Army. Afghan soldiers took them to a warehouse and showed them boxes of derelict AK-47s. The guns were rusting, dirty, missing sights. Over the preceding months, Afghanistan's warlords had surrendered more than thirty thousand weapons to the United Nations, and the guns were being stored in conexes like the one they now stood before. Their first sergeant, Dean Kimball, had accompanied the armament team. He said their job would be to ensure future peace by cleaning and fixing the old guns so that the Afghan government could hand them out to the Afghan National Army. They could save the Afghan government tens of thousands of dollars by repurposing the old weapons, Kimball said. They would identify which AK-47s might be salvageable, clean the weapons, fix those that could be repaired, and use the others for parts. It was important work, because they were helping to build a democracy. The transfer of weapons from the warlords to the Afghan army had a fancy name: NATO brass were calling it Disarmament, Demobilization, and Reintegration, or DDR. Michelle could never remember exactly what DDR stood for, so she just called it *Dance, Dance, Revolution,* after one of her favorite video games.

They drove back to Camp Phoenix in a convoy. A vehicle behind them broke down, and protocol required that their truck stop, too. They were still three miles away from Camp Phoenix, stranded and vulnerable. Some children approached, calling out, "Thank you! Good! Thank you! Hello, America!" Will and another soldier were ordered to pull security, which meant putting a bullet into the chamber and getting ready to fire. "The kids mostly want to come close but [we] have to lock + load + shoot if necessary," Debbie wrote in her diary that evening. The Taliban had been known to use children as suicide bombers. Afghanistan encompassed such harsh contrasts that it was hard to embrace it all; in a single day, they had recoiled at the sight of bombed-out buildings, rejoiced in the natural glory of the lofty mountains, suffered at the sight of such poor children, and then been told that it might be necessary to shoot them. Later that night, Debbie woke up to the feeling of her bunk being shaken. She thought Gretchen was trying to wake her up, but Gretchen protested that Debbie should stop shaking the bunk. It was their first earthquake. Afterward Debbie wrote, "I'm really missing my Maxxi a lot I need a dog hug badly."

Nobody on the armament team had worked on AK-47s before. The idea of learning how struck Patrick Miller as appealing, given that soldiers at Camp Phoenix were not breaking their own weapons often enough to keep his crew busy. In the days that followed, Debbie expressed enthusiasm for the new mission, and so did Will. Michelle felt torn: on the one hand, the AKs struck her as sinister, but on the other hand, she liked the prospect of traveling outside of the claustrophobic, regimented world of Camp Phoenix. Afghanistan was the first foreign country she had ever visited, and the brief glimpse of its strangeness that she had gotten made her want to know more.

2
Codependent

That fall, Afghans were attempting to elect a president by a democratic vote for the first time in their country's history. Originally the presidential election had been scheduled to take place in July 2004, but it had been twice postponed, and was now supposed to happen in October 2004. At the end of August, the soldiers living at Phoenix had been told to brace for unrest. "The elections are soon and they do anticipate trouble," Debbie wrote in her diary. In a letter to her father, Michelle shared that the atmosphere in Afghanistan had gotten "a little heated." Violence lurked all around. Soldiers found two unexploded bombs nearby. One had been placed inside Pol-i-charkhi, and the other had been discovered close to the gate of Camp Phoenix. After that, two Afghan National Army soldiers were shot, one in the neck and one in the foot; medics from Debbie's tent went out in the middle of the night to tend their wounds. And a Humvee got hung up on some piano wire that had been strung across the road outside of Camp Phoenix, at a height set to decapitate a soldier. That particular Humvee had a .50-caliber machine gun installed in its turret, however, making it impossible for the gunner to stand up. "Luckily the 50 mount was on or someone would have lost their head," wrote Debbie. "The warlords are active as it gets closer to elections."

From time to time, loud sirens blared across Camp Phoenix, signaling the descent of a rocket-propelled grenade. The soldiers in Debbie's tent handled the first such incident with aplomb; Debbie scrambled into her body armor and then chatted amiably with Gretchen as they waited for the all clear. "There was an explosion at the front gate no injuries," Debbie wrote afterward. "Still very scary. We have to stay inside the tent below sandbag level with all on till they give all clear."

The soldiers in Michelle's tent were younger, however, and the clanging sirens set them on edge. Desma distracted everyone by announcing that she wanted their help filling out a particularly dirty version of Mad Libs. By the time the all clear sounded, some of the young women had slipped into hysteria anyway. "I don't know what I'm doing here!" one of them cried. Somebody else said, "I want to go home."

They spilled out of the tent, a mess. Desma

had changed out of her blue flannel pajamas with white stars on them, back into her desert camo, and could see that she needed to take charge. Mary Bell was nineteen years old and she looked like she was about to bawl.

"All right, ladies, gather up," Desma announced. "Step into a circle. We're going to do the Hokey-Pokey."

And they did. *You put your right foot in, you put your right foot out; you put your right foot in and you shake it all about,* they sang. *You do the Hokey-Pokey, and you turn yourself around, and that's what it's all about!* Other soldiers stared as if they were kooky, but they did not care. Something about the way the words were ingrained and they did not have to think and the song had nothing to do with rocket-propelled grenades restored their equilibrium. They shook their right foot and their left foot and turned themselves around, and they got to the other side of the experience. Desma had put it behind them.

They found Afghanistan hard to explain to the people they had left at home. There was a nine-and-a-half-hour time difference, which made it challenging to find a good time to call, and if you said anything about bombs or booby traps to relatives, they got spooked. Desma called her children as often as possible, but made certain never to call on the same day of the week, never at the same time of day. It was easier on the family that way — they would not worry if they did not hear from her at the appointed hour. She hated the days when she called and caught the girls when they were tired, because then they would just cry. It made her feel as though she were making things worse by telephoning. She said nothing about sirens going off in the night. Instead she repeated the same refrain, over and over again. "I'll be home before you know it," Desma said. "I'll be home before you know it." It was like a lullaby. After a while she started saying, "You know when I'll be home." And Alexis or Paige would answer, "Before I know it." "That's right," Desma told them. "I'll call you again soon."

She got an email from her cousin Lesley, who felt she was not doing a good job. The girls were mad at her all the time, Lesley wrote. Apparently Paige had announced she was running away. Desma told her cousin that if the girls thought she was being too strict, then she must be doing something right. She coordinated trips for them to visit their father, to visit their grandparents. She called Lesley and said, "Josh wants to see Paige and Alexis, so he's coming to your house this weekend." It was long-distance parenting — trying to find a quiet corner on the post, at an hour when it made sense, arranging everything by cell phone.

Hearing about major change at home

unsettled the soldiers. Debbie was having trouble sleeping, which she mentioned to her grown daughter, Ellen Ann. Debbie was a night owl, but her tentmate Gretchen started getting ready for work at four in the morning, and Debbie often woke up to the sound of Gretchen rustling into her uniform, then could not fall back asleep. Ellen Ann sent her mother a care package with two movies, a pillow, and brand-new sheets. Combined with a Tylenol PM, the new bedding did the trick. "Tried my new sheets," Debbie wrote. "They are really soft. Feels so good. Wake up young again."

When she called Ellen Ann to thank her, Debbie learned that her daughter was pregnant. "Well it's great I'm finally a 'grandma' what a wonderful feeling my baby is having a baby," wrote Debbie in her diary. Ellen Ann's due date was in early May, however, and Debbie was not going to return to Indiana until the following August — she was going to miss the birth of her first grandchild.

At first Debbie and Jeff communicated exclusively by phone, but then Jeff figured out how to send and receive email, which delighted Debbie. "My honee emailed he loves me," she wrote in her diary. "Makes my night." At the same time, she worried about Jeff's well-being. Friends said Jeff had let his membership at the Moose lapse, and that it was hard to persuade him to leave the house.

Debbie urged Jeff not to hole up, and later he let her know that he had planned a weekend trip to go deer hunting. "My honee is going camping I'm glad he needs to get out more," Debbie wrote.

All of the soldiers in the 113th were struggling to cope with the radical changes in their lives. Shortly after they arrived, two of the battalion's soldiers had gotten in serious trouble for "huffing" — inhaling mind-altering vapors out of an aerosol can — and had their guns taken away. Then another soldier was caught with hashish, which he confessed he had acquired by trading with a local Afghan who worked on the post. Debbie had quietly begun drinking every day, if she could acquire alcohol — not too much, just one or two cocktails. She supposed there were worse habits. When the two guys were caught "huffing," Debbie observed in her diary that one of the soldiers was in complete denial about his addiction and hoped he would get help after he was sent to a rehabilitation program at Bagram Airfield, the largest US military base in Afghanistan, an hour's drive north of Camp Phoenix. She did not see her reliance on alcohol in the same light. She viewed it more as a sleep aid. "I'm awake off and on all night," she wrote in her diary. "I hate my sleep pattern. . . . What a few beers or a stiff drink would cure." Sometimes, however, she remembered to drink but forgot to eat. "Came back had the place to myself so I fixed a cocktail pretty good," she wrote one Sunday. "Watched a movie. Skipped breakfast and lunch."

Debbie asked Jeff to send more booze, and he mailed her a care package full of small airline-size bottles of liqueur. A colleague suggested they start pouring shots of Baileys into their morning cups of coffee, and Debbie figured why not start the day with a pick-me-up? In the evenings, she fell into the habit of taking a long walk with Will after dinner — they would go around the post's outdoor track for two miles or more — and then going to visit Gary Jernigan in supply. His office was tucked away in a remote part of the post, and it was deserted down there in the evenings; they could drink without fear of observation. Gary was happy to share his booze, and when they scored some alcohol they shared with Gary. After Ellen Ann sent a care package that included a large bottle of Early Times whiskey, Debbie wrote: "My box came today! What a mess. EA forgot to reseal the coffee container with tape, and the Rice Krispies and the popcorn were full of coffee. . . . But at least the goodies came. I've probably drank all the ET already but I shared with Will and Gary."

At work, however, Debbie maintained her enthusiastic disposition, and the people who worked alongside her had little idea of this other side of her life. Debbie was meticulously punctual and unflaggingly cheerful, and whatever insecurities she battled remained invisible to others. In some ways, the diary read like the inverse of her public persona, for in its pages she stored all the worry she never allowed herself to express out loud. With every passing week, Michelle relied on the older woman more and more for daily inspiration. Sergeant Miller tore her down and Debbie Helton built her back up. "I was always kind of a shit — like, I was never in a good mood," Michelle would say later. "And Debbie's really gregarious, and everybody's mom. Everybody loves Debbie. She's always happy, she's always in a good mood. And I'm always fighting with Patrick."

To learn how to work on AK-47s, the armament team apprenticed themselves to the Romanians, the most knowledgeable soldiers at Camp Phoenix about Soviet-style weaponry. Michelle discovered she was good at disassembling and reassembling AK-47s, and she took a certain amount of satisfaction in doing her work flawlessly, but she paid a heavy price for working with the Romanians. When it came to harassing women, they were the worst on the post, in her opinion. Some of the things that one particular Romanian officer said to Michelle were so vile she could not bring herself to repeat his comments even years later; anytime the officer got her alone, he told her disgusting things he longed to do in graphic, obscene detail. "The biggest pervert in the entire world," Michelle would say afterward. "I never heard anything like the stuff that came out of that guy's mouth. He was just a nasty, nasty, nasty dude."

Thankfully, the apprenticeship was brief. At the beginning of September, the armament team started a new routine. They met at 7:30 a.m., jumped into Humvees or Mahindra Boleros (a sports utility vehicle manufactured in India), and drove through the gates of Camp Phoenix, waving to Rambo on their way out. Rambo's real name was Jamal Undin. He had lost his wife and one of his children when a rocket hit his home in the 1990s, and he held the Taliban responsible for their deaths. He stationed himself at the front gate of Phoenix, wearing cast-off uniforms donated by American soldiers and wielding a lead pipe covered in red electrical tape. He used the pipe to smash the windshields of oncoming cars when the drivers approached the gate too quickly, or to beat locals if he thought they might be bearing explosives. It was handy to have somebody like him manning the gate — somebody fearless, somebody who could read the environment, somebody who spoke the local languages. Michelle counted on seeing him, even though he was not paid. "He would salute me every day when I left to go to work, and he would salute me every evening when I came home from work, and he stood there with his lead pipe and made me feel safer than all of the infantry boys at the gate combined," she would say later.

Michelle loved that moment when they drove through the gate, leaving behind the monochromatic world of the military post and entering the jumbled colors of the Afghan streetscapes, where they were surrounded by jingle trucks and three-wheeled taxis and horses with bright wool bridles. During the first week of the new routine, they passed by a funeral at a cemetery on the side of a hill. It was a sea of blue burkas: dozens of faceless women covered from head to toe in the same shade of evening-sky blue, with only a mesh window where their eyes should be. The strangeness of the hooded women — somebody hidden inside, looking out from that fabric prison — struck Michelle as barbaric. "Here the women aren't even allowed to show their faces in public," she wrote to her father. "They have to wear these blue gowns called birkas [sic]. . . . It's really sad and I am really glad that I'm from a country that allows me to be free. I couldn't imagine living that way."

Of course, they had their own strictures. The entire team was required to put on body armor before they left Camp Phoenix, just like everybody else who traveled outside the wire. The vests weighed enough to cause long-term physical issues for those who wore them daily. They were also hot, irritated the skin, and made the soldiers look lumpy and misshapen. But few of their colleagues got to pass through the post's gate as regularly, and the armament team treasured the privilege. While their colleagues remained stuck inside at Phoenix, coordinating the flow of vehicles or ordering supplies from identical prefabricated buildings, the armament team frequently worked outdoors, which made them much more aware of the weather. "We are outside this whole time I got some sun today," wrote Debbie in her diary. "We experienced the first real sandstorm. What a mess. The wind is still pitching a fit." They loved the constant sunshine, but after a while they all started to miss rain. Debbie wished for wet weather in her diary.

At first the armament team worked at Pol-i-charkhi, but Miller soon found them a better location over at the main storage and distribution center used by the Afghan National Army, in a nearby part of Kabul. At the ANA depot, Miller secured for them one corner of a cavernous warehouse. It was a cinder-block cathedral with a metal roof held up by steel girders. Skylights let in vast shafts of sunlight, and they entered the building through giant metal sliding doors that took two people to open. The warehouse was being used to store boxes of military goods, and they could work there largely undisturbed. With Miller urging them to work faster all the time, they started flying through boxes of AK-47s, turning broken weapons into functional weapons at a roaring rate. "We put three boxes up today," Debbie wrote proudly after one particularly busy day. Each box held about one hundred AKs. "Hey there big Daddy," Michelle wrote to her father. "I hope this letter finds you well. I am doing pretty good over here. I actually have a lot of work now; I've been working my ass off. I learned how to work on AK-47s. So we've got about 2500 of them to fix. Got about 500 done so far."

Michelle maintained that upbeat tone in all the letters she sent to her parents. In truth, however, she was grappling with conflicting emotions around the armament team's new project. The American-style semiautomatic assault rifle she carried had better aim, but the Soviet-style weapons she was fixing were cheaper and functioned better in adverse climates, such as the sandy places of the world, where weapons tended to jam. It had become the weapon of choice for poor people across the globe. The bullets fired by her M4 were lighter, and flew with higher velocity toward their targets, but the heavier rounds fired by the AK-47s penetrated farther into anything they hit — they did more damage.

Were things as simple as their first sergeant had declared? Would the guns be used only to help spread democracy? Michelle could not take apart and put back together an AK-47 without worrying how the weapon might someday be employed. It was hard to accept that the guns she was repairing would be used only for purposes that could be called noble. Guns had a way of changing hands. As she replaced the sights on a broken AK-47, Michelle asked herself who had used the assault rifle before and who would fire it next. Who would be hit by the large rounds? With her hands occupied, listening to music on her MP3 player (anything but the Dave Matthews Band, that was too close to home; she would never be able to listen to the Dave Matthews Band again), Michelle felt productive; at the same time, a black thread of worry pulled through her contentment. As satisfying as it was to make a broken weapon function, she had a lot of unanswered questions about the work she was doing.

While Debbie soothed her disquiet with a cocktail or two, Michelle developed other coping mechanisms. In a letter she mailed to Pete, Michelle assured her boyfriend that she felt no regrets about their relationship and apologized for being out of touch and said she had just gotten a new phone card and would call him that very night but in truth she had begun spending a lot of time with

Ben Sawyer. There were many reasons, among them that having him close kept other men at bay. While the young women who lived in Michelle's tent complained of feeling unfeminine, wearing their butch uniforms, they had nonetheless become sought-after commodities. The 113th Support Battalion included almost eighty female soldiers, out of a total of about two hundred and seventy personnel. But now they lived beside the all-male regiments that also belonged to the 76th Infantry Brigade — the very men their support battalion was intended to support — which rendered the ratio of men to women on the post even more highly skewed. Plus, most of the regular army and foreign NATO soldiers were men, too.

The male soldiers competed to see who could lift more weights, who could drink more beer, who could sleep with more women. Any attractive young woman living on the post drew intense scrutiny. The attention was fierce, omnipresent, palpable. The men on the post had left behind their girlfriends and wives and had taped pictures of barely clad women in their tents, and to these men Michelle did not look like a fellow human being so much as an opportunity for a kind of relief they were determined to find. Within weeks, male soldiers she did not know were greeting Michelle by name everywhere she went on post. She could not sit down in the dining hall without attracting a bevy of interested dining partners. Ben Sawyer assuaged her loneliness and also offered protection — he warded off other suitors. She started eating dinner with him almost every evening. Sawyer had never gone to college, he had bad teeth, and he was married. There was a tattoo of Jesus on his calf, a tattoo of Death on his shoulder, and on his arms he had inked the names of his son and his daughter. Michelle did not believe in Jesus, Death, tattoos, or infidelity, nor did she believe Sawyer was the right man for her, but he was a solid six feet three inches of warm muscle, and he was by her side. At home in Indiana, she had recognized Sawyer as being white trash, just like her half brothers, but after they got to Afghanistan, he made her feel safe. And so Michelle slept with him again.

It was Desma Brooks who came up with a system for when they could have sex. Debbie Helton's tent was close by, and she happened to witness the inception of Desma's system, because from where she put her chair in the evenings she could see the tent where Michelle and Desma lived. "The girls were funny last night," wrote Debbie. "They decided to hang out a white sock if someone was getting lucky. Desma did it for a joke at first and [then] everyone paid attention. Ziggy and her boyfriend took full advantage and went for it — they were allowed 30 minutes. These young girls have no shame. But they crack me up I could see me there about 10 years ago." Many of them used the white sock after that — Michelle for a tryst with Ben Sawyer, Desma for a tryst with the superior officer she'd been sleeping with since Atterbury, Mary during a brief fling with an infantryman who quickly moved along to other prospects.

After Michelle slept with Sawyer a few more times, she could no longer convince herself that it would not happen again. In her next letter to Pete, she struck a different tone. "I want you to live while I am gone," she told him. "You are not stagnant. Every day is yours and you should make the most of it. We will go on when I get home, so keep your life moving forward. I know wherever you go in this year I am much faster than you so I'll catch up!!" She could not bring herself to say in writing that she was not faithful, but she wanted to acknowledge the many kinds of distance that now divided them. Perhaps the letter was also an attempt to find a sense of coherence: she was still in love with Pete, and by sleeping with another man, she had split herself in two; Michelle was tortured by her deceit. She could neither stay away from Sawyer nor could she forgive herself for being so weak. But in truth without Sawyer at her side in the dining hall every evening, her time at Camp Phoenix would have been intolerable.

Early in September, a car bomb exploded outside Camp Phoenix. Perhaps as many as ten people were killed, including some children. Medics from Debbie's tent ran out to care for the wounded. The car bomb threw Michelle sideways, emotionally. "I hate days like this, when there is no mistaking that I am in hell," she wrote to Pete. "What really freaks me out is that I couldn't cry for them. I don't know why but I got so angry with myself because I don't want to be one of these mindless desensitized fucks that I am surrounded by. I don't know what's happening to me." It was still toward Pete that Michelle bared her soul, even though she was no longer calling as often. "I miss you a lot," she told him in the same letter. "I know I haven't called lately, and I'm sorry. They're supposed to be putting more phones in soon. I love you more than words can say." The car bomb seemed to trip something inside of Michelle, and she found herself filled with a wistful nostalgia for the life she was no longer leading — the life in which Pete was her partner, and there were no car bombs, and they could go eat at their favorite dive anytime they wanted. "Let's just walk down to Big Top for some onion rings and tea," she told Pete. "Before long it will be too cold to do it for a while."

By this point, however, her sense of commitment to Pete had taken on an unreal quality. He was so far away, and Ben Sawyer was so close. September 11 fell on a Saturday. It was yet another brilliant day, just like any other, but the leadership feared violence and the soldiers at Camp Phoenix were ordered to lock and load. They walked around carrying weapons that were ready to be fired, which made them tense. In their newsletter, called the *Wrench Daily News* (they were a battalion of mechanics, mostly), Jaime Toppe ran a special feature with soldiers saying why they thought they had been deployed. One soldier said that they were there "for a good cause," although he did not name what that was. Another soldier said, "The war on terrorism is a necessity. That's why we're here." A third said, "We must not lose our focus in extinguishing totalitarianism throughout the world." Debbie told Toppe: "I hope that we're going to make a difference and that we can accomplish everything we were sent here to do. Everything else is in God's will."

The day passed without incident, except that the brass brought in some camels for show. Especially aware of her own mortality, Michelle wrote several letters. She adopted her usual cheerful tone with her father: "I saw my first camel today!" she told him. "He was a scrawny bastard but I don't care. Because now that I've seen a wild camel, I have officially seen it all. . . . Try not to worry, Dad. I really am okay."

Her letter to Pete was different — reflective, intimate, almost elegiac.

My dear Pete

Talking to you on the phone today made me so emotional. . . . I miss you so much, I swear if it weren't for the pictures sometimes I feel like I made you up in my head. I miss everything about you. I miss lying in your arms, running my fingers through your hair, feeling the tickle of your mustache when you kiss me. I miss talking to you through the shower door, bitching about the bathroom sink, and your pit-stained white T-shirts. I miss brushing my teeth with you. Remember those times you couldn't get me out of bed and you'd just yank the covers off me? Man I used to hate that but I'd give anything to have that tomorrow morning. . . .

I guess I just want you to know that I am always thinking of you. We have so many good memories.

I will always love you.

Michelle

The idea of their relationship still warmed Michelle psychologically, but Pete was no longer a palpable part of her existence. When she wanted tangible warmth, she turned elsewhere. Afghanistan had torn them apart, and the September 11 letter was as close to a farewell as she could muster. She did not write again to Pete that calendar year, although he kept writing to her. At the end of September, when she turned twenty-two, Pete sent Michelle a box of homemade pot brownies. The box arrived several days before her actual birthday, and on Saturday, September 18, 2004, Michelle threw a party in her tent.

"Pete sent me brownies for my birthday," she told Desma. "And they're special."

"Woo-hoo!" replied Desma.

For strategic reasons, they decided to share the brownies with all of the women, so there would be a smaller chance that one of the others would turn them in for possession of marijuana. Half the tent declined to participate, but the rest consumed one brownie apiece. They packed a wallop. Mary, Desma, and Michelle were used to getting stoned, and huddled together giggling, but within an hour Karen Shaw was awash in paranoia. Moving slowly, with her eyelids halfway closed, she came over to consult with Michelle.

"What if I fall asleep and stop breathing?" Karen wanted to know.

"I promise you that I will check on you every twenty minutes to make sure that you're still breathing," Michelle said. "I will not let you die."

Karen crashed on her own bed. Michelle, Mary, and Desma stayed up for hours making a list about their relationships entitled "You Know You're Co-Dependent If . . ." and laughing until their sides hurt. That same weekend, Michelle received a card from her father, who had marked her birthday by going to a dive bar named PJs and getting all of the regulars to sign a card. "Tell everyone at PJs I really appreciate all the support," Michelle wrote back. "It was so nice to get something like that for my birthday, cause I was pretty homesick." She promised to have a banner printed up and to get everyone in her company to sign it, even as she winced that her father was such a barfly. On Monday, September 20, 2004 — her actual birthday — the skies opened, loosing a torrential downpour. Afghanistan was changing, the weather was changing, and Michelle was changing, too. They all were.

3
Rain

Tumult blossomed everywhere during the week leading up to the elections. The Taliban posted "night letters" (signs put up in the dark) across southern Afghanistan promising retribution against anybody who voted. Afghan authorities intercepted sixty guerrillas as they attempted to enter the country with the aim of mounting attacks at voting centers. The United Nations predicted fraud, intimidation, and violence; Human Rights Watch accused warlords of threatening women. President Hamid Karzai's running mate held an election rally in northern Afghanistan and his convoy was hit by explosives; two people were killed, although he escaped unharmed. Rockets hit various parts of Kabul, among other cities, while down in Kandahar, a dog trained to sniff for bombs uncovered a fuel truck filled with ten thousand gallons of gasoline that had been jerry-rigged to blow. The soldiers at Camp Phoenix expected rockets to fall but were spared. "On Thurs night we had some bombings in Policharky [sic] + Bagram + Kabul," wrote Debbie in her diary. "We weren't hit thank God."

Strangely, right before the elections, the post was blanketed in a thick, impenetrable fog. In her diary, Debbie likened it to something out of a Stephen King novel. The *Wrench Daily News* advised soldiers to be cautious: "With the elections approaching, be aware of possible threats. Let someone know your whereabouts at all times for the next few days for accountability." Toppe interviewed various soldiers about the upcoming elections. "I don't think a lot of people will vote, because they'll be scared," Mary Bell told the *Wrench Daily News.* "Especially women; they feel oppressed. I think there will be isolated incidents, like car bombs." Other soldiers echoed her comments, predicting a mix of violence and suppressed turnout. Only Debbie's bunkmate, Gretchen Pane, saw a more optimistic outcome: "The elections are going to be a great beginning for the Afghan people. It's going to liberate them. It's a new beginning."

On Saturday, October 9, 2004, a cold front moved through Kabul, bringing the first taste of winter. Neither the brisk weather nor the predictions of mayhem deterred the Afghan people: three-quarters of the country's registered voters cast ballots — a massive number, far exceeding estimations. Most of the voters waited patiently in long lines and picked their candidates without incident. Five Afghan National Army soldiers and fifteen election workers were killed, but the majority of polling places operated without disruption. It took more than a week for results to be announced — and even longer for the results to be ratified — but Hamid Karzai had been elected by a margin of 55.4 percent, after earning three times as many votes as any one of his competitors. "The people seemed really excited to vote," wrote Debbie two days after the elections. "Matula one of the workers for DFAC [the dining facility] showed me his card for voting he was so excited. I hope it's not in vain + it will help the people."

Although they played no direct role in securing voting sites, Debbie, Desma, and Michelle nevertheless felt proud for having been part of a military force that had ensured the elections could happen and that women could participate. Women made up two-thirds of the country's population, yet the question of what rights they should legally possess was a matter of heated contention. During the 1920s, a period of liberalization, women had gained the right to choose their own husbands and were encouraged to seek an education, but during the 1930s, strict Shariah law was reinstated. During the 1960s, another period of modernization, many Afghan women stopped wearing veils and some entered politics, and during the 1970s, the country outlawed child marriage. The 1980s, however, brought chaos. The Soviet Union and the United States struggled to control Afghanistan, and finally abandoned it to warring mujahideen, which led to the rise of the Taliban. In the mid-1990s, the Taliban instated a particularly severe version of Shariah law, requiring men to grow beards and women to veil themselves entirely.

After two months in Afghanistan, Debbie, Desma, and Michelle had begun to appreciate keenly the vast difference between their position in American society and the much more precarious station of the women around them in Afghanistan. Michelle thought it pure chance that she had inherited such largesse; she could easily have been born female into this society instead. Because she moved daily through the streets of Kabul, it was possible for her to imagine some of the privations that fate would have entailed. Not long after the election had taken place, Desma crossed paths with an Afghan family on the post. The medics at Camp Phoenix had provided care to their son, who had been injured by a land mine. The father was pushing his son's wheelchair, and in the traditional fashion, his wife was following five paces behind. The woman was holding a black headscarf across the lower half of her face. She looked at Desma, a female soldier wearing desert camouflage and carrying an assault rifle, and stopped walking. To Desma's shock, the woman knelt down before her. "Thank you," she said in English. "Thank you."

Unlike Michelle, Desma almost never left Camp Phoenix. She had been spending her days at the motor pool, also known as the shop. Including the mechanics, perhaps one hundred soldiers worked there. About fifty soldiers reported for duty during first shift, forty-five during second shift, and a skeleton crew stayed on through the night in case of something unexpected. "Night shift consisted of playing cards and drinking alcohol," Desma would say later. Most of the people who worked at the motor pool were men, and they had decorated the walls with pictures of women torn from magazines such as *Maxim* and *Sports Illustrated.* Desma worked first shift, along with Mary Bell. They started work at 7:00 a.m. Sometimes Desma finished at 3:00 p.m., sometimes at 5:00 p.m. It depended on how fast everybody else worked. Desma tracked the maintenance on the trucks that belonged to the 113th. The mechanics did top-to-bottom annual service checks on each vehicle, and some of those services took thirty hours to complete. A soldier who drove a vehicle outside the gates of Camp Phoenix did not want that truck to break down. That was the job of the motor pool, to keep the trucks running. The people who worked at the shop got covered in grease and their jobs were not glorious, but nobody could get anything done in Afghanistan without trucks, so they were proud of what they did.

When broken trucks came in for repair — maybe the engine had overheated, maybe something was wrong with the four-wheel drive — Desma made sure the mechanics had the right parts. Sometimes she made the hour-long run up to Bagram, jouncing over the potholes, dodging jingle trucks and donkeys, if they did not have the right parts at Camp Phoenix. In addition to tracking the maintenance of vehicles, Desma also ran software programs that tracked any repair work done on weapons, night vision goggles, radios, and other equipment. And she prepared reports about all of the maintenance work being done by the 113th for the battalion's leaders. Working nearby in the shop, her friend Mary belonged to a crew that dispatched trucks, recording the serial number and mileage of every vehicle that left the post and every vehicle that returned. When a truck broke down, Mary kept track of who went to get the damaged vehicle. Sometimes a team of mechanics drove out to fix a broken vehicle; sometimes they sent a wrecker. Every once in a while, if it was really far away, they sent mechanics out by helicopter.

At the beginning of every workday, Michelle visited the motor pool to let Desma know where the armament team would be working and what they expected to accomplish, and at the end of every day, she returned to say how many broken weapons they had fixed. Desma entered this information into her spreadsheets, documenting the work being done by the armament team. The motor pool was a hub of information and gossip, and working there put Desma in the position of meeting almost every new person who came through Camp Phoenix. Shortly after Michelle began repairing AK-47s, Desma had befriended two blond, good-looking Danish soldiers who had shown up looking for spare parts. They returned bearing a platter of Danish pastries to say thank you. Desma was good company and pretty soon Michael and Kristian were stopping by regularly. One day, Desma introduced the pair to Michelle. She was on her way to the PX to buy the new album by The Cure, and Kristian announced he was a fan of that band, too. The Danish soldiers started driving over frequently to hang out with Michelle and Desma. They worked at the military compound occupied by the International Security Assistance Force (they all called it ISAF), a ten-minute drive away. You weren't supposed to accept alcohol from the ISAF soldiers, but everybody did. In a letter to her father, Michelle confided that the two Danish soldiers had brought over some beer. "So things are looking up," she wrote. "I know I won't get in trouble because they're supplying all of my chain of command with whiskey."

One of the Danish soldiers was married, and Desma and Michelle were already having affairs with two other married men, so they kept things with Michael and Kristian fairly innocent. Typically they caught a movie (that month, Morale, Welfare, and Recreation showed *Shrek, Shrek 2, Rush Hour 2, Forrest Gump,* and *The Last Samurai*), or went for pizza at Ciano's. Michelle considered sleeping with Kristian, but she could not fathom the idea of cheating on Pete with Ben and then cheating on Ben with Kristian — so she kept the relationship platonic. Years later, however, she would say that she wished she had chosen to have her deployment relationship with Kristian instead, but Ben Sawyer had gotten there first. Desma, on the other hand, thought it was fun to make out with her Danish soldier and then sleep with her superior officer. She snuck dates with Michael early in the evening, then met up with Lieutenant Mark Northrup later at night. Desma said the Danish soldiers made the time go by faster; dating European men made the deployment more romantic.

In all kinds of ways, Michelle depended on Desma to make their drab lives more colorful. After they had been living in Afghanistan for about a month, Desma had announced that it was depressing to live in a green tent amid an ocean of identical green tents, and therefore she went online and ordered fifty hot pink plastic flamingos, as well as a sign that said KEEP OFF THE GRASS. Desma stuck the sign in a sandbag right outside their tent. Then she arranged the flock of flamingos around the tent's walls, sticking their wire legs between the sandbags. In that dreary place, the pink birds stood out, a shocking herd of whimsy. Michelle loved those crazy birds. The flamingos declared they would not conform — they were stuck here but they had not surrendered. Other soldiers seemed captivated by the sight, because one by one soldiers borrowed the birds. Desma saw one of them out on the highway, duct-taped to the front of a Humvee. She liked the idea of her flamingo traveling the length of Afghanistan.

When they got bored with filling out dirty versions of Mad Libs, they watched Disney cartoons together on their laptop computers, or swapped DVDs. Michelle watched every single episode in her collection of *Sex and the City* shows, and then loaned the DVDs out, exchanging them for other movies. Even Nose Hairs borrowed her *Sex and the City* DVDs. Then Michelle spent hours combing through the hadji movies at the bazaar, looking for entertainment. She found a hadji collection of Johnny Depp movies, as well as a copy of her beloved *Return to Oz.* The bootleg copies of Hollywood movies were sold at the bazaar for $2 apiece. The word "hadji" bothered Michelle, but everybody used it. Technically speaking, the word meant a person who had made the trip to Mecca — literally, a pilgrim — but Michelle noticed how the American soldiers used the word to separate themselves from Afghans, to keep their distance. Hadji movies meant blurry, cheap, bootleg movies; hadji workers did menial jobs. They had been instructed to use the term "local national workers" instead, but everybody still said hadji. Many of the American soldiers had had little exposure to foreign cultures and viewed the people they called hadjis with fear and contempt.

Debbie was a rare exception. She befriended local nationals just like everyone else, and was regularly chatting with the Afghans who worked at the dining facility. One Afghan man apparently believed they might be falling in love.

"Do you think it will rain?" Debbie asked him one evening.

"Rain?" he said. "Tomorrow!"

"It will rain tomorrow?"

He pointed to his finger. "Yes! Yes!" he said. "Gold ring! Tomorrow!"

"No, no, no!" Debbie laughed, backpedaling.

Camp Phoenix was bustling with activity involving local national workers, as the leadership at the post had ordered a variety of construction projects. Local workers were building a new dining facility, a new post office, a new laundry area, a library, a study room for soldiers who were taking continuing education classes, a television room with theater seating, an Internet café, and a food court with three new restaurants. Local workers were also building structures called B-Huts (short for Barracks Huts) that the soldiers were supposed to move into that winter, as well as more latrines and more showers. The wars were not going to end soon, the construction suggested — the soldiers were going to be here for a while. All of the construction posed an increased security risk, however, and soldiers in the 113th pulled hadji duty more and more frequently as the construction projects mounted. Being assigned to guard Afghan workers was considered an onerous task, but Debbie found it fascinating; she longed to understand more about the country around her, and she spent the time talking animatedly with the workers. "Well I did hadji watch not too bad . . . ," she wrote in her diary. "They make $6 a day which is a lot for them. They don't wear socks. Some young boys around ten, eleven. I gave one a pop tart he liked it. Was a cutie I could of adopted him."

One day the local workers she was guarding started a cook fire and made tea and flat bread. The Afghans offered to share their food, and Debbie fell in love with flat bread. The more she talked to the locals, the more her admiration grew. "One of the workers rides his bike one hour just to get here," she wrote. "No kid at home would do that for $6 a day!"

Debbie had also started visiting Michelle and Desma's tent regularly to cut hair, wax legs, and wax eyebrows. She told the other women that she would not take money; these services were what she had to offer to make them feel more at home. If they insisted on making some type of payment, they could pick up a scarf for her at the bazaar. Debbie had started off just cutting hair in her own tent, but soon she was getting requests from soldiers across the post; she spent more time doing beauty work inside Michelle and Desma's tent than any other. The younger women tended to be more concerned about their appearances. And Debbie could tell when a young woman started seeing another soldier, because that's when she would get a request for a bikini wax. Soon Debbie felt even more at home inside Michelle and Desma's tent than she did in her own. She spent hours listening to the young women chatter about their romances. Their tent had an intimate, lively atmosphere; it could also be wearying, as the young women indulged in a lot of drama. Debbie no longer wanted to take so many risks, nor suffer such large consequences.

The young women wanted so badly to feel more feminine. Because the soldiers were flush with cash and stuck at Camp Phoenix, Internet shopping became an obsession, and in Michelle and Desma's tent, the hot commodity became fancy underwear. Michelle and Mary started the trend, and then the other women followed suit. Within a short time, Michelle had matching lacy bra and panty sets in black, green, and gold. She hated wearing the male-looking uniform every single day, and liked the idea of Ben Sawyer finding the colorful underwear beneath her camouflage. Then she found a nail salon at Bagram where she could get a pedicure. Anytime Desma had to go get parts, Michelle tagged along and got her toenails painted. It struck even her as frivolous, but that was sort of the point. She wanted to hang on to the sense of being a woman, and that was hard to do as a soldier.

As the weeks passed the weather began to turn, and at night the lows started dropping down into the thirties. Ben Sawyer began staying overnight in Michelle's tent. All of the women had hung blankets around their sleeping areas, suspended from the top bunks, to create some privacy. For a time, the ten women had stuck to the rule that banned male visitors from spending the night, but at one point Michelle had innocently lifted up the blanket around another soldier's bed to ask a question, and to her shock had been confronted by the sight of that woman having sex with a male colleague. After that, the goings-on inside of the tent had become more of a free-for-all. Generally, the male visitors tried to tiptoe out of the tent by 4:00 a.m. It was widely understood that several of the battalion's senior leaders were having affairs with young subordinates, but it was also understood that nobody was supposed to get caught.

The battalion's soldiers split in their response to witnessing the affairs. Many soldiers were religious and attended a weekly prayer group, and some of the devout soldiers condemned the behavior as immoral and hurtful. Other soldiers shrugged it off as simply a by-product of having been sent to war. The Judge Advocate General's Corps lawyers who served as legal advisers to the battalion's command were perplexed about what to do, given that many of the relationships were clearly illegal. In previous wars, soldiers had found physical comfort outside their own barracks, with nurses or with local women. The current trend was a marked departure from past history and signified the first time that interactions between soldiers had become widely sexualized inside the barracks. What did it mean for the overall concept of military discipline when soldiers began picking and choosing which part of the Uniform Code of Military Justice they would heed? At one point Desma accidentally knocked over a folder in her company commander's work area and saw a memo from the JAG lawyers on the subject. Inappropriate relationships will not be tolerated, the memo declared. The commanders should crack down on the illicit affairs, and perpetrators should suffer punishment. Ha! Desma thought. That is not likely to happen, when half of the commanders are guilty themselves!

With a series of cool remarks, Michelle's tentmate Jaime Toppe communicated that she viewed Michelle's and Desma's habit of sleeping with married men as a sacrilege. Her own husband had deployed along with her, however — she was married to Jeremy Toppe, the soldier who had nicknamed Michelle "Poison Butterfly" — and she could sleep with him anytime she wanted. So Michelle shrugged off Jaime's scorn, concluding that with her own husband present, it was pretty easy for Jaime to resist other temptations. Who was she to judge?

As the days went by, Michelle grew accustomed to wrapping herself around Ben Sawyer's long body on her small twin mattress. In the dark she could not see his tattoos, and she used his chiseled proximity to tell herself that it was safe to fall asleep. She had no doubt that she still loved Pete, but he had vanished from view, and it was upon Ben that she began to depend for small daily assurances. It was Sawyer's arms that provided heart-pumped heat in the chilly tent as the nighttime temperatures began to drop, and it was Sawyer's long legs that reached down into the bottom of her sleeping bag and reduced her fear of the invisible camel spiders that still crawled across her skin.

As the temperature dropped, it also started to rain frequently; the seven-year drought had broken. They even got some hail. The Afghan man at the dining hall whom Debbie had befriended congratulated her on changing their weather. "Thank you for bringing the rain," he told her, as if she had actually brought the rain along in her duffel bag, all the way from verdant Indiana. "Honey, we didn't have a thing to do with it," Debbie replied. But he just said, "Thank you, thank you." And as it began to rain, they began to toughen up.

One day, the armament team took a break from working on AK-47s and fixed some broken rocket-propelled grenade launchers instead — the very weapons that were most often trained against them. While working on one of the grenade launchers, Michelle came to understand how crude the weapon was:

most of the RPGs she saw had no sights at all. It was a crapshoot, in other words, where the explosive device landed. That insight liberated Michelle from the fear of being hit by a grenade, which had dogged her since she had first arrived. There was no way to aim an RPG properly, she now saw; if she was hit, it would be an act of providence. The next time the blaring alarm siren sounded at the post, Michelle shrugged her shoulders at Desma, and they went on doing Mad Libs and eating Tostitos they had found at the PX. They put on their body armor and their helmets — "dressed for getting bombed," as Michelle liked to say — because otherwise they would get written up, but they did not worry about whether a rocket was going to obliterate their tent. It was too exhausting to keep worrying about that.

Later, during another air raid, Desma stuck her head outside and saw that nobody was around. "Hey, Michelle, let's go have a smoke," she said. They were supposed to hunker down below the sandbags, or else seek shelter in a bunker, but who cared anymore? They were outside smoking when a group of gung ho soldiers from Alpha Company ran by on their way to the bunkers with all of their battle rattle on over their pajamas. Desma gave them a round of applause and kept on smoking.

Over the course of that fall, Michelle

decided to stop allowing Patrick Miller to make her cry, and turned off the tears with stony determination. He continued to berate her, but when his rages no longer had any visible effect, he erupted less frequently. Maybe Miller could also see that he had to change his behavior. Accepting that Michelle would never show up on time, he assigned her the task of picking up their radios from the motor pool. This meant she had an extra half hour before she had to meet the rest of the team. And when Miller did yell, Michelle found ways to insulate herself. She brought her MP3 player to work every day, along with a pair of ear buds. The rest of the team would ask who she was listening to. If she answered Madonna, she was having a good day; if she said Nine Inch Nails, she wasn't. Often, if Miller was yelling at her, Michelle acted as though she could not hear what he was saying. "You could just tell, you know, that look on the face — she can hear Patrick yelling, but she's not going to answer him," Debbie would say later. "We were just dying laughing, because we knew what she was doing. She was just shutting Patrick out."

Michelle also learned to use the fact that she was female to throw Miller off. When he had served in the marines, he had had no women reporting to him, and he was still getting used to the idea. One day Miller gave the armament team a pep talk. He told everybody that part of his job was to make sure his soldiers were taken care of, and asked if there was anything they needed. "Birth control," Michelle said drily. It pleased her to see him blanch. (Much later, after she and Miller had grown close, Miller would reveal to Michelle that he had gone to her tent one day to give her a package from the post office, and had seen her lacy underwear strewn across the floor. He had never imagined *that* under a uniform — but once he had seen the garments, he could not get them out of his mind.) Michelle sensed that she had the power to make him uncomfortable and liked that it gave her the upper hand.

At the same time, she made herself useful. She saw that Miller could not function without his car keys and the small dark green field notebook in which he kept detailed notes about their progress. He kept misplacing both items. Michelle made it her business to know at all times the location of his keys and his notebook, and he began to rely upon her to tell him where they were. Also, Michelle and Debbie worked out a methodical system for documenting the stream of AK-47s that were passing through their hands. Miller drummed into his soldiers that they needed to be able to account for every single AK-47, but the AKs were sometimes hard to identify. Michelle and Debbie took over the task of deciphering the frequently eroded serial numbers on the sides of the weapons, and recording the identity of each gun they repaired. If the team got a difficult box, they all concentrated on disassembling and reassembling the broken weapons, and Debbie and Michelle documented the weapons after the repairs had been completed. If they got a box that was easier, however, then Will and Patrick focused on repairing the broken AKs, while Debbie and Michelle wrote down every symbol they could find.

The serial numbers typically began with a triangle or a square or a horseshoe, and such a sign would be followed by several letters and a series of numbers. Together the symbols indicated the country in which the gun had been made and the order in which it had been manufactured. At first Michelle copied down letters from foreign alphabets without understanding their significance; later she learned how to translate Russian, Chinese, Dari, and Farsi letters into the alphabet she knew. If they could not find a serial number on the barrel, they would look for a serial number on the butt stock or the trigger mechanism — although it was not considered as reliable, since these parts of the weapon could be replaced. Over time they grew fluent in the language of AK-47s. They came to know which countries had made more reliable versions, and which made versions that were more likely to be broken. The Chinese models were the worst, and they discarded large numbers of them. Other AKs held up astonishingly well over time. Some of the guns had been manufactured in the 1950s. "Those weapons last forever," Michelle would say later.

Typically, the sights would be missing, and the weapons mechanics would replace them. They also checked the function of the firing pin, making sure it would strike the bullet. They cleaned the gas tube and made sure it was not clogged. If the trigger did not feel right, they would replace the entire trigger mechanism. The safety — it often wasn't working. They used a punch to take it out, and put in another one. Frequently the springs were bad, and they replaced them; many times, Michelle had old springs pop out and hit her in the face. She accidentally got her fingers caught in various parts of the gun, too. But they were not terribly hard to fix. "That's the beauty of an AK-47," Michelle would say later. "It's a really simple machine." After all that, they would do a functions test, and oil the gun until it looked new. "We just got better as the year went on. You just get practice, and then you can do it in your sleep. Breathe, eat, and sleep AKs."

Did the various languages on the AK-47s map the shedding of blood around the globe? Michelle told herself not to think so much. Otherwise she would drive herself crazy wondering what role she might be playing in the globalization of war. Patrick Miller did not appear to let his mind wander in this fashion. He ordered the team to stack repaired AK-47s in groups of ten, and at the end of the day he counted how many stacks they had completed, and wrote down the total with satisfaction. He drove the team hard. So swiftly did they repair the weapons, a supervisor expressed doubt that Miller's team was actually accomplishing as much work as Miller claimed. Some brass came to the depot to conduct an audit, but Miller was able to account for every single assault rifle they had repaired, and proved the armament team was actually as fast as the prodigious numbers indicated. A major paused to inspect the documentation work that had been done by Michelle and Debbie. It was incredible, he said. He wished his guys were as good.

Michelle exercised furiously after work. She could not always restrain herself in the dining hall — it was hard to resist ordering an omelet in the morning, and she had become addicted to butterscotch pudding — yet she spent so many hours in the gym that she lost twenty-two pounds. She was proud of her flat tummy and her six-pack. By October she could do an hour on the StairMaster at level twenty. One afternoon, a guy they called Smitty walked up while she was working out. Michael Smith was a mechanic from Evansville who worked in a Toyota plant. He was smart, tall, and good-looking, and had a high-wattage smile; he was happily married, but all the girls loved him anyway.

"Have you ever seen *An American Werewolf in Paris*?" he asked Michelle.

"No," she told him.

"There's this scene where the werewolf murders a young woman," said Smitty. "And she is upset about getting killed because it took her four years on a StairMaster to get that body. When I look at you, that's what I think of. You look awesome!"

Michelle had been avoiding alcohol, but she made an exception that fall when Kristian and Michael smuggled over a bottle of vodka from the ISAF compound. Desma stashed the vodka in a secret hiding place, between the dark green canvas outer wall and the white canvas inner wall of their tent. Then Michelle decided to drink a little vodka with Ben Sawyer, and after they finished she put the bottle into Desma's footlocker, hidden under a stack of towels. Desma was supposed to stow it away in the more secure hiding spot after the rest of the women left the tent the following morning, but forgot.

A few days earlier, their tentmate Caroline Hill had received a care package. Michelle happened to be in the tent when Caroline had opened the box and pulled out a bottle of Southern Comfort. Later a female Alpha

Company soldier got so inebriated that she needed an emergency IV for rehydration. When questioned about how she had acquired the alcohol, the Alpha soldier confessed that she had gotten it from a Bravo girl, but refused to say which one. It seemed obvious to Michelle that Caroline Hill must have shared her bottle of Southern Comfort with the female soldier in Alpha Company, because the two women were close friends, but Hill denied doing so. "She told me that she got rid of this stuff by passing it along to the infantrymen even though her best friend had just gotten caught wasted," Michelle would say later. "It was kind of obvious that she was blatantly lying."

Several days later, Michelle went to the gym, took a shower, and returned to her tent. Then in marched Captain Nicholas Mueller, three first sergeants, and a female major named Foley. They announced they were doing a surprise inspection. Oh, shit, thought Michelle; the vodka. They found the half-empty bottle in Desma's footlocker right away. Desma was outside, smoking a cigarette. When she walked in, Major Foley made a show of searching her footlocker and acted as though she had just discovered the vodka.

"What do we have here?" Major Foley asked.

"That would be my Article Fifteen," Desma responded without missing a beat.

Article 15 of the Uniform Code of Military Justice allows a commanding officer to discipline a soldier for a minor infraction without a court-martial. Punishment could range from reprimand to loss of pay, extra duties, or reduction of rank. Desma would have to wait to learn her fate — all she knew was that she was in trouble. Within hours, Michelle and Desma learned that the inspection had additional consequences: Debbie Helton had also been caught with alcohol. News that Debbie and Desma were both in trouble because of a soldier from Alpha Company raced through Bravo ranks. Because the soldiers believed the wrong people were being punished, and because they did not like the idea that their personal belongings could be searched, the incident caused an uproar. Jaime Toppe ran a special news story in the *Wrench Daily News.* A total of six tents had been searched, she reported; Captain Mueller maintained that a routine health and welfare inspection had been planned even before the case of intoxication, and said the tents had been chosen at random. Mueller said he wanted the surprise raid to demonstrate that the leadership was serious about the ban on alcohol. "People need to be responsible," Mueller told the *Wrench.* "It could jeopardize the lives of others. We're in a combat situation and alcohol is not authorized."

Desma frequently acted in ways that her superiors considered inappropriate, and she was already in the process of earning a collection of counseling statements (written reprimands that constituted an official slap on the wrist) for being late, for being insubordinate, for having a bad attitude, and for failing to show up for remedial physical training as instructed. Desma pinned her counseling statements on the wall at the shop where she worked, right over her desk. As soon as she got the Article 15, she made it the centerpiece of her display. Debbie, on the other hand, felt angry and ashamed. "Way to go get busted," she wrote disgustedly in her diary. "If they would give us a three beer ration I would be happy but no. 76 sucks."

Bravo Company rebelled at the idea of Debbie Helton getting slapped with an Article 15. All the first sergeants had found were a few small airline bottles of liqueur with the seals unbroken, hidden inside a coffee can. Nobody thought that Debbie's stash had caused the soldier from Alpha Company to get sick. Even Dean Kimball, the first sergeant of Bravo Company, seemed to view the outcome as problematic. When Kimball crossed paths with the Alpha girl who had gotten drunk, other soldiers heard him yell, in a taunting tone, "Want a beer?" Other Bravo soldiers hassled the woman from Alpha Company, too — because of her, two of their own soldiers were getting punished. Debbie fretted about the pending judgment. "No word yet on our fate," she wrote miserably one day after the incident. Two days later she wrote, "Still no word I'm a little nervous."

At the same time, Debbie had other concerns, for she had learned in phone calls to her family that the condition of her childhood friend Jim was worsening. The following week, both Debbie and Desma had to appear before Captain Mueller, who told them they would be docked seven days' pay and get fourteen days of extra duties. Debbie savored a sense of relief that at least the sentencing was over. But when she went to check her email, she learned that her childhood friend had died. She had not gotten to see Jim after learning that he was sick, and the news made her distraught. "I feel so bad I should be doing something and I can't," she wrote in her diary. "I'm helpless over here!"

For the next two weeks, Debbie and Desma performed extra duties. They cleaned the shop where Desma worked, they swept the parking lot, they did extra time on local national watch. After a while, their supervisors eased up, and Debbie spent extra hours writing down the serial numbers of AK-47s, while Desma pulled extra guard duty, which actually meant she sat around playing euchre with Northrup and Mueller. Later, a soldier who worked in payroll quietly informed them that they would not actually lose any pay. Debbie spent some of her income on a surprise for her boyfriend Jeff. She renewed his membership at the Moose Lodge, paying his dues. Jeff sent an email in which he said it was a good thing Debbie was in Afghanistan or else he would have given her an ass-whooping. Debbie interpreted this to mean he was pleased. Then Ellen Ann mailed her a copy of the ultrasound that she had just gotten. "Well I'm having a Baby Girl," wrote Debbie. "As long as she is healthy it's okay. . . . I told EA the next one will be a boy. . . . I have to not shut Jeff out when I get back because I know I will want to be with the baby."

They could feel winter coming. They had been living at Camp Phoenix for three months, and they were not the same anymore: They were more capable, more cynical, less like civilians and more like regular army soldiers. They were a lot less scared, and a little more careless. At the same time, the war going on around them was changing, too. As the temperatures sank lower, their leaders said, the soldiers should expect a lull in the violence — generally, not much fighting happened in Afghanistan during the winter months — but they should not get complacent because spring was known as fighting season.

4
Translation

One day Patrick Miller went into the building where the armament team stopped to pick up its translators and came out with a young man named Akbar Khan. They had worked with various translators before, but none of them had been like this: Akbar Khan stood more than six feet tall, wore his black hair cropped short, and his face clean-shaven. He was movie-star handsome, with a square jaw, high cheekbones, chiseled lips, and an aquiline nose. He had been working at Camp Phoenix for only five or six days when Miller strode furiously into the room where interpreters waited to be assigned work. "He was a short, little, hyper person, and the first thing he did, he cursed," Akbar would recall later. "And then he asked for a person to assist him as a linguist."

Several other interpreters were waiting for a job, but Miller was so gruff and unvarnished that none of them replied. Akbar had already been told that he was going to Kandahar, a province in southern Afghanistan that was becoming known as a place where the Taliban appeared to be making inroads, but he had heard that Kandahar was a hellhole and that he should avoid going there at all costs. He felt weird that this person was standing there, all geared up to go, and getting no response from the other translators. He figured he should at least talk to the man. As soon as Akbar stood up, Miller said, "Okay! You! Get your ass in the Humvee!"

Because of the barbed comments Miller frequently made about black people, brown people, and hadjis, Michelle considered her boss a racist. Akbar Khan decided instantly that he liked Miller, however; Akbar thought that the team leader behaved in an entirely natural way, which he found reassuring. In Miller's brusque manner, there was nothing false. So Akbar got into the Humvee. Later, the other soldiers in the vehicle would say that getting to know Akbar was the single greatest thing that would happen to them in Afghanistan — he was what gave meaning to their deployment — but on his first day, Akbar made no significant impression. Akbar was not timid, but it was the first time he had ever been inside a military vehicle, the first time he had ever interacted at length with armed soldiers, and the first time he had been told to put on a seat belt. People in Afghanistan did not use seat belts, as a rule, and Akbar struggled to secure the unfamiliar strap around himself. "I had all kinds of feelings," he would say later. "The feeling of maybe if we get attacked en route, what should be my reaction? Especially when it comes to my own people, what is my place out there? Should I be hiding behind a tire, or protecting those that I'm working with? The question of who is the friend and who is the enemy — it's a very hard situation for us, especially when we have to decide which side to choose."

Akbar also suffered a mild sense of shock to see that two of the soldiers were women. He had been raised to revere women and to believe it was his job to protect them. He found it hard to grasp why a culture would put women in harm's way. At the ANA depot, the armament team taught Akbar the rudiments of their work. His primary task was to translate, but the need for translation occurred primarily when they were in transit, and as far as Miller was concerned, nobody should sit idle. But Akbar could see that Miller had qualms. "He was not feeling comfortable in my presence," he would say. "We were working on weapons. We had countless deadly weapons out there. Just one bullet was required to kill someone. He was very curious with my movements. He was paying attention."

Akbar proved reliable, courteous, and

highly intelligent, however — a vast improvement over the interpreters they had used previously — and from that day forward, he became their regular translator. After a little while, the armament team found him some cast-off BDUs (the dark green camouflage that none of them used anymore), which he wore with a white kaffiyeh jauntily draped around his neck. Akbar turned out to be fiercely proud of his culture but also relatively open-minded. He asked them all sorts of questions about America; they in turn asked all about Afghanistan. Akbar explained that he had grown up in a wealthy Afghan family that had fled during the rise of the Taliban; he had attended secondary school and college in Pakistan, where he had majored in sociology. After school, he had chosen to return to his country of origin, because Afghans were looked down upon in Pakistan. Rambo had recommended him as an interpreter, as they were relatives. Akbar spoke six languages fluently: Pashtu, Dari, Farsi, Punjabi, Urdu, and English. At the same time, he seemed naive about other aspects of life. Patrick Miller liked to discuss things such as women's anatomy in front of Akbar just to see him blush. Debbie, on the other hand, treated Akbar like the son she never had. "We have an interpreter with us now he's really nice his name is Akbar he's a hard worker . . . ," she wrote shortly after he joined the team. "Akbar is the oldest of his family + his parents are both sick so he's here living with his uncle and sending money back home to help his family."

Debbie asked Akbar Khan to explain everything she had been wondering about. Why did they never see any girls above the age of twelve or thirteen? They were kept inside, he explained. Above a certain age, it was no longer viewed as acceptable to play outside with boys, and they needed to learn the art of keeping a home. How young were the girls when they got married? Debbie wanted to know. More than half of the girls were married by age eighteen, Akbar told them. Some of the Afghan workers who moved inventory around the warehouse stopped by to talk. With Akbar translating for them, the Afghan workers plied Michelle and Debbie with questions. "Are you married?" one of them asked. "Do you have children? How old are you?" The Afghan workers seemed astonished to learn that Michelle was twenty-two years old and single. Debbie found it hard to explain her relationship with Jeff, so she lied and said they were married. "Then why did your husband let you come here?" one of the workers asked. Debbie laughed and said he hadn't been given a choice in the matter. Debbie enjoyed the conversation but it left Michelle feeling like a spectacle. "I would be like, I'm not a mother. I have no children. I have no husband. I'm a hussy little American. Like, I know that all the twenty-two-year-olds in your culture have five kids, but I don't. In their own polite Afghan way, they were asking: What the hell are you doing here? And I was like, I don't know! I didn't ask for this! And I'm not allowed to leave."

Akbar Khan tutored them in Afghan history. A monarchy had held the country stable for four decades, but since the 1970s Afghanistan had endured constant conflict. After the Soviet Union withdrew, leaving the country to be fought over by various warlords, one million Afghans had died and another three million had fled to other countries. Now that the United States had arrived, and was trying to stamp out the Taliban, hundreds of thousands of refugees were returning, in the hope that their once-thriving society could be reconstructed, but there was still not much of a local economy. Ninety percent of the government's budget came from international aid, and the warlords were running a lucrative opium trade, but otherwise most people lacked paying jobs. That was why Akbar Khan had chosen to support many members of his own family by working for the American military.

Akbar offered a door onto Afghanistan, a window onto Kabul. He was the first devout Muslim any of them had ever known. They watched him unroll a prayer mat every afternoon and make his prostrations. He was very pure, Michelle decided; all the virtue that she felt she had lost, she now ascribed to Akbar. They discovered that they were almost exactly the same age. Michelle concluded it was her job to protect this innocent young man from being corrupted by his contact with Americans. She chastised Patrick Miller for cursing around Akbar; she objected when Jason Kellogg joined them temporarily and teased Akbar for being a virgin; she got upset with Akbar when he drank Mountain Dew. Ramadan began on October 15 that year, and Akbar fasted for a month. Michelle brought Star-Kist tuna for lunch one day and worried that the strong smell must surely be increasing Akbar's hunger. Akbar viewed the intense young woman with bemusement. He had never met anyone like Michelle Fischer. "Are you a Christian?" he asked. Michelle said, "No." She tried to explain that religion played no role in her life, but this idea was impossible for Akbar to grasp. "You're a Christian," he told Michelle. "You come from a Christian country. Maybe you don't go to church, but the basis of all of your thinking is Christian." She tried but failed to repudiate this conclusion, and that was when she began to grasp just how central religion was to Akbar. He could not imagine a person without that basic orientation.

In certain ways, however, Akbar Khan

proved more worldly than his American friends. When the soldiers talked about the war with the Afghan translator, he did not speak of democracy or the rights of women or the satisfaction of liberating fellow Afghans from the yoke of the Taliban. He said, Don't you know that in our mountains we have one of the world's largest deposits of lithium? Cell phone batteries, that's what the war was about, Akbar believed. It was hard for the soldiers to trace the war's arc — hard to see the whole forest when they were so aware of each tree, each individual bomb blast. There were rumors of Taliban gains down in Kandahar and Helmand Provinces, but they had no way to gauge the scope of the opposition to the American presence. Over in Iraq, though, it seemed clear that things had taken a bad turn.

After Hussein had been removed from power, an intense struggle for control of Iraq had erupted between opposing Shi'a and Sunni factions, causing ever-increasing levels of sectarian violence. The Iraqi population had also turned against the US soldiers who had brought about this power vacuum and were waging a full-blown insurgency. Improvised explosive devices, or IEDs, were the weapon of choice. Meanwhile, US forces had been alienating the Iraqi population by sweeping through homes and rounding up all men of military age. "In the late summer of

2003 senior US commanders tried to counter the insurgency with indiscriminate cordon and sweep operations that involved detaining thousands of Iraqis," wrote Thomas E. Ricks in his highly regarded book *Fiasco: The American Military Adventure in Iraq.* "This involved 'grabbing whole villages, because combat soldiers [were] unable to figure out who was of value and who was not,' according to a subsequent investigation of the fourth infantry division's operations by the Army inspector general's office." Tens of thousands of Iraqis had been detained, and the US military did not have enough interrogators to process them in a timely fashion. The indiscriminate sweeps, which came about as a misguided attempt to rectify the lack of solid intelligence, only caused deepening animosity between the country's population and its invaders. Iraq had slipped into an ungovernable turmoil. US military commanders were trying to turn the situation around by implementing counterinsurgency tactics, but the ideas were foreign to many rank-and-file soldiers, as they involved restraining the use of force, and the new tactics were not yet proving effective. Instead soldiers were getting blown up in their trucks more and more often when they went out on patrol.

That fall, seventeen soldiers in Iraq refused to go on a fuel run in vehicles that they deemed unsafe and inadequately armored.

The soldiers were detained for their insubordination — news of which raced around other military bases. The army tried to dismiss the incident as an isolated problem, but the idea that US soldiers were being sent to war without adequate equipment took hold in public opinion. It was an election year in the United States, too, and by November of 2004 this question of whether soldiers were adequately equipped had become part of the ongoing debate between incumbent George W. Bush and his Democratic opponent, John Kerry. Likely voters were evenly split; it looked like it was going to be a close race. The two candidates argued heatedly over the wars, but in particular over Iraq; Bush's people had promised that the war would be short, but instead it kept on going.

That month, a military source leaked an internal document written by a top US Army official questioning the army's preparedness, citing concerns over a shortage of spare parts, adequate protective gear, and weaponry. At the same time, soldiers were filing lawsuits objecting to the fact that they were being kept in the military past the point when they had fulfilled the terms of their military contracts. Earlier that year, the military had instituted the "stop-loss policy," which allowed the armed services to keep soldiers past the point when their contracts expired if their unit was deployed to Iraq or Afghanistan. John Kerry took issue with the stop-loss policy, calling it a "backdoor draft." These debates were closely followed by the soldiers stationed at Camp Phoenix. Michelle mailed off her absentee ballot, casting another vote for Ralph Nader, while neither Desma nor Debbie voted. Most of the other soldiers they knew voted for George W. Bush.

Another big argument concerned the length of tours of duty. In the past, the army had typically sent soldiers overseas for six months at a time; it had upped its tours to twelve months after being asked to wage two wars simultaneously. Due to the length of its deployments, the army was now encountering difficulties with recruitment. The fewer new soldiers the military managed to recruit, the more often existing soldiers got shipped overseas. In response to the dismal recruitment numbers, the National Guard announced that cash bonuses for soldiers willing to reenlist for another six years were going to triple, from $5,000 to $15,000. Cash bonuses for new enlistees would jump from $6,000 to $10,000. That fall, the army's top officials began negotiating with the Pentagon to create more flexible rules about women in combat. The army asked for permission to place mixed-gender companies inside a battalion alongside companies of single-gender soldiers. Previously, the military had not allowed mixed-gender companies and single-gender companies to belong to the same battalion or regiment. The army argued that it was simply recognizing that male and female soldiers were facing similar threats from rockets, mortars, roadside bombs, and ambushes, regardless of job specialty. Women were seeing combat already, even if they weren't supposed to.

By November 2004, all the soldiers in the 113th had been on active duty status for six months and away from home for three months. They could feel the presence of the holiday season looming, and nobody was looking forward to spending Thanksgiving and Christmas at Camp Phoenix. "I've been really homesick lately," Michelle wrote to her father. "More than usual. But time is going by alright I guess. . . . I'm still living in a tent but we should be moving into a little building called a beehut in a few weeks. It'll be nice to have walls that don't flap in the wind. The girls that I live with have become like family to me; we are doing a secret Santa thing for Christmas. I'm dreading the holidays, everyone is going to be sad about not being home with their families. But we will get by. Just remember, they can't keep me here forever!"

Michelle asked to take a leave but was told she would have to wait — other soldiers had already applied. Desma Brooks and Mary Bell were planning a secret vacation to Italy.

They said nothing about the trip to their families back in Indiana; Desma desperately wanted a break from the crowded post, but she could not stand the idea of going home and then enduring another painful parting from her children. Desma did not want to take her leave so early, but it was the only time when she could get permission to go away with Mary. They flew to Kuwait successfully, but could not board their flight to Italy because neither Desma nor Mary owned a passport. Their military identification cards were considered insufficient to enter Italy. It seemed like a total catastrophe, but then Desma figured out they could fly from Kuwait to the United States and from the United States to Mexico using only their military IDs, and they successfully boarded a flight to Atlanta, where they connected with a flight to Cancún. "Heaven," Desma would say later. "White powdery sand, turquoise blue water, tart margaritas. Heaven."

Their hotel turned out to be low-end and located at the less desirable end of the strip, which suited Desma fine; the fancier places seemed intimidating. They upgraded to the "all inclusive" option; Desma was good at math, and she saw that the bracelets would prove to be a bargain. "I had never heard the term 'all inclusive' before that," she would say afterward. "I'd never been on a vacation before. I paid the extra $600 because it seemed to make more sense." They went snorkeling one day and the next day they went parasailing. They took a double-decker party boat over to Isla Mujeres, where they had too many bright-colored cocktails. Desma wound up riding a mechanical bull, barefoot in a little black party dress, and then on the way back she got sick over the side of the heaving party boat. They fended off a couple of French men by claiming to be lesbians. Toward the end of the trip, they shopped for souvenirs at the Flamingo Plaza, where they saw baby sea turtles the size of silver dollars. When they drove back through the gates of Camp Phoenix, and were confronted once more by the dreary starkness of the dusty post, Desma felt as though all of the joy had been leached out of the world. It was hard to be back, but she had no regrets about her decision. She knew that other people would think a mother should have gone home to see her children, but those people had never been to Camp Phoenix. A lot of soldiers snuck away on side trips without seeing their families. "It was hard enough to leave them the first time," Desma would say later. "And you do need a break. You need to take leave. Goddamn, I couldn't imagine going home and leaving them again, having to do that to myself all over again."

Bush had been reelected while Desma and Mary were in Cancún. When the soldiers at

Phoenix heard the news that Bush had won, Michelle received a stream of visitors to her tent ("people came in droves to, like, rub it in my face"). Michelle felt mystified by the support that Bush still held among her colleagues. "I was like, what is your problem?" she would say later. "Are you guys idiots? Like, do you want to stay here forever?" Knowing that she would be depressed by the election results, Pete mailed her a copy of *The Activist's Handbook,* by Randy Shaw — a guide to bringing about social change — which she devoured. Secretary of State Colin Powell announced that he was resigning, saying it had always been his intention to hold the job for only one term. Bush announced that Secretary of Defense Donald Rumsfeld would stay in his post. They kept hearing disturbing bulletins from Iraq, where thousands of marines were engaged in the Second Battle of Fallujah, a city held by the insurgents. Supposedly it was some of the ugliest urban combat since Vietnam.

The soldiers did what they could to distract themselves. Debbie stayed up late to catch live football games, which aired between midnight and dawn. Desma and her lover, Mark Northrup, became lethal at euchre, and were awash in pogs, the small cardboard counters that vendors used instead of coins to make change. Morale, Welfare, and Recreation showed *The Manchurian Candidate,* among other movies, and started a karaoke night. Desma got up and sang "I Got You Babe" with the new first sergeant. He had just taken over for Dean Kimball, who had been sent home because of a personal emergency. In an unrelated incident, the medics had discovered they were missing a significant quantity of morphine. Debbie's tent was searched twice, because of the number of medics who lived there, but nobody ever found the missing drugs.

Patrick Miller's wife sent a Christmas tree that arrived in the middle of November. It was plastic, dark green, and about three feet tall. The armament team set it up on a table at the ANA depot. Miller was battling increased guilt over his absence, because his wife had been caring for the baby by herself, and he felt terrible that he had done no parenting. "I don't feel like a father," he told the *Wrench Daily News.* "I miss what I'm missing. I miss her terribly. I feel sorry for her that I have to put her through this, that she's doing this by herself." When Toppe asked what was helping him get through the deployment, he answered, "My soldiers. People that look up to me, that respect me, that I respect. They're my family now."

The artificial tree bemused Akbar Khan.

"Why do you have a tree?" he asked.

"Oh, you know, we like to have a tree, we like to have lights," Debbie told him. "It's pretty. And we put presents underneath."

"But why a tree?" Akbar asked.

The soldiers were perplexed. Akbar had given them lessons in the history of Islam, he had told them all about Ramadan, but nobody could answer his one simple question.

"We have no idea," Michelle admitted.

Thanksgiving fell on November 25, 2004. Morale, Welfare, and Recreation organized a scavenger hunt, a flag football game, a volleyball tournament, and a horseshoe toss. The dining facility served corn on the cob, seasoned green beans, peas, broccoli with cheese, mashed potatoes, corn bread dressing, glazed sweet potatoes, four kinds of gravy, smoked turkey, roast turkey, turkey breast, glazed Cornish hens, baked ham, grilled steaks, steamed crab legs, and buttered lobster tail. The commander of the post invited Rambo to join them. He had never entered the dining room before and looked visibly uncomfortable. Then soldiers started waving and calling out thanks. "Thanksgiving! The DFAC personnel put on a very lavish spread it was really nice," wrote Debbie. "Even had an ice sculpture."

The following day, however, an Afghan man opened fire on a convoy as it was leaving the post. A French soldier shot and killed the man. The stark juxtaposition of the fatal shooting, coming so soon after the holiday meal, jerked everybody back to reality. The cooks had done a magnificent job of transporting them to some other place, but in fact they were still living in a war zone. To lift her own flagging spirits, Debbie was now hiding a puppy in her tent. Shortly before Thanksgiving, the armament team had been working at the ANA depot when they had heard shouting. Outside the depot, a group of children had been trying to sell some soldiers a puppy for $2, but the soldiers had refused to buy the dog, and the children had begun abusing the puppy. Debbie wrote:

> They were throwing her in the dirt and against the wall. She doesn't seem to be hurt but was very traumatized + shook all night. . . . She is probably only 3 weeks old. No teeth yet + her eyes barely open. So I've been feeding her with syringes + a formula they made up. She's up about every 2 hours. But she is so much better she has a lot more energy + her eyes are starting to shine so I hope she will make it. . . . Her back legs are weak so we hope there was no nerve damage.

They named the dog Diamond. A woman in Finance cared for Diamond during the day, and Debbie cared for the puppy at night. Every morning, before she met the rest of the armament team, Debbie secreted Diamond in a box and carried her over to Finance.

Every afternoon, as soon as Debbie finished her shift, she returned to pick up Diamond. The puppy required constant attention and could not be left alone. She also offered Debbie unconditional love. Debbie no longer went down to supply to drink, and no longer wrote about booze in her diary. She only wrote about Diamond.

> Well the baby is doing quite well I'm still Auntie Debbie the night nanny. Her back legs are moving great she has some sparkle in her eyes + is cutting some teeth. It's been tiring but worth it. I get up every 2–3 hours to feed her. . . . It's so nice to have her close by. I miss my Maxx a lot.

A few days later, Debbie's tent was ransacked again by staff sergeants who were continuing to search for the missing morphine, but Debbie got a heads-up and hid Diamond in another tent. The puppy required regular exercise, and it was hard to walk a dog and keep the animal hush-hush, so Debbie started getting up at four in the morning to walk Diamond around the post — an hour at which the only other people she encountered were the married soldiers who were sneaking out of tents in which they did not belong. None of them was likely to turn her in. Michelle found it hilarious that she was hiding Ben Sawyer, and Desma was hiding Mark Northrup, and Debbie was hiding Diamond. ("Her illicit relationship was with a dog," said Michelle drily.) "Baby girl got her first bath today," wrote Debbie in her diary shortly after Thanksgiving. "They are supposed to do a bed check tonight around 1:30 to make sure no one is practicing intercourse not sure what to do with Baby girl!"

It got cold and then it got colder. By the middle of December it was often dipping down into the twenties at night, and sometimes only climbed up into the thirties during the day. "Our heat acts like it's going out," wrote Debbie. "And no heat still at work." Patrick Miller complained that his people needed heat, and was told that a heater would be forthcoming, but weeks slipped by and it did not materialize. The armament team began burning old butt stocks inside the warehouse to keep warm. They mailed care packages back home and they also sent money. "Here is the money you needed," Michelle wrote to her father. "I hope it helps." Desma had been sending home child support to the people who were caring for her children every month, and now she mailed gift cards as well. Debbie sent money to her daughter, her brother, and her parents after they ran into various financial difficulties. "Jeff's worried I'm going to give all my money away before I get home," she wrote in her diary. "But it's my family + hard to say no. I really just want all my bills except mortgage to be paid off then I can concentrate on the next few years + try to retire early to enjoy. I don't need much just no bills . . . + Jeff if he decide[s] to stay."

The new post office opened in time to handle the holiday mail traffic. Every day for several weeks, trucks full of packages arrived, and the post office had to round up volunteers to unload all the boxes. The soldiers also flocked to the new PX, which carried a greater selection of magazines, food, DVDs, CDs, television sets, microwaves, refrigerators, Xbox consoles, PlayStation 2 consoles, and video games. Hamid Karzai was inaugurated as president of Afghanistan on December 7, 2004, and both Vice President Dick Cheney and Secretary of Defense Donald Rumsfeld arrived for the ceremony. Usually fighting ceased during the country's harsh winters, but US military leaders announced that because the Taliban was planning to disrupt the upcoming parliamentary elections, they were sending special forces out on raids throughout the winter. The midwinter push was being called Operation Lightning Freedom.

Ten days before Christmas, the Taliban retaliated with a series of attacks across Afghanistan. Mortar rounds rained down on a US base in Paktika Province; a rocket blast wounded other soldiers in Kandahar; inside the jail at Pol-i-charkhi, prisoners waged a ten-hour uprising during which inmates seized an AK-47 and killed four Afghan National Army soldiers. The next time the armament team went there, they were told they were not allowed to bring Akbar Khan inside the dining hall. Miller surprised the rest of the team by announcing that if Akbar couldn't eat in the dining hall, then none of them would. They ate lunch together out in their vehicles. It astonished Michelle; she had not expected Miller to evolve. But the daily contact with Akbar was having an effect on all of them — constant proximity to an Afghan who possessed so much dignity had changed the way they perceived Afghans in general. Even Miller did not make the same kinds of jokes about hadjis anymore. Akbar had brightened their days and they could no longer imagine their time in Afghanistan without him. Gift-giving was a significant part of Afghan culture, Akbar told them, and if they exchanged presents at Christmas then he wanted to give them something, too. But he puzzled over what would be appropriate. Were feminine things like earrings okay to give to a female soldier? Or should he get them knives?

Soldiers left Camp Phoenix to bring food, clothing, and medical supplies to families living in Kabul's crowded refugee camps. Michelle visited a local orphanage, and painted desks inside a school. She also started volunteering with a medical team that was providing health care to women living in local villages and refugee camps. Michelle played with their children while the mothers saw the medics. It was a small thing, perhaps, but later she would recall those moments as among the most rewarding of her life, and would search for a kind of work that would give her the same feeling of fulfillment. Soldiers who belonged to a different unit in the brigade got caught up in the story of a sixteen-month-old Afghan boy who needed heart surgery, and raised thousands of dollars to fly the boy back to Indianapolis to have a potentially lifesaving operation. Many people in Indiana attached great importance to the soldiers' effort, but Afghanistan was a place of harsh realities, and the boy died two days after returning home. The soldiers wanted to do good but it was not always easy to know how best to realize their intentions.

The air over Kabul grew acrid from smoke, because people were burning trash to stay warm. To cheer up the homesick soldiers, Morale, Welfare, and Recreation announced it was conducting a competition to see which tent could mount the best holiday decorations. It appalled Michelle to see generators being used to power Christmas lights when all around Kabul children were literally freezing to death. How could her colleagues happily fill the generators with fuel to light trees and displays and to pump air into blow-up Santa dolls? Michelle went on a tirade about it one day at work. "For some people, that's a morale lifter," Debbie tried to tell her. But Michelle would not listen. "It's so wasteful!" she cried.

Homesick, Michelle signed up for a video conference with Pete, Veronica, and Colleen. On the morning of the call, she woke early, and got dressed for work as usual — desert camo, ballistic vest, bulky Kevlar helmet, M4 assault rifle — then walked across the post to an office for the videoconference. There they were, waving at her, Pete and her two best friends, wearing homemade knit caps and stoner outfits. They had never seen Michelle in all of her gear. They had seen her in uniform, but they had never seen her carry a weapon. They should not have been taken aback, yet they were — the sight of her with the big gun, it was shocking. Plus, there was a glitchy time delay, and they kept interrupting one another. They tried for holiday spirit — "Merry Christmas!" Pete called out — but the call was an abject failure. They had hoped it might stitch them back together again but instead it left them feeling ripped apart.

The *Indianapolis Star* asked enlisted men and women to describe what they missed about home. One soldier said he missed being able to drive a car by himself. Another missed his La-Z-Boy recliner. The soldiers missed being able to watch football games at a normal time of day, missed arguing with their children, wearing civilian clothes, and ice cubes. They missed their own bathrooms. They missed Little League games and shopping on Black Friday. They missed fixing breakfast for their families on Sundays, and catching the holiday performances at their kids' schools. They missed spending hours finding the right Christmas tree and wrestling the tree into place and hanging ornaments on its branches. They missed shoveling their driveways.

One soldier from Camp Phoenix told the newspaper that the soldiers who were stationed there could look back over the months they had spent in Afghanistan and feel a sense of accomplishment. They had helped ensure the safety of the presidential elections, and they were training soldiers for the Afghan National Army. In their spare time, they had also tended to the sick, built schools, and brought clothes to refugee camps and orphanages. They believed they were making Afghanistan a better place. That month, residents of Indiana had sent tons (literally) of toys, clothes, coats, and blankets that the soldiers had distributed. "I realize that this may be the best example of the spirit of the season on Earth," wrote one soldier in a letter to the *Indy Star.*

Desma shopped for Christmas presents online. She got Alexis and Paige each a GoGo My Walkin' Pup, by FurReal Friends, fluffy white toy dogs that could walk and bark. She got Josh a new, tricked-out bike, had it shipped to his dad's house, and made sure his dad put it under the tree. There was no good time to call, given her work schedule, so she just phoned when she could, and wound up waking Josh in the middle of the night. It was two o'clock in the morning on Christmas Eve where he was, and he was only eleven, but Desma told him to get up and look under the tree. "Open up your presents, boy!" Desma said. "I got to go to bed." Josh was still half asleep and got confused by the box. "There's a bicycle inside," Desma assured him. "It's in pieces, but your father will help you assemble it." Once Josh woke up enough to realize that he was talking to his mother and she really had gotten him exactly what he wanted, Desma heard the sound of glee in his voice, and that was all she needed for Christmas.

Desma gave Michelle a clay pipe with a painting of a lizard on it that she had picked up in Cancún. Michelle gave Desma a bottle of Ralph Lauren "Romance" perfume. Ben Sawyer gave Michelle a large blue Yankees T-shirt, because the Yankees were his favorite team, and Pete mailed Michelle the final season of *Sex and the City,* because it was her favorite show. Michelle devoured the entire season in just one week. The DVDs got handed from bed to bed and only after the whole tent had watched the final season (by which point the DVDs were getting passed around the rest of the post) did Michelle and her tentmates finally talk about the surprise phone call from Big to Carrie.

Always outrageous, Desma also ordered vibrators for the entire tent, although the box got lost in the mail and did not arrive until after the holiday. When it finally came, she handed everyone a vibrator and announced, "You bitches need to chill the fuck out." The vibrators were small but powerful, with three rotating balls on the business end. Desma called them pocket rockets and promised they would deliver a real kick.

"Why would you buy this for me?" one of the other women asked.

"You need an orgasm worse than anybody I've ever met," replied Desma.

Michelle and Desma discovered that they could turn the vibrators on and race them down the aisle between the beds. Mary was still struggling to get the batteries inside her machine when Smitty walked into their quarters and announced he was doing a walk-through to see if they had any men in their beds. "Hey, Smitty!" Mary called out. "I need help! Can you open this battery compartment?" She thrust the sex toy at him. Smitty turned red when he realized what it was but got the vibrator working before he left. The vibrators, the flamingos, the vodka, the Article 15 — Michelle revered Desma. Without her, spending Christmas at Camp Phoenix would have been simply too grim.

Over in Debbie's tent, many of the women had gone home on leave, and she felt even more grateful for Diamond's company. "Diamond is growing I can't make her stay in the box," she wrote at the end of December. "She is my sanity saver she's my angel that's helping me through each day." At the same time, Debbie worried that Diamond would soon be discovered. The more active the dog became, the harder it was to prevent her detection. Debbie was not the only person who was hiding a pet — three other dogs and two cats had secretly been adopted by lonely soldiers — but it was against the rules. Meanwhile, Debbie felt increasingly homesick. "This is my first Xmas [away] from home it seems weird but then many soldiers before me have survived," she wrote. "I will too."

A big storm hit Indiana and Jeff wrote an email to say they got about twelve inches of snow. He was dreading the task of shoveling the driveway. "The wind is blowing, going to drift the snow, it is just 1 degree out," he wrote. "Twenty max today, and I got to get the truck out. Wish you were here we could cuddle up and not go out for 2 days." Debbie longed to be home to see the drifts out of her very own windows. She wrote in her diary, "Wish I was snowed in with him we would be snuggling." She did not have time to get depressed, however, as the armament team worked right through the holiday season. Afterward Debbie wrote, "Well what a week Xmas was okay just not home. We worked hard at the depot. Went through the rest of weapons stayed all day it was really cold."

Debbie's mother had mailed her a box of the old-fashioned peppermint sticks that Debbie always bought every year. They were the fat kind, with a hollow center. When she was little, Debbie's grandmother had taught her how to push the peppermint sticks into an orange and suck out the juice, and when Ellen Ann was little, Debbie had taught her daughter the trick, too. One day, Debbie brought the peppermint sticks and some oranges to the ANA depot, where she taught Michelle, Will, Patrick, and Akbar the same family tradition. They thought she was crazy until they tried it. Later, after they all got back home, that moment when Debbie had taught them to suck orange juice up through a peppermint stick would become one of the highlights of their time in Afghanistan, a little moment of joy they would treasure. The days had grown short and the nights were bitter, and they could not even agree about whether it was right to plug in a string of colored lights, and they had traveled miles and miles from who they used to be, and any hope of resuming their former lives now seemed tenuous, but in the coldest, darkest hours of their deployment, Debbie gave them the taste of peppermint and orange, winter sunshine in their mouths. They used the memory of that occasion to sustain themselves later, after much darker things happened.

5
Easter

What was strange about living at Camp Phoenix that year, as far as Michelle was concerned, was that you were neither safely at home nor properly at war. You were betwixt and between. Crazy things could happen — sometimes people strung piano wire across the road outside the post, sometimes RPGs whistled nearby — but Michelle could now see just how safe she was inside her tent. By the start of 2005, she had reached the midway point of her deployment, and she dared to hope that the support battalion might fulfill their year at Camp Phoenix without a single person getting hurt. She knew that the infantry soldiers they served alongside took much greater risks and saw much worse things than did the soldiers in her own unit. At the chow hall, they heard stories about the missions those soldiers went on, usually in the dead of night — breaking down the doors of people's homes, or ambushing insurgents holed up in the nearby peaks around Kabul. Most of the real action took place far away, but when they heard of an Al-Qaeda cell in the vicinity, the infantrymen at Phoenix were dispatched to capture or kill alleged members. Women never went on those missions, although anybody who left the post could encounter a land mine or an IED. Back in the United States, the idea of women being exposed to the worst hazards of war continued to be controversial. On January 11, 2005, Bush declared that the modifications being contemplated did not constitute any fundamental shift in position. "There's no change of policy as far as I'm concerned," Bush told the *Washington Times*. "No women in combat."

Yet they were surrounded by bloodshed. Almost every week, they got word of incidents that had taken place somewhere in Afghanistan involving either American soldiers or Afghan National Army soldiers. On January 3, 2005, for example, an American soldier was killed and three others were wounded near Asadabad, in far eastern Afghanistan, along the country's fractious border with Pakistan, after their Humvee hit an improvised explosive device, and a gun battle broke out. The wounded soldiers were evacuated by helicopter to Bagram. Forty-eight hours later, the soldiers at Phoenix learned that the individual who had been killed was Sergeant Jeremy Robert Wright, of Shelbyville, Indiana.

He was a Hoosier, too; he was one of them. But he was not National Guard — he had been regular army, with the special forces, and he had gone straight to Kunar Province. They were not over in Kunar; they were fixing trucks or AK-47s in the relative calm of Kabul. That same week, Morale, Welfare, and Recreation announced that they were offering swing dance lessons at Camp Phoenix. The following week, MWR opened a new racquetball court and showed *The Day After Tomorrow.* That was as close as most of her unit was going to get to real action, thought Michelle: watching it on a movie screen.

Over in Iraq, elections were going to be held at the end of January 2005, and the violence there intensified, echoing what had occurred in Afghanistan the previous fall but on a larger scale. On January 10, an unusually powerful roadside bomb destroyed a heavily armored Bradley Fighting Vehicle in southwestern Baghdad, killing two American soldiers and wounding four others. It was the second incident like that in less than a week; earlier roadside bombs had not been sufficient to blow apart an armored Bradley, but the insurgents had upped the power of their explosives. Bush and his advisers were still hoping that the elections would bring stability and the opportunity to withdraw quickly, but that looked increasingly unlikely.

At least from Michelle's vantage point,

though, war consisted of being stuck every night on a former Soviet air base where the biggest issue was boredom, wondering if she should take swing dance lessons or classes on personal finance, while knowing that people suffering from dire wounds were being flown to Bagram and that over in Iraq people were dying. By this point, Michelle knew she had it easy. She was not in Kunar; she had never been to Fallujah. The real soldiers (she sometimes thought) were dying in the mountains of Afghanistan and the cities of Iraq, and the biggest challenge she faced was the question of what to do with her time after she watched the last episode of *Sex and the City.* Even as she had these thoughts, of course, the military was altering its habits, as commanders became more desperate for replacements and less leery of putting women in harm's way, but it did not occur to Michelle that some future deployment might be different from this one, because she was too busy surviving her current ordeal.

Bored and restless, Michelle started off the year with several resolutions. "I haven't had a cigarette in about a week," she wrote to her father. "It was really hard at first but gets a little easier every day." And she enrolled in online courses that were being offered by the University of Southern Indiana to get a head start on her new life. "All of my free time goes to studying," Michelle said in another letter.

It didn't seem as though anybody at Phoenix would find themselves in harm's way, unless maybe they ran afoul of a land mine. Afghanistan was estimated to have ten million of the devices, making it one of the most heavily mined countries in the world. The list of countries riddled with mines (Egypt, Vietnam, Cambodia, Iraq, Iran, Kuwait, Somalia, Angola, Bosnia-Herzegovina) read like a history lesson in modern conflict. Mines had been used extensively in every war since 1938, and they never went away. They just abided, waiting to go off. According to the World Health Organization, no other country in the world dispensed to the victims of land mines as many prosthetic devices, crutches, and wheelchairs as Afghanistan. The social costs were immense. "Most land mine incidents occur in developing countries or regions where the victims are peasant farmers, herdsmen, nomads, or fleeing refugees," noted a World Health Organization bulletin. "Because of this, they rely primarily on their physical abilities for their basic subsistence. Many survivors never regain their ability to participate fully in family life or their society." Without mines, the authors estimated that agricultural production in Afghanistan could have doubled or tripled.

The mines were lurking everywhere, and it

was impossible to predict when one might be triggered. A group of soldiers from Camp Phoenix were returning from a visit to the ISAF compound when they saw a boy running through a field and suddenly the ground erupted. The soldiers jumped out of their vehicles and ran to tend to the boy, knowing there might be more unexploded ordnance hidden in the field. He lost both of his legs but they saved his life. The boy had not been targeted; the bomb was just a piece of military hardware left over from the other wars that had ravaged Afghanistan. His maiming was an accident.

But so far the land mines and the roadside bombs had let the soldiers be, and that January the main difficulty that the 113th Support Battalion encountered was precipitation. "The weather has changed it is really rainy + snowy," wrote Debbie in her diary, "but not like at home the snow doesn't last and it just floods because we are on cement." As the weather turned damp and cold, respiratory ailments spread through refugee camps, city neighborhoods, and across Camp Phoenix. Half the battalion fell sick; even Akbar Khan got pneumonia. Ben Sawyer came down with a fever so fierce that when Michelle wrapped herself around him, she was alarmed to feel the amount of heat coming off his burning body. It kept her warm, though. The generators that powered their heaters often quit during the night, leaving them without heat for hours at a time. Michelle, Desma, and Debbie started wearing footies and multiple pairs of long johns under their flannel pajamas when they slept. But they could hardly complain when they were not being asked to fight in Kandahar or in Kunar. How could they whine about the cold when they knew they were not carrying the war's true burden? And all around them, people lived in far worse conditions. "I'm still seeing the kids along the way to ANA without socks or shoes it just kills me," wrote Debbie. "I wish I could save them all. People back home can't imagine."

Debbie decided to work through the entire deployment. It felt wrong, she thought, to go on a vacation. She would not be able to relax, knowing that two wars were being waged and that other people were bearing the brunt of the fight. Plus, if she worked straight through the year, she would be able to take a leave when she got home, instead of having to go straight back to work at the beauty salon. Patrick Miller told her that spending an entire year at Camp Phoenix without a break would not be healthy, but she refused to listen. Then Miller engineered matters so that she "won" a free trip to Qatar in a rigged lottery. "Maybe I will get off post after all," wrote Debbie. "I need a beer I'm sure they don't have Coors Light but I hope they do."

Debbie left for Qatar on Monday, January 10, 2005 — the same day they got news of the second roadside bomb destroying an armored Bradley over in Iraq. She turned in her weapon, caught a ride to Bagram, and waited for a plane to take her to the Persian Gulf, feeling badly about leaving Diamond. At 5:30 p.m. she boarded a plane for Qatar, along with a group of commissioned and noncommissioned officers she recognized from Camp Phoenix. Debbie imagined they might all go bar-hopping. She felt excited about the idea until they arrived at Camp As Sayliyah, the US Army base outside of Doha that served as an R&R facility for troops serving in Iraq, Afghanistan, and Kuwait. The post strictly regulated access to alcohol, Debbie learned at a briefing; visiting soldiers were given three tickets per day, allowing them at most three drinks in a twenty-four-hour period. And the bars on post only served alcohol between 6:00 p.m. and 11:15 p.m. Qatar was not going to be the free-for-all she had envisioned. "Have to wait for drink tomorrow, too late tonite," she wrote in her diary. "Plus can't get your drinks until [evening]. How crazy no drinking during the day."

The following morning, the soldiers she had traveled with went their separate ways, but they joined up for lunch at Chili's. "Food really good," Debbie noted later. "No alcohol." After lunch they marveled at the lush, manicured grounds around the post's fancy hotels — they had not seen anything green in months. "Trees, grass, flowers even," wrote Debbie. "You know 'stopped to smell the roses'? We stopped to smell the grass."

In the evening, Debbie met the same soldiers back at Chili's. The enormous post was strange, and the chain restaurant offered the reassurance of being familiar. They hit the bars after dinner. Debbie obsessed about the fact that her colleagues ordered only one alcoholic beverage apiece; the colonel and the NCOs did not seem concerned about using their allotted alcohol ration. Would they offer her their unused tickets? She longed for them to do so. "But no one is offering so I guess I'm stuck with my 3," she wrote in her diary.

The following day, Debbie bought some earrings for her daughter and coveted but did not buy a pair of pewter goblets. "I miss my Diamond Girl!" she wrote. When she met up with her traveling companions, they talked her into joining them on a boat ride in the Persian Gulf. From the deck of the craft, the soldiers could see a string of construction cranes hugging the shoreline; the area was booming. The sky clouded over and the temperature dropped and the soldiers shivered as they stood on the ship's deck. They watched a bunch of marines who'd been serving in Iraq cutting loose; of course Debbie befriended them. The marines decided to pile on top of each other to stay warm, and their colonel stacked rugs and mats on top of his men to shield them from the cutting wind. Debbie envied the evident bond between the members of the unit and their leader. Later she wrote: "He is so cool, wish he was over us!"

On their second-to-last day in Qatar, the soldiers from Camp Phoenix paid to go on a safari. Guides drove them all over an astonishing ocean of sand dunes. Debbie raved about the experience:

> Oh my what an awesome day. It's the best $21 I've ever spent. We were in Land Cruisers and they had to let the air out so they ride right. It was just like a roller coaster ride my stomach was doing flip-flops I was sure we would roll over but we never did. It's just an awesome feeling to be in a real desert and we were right by the Persian Gulf again we had a cookout with a big tent, chairs, tables, bonfire + beautiful sunset. . . . It's just beautiful like on vacation. They lit Tiki lights + it's just great if only we could stay longer.

But their leave was almost over. Debbie hoped that finally on their last day she might receive some of the unused drink tickets belonging to the other soldiers, but she was disappointed again. "Carpenter still won't give me his tickets oh well it's OK," she wrote. "I had Carlsberg tonite not bad beer really!" The group decided to return to Chili's again for their last meal. After they finished eating, the others were ready to head back to the barracks, but Debbie still had tickets to use, and the alcohol blanketed her in a comforting fog and helped her find sleep, and it would not be so easily available once she returned to Camp Phoenix. She wrote afterward, "Everyone left + I stayed to finish my beers."

The next morning they had to be in formation by 4:00 a.m., then caught a flight back to Bagram. Debbie's thoughts shifted to her pending reunion with Diamond. "Not sure if we have work or not I'm hoping I get my day off on Monday. But if not I will still go see my Baby!" They got stranded at Bagram Airfield for lack of a convoy to Kabul, but made it back to Camp Phoenix one day later. Debbie got the day off on Monday and used the time to distribute gifts to various local national workers and to visit Diamond. "She's grown so much," wrote Debbie. "She did fine while I was gone but she missed me. They didn't take her out at all. So I'm picking her up at night + walking her for 2 hours around compound hopefully that will help."

That week, Debbie did three haircuts and

three leg waxes, making up for lost time — her services were in demand, as her clients had missed her while she was gone. It pleased her to be needed. At the same time, Debbie was characteristically delighted when Patrick Miller took the armament team to the range to fire SPG-9s, a recoilless Soviet antitank gun. They had been fixing SPG-9s instead of AK-47s and wanted to be sure they were doing the job right. The only way to know if you had fixed a gun properly was to fire it, Miller said — so they did. Everybody except Michelle Fischer. She announced that she was trying to get through her deployment without firing a weapon and boycotted the exercise. The others were thrilled to fire the unusual weapons. "What a blast," Debbie wrote in her diary. "It's really quite a boom + really shakes your legs + insides."

In the chow hall, people were talking about multiple deployments. Earlier that month, Fox News had reported that the army was considering a change in its use of reserve and National Guard soldiers: at the moment, part-time soldiers could not be asked to serve on active duty for more than twenty-four months, meaning that for the entirety of their time as soldiers, they could not be asked to spend more than a total of two years overseas; the proposed change involved rewriting the sentence to say the army could deploy part-time soldiers for no more than twenty-four *consecutive* months. The effect of the one-word change would be to allow the army to deploy part-time soldiers for up to two years at a time on multiple occasions, rather than sending them overseas for a cumulative total of two years. The new policy would allow the army to deploy its part-time soldiers for much longer periods of time and far more frequently. And the 113th Support Battalion was being told to expect a deployment to Iraq at some point in the future.

The policy allowing multiple deployments in a single conflict was controversial — even during Vietnam, which had lasted for ten years and was at the time the longest war in US history, soldiers were done after one tour of duty, unless they volunteered to return — and nobody in the Guard had foreseen repeated lengthy deployments. By this point, however, American soldiers had been fighting in Afghanistan for more than three years, and in Iraq for close to two. So reliant on the National Guard had the army become that it had already deployed or put on notice of plans to mobilize during the coming year fifteen of the Guard's combat brigades. Not every soldier would be deployed — as chance would have it, Michelle's two former boyfriends, Noah Jarvis and James Cooper, were sitting out the wars at home, because their particular job specialties had not been required — but almost every brigade would be affected. The Guard was no longer serving in an emergency capacity, in other words; it had become an essential part of the country's war machine.

Military leaders were debating whether it was advisable to rely so heavily on the National Guard. Most of the "citizen soldiers" had not foreseen long deployments when they signed up and were not really ready for them. Neither were their families. In a memo to the army chief of staff that was leaked to the *Baltimore Sun* that January, Lieutenant General James R. "Ron" Helmly, the chief of the army reserve, called Bush's policies "dysfunctional" and expressed his "deepening concern" about the readiness of reserve troops. He warned that his branch of the military was being overused and said the reserves were "rapidly degenerating into a 'broken' force." He said the Guard could no longer regenerate itself in a viable fashion. Indeed, all of the publicity over multiple deployments had caused recruitment efforts to slide: that January, the National Guard met only 56 percent of its recruiting quota. Noting that recruitment was failing to meet expectations, Secretary of Defense Donald Rumsfeld conceded that the US military was "clearly stressed."

Embroiled in two wars that kept thundering forward, however, Pentagon leaders believed there was no other way but multiple deployments to keep troop levels sufficiently high — at least not while maintaining the idea that the United States was using an "all-volunteer" force. In the weeks that followed, the army did adopt the one-word change in policy, although the decision proved so unpopular that Pentagon officials almost simultaneously vowed not to use their new authority. "No individual will have more than twenty-four months cumulative on active duty, Guard or reserve," General Peter Pace, vice chairman of the Joint Chiefs of Staff, would tell the Senate Armed Services Committee. "Right now we're able to stipulate that anyone who has already been called to active duty will not be recalled." But the soldiers at Camp Phoenix suspected that this vow would prove untrue.

As they debated the issue of multiple deployments, a series of blizzards pummeled the region. It snowed on both January 20 and January 21, which happened to be the first two days of the Muslim holiday of Eid al-Adha. Also called the Greater Eid, or the Feast of the Sacrifice, Eid al-Adha was a different holiday than the Lesser Eid, which had marked the end of Ramadan. During the four-day holiday, Muslims honored the willingness of Abraham to sacrifice his son, before God let him sacrifice a lamb instead. Camp Phoenix announced that most of the soldiers on the post did not have to work. They all enjoyed the holiday atmosphere in their own ways. Debbie slept late and hung out at supply, drinking. Desma drove to a nearby orphanage in Kabul to deliver clothes and shoes, on a day when the sun was shining, and everything glittered. Michelle studied for her online courses and had a snowball fight with Ben.

President Bush delivered his second inaugural address on Thursday, January 20, 2005 — also the day that snow began falling in Kabul, and the day that Muslims began celebrating Eid al-Adha — to an audience that included soldiers who had been wounded in Iraq and were being treated at a nearby military hospital. Bush thanked the men and women who were serving in the armed forces. He talked about freedom and liberty. "Across the generations we have proclaimed the imperative of self-government, because no one is fit to be a master, and no one deserves to be a slave," Bush said. "Advancing these ideals is the mission that created our nation. It is the honorable achievement of our fathers. Now it is the urgent requirement of our nation's security, and the calling of our time. So it is the policy of the United States to seek and support the growth of democratic movements and institutions in every nation and culture, with the ultimate goal of ending tyranny in our world." Maybe the elections in Iraq would make everything there all right, he seemed to be saying. Shortly afterward, the

Bush administration requested another $80 billion to pay for the wars in Iraq and Afghanistan.

Then it snowed more. In Kabul, it snowed lightly on January 24 and much more heavily on January 25 and January 26, when a blizzard dropped two feet of snow on the post. Workers were sent out all night long to get the weighty snow off the tents, to make sure they did not collapse. Desma, a light sleeper, woke up over and over again to the sound of squeegees scraping across the frozen canvas; Michelle, a heavy sleeper, never stirred. Then it plunged down to thirteen degrees one night, and the following night down to a cruel eleven. Local national workers took away the sandbags around the outside of the tent because they were soon to move into a B-Hut, which was how they learned that the sandbags had provided insulation. It was so painfully cold that they found it impossible to sleep, no matter how many items of clothing they wore. Any water left standing on the post's concrete landscape turned to ice, and much of the ice was hidden under snow. Desma was walking a group of local nationals over to the dining facility when her legs went out from under her. She fell hard and broke her right arm. The medics X-rayed it on a dental machine and then set the bone. Meanwhile, everybody felt unsettled at the news that an Afghan soldier down in Helmand Province had turned on his colleagues and opened fire, killing five fellow Afghans and wounding six others; the rampage was attributed to mental illness. Nobody wanted to believe that it might mark the start of a trend. They were arming Afghan soldiers and they had to trust that the Afghans would remain their allies.

Desma celebrated her twenty-ninth birthday on January 28, 2005. She did not let her broken arm prevent her from throwing a party; she got away with staging a birthday party during work hours by calling it a "maintenance appreciation celebration." Jaime Toppe advertised the party in the *Wrench Daily News:* "Refreshments, games, music, and more!" Desma's friends decorated the shop with pretty pink streamers — actually, the ubiquitous pink crepe Chinese toilet paper found in every bathroom on the post. They played a hilarious game of Twister, with Desma manning the spinner. They couldn't serve any booze because Desma's boss was there, but there was something delightful about the low-key manner in which most of the soldiers whom Desma liked dropped by the party; she found it hard to say why, but the toilet paper streamers and the game of Twister and having a party at the shop somehow amounted to one of the best birthdays she ever had.

They moved that weekend. Desma, Michelle, and the eight other women they lived with carried their belongings out of the drafty canvas tent and into the brand-new plywood B-Hut that would serve as their home for the rest of their time in Afghanistan. Tent by tent, Bravo Company had been moving for weeks; as fast as the huts could be constructed, soldiers were filling them up. When construction workers tore down their emptied tent, Desma and Michelle were disgusted to see black mold covering the bottom-side of the floor, and scum oozing over the concrete underneath. The B-Hut was entirely clean; the wooden walls and ceiling embraced the warm air of the heaters more thoroughly than the canvas walls of their tents. They moved just in time. That night, the temperature plunged to a new bone-chilling low of one degree, the coldest day of the entire year they would spend in Kabul. That same weekend, Jaime Toppe started running a daily joke about life at Camp Phoenix in the *Wrench Daily News* under the headline "How to Prepare for an Afghanistan Deployment" (similar things were being emailed from soldier to soldier). Her first suggestion: "Sleep on a cot in the garage. . . . Replace the garage door with a curtain. . . . Six hours after you go to sleep, have your significant other open the curtain, shine a flashlight in your eyes, and mumble, 'Sorry, wrong cot.' "

The jokes immediately became Desma's

favorite thing to read in the *Wrench.* She read them out loud to Mary and Michelle: "Stop using your bathroom and use a neighbor's. Choose a neighbor that's at least a quarter mile away." And "Leave the lawn mower running in your living room twenty-four hours a day for proper noise level." That's exactly what it had been like, living in a tent that was too close to a generator. After five months of that a plywood hut struck them as luxurious.

Meanwhile, Debbie was still shivering in her tent — she would not move into a B-Hut for several more weeks. And right after Desma's birthday party, Debbie heard that a dog that hung around the front gate had been taken to Bagram for routine vaccination shots and had supposedly "gone crazy." This sparked talk of rabies. "So now they can get rid of all the animals," wrote Debbie disgustedly. "They were saying Diamond came from that litter [the same one as the dog at the gate] but she didn't." Company commanders rounded up every pet the soldiers were concealing. They kept the dogs at the motor pool, where Desma and Mary could keep an eye on the animals while Debbie was at work. It broke Debbie's heart to see Diamond locked up but she visited as often as she could. "I let her in the office to play + took her out to potty," wrote Debbie. "I came back next morning so she could get out to potty + eat. She was so scared + confused as to why she had to be in the cage."

The soldiers were told that the animals would be held in quarantine, probably at Bagram Airfield. If they proved not to develop rabies, supposedly they would be returned. "I suspect they are lying," wrote Debbie grimly. "They are not coming back." Later that week, Mary Bell told her that Diamond had been moved, and she did not know where. Debbie learned that all of the dogs were now being held in the welding shop and were about to go to Bagram. She got to see Diamond once more.

> I found out where she was + went to see her + asked if they had let her out to potty or eat they said they were not allowed to let them out. . . . So sad they were so frightened. Dia was so restless I knew she had to pee + poop. She finally did so I cleaned it up + her blanket was wet either her water or pee. I dried her blanket. I couldn't take her out so I sat a chair in front of the gate + got half in + petted her + rubbed her to try + give her some comfort. I brought her back steak for dinner. . . .
>
> When her blanket dried I put it back in and she started to wind down a little. I brought some of her fav toys she played with them she finally was tired so she laid close to me and I just petted her till she fell asleep. . . .

That was the last time I had with my Baby girl. I miss her a lot.

Debbie never found out exactly what happened to Diamond; she simply never saw the dog again. The soldiers assumed their pets had been euthanized. "Needless killings," Debbie fumed in her diary. A dog named Cherry had escaped the roundup and was still at Camp Phoenix. Cherry had been there when they arrived and would be there when they left — that dog had achieved the status of an unofficial mascot. If they could spare Cherry, why not Diamond? Debbie could not speak of anything else in her diary for several weeks, while around her colleagues and friends she lapsed into an uncharacteristic silence and did not speak at all. She was furious with the brigade's leaders. "As usual if you're having fun it will be taken away," she wrote in her diary. "76th sucks." Soon Debbie resumed her habit of taking long walks in the evenings with Will, and going down to see Gary. "Will came up with some Southern Comfort so we trekked to Supply + had a nice cocktail for the evening!"

As the cold snap intensified, conditions in the unheated warehouse where the armament team worked became almost unbearable. On many days, the ink in Michelle Fischer's pen froze, making it impossible for her to write down the serial numbers of the AK-47s until she warmed the ink back into liquid form. Patrick Miller let them burn old butt stocks in an oil barrel, and they warmed their hands over the fire. They wore four layers of clothes: thin black nylon long underwear known as ninja suits; then the uniform itself; over that, they wore bear suits, as they called the heavy black fleece overalls and matching black fleece jackets; the final layer was a lined Gor-Tex overcoat. Debbie also made certain to wear earmuffs every day, but several hours in the penetrating cold still left her numb. Eventually Miller decided it was inhumane to keep the group inside the frozen warehouse for an entire day, and announced that he was implementing an unauthorized winter schedule: they would work until they had fixed one hundred weapons, or until 2:00 p.m. in the afternoon, whichever came first, and then return to the post and lie low. Motivated by the desire to get warm, they hustled and finished one hundred weapons by midday. "Go hide," Miller urged back at the post. "Fischer, don't go to the gym before four o'clock. Don't change your clothes. Just go back to the barracks."

And then it really began to snow. Early in February, the sky clouded over and stayed gray for two weeks, while a series of storms dumped another several feet of snow on Kabul, paralyzing the city. Kabul had not experienced so harsh a winter for half a century, said the oldest residents of the city. Many Afghans welcomed the precipitation as likely to assuage the devastating impact of the drought, but the harsh weather also caused a rash of injuries and fatalities. Doctors reported seeing 30 percent more leg and arm fractures than usual that month, and saw a sharp rise in cases of serious respiratory diseases, particularly among children. "We have to have two children to a bed," Mohammed Hamid Nazim, a doctor in a pediatric hospital, told the Environment News Service. "The number of patients is simply too great."

All of the highways leading into and out of Kabul shut down — the city did not own enough plows to clear the roads, and the machines they had were malfunctioning due to the freezing weather — and officials found eighteen people dead in their vehicles after they were stranded for an extended time on the Kabul–Kandahar highway. Truckers had to abandon tankers full of aviation fuel, causing airlines to cancel dozens of flights. And at the airport, workers could not clear the runways. During the worst of the snowstorms, the Kabul airport turned away a Boeing 737 from Herat that was carrying 104 passengers. The plane went missing. Rescue teams located wreckage in the steep mountains, but when they finally reached the site, they found nobody alive.

Debbie moved into a B-Hut in between the

two biggest snowstorms. Something about the new surroundings and the fresh plywood lifted her spirits, which had been low ever since she had lost Diamond. Gretchen was away on leave, and Debbie packed her tent-mate's gear for her. She arranged their beds in a corner of the B-Hut, with a small table where they could use their laptops. "I'm pretty well settled," Debbie wrote in her diary. "I like it + do have more room + a window. I'm going to make a flowerbed at my window."

Debbie and Michelle both stayed up late to watch the New England Patriots take on the Philadelphia Eagles in the Super Bowl, which aired in the chow hall at the painful hour of 2:30 a.m. on Monday, February 7. Then Debbie spent many evenings crocheting a blanket for her grandchild. Ellen Ann and her husband, Jay, had settled on Jaylen — an amalgam of their names. "I'm almost done with her blanket but I don't think it's going to be big enough after all so not sure what I'm going to do," wrote Debbie. She worried about whether Jeff was getting out of the house. "Today is Nascar day I hope he goes to the party but I bet he won't," she wrote. "I'm making valentines for the DDR team tonight but I also want to check on the race." Using glitter pens and construction paper sent by Ellen Ann, Debbie made cards for everybody on the armament team, including

Akbar Khan, as well as an Afghan worker at the depot named Daoud.

Valentine's Day — another holiday away from home. By this time Michelle had been cheating on Pete for six months, and still had not summoned the nerve to tell him. Later she would say she did not want to break the news to him in a phone call — she wanted to tell him face-to-face — yet she had not been able to schedule a leave until March. Perhaps it was also true that she could not wrap her mind around how her universe had been split by the war; in some ways it seemed as though she were leading two separate lives — a military life that was unfolding in Afghanistan, and a civilian life that had once unfolded and would someday unfold again back in the United States. And possibly Pete had become so unreal to her that she could somehow reconcile maintaining a theoretical relationship with him even as she engaged in an actual relationship with someone else. All around her she saw other people who were behaving in similarly divided ways. It was what a deployment did; it fractured reality.

Meanwhile, Ben Sawyer had practically moved into Michelle's B-Hut. He spent virtually every night there, and Michelle no longer dismissed their interactions as insignificant. Ben was like a fixer-upper, she had decided; he had potential. Maybe she could turn him around, maybe she could help him figure out what to do with his life. They had begun discussing the possibility of a future together — sometimes they talked about finding a place to share in Indiana. Ben had a volatile temperament, however, and when they fought he got mean; it scared Michelle. One day she came to work in a huff following a bad fight. She mentioned the spat to Patrick Miller. "Well, if you ever want to make Ben jealous," Patrick said — then he raised one hand into the air — "pick me." Great, now her boss was hitting on her, thought Michelle. That's life in the army for you. But she trusted Patrick — he would never force her to do anything she did not want to do. It never crossed her mind to report his comment. By now she thought of him like a brother.

Meanwhile, she still received letters, post-cards, and care packages from Pete — he was going to Seattle, he told her, to check out their future home. For Valentine's Day, Pete mailed Michelle a bottle of Southern Comfort. Afraid to drink it, Michelle gave the liquor to a soldier from Bravo Company named Aaron Schaffer, who sometimes joined the armament team if they were short of personnel. He drained the entire bottle in one sitting and became so obviously drunk that she feared the alcohol would be traced back to her. But Schaff just slept it off and nothing happened. Michelle sent Pete two Valentine's Day cards. The first had a white background with a red valentine cracked in two by a jagged line — a broken heart. "This is me," the card declared, "without you." Inside, she wrote:

> Hey baby,
>
> Valentine's Day is a fucking commercialized bullshit holiday. But I still hate not being with you for it. I miss you and love you more than you could ever know. . . .
>
> Well, let's look on the bright side. I'll see you in a few weeks!!
>
> I love you sweetie.
>
> Sorry the card is so corny, not a huge valentine selection in Afghanistan.
>
> Love you always
>
> Michelle

Then she sent a second card that showed Piglet handing Winnie-the-Pooh a red valentine. "Being with you," the card said, "is what I love best." Inside Michelle scrawled:

> Ha ha you're so awesome you get <u>two</u> lame VDay cards! I really miss you I hope that Seattle was fun. Chin up because baby I will see you <u>soon!</u>
>
> Love Always
>
> Your Girl
> Michelle

As long as she remained in Afghanistan, she could sustain this state of irresolution, where she never had to confront the truth of what she was doing. She could see Ben in person and interact with Pete as an almost fictional being — but it was crazy, she knew. And it cost her emotionally in ways she had not even started to tabulate, trying to inhabit both worlds at once.

Desma cherished no illusions about her significance to Mark Northrup. She would have liked to hold on to a man of his caliber, but it was not going to happen, and she knew it. Sometimes he went out on the road with Voodoo Child — as his roving maintenance team liked to call themselves — to rescue other soldiers who had gotten stranded in bad situations. Then she might not see him for several weeks. When he was on the post, they slept together fairly regularly, usually about once a week. They had sex in her hut, his hut, Mueller's office, an ambulance, the back of a van. Once Northrup asked her if she would have sex with him inside a Porta-John, but that was where Desma drew the line. "I think this affair is over if you think I am to the level where I will have sex with you in a Porta-John," she told Northrup. "I am not that person, and you really do not need me to be that person."

But he was not going to leave his wife, he was not going to marry her. Desma did not even dream that would happen. Nobody was supposed to find out about the affair, but it had become an open secret. At about this time, somebody posted a picture of Desma and a mechanic together on MySpace. Because of Desma's reputation, the mechanic's wife jumped to the wrong conclusion. "Apparently she totally flipped out, and thought we were sleeping together," Desma said later. "And that was so not the case. Well, then, in his defense, bless his heart — I'm not mad at him, but he really shouldn't have handled it the way he did — he told her, 'No, I'm not sleeping with her, Northrup is.' " The photograph of Desma and the mechanic had been on MySpace for only twenty-four hours when Desma got a phone call from Stacy Glory, back at the armory in Bedford. Stacy called Desma at the motor pool (they were supposed to use the phone line only for military purposes, but sometimes they used it just to catch up) to warn her that the comment had made the rounds of the Family Readiness Group. The wives could be vicious. "Northrup's wife pretty much put it out that I was sleeping with everybody," Desma said. "I wasn't." After that, she and Northrup tried to be a little more discreet.

T.J. told Debbie that she was mailing her something really sexy that she could do all by herself for Valentine's Day — it turned out to be a blow-up guy, and he got passed around

Debbie's hut — but Jeff forgot about the holiday entirely. When he realized that he had neglected to send a card or a gift, he wrote Debbie a heartfelt email saying "it's your dead beat honey" and promised he was going to show her such a good time when she got home that "you might want to wear your body armor when you get back just to be safe." As it happened, the power had gone out that day and most of the meat he had stored in the freezer had thawed. "Maxx will eat good for a couple of days, I'm telling you," he said. "Maxx is okay he will love my pork chops the big butt head." Debbie told her daughter to make sure to take Jeff to Pizza Hut for Valentine's Day so that he wouldn't spend the holiday alone. Debbie was a little envious of all the action the younger women were getting. "Terry told me to write something juicy about her but we all laughed none of our immediate group are getting any juiciness of any kind. In our dreams." But she also felt grateful that her life was not so tumultuous.

Later that month, the armament team drove to a new location: a facility known as the Kabul Military Training Center, where a *kandak* was about to be deployed to another province. *Kandak* meant brigade. One of the principal training sites for Afghan soldiers, the KMTC sat in rolling foothills on the outskirts of Kabul. There were no trees; the landscape was an undulating expanse of tan-colored sand and gravel, interrupted by hardy brown grass and occasional shrubs. Soon it would be fighting season, and the newly trained soldiers needed weapons. Michelle, Debbie, Will, and Patrick worked in an unadorned cinderblock room painted white, where they sat on red plastic chairs and used overturned metal drums as tables. Hundreds of AK-47s had to be repaired in a hurry. Their job remained similar — they sorted through the reclaimed guns, fixed the ones that were broken, and documented everything — but these AKs were in much better shape than the others they had been repairing. Debbie, Will, and Patrick flew through the boxes while Michelle sat to one side, furiously writing down serial numbers. Afghan soldiers watched them intently, including a bearded man of high rank. The Afghan men seemed taken aback to be interacting with female soldiers. "The young recruits were very curious about Michelle + me," wrote Debbie afterward. "I think [they were] fascinated they stare continuously." Michelle retreated to their Humvee to eat her lunch, unable to tolerate the degree of attention she attracted.

For the rest of the deployment, the armament team alternately fixed broken AK-47s at the ANA depot and at KMTC, and eventually they also started giving classes on how to maintain and repair AK-47s to the deploying Afghan soldiers. As they spent more and more time over at KMTC, the Afghans showed them greater hospitality. "They served us chai + a really great cake taste a lot like our pound cake," wrote Debbie. "Then they fed us lunch 'Afghani style.' Rice, beef, cauliflower. [It] was really good! Michelle + I love those cakes." Finally they got heat at the ANA depot; mechanics arrived and installed a generator outside the building, then ran a metal tube in through a window. If the armament team stood directly underneath the tube, they could feel a river of warm air. It did not really heat the warehouse, but you could stand under the tube and take a heat shower. Miller kept driving them furiously. At the end of February they learned that their superiors considered their productivity so prodigious that they were being given a special commendation. "DDR received medals for our work apparently very prestigious awards not usually given out they were signed by a two-star general!" wrote Debbie. "Not many of these will be given out pretty cool."

Sometimes Patrick Miller lost control of his temper when he could not get the Afghans to do his bidding. At one point after they had returned to the ANA depot, he jumped up on the back of a truck and started yelling and waving a knife around when he could not get a group of Afghan soldiers to clean their AK-47s to his liking. He said the Afghans should clean the AKs immediately, or else he would cut their balls off. Michelle and Debbie could tell that Akbar fudged the translation. ("I just said he is requesting with great vehemence that you do this task," Akbar would say later, confirming their sense.) The armament team figured Akbar had saved their lives. "Miller acts like a beheaded chicken," Debbie wrote in her diary. "He drives us crazy at times."

The harsh winter was followed quickly by an unusually mild spring. On March 13 — the most unusually warm day of the entire year, in terms of the relative increase over previous years — the temperature rose to seventy-two degrees Fahrenheit, twelve degrees warmer than the previous average. But the skies did not clear. It rained more in March than it did during any other month that year. The soldiers reveled in the warmer temperatures. Even Patrick Miller softened with the change of weather. Since the work of his team had been formally recognized, he visibly relaxed, and let them goof off. In the middle of the warm spell, he let the whole team stop work to watch Akbar Khan fly kites.

Both Debbie and Michelle had read *The Kite Runner,* which had led them to ply Akbar with questions about the Afghan tradition of kite fighting. Young men battled with kites that had sharp pieces of glass fused into the string, making their kites dive to cut each other's lines. Akbar told them it wasn't kite season — kite fighting tournaments were held in the dead of winter, when children stopped going to school because of the cold — but the soldiers begged him to show them how kite fighting was done anyway. He brought two kites to work; one was lime-green and aqua-blue, with long streamers, while the other was purple, fuchsia, and yellow. Akbar launched one of the kites. He stood in place, and tossed his kite in the air, flicked his wrists, and suddenly the kite was airborne — a bright flower of color leaping above the drab brown conexes. "We had a great day at the depot," Debbie wrote that evening. "Akbar brought 2 kites. We watched him fly it was really something. . . . One of the other boys said he knew how to fly so he + Akbar had a kite fight. They use glass string and he cut the other kite's string so quick we missed it. They don't run [but] stay still + use a lot of hand movements. We are going to have a Kite Day + learn how to fly it right maybe I can teach Jaylen!"

While explaining his country, Akbar had also taught them a lot about themselves, about what it meant to be Americans who traveled in foreign places. They could no longer bear the idea of leaving him behind. "He told Q. that he really loved his mother but I was like his mom here because I mother him I guess," wrote Debbie. "He's such a great person. We all want him to come to America! So innocent. So smart." They had asked to meet some of his relatives, but had been told by their superiors that it was not permissible. The following week, however, as they were driving back to Camp Phoenix, Akbar pointed out some men who were working in the fields. He said one of those men was his uncle, he was planting wheat. It was unusually early, but the weather had warmed so quickly that his uncle had decided to put seeds into the ground now, while the dirt was soft and wet. Stop the truck, said Patrick. Let's say a quick hello. They were violating all kinds of prohibitions. If anything had gone wrong, it would have been the end of Miller's career. But nothing went wrong. It was just Akbar's uncle, a man with a weathered face, one piercing brown eye, one eye that looked dead, and a long gray beard, who wore a set of cotton trousers with a long, dress-like top made from matching fabric. He was delighted to meet the Americans his nephew had told him about — why didn't they come over for tea. They doubted if they would be allowed to accept but told him they would love to have tea someday. "We had to stop + pull security," Debbie wrote later. "But I didn't feel scared it was like a natural thing to do. We can't go to Akbar's so I'm not sure what we will do about tea but it would be nice to have conversation. Akbar told him I was his American mama!"

The following week, Akbar wanted to feed the team a proper Afghan meal. Miller gave him the equivalent of twenty dollars and Akbar left to pick up the food at a restaurant in downtown Kabul. Hours passed and Akbar did not return. They trusted the young man completely, but wondered if something dire had happened. When he finally returned that afternoon he explained that his cab had gotten a flat tire, and he had helped the cabbie change the tire. He had brought kabob (lamb, in this case), *kafta* (ground meat mixed with parsley and onions), and *kabuli* (rice cooked with carrots, raisins, cabbage, and beef). The following day was Gary Jernigan's birthday, and because Debbie and Will knew that Gary had fallen in love with the colorful, noisy jingle trucks, they had asked Akbar to help them secure a special birthday gift: a set of jingle chains that Gary could affix to his own truck when he got back to Indiana. "I want some for the dogmobile," wrote Debbie enviously.

Akbar had a way of knowing what would touch another human being, and by this point he had touched them all. Even Miller. One day that spring, when they radioed to Camp Phoenix that they were on their way back to the post, they learned that there had been trouble on the road. Miller warned everyone to be ready. He pointed to the 9mm that he carried, in addition to his M4 assault rifle.

"If we have any trouble, I want you to take this gun," he told Akbar.

"Oh, no, Mr. Patrick," Akbar said. "I'm not allowed to do that. I can't touch a weapon."

"You will take the gun," Miller told him. "If it means you can save someone's life, you will take that gun."

Later on, Michelle and Debbie marveled at the exchange. It meant that Miller's trust in Akbar had become complete.

As the air grew warm, the soldiers at Camp Phoenix found their thoughts turning toward home. "Miller heard we will be home by July 4 they want to have a celebration at the Hoosier Dome or somewhere," wrote Debbie. "That's good!" Michelle wondered what going home would mean for her and Pete, for her and Ben. What was she going home to? Other soldiers had already disclosed their infidelities, and so many relationships — even some marriages — had broken apart that Debbie had come to believe she should not expect Jeff to remain faithful. She had written a letter telling Jeff he was free to do as he pleased. What she was trying to say was that she loved him, but did not expect him to remain celibate for an entire year. When Jeff got the letter, however, he read her words to mean that *she* no longer wished to remain faithful. He decided the honorable thing to do would be to move out of her house. Debbie heard from Ellen Ann that Jeff was packing his belongings because she had a new boyfriend. Debbie immediately phoned Jeff to set things straight and they talked for more than an hour. Jeff sent Debbie a pungent follow-up email in which he reminded her that he had served in the military, too:

> your my honey get out of the sun its frying your brain our something, it will be the same when you get home you forget i know where your comming from i did my time 20 years back maybe thats why we get along so good and every body else is just fuck in the head . . . im proud of you honey your the best so keep your little ass safe till you get back, maxx said hi and he cannt wait till you get home dads no fun . . . just one more thing if you talk to me reel nice when you get back i may let you suck my dick on the way home ha ha ha
>
> love you honey kiss kiss kiss

Jeff had proved himself to be constant. In some unexpected way, it felt as though the deployment had actually strengthened their relationship. Debbie mulled over the idea of a deeper commitment — but would a second yearlong deployment pull them apart? "I'm so thankful for my Honey . . . ," she wrote.

"Too many people here are having trouble back home. I am thinking about kidnapping him + maybe even getting married yea don't faint. But . . . there's the Iraq thing before I can retire." Meanwhile, Diamond or Maxx — Debbie longed for the company of a dog. In one of their phone calls, Jeff told her that he started her car, to make sure it was running fine, and gave Maxx the false impression that Debbie was home. "Jeff said Maxx went crazy in the house scratching the doors," she wrote in her diary. "When he let him out he ran around the car + looked in the windows for me. . . . He is getting old for his breed I hope he lasts a lot longer I sure miss him a bunch!"

On Friday, March 18, 2005, a huge hailstorm pounded the region. Black clouds obscured the sky, and lightning forked down. It rained again on Sunday. On Monday, it started raining so hard that Patrick decided it wasn't safe to make the drive to the depot. They waited out the torrential downpour inside the motor pool, listening to the rain make a drumroll on the metal roof. "Rained so hard we left hour later [than usual]," wrote Debbie. "It was really pouring sounded great!" Michelle was in a good mood, because she was about to go on vacation in a week's time — she and Ben Sawyer had decided to sneak away for a quick break in Florida before they both returned to visit their respective families. The armament team worked hard that day, and Miller let them leave work ahead of schedule. "Came back early we had pizza, me, Akbar, Miller, Kellogg, Michelle," wrote Debbie afterward. "It was fun. . . . Went to help Gary in supply for a little while + had happy hour. Well, it's almost Easter hard to believe another holiday down."

On Friday, March 25, 2005, two days before Easter, Michelle Fischer and Ben Sawyer left in a convoy for Bagram, hoping to catch a flight out the following day. On Saturday, March 26, another convoy left Camp Phoenix, headed in a different direction. A group of soldiers from the 151st Infantry Regiment — another part of the 76th Infantry Brigade — left to scout out a new location for a shooting range for the Afghan soldiers they were training. They were about thirty miles south of Kabul when one of the vehicles exploded. It was a road the soldiers had traveled over and over again — a road they thought safe. The Taliban claimed credit, saying they had placed a bomb by the road, but military investigators determined instead that the foul weather had caused significant erosion, probably unearthing a piece of Afghanistan's lethal past — a long-buried Russian land mine. With brutal efficiency, the device had killed all four of the truck's passengers: Todd Fiscus, thirty-six years old; Brett Hershey, age twenty-three; Michael Hiester, thirty-three; and Kyle Snyder, twenty-one. Debbie wrote:

> This was not the best day for Phoenix. We lost four of our soldiers due to a land mine. . . . With all the rain + snow there have been a lot of mines uncovered that have been buried for many years. It's so close to going home but we still need to be alert. There's a memorial service tomorrow I will attend. A really sad Easter Sunday.

Fiscus and Hiester had been close friends; they had served together in Bosnia before being deployed to Afghanistan. Hiester had been a volunteer firefighter; he was married and had two children. Fiscus was also married and also had two children. The younger pair, Hershey and Snyder, were also close friends; they had roomed together. Snyder had been raised by a single mother who could not afford to send him to college, and he had signed up for the National Guard to obtain college tuition. He had been planning to enroll at Indiana State University in the fall. Hershey was already enrolled at Indiana University.

The loss of four colleagues at one time knocked the other soldiers sideways. Because Hershey, Snyder, Hiester, and Fiscus had belonged to the 151st, their closest alliances were there; they were not as well known to the 113th Support Battalion. Yet everybody who was part of the 76th Infantry Brigade got swept up in the sense of loss. "We lost four brothers," Karen Shaw told the *Indy Star.* "Even though we weren't directly related, they are your brothers. They are your friends. They are who make you laugh. They are the only people you have in the midst of absolutely nowhere." Debbie went to evening Mass on Easter Sunday, even though the service was in French. She did not know what the priest was saying but recognized key moments in the familiar routine. Questions beset her mind. How many times over the past few months had she driven over a land mine? One that was buried just deep enough? And why had she been spared? It pained Debbie to think of how young the soldiers were. They should have had their whole lives ahead of them — two of them were only in their twenties. And the other two had children to raise. I've had my fun, thought Debbie; I've raised my daughter. Why not me? It would have been better, and I would have been willing to go.

Desma had known three of the soldiers who died. Working at the shop — it was the post's central hub, and Desma talked to everyone. Michael Hiester had belonged to the post's firefighting team and had helped sweep the post for fire hazards. Every time he had come through their tent, he had told Desma patiently that she had to take down the blanket hanging around her bed; she always put it back up again after he left. She had watched Brett Hershey play in the post's basketball league. But it was Kyle Snyder, the youngest, whom she knew best. Back at Camp Atterbury, he had flirted with Mary Bell. One night, over in the Romanian part of Camp Phoenix, Desma had bumped into Snyder. Neither one of them was supposed to be there, but it was fun because they served booze. Snyder was hanging out around a fire with some foreign soldiers. They had talked for a couple of hours. It had been something different, a break in the routine.

Snyder had just gotten back from leave. He had gone to Australia, and that seemed noteworthy to Desma — that he had squeezed in a final hurrah. Australia struck Desma as a once-in-a-lifetime kind of trip. It must have made him happy, she thought. It was not unusual to skip going home, because going home was hard. Soldiers who returned from a trip to Indiana came back saying you had to deal with everybody else's emotional needs, never got around to your own. Many of them chose to grab some R&R in a faraway place rather than confront the heartache of a reunion followed too swiftly by another farewell. They wanted to go home too badly to go home for just a little while. Desma had done that herself. She applauded Snyder for going to Australia, even though it meant that he had not seen his mother. You had to live for the moment, she thought. Because you never knew when it was all going to end.

Everybody in the 76th lined up in formation for the memorial service. Four sets of boots, four helmets, and four rifles stood on a platform. It was early in the morning and the weapons cast long shadows. Dog tags hung from the trigger mechs. Boots, guns, dog tags, helmets — almost a soldier. All that was missing were the men. They filed past to say good-bye, soldier by soldier. It hit the entire brigade pretty hard, the idea that they were not so safe after all, the idea that the war could reach into their ranks and claim any one of them in an eyeblink.

Three of the coffins went back to Indiana. Hershey's parents had moved to Pennsylvania, and his coffin went to that state instead. Out on the tarmac near the cargo building at Indianapolis International Airport, members of the Indiana National Guard wearing blue dress uniforms carried one coffin at a time off the airplane. There were no speeches, nothing was said. Snyder was first, and they carried him past his mother and over to a gray hearse. They carried Hiester to another gray hearse. Fiscus's father saluted the coffin that held the body of his son. The only sound that could be heard was the deep rumble of jets taking off and landing all around them.

People back in Indiana seemed inclined to believe that the Taliban could strike down their soldiers; it was hard to grasp how a land mine from a previous war could have caused such a catastrophe. But everyone who had spent the past eight months at Camp Phoenix found it plausible that the ground might have betrayed them. They had seen children missing legs, or hands, or other body parts. They had watched a boy run across a field and nearly die. And they thought of the Taliban as a ragtag sort of enemy. In either case — land mine or IED — Afghanistan had reminded them that it was a dangerous place. But they could not go home yet; they had several months left in the deployment.

6
SEA WORLD

Michelle never saw the empty boots, she was not present for the memorial ceremony. By the time the service took place, she and Ben Sawyer were in Kuwait. They had heard about the explosion while they were still at Bagram. Michelle had caught sight of Desma and Mary's platoon sergeant, looking harried. Why was he wearing his ballistic vest in the middle of the day when there were no sirens blaring? Four guys just died, he told them curtly. There were two theories: the Taliban or the rain.

Michelle thought about how much rain had fallen, and figured it was likely the deluges could have caused some long-buried land mine to migrate. Still, for weeks afterward, she found herself wondering if the official story was fiction. Truth seemed elusive in a war zone, and both sides had motivation for their theories. Could the US military be using false narratives as well as armor and bullets? She didn't want to think so, but she had read a lot of left-wing periodicals. Maybe her commanders wanted to blame the weather to make the Taliban seem less powerful. In the years that followed, charts of violent incidents would show that during the months of March, April, May, and June 2005, there was a sudden spike in the use of IEDs across Afghanistan. That year's fighting season was when the war took a darker turn, in other words. Later — when it would become clear that Afghan insurgents had gotten much better at building bombs that particular spring — it would seem more likely the Taliban might have played a role, but by then the families had already been told the official story about the rain.

Meanwhile, Michelle and Ben had concocted a false story of their own. Both of them were expecting to return to stressful scenarios in Indiana. While they were still in Afghanistan, Michelle had called her father from Ben's cell phone and he had let her know that he had been arrested for dealing methamphetamine (although he would later plead guilty to a lesser charge, possession of methamphetamine). He and a friend had been busted for running an illegal meth lab on his property, according to Michelle. He had needed money for bail and Michelle had sent him several hundred dollars. She was dreading her return both because she would have to confront the sordid mess her father had gotten into and because she was planning to tell Pete the truth about the affair.

And Ben Sawyer told Michelle that he had been watching his bank account be drained from afar, presumably because his wife was spending the money he had been earning. Because he had been amassing combat pay, he kept depositing significant amounts into the account, and he had been spending hardly anything, yet Michelle got the impression that the money kept melting away. Ben told Michelle that his wife had supplied vague answers when he had asked where the money was going, but his friends had shared their suspicion that in his absence Amanda had grown reliant on OxyContin. The military had required that Ben give his wife access to his earnings, to make sure she would be able to support their children while he was gone — it was standard practice — and he had no authority to take that access away from Amanda as long as they remained married, because she and the children were his dependents. By this point, however, his wife seemed to have spent tens of thousands of dollars, and Ben told Michelle that he feared much of the money might have gone to pay for drugs.

Neither of the two was looking forward to going home — although they both felt compelled to return — so they had lied to their families about the duration of their leave and said they had been given only ten days, when in truth they had been given two weeks. This allowed them to steal five days for themselves, five days when they would answer to nobody, and not wear uniforms, and not have to confront any of the difficulties waiting for them. They took military transport all the way to Louisville, Kentucky, but did not leave the airport. They walked through international customs, went to a different terminal, and caught a commercial flight to Orlando, Florida. They stayed at a fancy resort, ate big meals, drank a lot of booze, went shopping, and lazed on the beach. Michelle looked spectacular in her bikini. Then they went to Sea World. It was free for military personnel, and Michelle, the nature lover, had always wanted to go. Ben was happy to go anywhere with Michelle as long as it meant that he could defer the impending confrontation with his wife. They saw beluga whales and bottlenose dolphins and sea lions and manatees. They saw schools of tropical fish — silver, yellow, orange, green — that whirled in stunning unison. They did not like the crowds, but as long as they were looking at sea creatures they had a sense of being transported to a place where nothing bad would happen. Then Michelle and Ben flew back to Louisville and feigned an arrival straight from Afghanistan.

Michelle told nobody about the five stolen

days in Florida, not even Veronica, who met her at the airport. While they drove to Evansville — past gray fields stubbled with last year's corn, as a gray sky hugged the gray landscape — Michelle did tell Veronica everything else. She described how Ben had shadowed her, and how other men had called her by name even though she did not know who they were, how she had slept with Ben by accident, and how it just kept happening. Michelle described how cold it had been and how warm Ben had kept her. As Veronica sped along the highway, Michelle speculated about whether the new relationship might continue after the deployment. Veronica just listened. She did not show surprise or criticism. For that, Michelle was grateful. She felt unburdened for the first time in months.

Veronica drove her straight to Pete's apartment. He still lived in the same place, the one they had shared. Michelle was not naturally a deceitful person — she was needy, but not untruthful — and hated herself for hiding the affair for such a long time. Now that she was seeing Pete face-to-face, she could think of nothing else except telling him about Ben Sawyer, but it was late by the time she arrived and when she walked into the apartment she found Pete and Halloween asleep in bed. So she just climbed into bed with them and fell asleep, too. She was home, she thought, as she drifted off. In the morning, she told Pete everything. He shied away from the subject of her infidelity, as if it disturbed him too much to discuss, and just said in a tone of wondering dismay that she had changed in so many ways he felt as though he hardly recognized her. Where was the Michelle he knew? Even her body was different — she had grown so muscular. Michelle bristled. She was proud of her body, she told Pete defensively. She had worked hard to look like this. You've become vain, Pete said. And you don't even smell the same.

They got into an epic fight. Michelle stormed out the back door and sat down on the chipped concrete steps. She hunched over to make the tightness in her middle go away, but it was a stubborn kind of tension. After a while, Pete came out and sat down beside her.

"I'll forgive you," he said. "I'll forget all about this, if you'll just stay with me."

"I can't," Michelle told him. "I love him."

She spent the rest of the week at her mother's place.

Irene had moved again while Michelle was gone and was now living in the middle of nowhere, without a telephone. Her half sister Tammy and her two kids were living there, too. Michelle had no way to call and let them know when she was going to arrive, so she just showed up. Her mother was reading in the bedroom, Tammy was occupied in the kitchen, and her nephew Cody was playing by himself, wearing only a diaper. "Hi, Michelle," Cody said brightly when she walked into the trailer, as if she had been gone for only a few hours. Tammy gave Michelle a tight hug and whispered to be quiet so they could surprise their mother. Irene melted at the sight of Michelle.

Later Colleen and some other friends took Michelle to a male strip club and made sure that she got spanked onstage. It somehow seemed appropriate at the time — how else did you celebrate having stayed alive? She did not know what she actually needed, so she went along for the ride.

At various points during the week Michelle returned to the apartment where Pete was living, because she needed some of her belongings, or because Colleen and Veronica lived upstairs and she just happened to be in the building. Pete had taken the entire week off work, expecting to be able to spend it with Michelle, and instead she had dropped that bombshell on him. Each time she returned to see how he was doing, she found him sitting on the sofa in his boxers, in a catatonic state. She did not want to be responsible for putting a human being in that position so she told herself that Pete had conflated her abandonment of him with his mother's decision to leave him for an entire year when he was just a child. And who knows, maybe there was some truth in that explanation, or maybe she was just using it to make herself feel better about an awful, awful thing.

Strangely, the person she found it easiest to be around was her father. He took her to PJs and got her drunk and then they spent a day drinking together in his party trailer with relatives on his side of the family. Her father had parked a second trailer beside the trailer in which he lived, and they used it for any kind of celebration. For once there was no conflict, and it was easy. Her father and her uncle and her other half sister Cindy all seemed to look at her differently — with a rosy glow of appreciation. It had never been like that with her father before. He had always taken her for granted, but somehow she had become special.

Michelle saw Ben Sawyer again back at the airport in Louisville. He said his wife was down to ninety pounds, and his kids had wandered into and out of the house essentially uncared for while she lay sprawled across the sofa. The house had smelled bad, and there had been dirty clothes mounded in the bathtub. They got stuck in Kuwait for several days, and arrived back at Bagram almost three weeks after they had left, in the middle of April. Fighting season was in full swing and they spent the night in Bagram's transient housing area, lying side by side on cots in a cavernous, domed tent, filled with an ocean of cots occupied by innumerable other soldiers, all wearing Kevlar helmets and ballistic vests, listening to RPGs explode around them. Michelle listened to the big booms, crying as quietly as she knew how. She was afraid for her life, and she had forgotten what that felt like — it was as though she had never before been to a war zone. During those nights when she had done Mad Libs with Desma, she had grown numb to the idea that an RPG might snuff her out, but the women who shared her tent were not with her, and Michelle felt alone in the sea of strangers. She had never been through an RPG attack without Desma before.

Only after they returned to Camp Phoenix did Michelle finally realize the enormity of what she had missed: the four deaths had fundamentally altered the atmosphere at the post. There was a shared sadness in the air and she was out of place, out of step with everyone else. While they had been grieving, she had been at Sea World; in retrospect, the vacation that she and Ben had stolen seemed selfish, wrong. Michelle felt like a stranger in her own tent.

While Michelle had been gone, Debbie had been forced to confront her own mortality. Shortly after Michelle and Ben had left, Debbie had gotten a cold, which had turned into a sinus infection. She had gone to see a medic, who did a routine examination and discovered that Debbie's blood pressure had jumped to 155/99. The last time the medics had taken a reading, her blood pressure had been 110/80, in the normal range. She had a mild case of hypertension. The medics conferred among themselves and decided to monitor Debbie's blood pressure daily. "I've never had any problems so I'm supposed to go back the next 3 days around the same time," Debbie wrote in her diary. "Didn't go anywhere just laid around don't really feel like too much." In the days that followed, however, Debbie's blood pressure went up, not down. She scrawled with frustration: "Went to get it checked around 3:30 it was higher today 158/102 what's up he said if it's still high tomorrow medicine I guess my 50s are not going to be nice to me."

Debbie spent hours crocheting, hoping the soothing activity would lower her blood pressure. It was almost time for the baby's birth. "I talked to mom EA is one and half cent dilated but could stay that way for a while," Debbie wrote. "She's two weeks away." She finished Jaylen's blanket. "It doesn't look too bad now to mail it off." She was hoping the blood pressure issue would resolve of its own accord but when she saw the medics again she learned otherwise. "Didn't have as much headache so I thought maybe it would be better but it was worse I don't get it. It was 158/110 today." The medics started Debbie on blood pressure medication. Afterward, Debbie cheered herself up by going down to Morale, Welfare, and Recreation with Gretchen and some other friends. They ordered a pizza at Ciano's and then went to the new Dairy Queen that had just opened up on the post. It was comforting to linger over a beverage that reminded her of home. "Orange Julius was great haven't had one since they left the mall," Debbie wrote.

The group gossiped about the fact that two women in the battalion had learned they were pregnant. Living in such close quarters, they had few secrets, and many people knew that a married woman from Charlie Company had conceived a child with her husband while she was home on leave, and an unmarried woman from Bravo Company had conceived a child with someone else on post. Ten days later, the young woman from Bravo Company left for Germany, supposedly to seek treatment for bowel trouble. "Heard [name deleted] was sent to Bagram for bowel trouble but not!" When the young woman returned, looking wan and strained, she turned to Debbie for consolation; it was always Debbie, she mothered them all. The young woman confessed that she had found reentry into the gossipy world of Camp Phoenix excruciating. Debbie confided something she rarely discussed: she had once gotten an abortion herself, more than twenty years earlier.

She got back today she feels strange like everyone is judging her I told her it was her business anyway no one else's. Her dad went to Germany to be with her for a while it was a wise decision she just doesn't know it yet! It was hard for me + I still have hard feelings every once in a while but it was the right one!

Encircled by younger women, on the verge of becoming a grandmother, and feeling powerless as she watched her blood pressure rise, Debbie faced the unavoidable truth that she was aging. So were her parents; that month, her father turned seventy-nine. She called him on his birthday; they had always been close. She wrote wistfully in her diary that at least she would be home the following year, when he turned eighty. Becoming older herself confounded Debbie. She still found herself attracted to men who were half her age. ("Some people were visiting from Kabul University boy was there a cutie I've been here too long he looked a lot like Keanu Reeves . . . he was gorgeous.") Yet her body was betraying her in a fashion as elemental as the way her blood ran through her veins. She wondered about the possible reasons for her hypertension: Was it age? Could it be the altitude? The stress of the deployment?

Her blood pressure varied but stubbornly remained higher than normal, despite the medication. During her daily visits to the medical area, Debbie grew attached to one doctor in particular, a tall, blue-eyed, sandy-haired medic who had an attentive bedside manner. During one of their consultations, the doctor noticed Debbie's tall and slender build and asked about her diet. Was she eating enough food? Debbie said she was. Drinking excessive amounts of alcohol can raise blood pressure to unhealthy levels, but when the doctor asked, "You haven't been drinking while you're here, have you?" Debbie said, "No, sir." The doctor changed her medication. The following day, Debbie felt worse, not better. "Well I go back today to check the BP I think it's still up I have a constant headache + I felt like I was in a fog last night + this morning," she wrote. Indeed, her blood pressure had climbed even higher, to 162/99. Several days later, however, her blood pressure dropped to 138/100. The medics continued to monitor her closely, but they were encouraged — the new medication seemed to be working.

Shortly after starting the second medication, Debbie went down to supply for an impromptu party after being tipped off that other soldiers had made a run to Supreme Foods. The store was part of a chain founded by a former army food service worker; it sold liquor as well as groceries, and had outlets near American bases in the Balkans, Sudan,

Somalia, Iraq, and Afghanistan. Soldiers from Camp Phoenix had discovered a branch in Kabul. The armament team had begun radioing in false departure times from the ANA depot or the KMTC so they could stop there to stock up on liquor. "The boys got to make a Supreme Run for the First Sergeant," Debbie wrote in her diary. "Me + Terry went down around 3:00 started having fun early too early skipped dinner don't remember coming home. Got sick felt like shit most all the day not like my normal hangovers." The following day she went back and allowed herself only one alcoholic beverage, but soon she was drinking at her usual rate. She shrugged off her brush with ill health. "Okay my BP 130/78 so I think that's fine," she wrote. "I think it was a fluke with the sinus + throat thing. I'll finish this med + then have it checked + see about going off of it in case I don't need it!"

When Michelle Fischer returned that week, Debbie greeted the young woman with her usual stream of chatty affirmation, wanting to know how everything had gone, buoying Michelle up by saying she had done the right thing, telling Pete in person. Debbie mentioned dealing with some issues related to blood pressure but quickly changed the subject. Only in the pages of her diary did Debbie reveal worry, fear, anxiety, or dependence; otherwise she concealed her vulnerabilities. Debbie had missed Michelle while she was gone. She enjoyed the girl's liveliness, her daily dramas, and her compelling way of putting it all into words, entertaining everyone in the process. Although Debbie thought it was her job to take care of Michelle, who struck her as too young to be in Afghanistan, oddly she found herself less anxious when she heard the girl's bell-like laugh peal out again as they fixed another batch of AK-47s. Patrick Miller had gone home on leave to visit his wife and baby, who was now six months old, and had left Will Hargreaves in charge of the armament team. Will was not a hard-driving taskmaster, and Debbie and Michelle enjoyed his more relaxed style. The air grew mild, and wildflowers carpeted the hills around them. "The weather has been beautiful I'm getting spoiled working outside every day!" Debbie wrote. She picked some of the wildflowers and stuck them into the pages of her diary. Meanwhile Michelle and Desma bought some hash and got stoned in the tent, hiding under their bedclothes, blowing the smoke into dryer sheets in an attempt to hide the smell. They thought they were very clever, but Caroline Hill came in and said, "You know I can smell that, right?"

When Patrick Miller returned he got them all working double time again. He kept meticulous notes about their progress, including a precise count of the number of assault rifles they had fixed — he proudly told the armament crew that by his tally, they had overhauled almost twenty thousand AK-47s so far, and he thought they could do twenty-two thousand before their deployment was over. They could feel their time together drawing to a close. At the end of April, Miller told them that some of them would start going home in June and the rest would follow in July. At the same time, Miller cautioned the soldiers to remain vigilant. They all took a mandatory class on improvised explosive devices, because of the frequency with which they were now being used across Afghanistan.

The soldiers were exhausted and raw, and the final months of the deployment unfolded messily. In quick succession, the post endured two scandals. A woman from Charlie Company had been having an affair with a lieutenant; unwisely, they had made a sex video, which showed her performing fellatio. The video passed from tent to tent via jump drives, and everyone watched the spectacle. Only days after word of the video spread across the post, an Alpha girl from Evansville accused a soldier from Bravo Company of rape. "[Name deleted] supposedly was raped by [name deleted] at a b-day party at one of the connexes," wrote Debbie. "She woke up + he was on top of her." The young woman was viewed as unreliable by her peers, however, whereas the man she accused was well liked. The rape charge ignited a stormy controversy, with most of the troops lining up behind the accused man. There was little support for the young woman's position, partly because she had been drunk. Desma Brooks told others that the male soldier who was involved in the incident had once made a pass at her, and had been pretty pushy, but after she firmly told him no, he respected her wishes. She speculated that maybe the young woman had been too drunk to say no.

While all of the female soldiers in the battalion were aware there was a risk of getting raped while living on the post, the soldiers did not yet fully appreciate the extent to which sexual assault had become epidemic across the two war theaters. Like the use of improvised explosive devices, "military sexual trauma" was on the rise — eventually as many as one-third of the women who served in Iraq and Afghanistan would report having been subjected to a sexual assault of some kind during their deployments. Statistically, in other words, it was unlikely that the 113th Support Battalion could have been in Afghanistan for a full year without a serious assault. However, Desma and Michelle both felt greater fear of the male soldiers outside of their mixed-gender battalion than those in it. They maintained they received much worse harassment from regular army soldiers, or from Guard soldiers who served in all-male units, compared with soldiers who were used to having a significant number of female colleagues. The soldier accused of rape was ultimately convicted of adultery, according to people who knew him in Bravo Company. The other soldiers treated the young woman who had lodged the accusation as a turncoat; the idea was that a loyal soldier would not do that to another member of the same battalion. Her commander assigned her to the third shift of local national watch for the rest of the deployment. Nobody else who had been caught drinking had been made to work nights for such a long time. Michelle wondered, what exactly was the woman being punished for?

Even while the rest of the battalion was struggling to understand what had taken place between the Alpha girl and the man she had accused of rape, Debbie became preoccupied with the fact that Ellen Ann was about to give birth. Doctors had begun monitoring Ellen Ann closely, because her blood pressure had started to climb, indicating the possibility of preeclampsia. As the baby's arrival drew near, Debbie found her thoughts always turning to her daughter. "I may try tonight to reach her," she wrote in her diary. "Hope everything is okay!" Four days later, Ellen Ann was still at only one and a half centimeters. Debbie wrote, "She is a week out so could happen any time."

A few days later, Debbie spoke with her daughter, and Ellen Ann said her cervix was now three centimeters dilated. She was experiencing mild contractions. The doctor had said he wanted to induce the birth on the following morning if she didn't go into full labor that evening. Ellen Ann had packed her things and put the baby seat into the car. Debbie felt anxious and far from home. Gretchen Pane loaned Debbie her cell phone, which Debbie took to work with her the following day, but she got no news from Indiana. That night she used Gretchen's phone to get the latest update.

> I called the kids + they're in her room at the hospital. They gave her the meds + broke her water. Her dad came I'm glad I know that will make her feel a little better. She is having contractions + a lot more pain. They are bringing her an epidural soon but it still could be a while. I'm afraid to lay down + I am hating life about now by not being there but she has a lot of support but hopefully she is missing me a little bit. I can't wait to hear her voice. I bought some cigars. Swisher Sweets.

Unable to sleep, Debbie called Ellen Ann again at 3:30 a.m. in Afghanistan and learned that her daughter had received the epidural.

Three hours later, when it was about 7:00 a.m. in Kabul, Debbie got the phone call she had been waiting for: Ellen Ann had just given birth to a healthy baby girl, seven pounds, fifteen ounces. "Had problems in canal her shoulders were too big almost had to take her C-sect but gave one last hard push + she did it. . . . I probably should of been there."

Ellen Ann said the baby wanted to sleep all the time, and she had to wake her up to feed. Debbie said she had to do the same with Ellen Ann. Jeff had gone to the hospital, which made Debbie glad because it felt as though Jeff had stood in for her. "The kids are great + Jaylen is doing fine with Mom-Dad in her room," wrote Debbie in her diary. "I might have pics tomorrow. Well I haven't been to bed yet too excited so I need to try + sleep."

The next morning, Debbie checked her email and was thrilled to see the first pictures of her granddaughter. "She is a beauty looks like EA with those fat cheeks of hers," Debbie wrote. She bought a carved wooden chest at the bazaar and mailed it to Jaylen; it seemed romantic to send such an exotic gift from halfway around the globe. Someday she would tell her granddaughter that she had been doing important work in Afghanistan at the hour of her birth. Bravo Company surprised Debbie with a celebration to mark the occasion:

> My what a great night. A Granny Party for me. . . . I was so surprised. . . . [W]hen we got to MWR we walked in + I noticed it was crowded but still didn't get it. . . . So I stopped looked back again + everyone was clapping taking pictures + I started forward + they said this is for you + I said for me? A Granny/Jaylen shower party. So I had a blonde moment. But it was so nice because they know I would like to of been home but it was nice of my family here to do something so nice. It really was great!

And then it was May. They still had to survive two more months but it already felt like summer. Debbie asked Akbar to build her a flower box, which she hung outside the window of her B-Hut. An unexpected hailstorm filled the flower box with hailstones, but her seeds sprouted anyway, small tufts of green poking up from the black dirt, signs of new beginning. Debbie started playing softball in the evenings, instead of going down to supply. The battalion also began the monumental task of packing up to go home — some soldiers were going to depart in six weeks, others in nine, and the final group in twelve, but the first conexes full of gear were going to ship out that month. The soldiers combed the bazaar for souvenirs: Michelle bought marble tea sets; Desma bought a blue burka; Debbie bought rugs, scarves, jewelry, gifts for everyone she knew.

The act of packing up unsettled Debbie. "I'm leery about going home," she confessed to her diary. "Don't know why I am [not] ready I just feel like I haven't been here long enough yet I'm sure next month will seem different." It was not the idea of returning to Jeff that felt off-putting; she longed to embrace him. They were planning to rent a hotel room to celebrate their reunion. "He also said that a hotel would be an expensive 5 min but I told him we would just do it again + again + again." And she could not wait to meet her granddaughter. She could not put her finger on what was troubling; she wondered if perhaps she did not feel ready to leave because she had not bought enough souvenirs. But it could have been something to do with taking off the uniform and becoming the manager of a beauty salon again; maybe it had to do with self-worth, and the ways in which she felt more valuable as a soldier.

On Mother's Day, Akbar Khan told Debbie that she was like a real mother to him and gave her a gold watch set with cubic zirconia. "It's really nice," Debbie wrote afterward. "I will be able to wear it at work it's very dressy. He is such a sweetie. Florida group better treat him right." Florida would take their place just as they had followed Oklahoma. They all wondered how Akbar would be treated after they departed. Would others appreciate him as they had grown to do? Meanwhile, Akbar struck them as unusually withdrawn. Concerned, Debbie asked what was wrong, but he said it was nothing. Michelle also noticed his distance, but also failed to draw him out. Maybe he was worried about his father, Debbie thought; maybe there had been some sort of setback with his health. Then one morning, as they waited together by the motor pool, about to start their workday, Akbar turned to face them. "I need to talk to you," he told the team. "I know you've been asking me what's bothering me, what's wrong. I want to explain: I have to get married."

It was his mother's idea; she had selected the young woman. He didn't want to get married, but was trying to resign himself to the plan. The rest of the armament team knew that their translator hoped to return to school for a graduate degree; complying would mean that Akbar and his new wife would move in with his mother, and instead he would work to support the extended clan. They objected, saying he should not accede to his mother's wishes. "This is what we do here," Akbar said. "My mother is getting older, and my sister will probably leave the home soon — she will get married herself, and she won't be there to help my mother. And that leaves only the boys, my younger brothers, and it's not their place to help in the home. So the eldest son needs to take a wife."

The team got into two vehicles and drove to the ANA depot, and opened up another box of AK-47s. The conversation about Akbar's predicament continued. They could not believe he was planning to marry a woman he had not even met. They asked how his mother had arranged his match and he said she would have sent a basket full of significant gifts, a certain kind of fruit, a particular type of candy. At one point Akbar mentioned that his mother had selected a young woman with a stellar reputation — her sister's daughter.

"Akbar, you can't do that," Debbie interjected. "That's your first cousin."

"This is what we do here," Akbar replied.

"No, Akbar! You can't marry your first cousin," Debbie insisted. "You'll have idiot children."

He glowered at her, fell silent. After a moment, he said, "Mama, I have to tell you something. My parents are first cousins."

In any event, they all understood that the marriage meant the end of Akbar's dreams. His mother had made all of the plans from Pakistan; her sister still lived in Afghanistan, in the city of Mazar-i-Sharif, and it had been arranged that Akbar would meet his cousin there soon. They would meet at their own engagement party. None of the others could believe what Akbar was saying; they had heard of arranged marriages, of course, but it was another thing entirely to watch a young person they cherished bend to his mother's will. "Me, personally, being the same age as him, I mean, it just blew my mind to think about if my mother or my father got to choose, no discussion, no anything," Michelle would say later. They had come to the crux of the difference between their two cultures — the Americans kept saying things that spoke to their individualism, while Akbar kept trying to explain that for Afghans the basic orientation was communal.

The armament team viewed Akbar's forthcoming marriage as a disaster. He was not calling it that himself, but they sensed his devastation, and they responded as if a battle buddy had gotten caught in crossfire. They were a team, and you did not leave a fellow soldier behind. How could they save Akbar? Patrick Miller decided that if Akbar needed to get married, he should marry one of them. "Akbar, you should marry Michelle!" urged Miller. "Then you'll be able to move to the United States." This struck everybody else as a good idea; Debbie loved Akbar, and she loved Michelle, it delighted her to think of the two of them getting married. Akbar looked at Michelle, and Michelle looked at Akbar. They had both been feeling an unspoken attraction to one another, and now it had been spoken, but not in the way that either of them had imagined.

"I would do that for you," Michelle said.

Akbar shook his head. "She's not a Muslim," he told everyone else. "It's not allowed for us to get married."

Later, when they spoke privately, Akbar confessed to Michelle that he had strong feelings for her but he would not let her marry him out of pity. She didn't quite know how to respond — her life was already so complicated — so she just reiterated that they could get married if it would be helpful. He said no.

For the rest of the month, the armament team became fixated on Akbar's dilemma. He kept them apprised of every development. First his mother was traveling from Pakistan to help with the engagement party. Debbie wrote:

> Akbar's mom is coming today to talk with him about getting married but he's not ready + doesn't know how to tell her because of traditions + culture. It's even his 1st cousin which makes it worse. Michelle + I told him he could have idiot kids. He is so afraid of hurting his mom's feelings + if he refuses he is shunned by the family. I told him he will have to come to America then. . . . Michelle said she would marry him so we could get him to the States!

Akbar left for Mazar-i-Sharif on May 19, 2005. He spoke to Debbie by phone shortly after the party. "Akbar has pictures she did not wear a burka I'm so glad that he would not say if she was pretty or not!" Debbie wrote. Several days later, when Akbar returned to Camp Phoenix, the armament team peppered him with questions. Jason Kellogg accompanied them to the depot that day, too. Akbar explained that his fiancée had been chaperoned at all times by her brother; at the party, Akbar and his fiancée had been seated at opposite ends of a crowded room. They had been able to see each other but could not talk. Afterward, however, Akbar's fiancée had been given a cell phone that her brother monitored. Akbar could call, and if the brother granted his permission, speak to his fiancée by phone. The armament team clamored to see what his wife-to-be looked like. Akbar took out a photograph and they all passed it around. They saw a young woman with a round face and masses of dark hair, who was wearing a brilliant blue dress.

"She's a knockout!" Patrick Miller pronounced.

"She's really pretty, Akbar," Debbie confirmed.

"Well, how big are her boobs?" Jason Kellogg wanted to know. "You got to look at the whole package."

"I don't know," said Akbar stiffly.

"Akbar! You have to try her out," Kellogg advised. "It's like test-driving a car before you buy it."

"No, no, no," said Akbar.

Michelle told Kellogg to shut up.

Eventually the armament team accepted that Akbar was not going to marry Michelle, and that he was going to do as his mother asked. "Poor Akbar still getting married to his cousin we can't help him," wrote Debbie at the end of May.

The first soldiers left in June. The armament team found it painful to separate from Akbar, so they said good-bye twice. Patrick Miller came up with the idea of staging a formal ceremony to thank the translator for his work; they asked the company's XO to present him with a certificate of appreciation. They held the ceremony at Camp Phoenix on June 7, 2005. "We gave Akbar his certificate, he was really surprised," Debbie wrote afterward. But it did not seem like enough. He had given them so much — knives, a watch, jingle truck chains, traditional Afghan meals, a moment with his uncle, the sight of those kites, and most of all, an understanding of this place, a sense of its deeper meaning. Michelle had the idea to buy Akbar a computer as a parting gift, and found a refurbished fourteen-inch Compaq Presario laptop at the PX. The entire team pitched in. They gave the laptop to Akbar as they stood together by the gate to Camp Phoenix, when they were seeing him for the very last time. "Busy now getting everyone ready to leave," wrote Debbie. "We gave Akbar his computer he was speechless. Put our addresses + pictures on it."

Akbar Khan valued the gift more than the team could know, because it opened up a new world. And it allowed them to stay in touch. "The financial status I had at that time was not really good," Akbar would say later. "I was struggling with financial stability. The first computer ever that I owned was the one that was gifted by the team to me — think about that, how much would that mean to me. In Afghanistan, we have this mentality, if a person helped me stand up in a certain area, no matter how much I achieve or what I become out of that help, still it is them who should always be thanked. I might go to a college and study professionally with computers, software, and hardware. But I cannot forget about that. According to our society, if I purchased a computer for every single one of them I cannot pay off that. It's a debt on my soul."

Akbar vowed to come to the United States to visit, but nobody knew if this would transpire. It seemed implausible — but Akbar had grit. They watched him walk through the gate of Camp Phoenix, asking each other if they would ever see the young Afghan again.

And what of his country? They wanted to believe the year they had spent in Afghanistan had made some kind of difference, that they had done some good. That all those weapons would be used to further some cause in which they could believe. And they wanted to have faith that the other relationships they had forged here would also continue. As she watched Akbar walk away, Michelle wore a new silver band on her ring finger. She had wanted a souvenir that would memorialize the time she had spent in this place, and she had asked Akbar to accompany her to the bazaar, to help her buy the ring. He had translated for her the words she had wanted inscribed on the inside of the band. "My heart belongs to Ben," the ring said in Dari, in a beautiful flowing script that she could not read. Those were the words she would wear next to her skin when she got home. It was her attempt to fix things in place, to secure this moment, to create something permanent out of all this change as she stood at the gate that divided Akbar's world from hers, on the brink of yet another journey.

■ ■ ■ ■

III
Indiana, 2005–2007

■ ■ ■ ■

1
Welcome Home, Dad

Michelle Fischer had forgotten that anywhere could be so green. Bright emerald grass and the pale lime floating leafiness of trees and the dark olive profusion of bushes, it astonished her to see such fecundity. They were riding on a school bus from Indianapolis International Airport to a National Guard armory located ten miles away, on the west side of the city. It was the middle of the day. The school bus had been painted white, and its windows were latched halfway open. Michelle was struck with wonder at the smell of summer: humid, verdant, sweet. Had it always smelled so fragrant in Indiana, and she had simply never noticed? The trees seemed larger than trees had before. They towered over the highway, pressing forward with startling abundance. She caught sight of rows of young corn, still ripening and not yet ready for harvest.

Michelle had left Afghanistan with Mary Bell on a C-17 that had taken off from Kabul

International Airport. They had handed over their assault rifles and ballistic vests right before they boarded the plane — rifles carefully counted and put into one box, vests carefully counted and put into another, and the boxes loaded onto conexes. As the plane had taken off, Michelle had folded over and put her head down between her knees and wept, stricken at being separated from Ben Sawyer, who was returning later. There had been no sit-down toilets on the plane; male soldiers had urinated into hip-level funnels built into the side of the craft, while female soldiers had squatted over a bucket behind a curtain. The curtain had offered inadequate coverage, and Michelle had waited until Kurdistan, where she had said, "Somebody who lives here has to sprint me to a bathroom." They had changed planes several times in various countries before they had touched down in Indiana. The rest of the battalion would follow, returning in staggered groups over the course of the summer.

The white school bus pulled up at the National Guard armory on West Minnesota Street. The soldiers were told to drop their bags and stand in formation; they could hear people screaming from behind a set of rolling doors. There was nobody waiting for Michelle behind those doors, because she had not told her family when she was coming home. Mary also had not informed her family. The soldiers were being given two days of freedom before they had to report to Camp Atterbury for a week of demobilization, and Michelle and Mary were planning to spend those two days in Bloomington. Michelle's friend Veronica was living there now, in a house she shared with her boyfriend, Russell, and their friend Philip. Veronica had transferred into Indiana University, partied too much, gotten kicked out, and was now taking classes at Ivy Tech instead. The idea of getting drunk with Veronica seemed more appealing than an emotional reunion with tearful relatives, and they figured that no harm would be done, since their families did not know when they were due back. But when the doors opened, the soldiers marched into the armory's gymnasium, where they were swiftly enveloped by the hungry, screaming crowd, and out of the maw came Mary's mother. She said the Family Readiness Group had let her know.

Mary's mother gave Michelle a ride to Columbus, where they dropped her off at a gas station. It was hard to be severed from Mary; whenever they had left the post, they had traveled in pairs, and Michelle thought she needed a battle buddy. But the civilian world had other routines. Veronica picked her up, said it was karaoke night at a bar called the Office and that a group of friends were gathering there to celebrate her return. Michelle no longer fit into her civilian clothes

— over the course of the deployment, she had dropped several sizes — so they went to the mall. There were no windows, there were too many stores; it was overwhelming. Disoriented, Michelle hardly paid attention to what they bought. It did not matter what the purchases cost, because she had $20,000 in her bank account. When Michelle put on the tube top and the tight jeans Veronica had chosen, she liked the way the clothes emphasized her new figure but hated the way they revealed her farmer's tan. She imagined that every other person at the bar would look at her brown neck and forearms and her white shoulders and know that she had been in the military. She got falling-down drunk. It was a relief to know that she could drink and not worry about running into an infantryman on the way home.

Then she returned to Camp Atterbury for five days of demobilization. Back again amid that sea of identical yellow cinder-block buildings, Michelle filled out reams of paperwork. One of the forms was a questionnaire called a postdeployment health assessment. None of the soldiers wanted to admit to any difficulties, which would only get them tangled up in the army's cumbersome bureaucracy. Michelle could not wait to put aside her desert camo uniform and raced through the form in a way that was not entirely truthful but was intended to convey the impression that she had sailed through her deployment. No, she had not seen any dead people. No, she had not seen anyone get wounded. No, she had not been engaged in direct combat. No, she had not shot anybody. All true. No, she had not experienced any diminishment in pleasure (although she had). No, she did not have nightmares (although she did). No, she was not feeling depressed (although she was). If she answered yes to any of those queries, Michelle thought, she would only get stuck at Atterbury. Better to claim that she was entirely cheerful, that she had no bad dreams. She did admit to having been exposed to burning trash, loud noises, and vehicle exhaust fumes. But she did not admit to any critical feelings about the military. Did she think her unit leadership had taken care of her during this deployment? "Yes," Michelle wrote. What events made her feel this way? "Good chain of command."

The same form asked if the soldier was presently in a committed relationship. Michelle said she was, thinking of Ben Sawyer. She was asked to rank, on a scale of one to five, how she felt about the following statements. "My relationship with my partner is more important to me than almost anything else in my life." Five out of five, answered Michelle. "I want this relationship to stay strong no matter what rough times we may encounter." Five out of five. The form offered more such statements, but changed the rating scale from one to seven. "I believe we can handle whatever conflicts will arise in the future." Five out of seven, said Michelle. "I feel good about our prospects to make this relationship work for a lifetime." Six out of seven, said Michelle. "I am very confident when I think of our future together." Six out of seven.

Then she headed back to Evansville. Michelle did not feel ready to enroll at Indiana University that fall, but planned to resume her college education there the following semester, in the spring of 2006. She was not sure exactly how she was going to occupy herself until then. As it turned out, not much held her interest. With no medics around to write new prescriptions, Michelle gave up the pills that she had been taking nightly, but began consuming a lot of alcohol. She slept on Colleen's couch. Her friends had busy, civilian lives, while she had mislaid hers, and the month of July passed by in a foggy blur of hangovers, Advil, and beer.

At some point she called Pete to let him know she was back from Afghanistan. She said she knew that she needed to remove her belongings from his apartment as soon as possible, but she didn't yet know where she was going to live. "Don't worry about it," Pete said. "I promise not to pee on your clothes. You can get them when you're ready." In the weeks that followed, Pete figured he should wait and see if she called. She did, but not often. There was this looming army guy in her life; the soldier assumed enormous significance in Pete's mind. Then he got a phone call from a friend who was living in Los Angeles and working on a movie. The friend said he could get Pete a job on the set. Why not? There was nothing keeping him in Indiana. Pete asked Michelle to keep Halloween for a little while, until he got settled in L.A. Somehow the cat had become his while she was gone.

Michelle was unprepared for what her uniform was going to mean to other people. She still thought of herself as someone who loved alternative music and hated George Bush and voted for Ralph Nader, but to some members of the extended family she had become a symbol: a soldier, a veteran, a hero. A great-aunt she did not know had started emailing and was signing her notes "love in Christ." She also sent Michelle a picture of her daughter with George W. Bush. The woman seemed to view Michelle as the personification of a whole confluence of matters that were hugely meaningful but she also seemed to have a hard time seeing the actual Michelle. "This woman never met me, she didn't know me at all," Michelle would say later. "I'm not a Christian, I'm not a Bush fan. She was the opposite of everything I was." Meanwhile, Michelle's mother's first husband, who had served in Vietnam — her father's first cousin — asked if she would join him in a parade at a 4-H fair in Evansville. Michelle said yes, because she felt obligated. But as her father was driving her over to his cousin's house, she held the familiar desert camo in her hands and was filled with dread. She was going to have to wear the uniform again at drill, which would resume three months after her return, but she had not put it on since the deployment.

"I can't do this," Michelle said. "Dad, I can't put this uniform back on."

"That's okay, honey," Fred Fischer told his daughter. "Let's turn around. We'll go to Denny's instead."

Not many people accepted without query that she might have gone astray, but she never had to explain the difficulty of finding her way back home to her father. Being lost, that he understood. Michelle gave him the medals she had earned. Everybody in the battalion had been given a combat action badge because of the RPGs that had been fired over their compound (although Desma had immediately scoffed, and swore she would never wear hers, saying the tour had involved no actual combat). Michelle gave him that and the special commendation for all the AK-47s. She didn't want them, but she didn't want to throw them away, either. Otherwise, some of the interactions she had with family members proved jarring. She had been gone for a long time, and they could not fathom where.

"This is my sister — she just got back from Iraq," her sister Tammy told a friend at one point.

"Actually, I was in Afghanistan," Michelle said.

"Where in Afghanistan?" asked her sister's friend.

"I was in Kabul."

The friend looked blank-faced.

"It's the capital," Michelle snapped. "Look it up sometime."

Nobody at the parties that Colleen brought her to had heard of places like Kandahar or Helmand, and they could not say if Mazar-i-Sharif was a city or a province. Michelle remembered with a sense of shocked recognition that the wars were incomprehensible to most Americans. They could not list the major developments in either narrative. A few people had heard that there had been an election in Afghanistan, but none of them knew the name of the man who had been elected. "You think people are really stupid and fat and lazy," Michelle would say later. "They just work to buy shit they don't need. Over there, everything is really simple. You get back here — we make our lives really, really complicated. You meet people here in

America and it's like, nothing is ever enough. They want to make more and they want to be more and it just seems so irrelevant and trivial and pathetic, and it's really hard to be around people. It's like, You really have no priorities, you ought to just go sit in a third world country for a while, and then you might feel a little better about your life."

For weeks, the only human being whom Michelle could bear to be with was Mary Bell, who came to see her in Evansville several times. On one of those visits, Mary accompanied Michelle when she went to buy a used Cabrio. Afterward, Mary taught Michelle how to drive a stick shift. Mary was easy to talk to, and she got mad about all the same things — the stupid questions, the obliviousness, the lack of recognition. Then Desma came home at last, at the end of July. Mary and Michelle drove to Indianapolis to greet her inside the same armory on West Minnesota Street. The armory's gym was filled with balloons and flowers and flags, as well as homemade signs, many of which said, WELCOME HOME, DAD. The din made Michelle flinch. The soldiers marched into the gym and then dissolved into the crowd. They spotted both Debbie and Will but lost them quickly in the pandemonium. Finally they saw Desma, looking travel-worn and weary in a wrinkled uniform. They had forty-eight hours before she had to get on the bus that would take her to Camp Atterbury. "Let's get the fuck out of here," Desma said. They drove to a hotel and they ordered takeout food and they did nothing but watch movies on TV for two whole days.

It was strange, once they were all back, because Michelle felt as though Debbie and Desma were now her family, yet they lived in far-flung places. Debbie lived two hours to the north of her, while Desma lived almost an hour to the east. They did not have to return to drill for three months, and Michelle did not see anybody from Bravo Company unless she made a special effort. It was odd to wake up and not see those familiar faces in the dining hall over breakfast. Estranged, Michelle called Debbie and Desma constantly. They spent hours on the phone, because nobody else understood. Michelle missed her unit terribly.

And she craved Ben Sawyer in a famined, visceral way. Previously they had eaten dinner together every evening and spent every night intertwined on a narrow bed, but now they lived two and a half hours apart and could barely manage to speak on the phone. He lived in a town 140 miles to the east, and had returned to his wife after he got home that summer. Ben told Michelle that he had nothing left in his bank account to show for Afghanistan — his wife, Amanda, had torn through all of his combat pay, he said, every penny. His life struck Michelle as so unfair.

Yet now Amanda took precedence in a way that had not been true during the deployment. Suddenly it was almost impossible for Ben and Michelle to see each other, and even difficult to speak. Ben and Amanda shared a single cell phone, and Michelle was only supposed to call when Amanda was at work. One day she phoned at the wrong hour. When Amanda answered, Michelle hung up without saying a word, but Amanda barraged her with texts. Who is this? she wanted to know. Sorry, wrong number, Michelle replied. I know who you are, Amanda wrote back. Ben was irate.

The rules were so different all of a sudden. In Afghanistan they had not hidden the relationship from their colleagues, except at the beginning of the deployment. By the end, everybody had known they were a couple. The rest of Bravo Company had gotten used to seeing married people in deployment relationships; they were all just trying to get through the year. Now Ben had returned to his family and it was hard for Michelle to adjust. During the deployment she had functioned more like a wife than a mistress; now the wife role was Amanda's position once again. What did that make Michelle? A home wrecker?

Michelle said Ben needed to make up his mind. He could stay with Amanda if he wanted to save his marriage, or he could try to make a go of it with Michelle, but he needed to make a choice. Otherwise they should stop seeing each other. At the end of the summer, Sawyer left his wife and petitioned for custody of his children. Michelle started visiting him on the weekends, and they took the children out to places like Chuck E. Cheese's. Meanwhile, Michelle decided to move to Bloomington that August. She wanted to take her time getting settled there, before she started school in the spring. "It took me a while to pick myself up, and get the guts to go back to school," she would say later. "I gave myself some time. I had plenty of money in the bank, so I didn't need to work." When it came time to move, she called Pete, who was about to leave for California. Could he help her move her things to Bloomington? He had a big truck. If she tried to move everything herself in the Cabrio, she would have to make several trips. Pete said sure. Michelle took Halloween and her clothes in her new car and Pete took her bed and her desk in his truck, and they drove up Highway 41 in a caravan. When they got to Bloomington, Pete helped Michelle carry her belongings into the house that she was going to share with her friend Philip. Philip had been straight when Michelle had left the United States but he was gay by the time she got home; he understood what it meant to live through a hard turn in one's identity. In the months that followed, he would become the only civilian Michelle could talk to without difficulty.

Pete and Michelle went to Target, because there were all kinds of things Michelle needed — cleaning supplies, shampoo, toilet paper. Inside the store, Michelle grew edgy. There were too many things for sale and she did not know which brand was best. She slowed to a halt in the toilet paper aisle. There were an awful lot of different kinds of toilet paper. How did you choose? She thought of the pink crepe toilet paper in Afghanistan; she remembered giving a roll of it to one of the Afghan workers at the depot, who had considered it a grand luxury. It made Michelle a little queasy to behold an American display of toilet paper with her Afghanistan-schooled eyes. Was this what the war had been about? Protecting this sort of abundance?

Questions like these thronged her. She understood why the United States wanted to prevent terrorist strikes, and she knew that Al-Qaeda had established training camps in Afghanistan, yet she could not always fathom how the work they had been doing at Camp Phoenix was related to all that. And she had never understood why it had been necessary to invade Iraq, when the blame for 9/11 lay squarely with a small group of men who came primarily from Saudi Arabia. And how exactly had the two wars mushroomed into their present, bloated forms? Was she the only one who wondered why the military had strayed so far from its original goal of finding Osama bin Laden? When would it all end? There was always the thought that she might be sent on another deployment. The longer the wars continued, the more likely this seemed. Meanwhile, the part of her intelligence that constantly analyzed things was waking up again and sometimes she felt filled with horror, wondering about the meaning of her deployment. What had it signified, that she had spent a year fixing broken AK-47s? Often she had a hard time staying in the present. She was standing in Target, she reminded herself; she was supposed to buy toilet paper. It was just hard to make up her mind.

"Stay here," Pete said. "I'll be right back."

He vanished, leaving her alone.

Panic. Her peripheral vision blackened, her sense of hearing dropped, her heart thudded in her chest. Primeval questions blared across her mind: Am I safe here? Is this a good place? She could not have justified why in rational terms, but it seemed to her that there was something fantastically amiss — something malignant, even — with a store that sold twenty-five different brands of toilet paper. How could this level of material abundance be morally acceptable, given the poverty on the other side of the globe? And now that the flesh of reality had been peeled back and she could look underneath the surface of things, she could see that she was utterly, utterly abandoned and surrounded by a yawning, nameless danger. Michelle began crying uncontrollably, heaving sobs, terrible sounds. By the time Pete found her, she could barely function. "I'm having a panic attack," she managed to say. "Get me out of here."

They left without buying anything. Afterward Michelle thought the timing of the panic attack had been curious. She had survived the sound of nighttime rockets whistling around her at Bagram, only to be felled by a trip to Target? Why had that pushed her over the edge? Maybe some part of her recognized that on home soil it was permissible to go to pieces, or maybe coming home was simply much harder than she had anticipated, or maybe the transition from Evansville to Bloomington had been the last straw. Michelle unpacked her clothes and put the marble tea sets that she had bought at the bazaar in Afghanistan on the bookshelves. This was simply going to take some time, she told herself.

Desma Brooks had not wanted to meet her children in the crowded, noisy armory because she thought she might fall apart. Instead she had waited until after the five days of demobilization to call her cousin

Lesley. She arranged to meet Lesley and the children at a McDonald's near Lesley's house. Lesley brought all the children, including her own, to the restaurant. Desma walked over and sat down at their table and for one split second she marveled at how much Lesley's son had grown. Then he said, "Hey, Mom." It was Josh. He had been round and pudgy when she had left, but now he was all angles. "Where?" one of the girls said in response. "Where's Mom?" Desma had not recognized Josh; the girls had not recognized their mother. It had been a long time.

Desma told the children that she needed some time to unpack, and then two days later she drove to her cousin's house and her ex-boyfriend's house, collected her three children, and tried to pick up where she had left off. She was a mom; she should cook dinner. At Camp Phoenix the staff had cooked her meals, done her laundry, cleaned the bathrooms, mopped the kitchen floor. Her life had been highly regimented; she had been told where to be and what to do. Go to the motor pool, track vehicle maintenance, eat dinner, play cards, sleep; go to the motor pool, track vehicle maintenance, eat dinner, sleep. Each day mind-numbingly similar to the previous one. Now there were three children running around in a state of overexcitement and a grown man waiting to be fed and nobody to tell her what was on the menu.

Desma opened the refrigerator and saw that it contained only condiments. Okay, there's no food in the house, Desma said to herself. I've got to go to the grocery store. She drove over to the Buy-Low, and it was just aisles and aisles of stuff. "And I'm like, I don't know what I need," she said later. "I don't know what I'm supposed to cook. I don't know how this all works. It was like, What do they eat? What do they like? I haven't been here in over a year."

Tunnel vision, racing heart. She abandoned her shopping cart in the aisle and went outside and called Stacy Glory. Stacy talked to Desma the entire time as she drove the fifteen miles to the Buy-Low, and then she accompanied Desma as she walked back into the store. After that, for a period of several months, Stacy went with Desma whenever she ran errands, made sure she was never by herself. "She would go grocery shopping with me so I didn't freak out when I didn't know what to get," Desma would say later. "I tried to come home and pick up my life, and I was like, I don't know what I'm supposed to do." Stacy told her it was normal to be bewildered; she just needed time to adjust. That was reassuring, because otherwise Desma found her difficulties inexplicable. Nothing dire had happened to her in Afghanistan, so why did she stand in the cereal aisle for an eternity, staring at a box of Honeycomb, asking herself how it could be true that when she had left, the box had cost less than $3 and now the same box cost almost $4? Sometimes she got lost in her own head, puzzling over her place in the universe. "I came back and I realized how small I was in the whole scope of things," Desma said later. "I was sitting at the picnic table in my backyard and I look up and there's a plane flying overhead and it's full of people and I don't mean jack shit to anybody. It was a huge problem when I first got home."

One night her sense of being insignificant grew so acute that she called a suicide hotline. The woman she spoke to struck Desma as useless, and the phone call was more annoying than helpful. The interaction served a purpose, though — it made her want to speak to somebody who would not talk in platitudes. So she called Mary Bell, who came over and stayed with her until she regained a sense of worth. Desma felt like a freak, but she could say this to Stacy, or Mary, or Michelle. And Stacy kept telling her, Des, this is just what happens. You'll get used to going to the grocery store again. It's overwhelming at first, but you'll get used to it again. Everybody feels this way when they get back. But it was impossible to explain to civilians.

"You are different," Jimmy said. "What happened to you?"

"I dunno, there ain't nothing wrong with me," Desma told him.

Suddenly it was time for the kids to return to school. Alexis was starting kindergarten that year, and Paige was starting second grade, while Josh was going to enter the seventh grade, in a different middle school than the one he had attended while she was gone. She bought them new shoes and new clothes and new backpacks and then she looked at her bank account and realized that if she did not go back to work soon the money would run out. She had been paying $600 to her cousin and $300 to Josh's father every month the whole time she was gone, and had ordered gifts and necessities on the Internet for the children as well, so she didn't have nearly as much money saved as her childless friends. Desma still felt dazed by basic domestic routines and not yet competent at civilian life, but she returned to work anyway.

While she was gone, the truck stop had turned into a strip joint, so she didn't go back there. Instead she returned to her part-time job at the Kentucky United Methodist Homes for Children and Youth, and tried selling life insurance on the side. She gave up the life insurance gig after she figured out that the clients were even more broke than she was. Then Kentucky United got a big grant and promoted Desma to full-time and boosted her hourly pay to $10. Trying to work forty hours a week, run errands, clean the house, and feed the kids, Desma could not manage. "I had a back porch area — it was enclosed, and I had my washer and dryer out there," Desma said later. "They had so much laundry, and I had a full-time job. I could not keep up with it. Then it was mounding in these baskets and I didn't know how to take care of it." It baffled Desma to watch herself fail to cope. She had not been shot; she had not seen anybody get blown up. She had spent her days at the motor pool. Why could she not do the laundry? But there was so much of it, and she hadn't done any for a year. Among Jimmy, the three children, and herself, the household produced an extraordinary number of tasks. In those early days, it just felt like too much. Everything felt like too much.

Desma slept with Mark Northrup once or twice more, and then the relationship fizzled. The end came after he broke the rules, and called her from his home phone — although they had agreed they would only communicate on drill weekends. Northrup's wife must have grown suspicious, because one Saturday afternoon Desma started getting phone calls from Northrup while she was sitting in a movie theater with nine teenagers from the group home. She was working that day, and the teens had earned the privilege of an outing. Perplexed to see that Northrup was calling when it was not a drill weekend, Desma let several calls go to voice mail, and then she received a text message saying, You really need to call back. When Desma called back, Northrup put her on speakerphone. He said he was sitting with his wife.

"Oh, okay," said Desma. "What's going on?"

Northrup announced that he had told his wife about all the flirtation and the connotations, and said it had to stop. Desma played along, for the sake of his marital harmony, although she could not believe what he was doing — denying the affair, pinning the whole thing on her, taking zero responsibility.

"That's cool with me," Desma told Northrup. "I didn't mean to cause any harm. It was all in fun. I know you're married. I didn't figure I could take you home."

"Well, it has to stop," Northrup said again.

"Fine," Desma said.

She never slept with him again. "I was beyond done," Desma would say later. "He could kiss my ever-loving ass — you know, put me on speakerphone with the wife. Own up to your own shit, and let's not blame it on me."

When Debbie Helton had arrived home, Ellen Ann had been waiting for her in the crowd at the National Guard armory, and she had brought her baby along. Both of Debbie's parents had been there, too. Debbie wound up on the front page of the *Indianapolis Star* after a reporter had learned that she was meeting her granddaughter for the first time. Jaylen had reached for the name badge on Debbie's uniform as the *Indy Star* reporter questioned Debbie about her age; because the military needed additional recruits for the war effort, the Pentagon had just asked Congress to raise the age cutoff for new enlistees to forty-two. Debbie suggested people should think hard before they enlisted but told the *Indy Star* that she had not allowed her age to stand in the way of her dream to become a soldier. "I was determined enough that I wasn't going to fail," she told the *Star*'s Rebecca Neal. "If you're determined, if you want to do something, put your mind to it and you can."

Jeff had not met Debbie in the big crowd. "He was going to meet me later because he felt like that was the time I should be meeting with my mom, my dad, and my daughter, and for the first time meeting my granddaughter," Debbie would say later. "And he felt that he would rather wait until I got settled and then he would come and get me. And then we would do our own thing." Jeff picked up Debbie and Will after they received their two-day passes — Will had no plans and had been at loose ends — and drove them around Indianapolis. They meandered up and down the city's streets, looking for a decent place to stay. Jeff said he wanted to find the right sort of hotel, although Debbie said they could spend the night in a tent and she would not care. They wound up at a Holiday Inn. What Debbie did not say was that she was finding the reunion to be more fraught than she had anticipated. "It had been over a year," she would say later. "You're a little apprehensive, because you haven't been with this guy for a year, and is he going to think you're just as attractive as you were then, or are you going to think he is? Are you going to feel different? Are you going to feel attracted to him when you see him? Are you going to feel sexual? Or not? Oh, yeah, totally overwhelming. And then what if you sit there and you have a conversation and you don't like the person anymore? You change, you change, and even though you talk and you say the same things on the phone, and you write emails, when you meet in person, you're like, Oh, my God, he might not like me anymore."

They checked in at the front desk.

"I'm going to go to my room and get settled," said Will. "I know you two have a lot of catching up to do."

Jeff said drily, "Well, I doubt that's going to happen right away."

In the hotel room, Debbie and Jeff sat on the bed and talked about nothing, just talked about the flight, and about the day, and about her granddaughter. Debbie decided maybe nothing had changed after all — "it had changed but it hadn't changed." Jeff asked what she wanted to do. "Honey, you probably want to get out of them clothes," he said. "You've been in them for twenty-four hours. Would you like to take a hot bath?"

"Yeah, but I want you to come with me," Debbie said.

"Well, I don't have to, if you want to take a bath by yourself, I understand."

"No, I think I want you in there."

They lazed around in the tub for an hour, then called Will.

"Are you ready to go eat dinner?" Debbie asked.

"Yeah, I'm starved," Will said.

They found a steak place nearby. Will came back to their room, had a few beers, but did not stay long. "Aw, I'm beat, guys," he said. "I'm going to bed." By the following day, Debbie was not worrying about whether she and Jeff would stay together, because he kept making everything easy. It was all about her. What did she want to eat? Where did she want to go? He made no demands. It meant a lot to Debbie that Jeff had let Will join them. So many men would have gotten upset at the request to bring another man along. But Will had been her closest friend during the deployment, and Debbie had not wanted to leave him alone. Maybe Jeff could also see that Debbie needed Will; it would have been jarring for her otherwise, to leave the rest of her unit behind, and spend two nights with a man she had not seen in a year.

Shortly after they returned to Bloomington Debbie walked into a Kroger grocery store, realized immediately that she could not handle the experience, and turned around and left. She did not stay long enough to become panicked, and few people knew that Debbie struggled to get used to being home again. But she did, because she missed Afghanistan terribly. The life she had returned to struck her as meaningless by comparison. "When I got back, I felt pretty worthless," she would say later. "Like, What am I doing? I'm just back working at a hair salon, and that's nothing. Well, yeah, my clients like it, but where's my life going?"

She slept poorly and some days it was hard to get out of bed. The question of what clothes to put on perplexed her; she had liked just knowing to put on a uniform. Debbie had always remembered everything about her clients — their names, the names of their spouses, the names of their children, even their pets — but at this point she found herself frequently going blank when she was greeting a client. She covered up her memory lapses by calling her clients "honey" and "dear" and hoped they did not notice. Her colleagues saw that she had trouble stocking the inventory, however, as she failed to order critical products when they ran low. Before the deployment, Debbie had been able to glance at the shelves and know instantly which products needed to be ordered, but now the shelves read like a foreign language; she could not remember which shades of hair dye were the most popular and needed to be stocked in greater quantities. When she did the payroll she found she could no longer perform basic math, and she had to count on her fingers to determine that 8 plus 7 equaled 15. Debbie was frightened to see how many facts that had once moored her had unaccountably slipped away.

At home she had crying jags. It was unlike her, and it startled Jeff. He noticed how much better she seemed after speaking with Will, however, and urged her to call Will more often. And it was true, speaking to Will always helped. Debbie needed that particular connection — she needed to talk to someone who had been with her in Afghanistan, preferably another member of the armament team. Will or Michelle, their voices produced the right chemistry. They were the ones who could lift her out of a black mood or restore her sense of having value. "I'm just having a really bad day and I just need to talk to you for a little bit," Debbie would say. The first time Michelle got one of those phone calls, she was caught off guard — it was so unlike Debbie. And Debbie hated not being herself, hated being needy. She criticized herself for losing perspective, for lacking self-control, for letting in the blackness. She thought she was supposed to be strong, like her father. She did not want to be like her mother, who had suffered nervous breakdowns. She did not want to be weak. But Debbie had to admit out loud that she was struggling to find any relief. Soon Michelle and Will got used to Debbie's calls, because she frequently needed to talk.

"I just don't know why I'm here," she said to Will at one point. "I wish I could be back over there. I feel useless here, like I'm not accomplishing anything. I think I could accomplish more if I went back over there."

"Well, are ya crazy?" Will replied. "You miss all that sand? You're right where you need to be. You need to be right here, at home."

And that's all it took, hearing Will's voice say those words. It was like swimming in a cool lake on a hot day, it was like eight hours of sleep. She found herself refreshed, she calmed down, the blackness retreated. Jeff could say the same thing and it would not work — it had to be Will. She had to hear the voice of someone who knew about the AK-47s, and the B-Huts, and the sandstorms, and what it was like to take a shower inside a conex. Debbie apologized to Jeff. She said she was sorry that talking to Will helped and talking to him did not. But Jeff said, "Don't worry about it, that's all right. I wasn't there. You just needed to talk to somebody who was there. It's okay."

Debbie said maybe they should get married after all. Jeff had asked once before, but she had put him off. "Oh, no, I'm not interested now," Jeff told her. He let her stew for three days, and then gave her a blue topaz ring. They flew to Mexico and eloped. When Jeff's daughter was about to have a baby, she asked Debbie if she would like to attend the birth. Debbie said no, she didn't have to be there. But her daughter-in-law said she had missed the birth of her own granddaughter — she should come. So she did, and it was miraculous. After Mallori was born, Debbie and Jeff began having their granddaughters sleep over at the same time, and although Jaylen and Mallori shared no blood, the two girls grew up like cousins. Debbie's days filled up fast: she had appointments at the hair salon, she cared for one granddaughter or the other, and she tended to her mother, who had been sliding into ill health. She never felt quite the same sense of fulfillment that she had obtained from being a soldier, but she did not feel entirely worthless. And Debbie spent untold hours with Michelle, whom she practically adopted after Michelle moved to Bloomington. Michelle seemed thirsty for attention, for as usual her life was full of drama.

2
Out of Uniform

When the shock of coming home wore off, they had to confront the question of which relationships to keep. Which friendships, forged in Afghanistan, would last back in the United States? The apartment Michelle shared with her friend Philip was across the street from the mall where Debbie worked, and after she moved to Bloomington, Michelle began dropping by the hair salon all the time. Sometimes she popped in to say hello and sometimes she made appointments to see Debbie for the same services she had gotten in Afghanistan. Then Michelle started visiting Debbie at home, too, where she got to know Jeff. Soon she began introducing Jeff and Debbie as her surrogate parents.

That fall Michelle drove her Cabrio down to Evansville to pick up some more of her belongings, and while she was down in southern Indiana, she took a detour over to Rockport to see Desma. They had spoken endlessly by phone but they had not seen each other in person for a while. This was the first time Michelle had visited Desma at home. It was like old times, it was like seeing a sister. They laughed about smoking hash under the bedcovers and blowing the smoke into dryer sheets and about the vibrators and the vodka. Desma wanted to know how things were going with Ben Sawyer, and Michelle said she had loaned him a lot of money. They were still sitting in the living room when Desma's children got home from school.

"All right," Desma said. "What kind of homework you all got?"

Paige and Josh listed the homework they had to complete that evening. Alexis did not have any homework, as she was only in kindergarten.

"Go sit down at the kitchen table, get yourselves a snack," Desma said. "I'll be there in a minute."

She turned back and saw that Michelle looked stricken.

"I can't take this," Michelle said, and she fled.

Desma could not fathom what had gone wrong. Later Michelle called to apologize. "I've never seen you as a mom before," Michelle said. She had only known Desma as a badass soldier — the stubborn individual who would not use a regulation army wool blanket, who had said to take one Valium and one

Ambien before a combat landing, who had brightened the drab surroundings of Camp Phoenix with a flock of pink flamingos. It had spooked Michelle, the sight of Desma as a mother — she had felt as though she were watching a Desma that was not Desma. Of course Michelle had known that her friend had children, but she had never confronted the children's actuality, never witnessed the vulnerability written on their faces. To see how needy the children were, to watch the way they depended on Desma — it seemed unbearable to Michelle that Desma had left them for a year. Desma understood: everything was too much, when they first got back, all the ordinary things, toilet paper and cereal and laundry and the sight of children.

The uniform had erased so many of their differences, Michelle realized. It had made the soldiers seem more alike than they really were. It had taken away their origins and their destinations, their past and future selves, and left only their basic personalities, absent all the other signifiers that said who they were back home. She had never had to confront the reality that Ben Sawyer was married to Amanda, or that he was a father, or that he came from a family that was awash in addiction. She had never seen Debbie Helton inside of the beauty salon or at home with Jeff Deckard. She had never witnessed how badly Josh and Paige and Alexis needed

Desma to be there when they got off the school bus. It was jarring, how much Michelle did not know about these people she thought she knew so well. She was astounded to glimpse who they had been before they had spent a year together on a former Soviet air base in Afghanistan, and who they were in the process of becoming again.

Ben Sawyer sprang from poor soil. After he returned home, he found himself girdled by people who depended on drugs, and Michelle felt her impulse to fix Ben up countermanded by others who pulled him down. Some members of his own nuclear family abused pills, but Sawyer nevertheless occasionally depended on them to help with his children. Rose and Ryan were three years old and five years old, respectively. One day that fall, some friends from Bravo Company invited Ben and Michelle to go out to dinner. Ben left his children with a close relative. Toward the end of the meal, he got a call on his cell phone: Rose had been rushed to the emergency room. She had swallowed an OxyContin that she had found on the floor of the relative's house, and doctors were going to pump her stomach. Michelle drove from Indianapolis to southeastern Indiana, with Ben decomposing in the passenger seat of her Cabrio. At the hospital, they found Rose white-faced and unconscious. The medical staff had inserted a tube down into her stomach and had suctioned up its contents, and then had given Rose charcoal to absorb any harmful substances. Rose threw up black bile, and it streaked across her white face. Seeing his small daughter in such distress undid Ben, who shook, bawling. "It was the saddest fucking thing I've ever seen," Michelle would say afterward. "That was one of those moments where I was like, it's just not ever going to be okay for him. Like, he's not ever going to get a fair shake, because he has nobody to count on."

Michelle thought maybe Ben could count on her. She wanted to help him build a better life. So she bought him a car, a used black VW Jetta that cost about a grand. It did not seem fair that Amanda had blown through all of Ben's combat pay; plus, Michelle wanted Ben to visit her in Bloomington. "I always spent a lot of money on Ben because I had it and he didn't and I felt bad for him," she said later. "We were the same rank. He worked as hard, he went through all the same stuff I did, and Amanda spent all his money on drugs. So I did a lot of stuff for him. And I didn't think twice about it."

At the same time, however, Michelle was moving away from the soldier she had been. She resumed her friendships with people she had known in high school who were now living in Bloomington. Hanging out with her old friends, she started to remember that she was only twenty-three. During the deployment, everybody else had been older: Debbie was fifty-three, Desma was twenty-nine, and Ben Sawyer was twenty-eight. They all had children, but none of her friends in Bloomington were shouldering those kinds of responsibilities. They did not have mortgages, or ex-wives, or daughters who had to be taken to the emergency room. As Michelle began spending more time with people her own age, she gained perspective on her relationship with Ben. Perhaps because he felt her pulling away, Ben grew increasingly possessive. He started asking questions about how she was spending her time. In October, when Michelle told her boyfriend that she had been invited to a Halloween party, he made clear that he wanted to go, too; Michelle wound up inviting both Ben and Mary Bell. She was planning to go as Wonder Woman; Mary was going to be a Native American squaw. Ben said he might not be able to afford the gas for the drive to Bloomington, however, because he was barely making ends meet. Later he called to say he had found a solution: he had bought some weed, it was in the trunk of his car, and he was planning to sell it for a tidy profit.

"You're driving around in the car that I bought you with weed in the trunk?" Michelle asked in disbelief.

"What about it?" Ben said.

"You have two children that have one good parent," Michelle told him. "And if you got pulled over right now, they would have nothing. And you're doing all of that because you want to come to some party with me?"

But he was slipping beyond her sphere of influence. They no longer ate dinner together every evening, nor spent every night on her twin mattress. There were other forces at work on him, and they were more powerful than Michelle. Sawyer did not remain a model soldier. He did not enroll in school and use the GI Bill to get ahead. Instead he was slowly reverting to the person he had been before he had worn the uniform every day, someone who took shortcuts. It scared Michelle, the idea of dating a man who would risk a felony conviction for a quick buck. She broke up with Sawyer over the phone.

He called her repeatedly in the days that followed. Michelle tried to explain. She said they had been able to make things work in Afghanistan because they had more in common there, such as the post itself and the chow hall and the uniform and the routine and a common circle of friends, but once they got back home they had begun moving in different directions. They were living in different places, they were different ages, they had different friends and different lifestyles. He was twenty-eight and she was twenty-three; he was a working father and she was a college student. They just did not have as much in common. Sawyer did not agree, however, and starting in October, they had to go to drill together. After moving to Bloomington, Michelle had begun reporting for drill in Bedford. That November, when Michelle showed up for drill weekend, she saw Sawyer in the parking lot. He grabbed her and started yelling that they could not separate. Michelle tried to reason with him, but her words only fanned his fury. At one point he hurled his cell phone down on the ground with such force that it shattered into pieces.

The encounter left Michelle afraid for her safety. How unstable was Sawyer? At the end of that weekend, he stopped by Michelle's apartment to pick up some of his things. When she opened the door, he spat directly into her face; she was wearing her glasses, and his spittle landed all over the lenses. Mary Bell had slept over the night before but was not yet awake. Mary had been going through hard times — the man she had married right before they deployed now had another woman living with him. She was in the middle of getting a divorce. As Michelle stood in the doorway, trying to decide whether it would be safe to let Sawyer enter, she wished that Mary would wake up, because she feared Sawyer might hit her. But Mary kept sleeping, and Sawyer got his stuff and left without striking her. When Mary finally woke up, Michelle told her about the encounter. She said that she could no longer wear the silver ring Akbar had helped her buy at the bazaar, the one that said *My heart belongs to Ben.* Mary said she would take the ring; it was too beautiful to throw away. Michelle had grown closer to tall, slender Mary Bell; by this point she felt as close to Mary as she did to Debbie or Desma. Consequently, Michelle did not expect what happened next: Mary Bell began sleeping with Ben Sawyer and wearing Michelle's ring. Michelle stopped speaking to Mary after that.

Desma depended upon Stacy, Mary, Michelle, and Debbie, in that order, and she wished that Michelle would forgive Mary so that they could all hang out together again. But Michelle was stubborn, and she would not relent. That fall, after she signed up for the college classes that she would take in the spring, Michelle joined Facebook. She used the social networking site to reconnect with other people she had known from high school and from her years at the University of Southern Indiana, as well as people who were going to Indiana University at Bloomington. (At first nobody she knew from the military joined Facebook, but one year later she would become Facebook friends with both Desma Brooks and James Cooper, her old flame from Aberdeen Proving Ground.) She was moving into more civilian circles, and she might have put Afghanistan behind her, except that she emailed with Akbar Khan almost every week. He had decided that he wanted to move to the United States, and was applying for a visa to make this possible. Michelle got the XO of Bravo Company to write a letter of support.

That November, Pete flew back from California for Thanksgiving. He drove up to Bloomington to see Michelle and to pick up Halloween. Michelle could not see Pete without thinking of all that might have been, and at the same time seeing Pete reminded her of her own infidelity. A war had come between Michelle and Pete, and she could not imagine how to put back together what the deployment had pulled apart. To complicate matters, she had just met a young man named Billy, who had begun pursuing her avidly after they had crossed paths one night at a bar and again at a party. Pete did not have much luck with Michelle or the cat. Halloween behaved as though Pete were a stranger, hissing and backing away. "Man, that cat was my best friend!" Pete would say later. "And now he won't even say hello." They decided that Halloween should stay with Michelle after all. Then it was time for Michelle to go back to college.

3
Answered Prayers

They settled back in, they moved on with their lives, they became civilians again. They acted as though there would not be another deployment. Wasn't it likely the wars would end before their battalion got sent anywhere else? In January 2006, Michelle began taking classes at Indiana University — her dream come true. She had transferred into IU with a total of sixty-one credit hours (forty-two credit hours from the two years at the University of Southern Indiana, six credit hours from the misbegotten semester at Purdue University in Fort Wayne, and another thirteen credit hours that she had earned for her military service in Afghanistan). Her plan to major in environmental science looked too daunting, as she could not stomach the idea of retaking all of the required science courses she had tried and failed to complete back in the spring of 2004. Instead she opted for a bachelor of science in public affairs, with a major in nonprofit management. Her dream, trimmed a little. That first semester she took four classes: Introduction to Computers, Finite Mathematics, National and International Policy, and Urban Problems and Solutions. She also started seeing Billy.

Two years older than Michelle, Billy had already completed one undergraduate degree and was working on a second. He had gotten a degree in economics from Wabash College, as well as a minor in religious studies. Then he decided to get a second undergraduate degree, in international relations, from the University of Evansville. There he considered himself "kind of an outsider," because he was older than most of the students. Michelle and Billy had this in common — not quite belonging. They were also both highly intelligent, and held political views that put them to the left of the mainstream. Back in 2003, when the Iraq War had begun, as chance would have it, Billy had been in Turkey with other students from Wabash College who were taking a class on world religions. It had changed his life, to be in Istanbul when George W. Bush had told Saddam Hussein he had to leave Iraq within forty-eight hours or else. The Turkish people were not happy. Billy had glimpsed what his own country looked like from another vantage point, and Michelle knew what the United States looked like from Afghanistan. "We were both outside the US bubble," Billy would say later. He was also tall, handsome, and charismatic. He had olive skin, dark red hair, hazel eyes, and a warm manner. He had an unusual capacity for emotional intelligence. He told Michelle he could not believe the United States was sending single mothers and grandmothers to war. It was a sea change, he said. He could not believe that he had gotten to stay at home while somebody such as Debbie had been deployed. Michelle would say later that he had brought her back to life.

Going to school in Bloomington proved all that Michelle had hoped for, in certain respects. One year before, *Newsweek* had named Indiana University the "Hottest Big State School," in part because the institution had embraced the information age and was offering fast networks, extensive wireless capability, and superb computer support services. Michelle loved the school for other reasons — she found the setting spectacular, thanks to the original woods that still flourished at the heart of the campus. The Olmsted brothers, who had designed Central Park in Manhattan, had laid out the campus, and they had decided to keep Dunn's Woods intact. After the university embraced the idea that a forest should stand at the center of the campus, the vast thicket of trees became a defining attribute. "There are few places in the world where great laboratories, classrooms, libraries, auditoriums, and other such centers of intellectual and artistic creativity are located in an environment which retains its primeval character — few places where one may so quickly and so completely cast off the tensions and anxieties of this complex modern world in quiet meditation," wrote Paul Weatherwax, a botanist and a longtime member of the faculty. Michelle found constant replenishment walking through Dunn's Woods, under the boughs of ash, beech, buckeye, hickory, maple, red oak, sycamore, and walnut trees. Because her school protected the woods, and was literally built around the trees, Michelle understood the university to be a place that shared, at its core, her values. And the buildings themselves, built of locally quarried limestone, spoke of soaring ambition and lofty goals; they had been built to last, and built to inspire.

At the same time, Michelle struggled to complete her schoolwork. Indiana University was more demanding than any other institution she had attended, and the class material seemed so abstract compared to the concrete, practical tasks the army had asked of her. Thinking critically, synthesizing information — she was rusty. While serving in the military, she had shut down the part of her brain that engaged in critical thinking. A soldier had to react fast, respond quickly in a predictable manner; a soldier was not supposed to overthink. Writing her midterm papers, in March 2006, proved excruciating.

Indiana University was also big. Forty-two thousand students attended classes at the flagship campus, four times as many as at the University of Southern Indiana. Socially it was hard for Michelle to get her bearings. She had studied a map of the physical campus and familiarized herself with the names of all the buildings, but nobody could give her a map of the campus's social groupings, and she was jumping into the mix as a junior — after other students had already spent two years forming close alliances. Also, she was several years older than the norm, because of the time she had spent in basic training and the time she had spent in Afghanistan. Her present classmates were twenty or twenty-one, and when she mentioned that she was twenty-three the other students seemed put off. It was not a big age difference, but in that setting it mattered. When the subject of her military service came up, however, Michelle found the conversation tended to slip sideways. Her roommate Philip had an extensive network, and at one point a friend of his who was an art major dropped by. When she caught sight of Michelle's marble tea sets, she crouched down to admire them.

"These are beautiful!" the art student exclaimed. "Where are they from?"

"They're from Afghanistan," Michelle said.

"What were you doing in Afghanistan?" the art student wanted to know.

"I've been in the military," Michelle said. "I was deployed there for a year."

The art student left soon after, and Michelle could see that she had been written off; any possibility of friendship had evaporated. Bloomington was like that — it was a town filled with young people who thought of themselves as open-minded, yet were closed on the subject of the military. They hated George W. Bush, and they hated the wars; by extension, they thought they knew better than the kind of people who had signed up. Michelle could see clearly all the ways in which the art major was like the rainbow-hemp-wearing person that she had been before her deployment, but she could also see clearly that the art major came from a different socioeconomic background. She was rich; Michelle was not. And Michelle had been changed by the deployment. She had spent a year serving alongside Patrick Miller and Debbie Helton and Desma Brooks. Michelle could not look down on the kind of people who joined the military. Nor could she look up to students who had never considered bartering their freedom for tuition. What Michelle could not forgive was the obliviousness that accompanied the art major's privilege. "This girl had never known anybody in the military," Michelle would say later. "And she obviously did not care. I almost hated her. Look at what I went through! And you're not going to ask me any questions? Meanwhile, your dad's paying for your liberal arts education. That's nice."

The subject of the wars proved touchy. Other students knew too little and Michelle knew too much. If she revealed that she had spent a year in Afghanistan, the other students asked if she had killed anybody, or if she had seen anybody die. She did not want to entertain them; they were too ignorant. The other students had only a hazy sense of current events and could not keep the two wars separate. "People get it wrong," Michelle would recall. "You say you went to Afghanistan and ten minutes later in the same conversation they say Iraq, and you're like, No, I went to Afghanistan." On this topic her classmates seemed unknowing, pampered, parochial. And while she shared their liberal bent, she did not share all of their opinions, not anymore. The memories of her deployment brought up a welter of emotions, and somewhere in that mix, surprisingly, lay pride. She still hated Bush, and she still thought the invasion of Iraq unwarranted, but she had fallen in love with Afghanistan. The other students wanted her to say that being sent to Camp Phoenix was the worst thing that had ever happened to her, yet she could not disavow her experience. How could she wish for a comfortable life in which she never saw women wearing head-to-toe blue burkas or shoeless children thrusting their thumbs up in thanks or Akbar Khan flying a kite with a glass-encrusted string? Michelle could not say that she regretted Afghanistan because there she had known some of the most meaningful encounters of her life. And when she tried to explain this to the twenty-year-olds around her, they responded as if she were some kind of warmonger. So Michelle started hiding the truth. She stopped saying how old she was, and she stopped disclosing that she was a veteran. "I didn't tell in class, I didn't raise my hand," she would say later. "I didn't want to be identified as older, I didn't want to be singled out. I didn't want to have to explain it. And I didn't want the really stupid questions. It was a very liberal crowd, people make assumptions. The stereotype that goes along with being a veteran, it didn't serve me well."

In her first semester, Michelle earned mostly Bs. She thought she could do better, but forgave herself for getting off to a slow start — she had been through a lot. Sensitive about being older, she decided to finish college in the shortest time possible. She went to school full-time throughout the summer of 2006, completing another four courses while most of her classmates took their summer break, and in the fall of 2006 she signed up for a total of seven classes, and managed to earn As and Bs in all of them. "I was all business," she would say later. "I didn't take a break the whole time I was at IU, because I was already having a hard time with how old I was going to be when I graduated, and how competitive I was going to be in the marketplace. I saw it as a giant flaw. I didn't see it as a strength. It took a long time before I could see it as a strength."

On drill weekends Michelle left behind the world of the campus and reentered the world of the military, which now offered her a sort of respite. After they finished the obligatory exercises, she threw herself into socializing with her fellow veterans. She slipped back into her original friendship with Patrick Miller, once he was no longer her boss. Miller represented the antithesis of the sneering, privileged students back in Bloomington — he wore Wrangler jeans and chewed tobacco and bragged about his days as a bull rider — and this was refreshing. One night at Shorty's, the bar in Bedford where many of the soldiers in their company liked to hang out, somebody put Willie Nelson on the jukebox. Michelle was already fairly drunk and Patrick knew how to dance. He spun her around so that her long blond hair fanned out in a circle. Michelle could have kept dancing with Miller all night long, but Ben Sawyer stepped forward and asked to cut in. Apparently he had been watching them dance for a while.

"I still love you," Sawyer told Michelle.

She tried to smack Sawyer in the face but she had drunk too much and she missed, swatting only air.

"You don't love me!" Michelle yelled. "You don't know what love is! If you love me, then give me my fucking money back!"

Desma Brooks swooped down and wrapped her arms around Michelle's waist and hoisted her out of Shorty's facing backward with her arms and legs flailing. Michelle threw up on the ground, while a soldier whose given name was Richard held her hair out of her face. They all called him Big Dick. (One day back in Afghanistan Smitty had walked into the motor pool and said, "Have you seen my Big Dick?" to Desma, a story she loved to tell.) Big Dick carried Michelle over to Desma's car and laid her out on the backseat. The people she had deployed with watched out for her in a way the college kids never did. As best they could.

Michelle never knew when Ben Sawyer might show up at her door. He had been appearing at random intervals, ranting and irate. Later, when Sawyer started failing to show up for drill regularly, Michelle felt a selfish relief because it was easier for her when he wasn't around; yet she felt sad, too, because failing to show up for drill was a violation of his contract with the military, and it meant he was diving into trouble. When Sawyer did show up, Debbie Helton told him, "Get it together, son." Sawyer told Debbie he was going to start showing up every month, but instead he stopped coming at all. Then he did time in jail for dealing meth. Michelle thought of Rose and Ryan growing up the hard way, and asked herself if some piece of their struggle might be her fault. She did not want that to be true, but it seemed hard to assign responsibility cleanly, when for a while she and Ben had lived so closely intertwined, and everything had gotten so jumbled.

In this way, Michelle led two separate lives. There was her primary life, as a college student, where she worked tremendously hard and made few close friends. And there was her secondary life, as a National Guard soldier with one deployment under her belt, and a big, dysfunctional family of fellow veterans to whom she felt intimately bound. The two worlds didn't align much, except that anytime she needed to, Michelle could walk out of a class and over to the beauty salon and get a hug from Debbie. And she could text Desma at any hour and get an instant response. Michelle found solace in her burgeoning relationship with Billy — he told Michelle he had never been in love before, not the way he was with her — although her ties to the military occasionally proved a source of conflict. Billy sometimes found it threatening that Michelle liked to socialize with male soldiers, and because he avidly opposed the two wars, he sometimes wondered if her friendships with other veterans were healthy. He would have wished for Michelle that she never had to be part of the military at all.

On rare occasions Michelle achieved a moment of harmony between her two worlds. When she took a psychology class called Managing Behavior in Public Organizations, Michelle struck up a warm relationship with the professor. At one point she went to see him during office hours, and confided that she had served in Afghanistan. He responded with curiosity, and she found herself telling him about the work she had done. At the end of the semester, when she sat down to take the final exam in that class, she saw on the last page that the professor had included an extra credit question. It was a picture of an assault rifle, and he asked the students if they could name the person who had invented this particular type of gun. "Mikhail Kalashnikov," Michelle wrote confidently. She knew the professor had included a question about an AK-47 solely for her. At least one person at the university recognized that in Afghanistan she had obtained an education of a different kind and that it should be acknowledged.

And in a class called Poverty and Public Policy, Michelle asked for permission to write her final paper on poverty in Afghanistan. The scope of the class was domestic poverty, but her professor granted permission for her to write about a foreign country after she explained that she had spent the last year living on a military base there. Michelle summarized the history of Afghanistan since the reign of Muhammad Zahir Shah, described how after his monarchy had ended in 1973 the country had been gripped by turmoil for the next three decades, sketched the destructive roles played by the Soviet Union and the United States during the 1980s as they struggled for control of Afghanistan, showed the rise of the mujahideen, and then described how they tore the country apart with their squabbles and paved the way for the Taliban. In the process, the Afghanistan economy had fallen apart, and its people had grown poorer, and their country had become less able to govern itself. Warlords traded in opium, heroin, and morphine, but otherwise there were few legitimate exports. She listed the stark statistics describing how meager life in Afghanistan was after this ruinous history: that 70 percent of the country's population survived on less than $2 a day, that life expectancy there was twenty years lower than in neighboring countries, that more than 80 percent of Afghan women were illiterate, that more children died than in almost any other country on the globe, and that the leading causes of death among children were preventable ailments such as diarrhea and respiratory illnesses. Michelle wrote about efforts to salvage what was left of Afghanistan, to rebuild a viable nation so the country would no longer serve as a breeding ground for terrorists, including the UN attempt to disarm the warlords and transfer weapons to the Afghan National Army through the program known as Disarmament, Demobilization, and Reintegration. "Enhancing security and rule of law through vigorous security sector reform and capacity building (with emphasis on the Afghan National Army, police force, and justice system) are necessary to keep the country moving in the right direction and keep insurgencies low," wrote Michelle. "Without security not much progress can be made."

Her paper was twenty-one pages long, well researched, and cogently written. She got an A. Michelle felt as though she had been carrying around thousands of puzzle pieces and could only now see how they fit together — why she had been living on a former Soviet air base, why the warlords had possessed so many AK-47s, why she had been asked to repair those weapons, why all the children they had driven past had lacked shoes. Michelle emailed the final version to Patrick

Miller, George Quintana, Debbie Helton, and Akbar Khan — the armament team. She would have sent it to Will Hargreaves as well, but she didn't have his email address. "That was the first time I tried to intellectually synthesize what I had gone through," Michelle would say afterward. "That was the first time I tried to put it in the context of history. You know, when I first got home, I didn't want to touch the subject. I didn't want to look at anything that reminded me. I just wanted to pretend like it didn't happen. I wanted to go back to college and be a college kid. But it just doesn't work that way. It's impossible."

Shortly after coming home, she had been reduced to panic in the aisles of Target, without the ability to articulate what was wrong. Now fourteen months had passed, and she could say, in a term paper, exactly what had happened in Afghanistan — what she had witnessed — that would reduce her to such a state. She had achieved her dream of going to the kind of college that had trees and demanding professors, and at the same time she had discovered that the means by which she had paid for that dream also rendered it impossible for her to fully enjoy college in the way that she had once imagined. Because of what she had been through, she did not truly fit in. But she moved past that when she wrote the paper on Afghanistan, because she discovered that she could use the tools of the classroom to make sense of her journey, and it did bring her some catharsis.

Michelle began her senior year at Indiana University in January 2007. She was planning to graduate that December. On drill weekends, however, there was talk of another deployment; Michelle could hardly bear the idea of her college education being interrupted once again. As it happened, she reached the end of her commitment to the National Guard in March 2007 — six years after she had first sat down with Sergeant Wilber A. Granderson — without receiving orders to deploy. Michelle felt so finished with the Guard that after her last drill weekend she folded up her military uniform and hoped with a fierce intensity that she never had to put it on again. She and Billy had started talking about moving to Colorado. All that Michelle wanted was the chance to start over in a new place, without the military stealing another year of her life. It seemed her prayer might be answered.

Two weeks after she completed her last drill, however, the majority of the soldiers in the 113th Support Battalion got official word of the next deployment. Almost everyone whom Michelle knew in the National Guard was going to be sent to Iraq. The soldiers would go on active duty status at the end of that calendar year, they were told. It took nine months for everybody to get their assignments — nine long months of knowing they had to go, before they actually left. Later, Desma Brooks would say she honestly didn't know which was worse, not being given any notice at all that she had to leave her children for an entire year, or knowing for nine whole months that she was going to have to leave them. Debbie Helton was told that she would stay back, but that is not exactly how things unfolded.

And then that summer, while everybody in her old unit was doing extra training to get ready for Iraq, Michelle got a phone call from James Cooper, her ex-boyfriend from Aberdeen, with whom she had stayed in contact. Cooper told Michelle he had just gotten his orders: he was being sent to Afghanistan. The level of violence faced by US troops in that country had escalated dramatically since Michelle had left. Although the Afghan war had gotten off to a successful start, subsequently several things had gone wrong. Leaders of the Taliban and Al-Qaeda had been permitted to flee to Pakistan, where they had established strongholds, and from there they began orchestrating missions inside Afghanistan along its southern and eastern borders. Meanwhile, Afghans had grown increasingly disenchanted with the democratic government that the United States had helped establish, due to rampant corruption. And as the war in Iraq had turned to mayhem, that conflict had siphoned off critical resources from the war in Afghanistan. For several years, Iraq had been receiving the bulk of military equipment and attention. "The ratio of key ISR [intelligence, surveillance, and reconnaissance] assets divided between Iraq and Afghanistan was typically 4 to 1 or 5 to 2," wrote Seth G. Jones in his book *In the Graveyard of Empires: America's War in Afghanistan.* "That is, for every four Predators that were shipped to Iraq, one went to Afghanistan. Or for every five Predators shipped to Iraq, two went to Afghanistan. Special operations forces were also reallocated. . . . Low levels of money, energy, and troops made it nearly impossible to secure Afghanistan after the overthrow of the Taliban regime and almost certainly increased the probability of an insurgency." Whereas the Iraqi insurgency had spread with rapid intensity immediately after the United States had invaded, opposition to the US presence in Afghanistan instead built slowly and quietly. American soldiers had only felt the full brunt of the resistance perhaps four years after the start of the war in that country. From that point forward, however, violence had started to bloom quickly. "The increase in violence was particularly acute between 2005 and 2006," noted Jones. "The number of suicide attacks quadrupled, remotely detonated bombings more than doubled, and armed attacks nearly tripled between 2005 and 2006. The following year would bring more of the same, as insurgent initiated attacks rose another 27%." Billy comforted Michelle while she fretted about the well-being of a man she had once slept with, many years ago, and who was now being sent to Kandahar. There was a full-blown rebellion raging there by this point, and it was the scene of some of that war's most intense fighting.

The orders that she had so narrowly missed and the news from Cooper made Michelle realize how painful it was going to be to watch her wish come true. She would remain at home, as she had fervently hoped. But almost everybody she cared about in the Guard was going to be sent somewhere dangerous, and she would worry for the entirety of the time they were gone about whether they would make it back. She was going to be given a life of ease while everybody else would suffer. It felt entirely wrong. She was young and had no children, while Desma was a single mother with three kids, and Patrick Miller's wife had just given birth to a second child. Michelle had imagined that being released from her commitment to the Guard would offer sweet relief — and, briefly, it had — but she had never imagined being left at home while her entire battalion shipped off to Iraq. She considered herself less encumbered than many of the soldiers who were getting ready to go, and she was nonplussed to realize that she would have traded places willingly with any of them, if only she could spare them what was coming. The one person Michelle cared about who was not going to Iraq was Noah Jarvis. When he had heard a deployment was likely, he and his closest friend in the Guard had hastily transferred into another unit that was based in Louisville, Kentucky. Everybody in Evansville was derisively calling Jarvis and his pal the Kentucky Flyers (after a local cycling club), but Michelle did not blame him for ducking a war he did not support. She would not have been able to shoulder the guilt if he had come back maimed or hurt or not at all, given that she had persuaded him to enlist in the first place, six long years before.

▪ ▪ ▪ ▪

IV
Iraq, 2008

▪ ▪ ▪ ▪

1
Look, Fuckers

Becoming soldiers again, that was the task. This time they were given almost an entire year to prepare. Desma had been telling her children for months that there might be a deployment coming, but when she said it's definite and it's Iraq and it's happening this year they were shocked. "You're just going to leave again?" Josh asked in disbelief. "It's not like I have a choice," Desma told him. "You'll understand when you're older." That fall, Alexis was going to start second grade, and Paige was going to start fourth grade, while Josh would begin his freshman year of high school. All of them were old enough to anticipate what a year's absence would be like, and they had three-quarters of a year to fret. The girls grew clingy; Josh kept his distance. He said, "I want to finish high school where I start high school. I'm not going to keep moving around." Desma said all right, he could stay with his surrogate father Keith in Gentryville during all four years of high school, although it kind of broke her heart. Then she spoke to her cousin Lesley about minding the two girls again. Lesley said she would do it if it was what Desma really needed, but she had a lot going on. Desma understood: it was too hard. So she made other arrangements. Her daughters would stay with their paternal grandparents, who lived close to the girls' father, down in Spurgeon, Indiana.

It was the same town in which Desma had been raised. The girls' grandparents lived in a house that Desma remembered being occupied by some boys who used to pick on her when they rode the school bus. Spurgeon was about an hour's drive from Rockport, where Desma lived, and Desma had maintained a close connection to her in-laws even after her divorce from their son, Dennis Brooks. Like everybody in southern Indiana, it sometimes seemed, they had fallen on hard times; Desma's father-in-law, Ray Brooks, had worked for a company that had closed, and had started over with an entry-level job at a furniture factory in Jasper. The girls had a particularly warm and affectionate relationship with their grandmother, Paula Brooks, whom they called Ma-maw. Desma thought it would be a good arrangement. "She loved the girls," Desma would recall. "They were her pride and joy, kept her going every day. She never faulted me for our divorce, she loved me very much. And was thankful for the opportunity to spend as much time as she got with the girls."

Desma had to report to Camp Atterbury for two weeks of training each month in May, June, July, and September 2007. She tried to hang on to her full-time job at the Kentucky United Methodist Homes for Children and Youth, but eventually asked for a leave of absence. Her boss said he would keep the job open until she got back, and her coworkers made her a quilt. The coming deployment pretty much ended Desma's relationship with Jimmy. He said he had endured one yearlong absence already and would not do it again. If she went to Iraq, she would not find him waiting for her when she got home. Jimmy said she had chosen the military over him. Desma said that was fine with her, he should not wait. Her lease did not run out until July 2008; Desma wrote enough checks to cover the rent until then, and gave them to Jimmy to mail as the months went by. She told Jimmy he could stay in the house while she was gone. All she asked was that he look after her dog, Goldie. Mary Bell had given her the dog — a pug and beagle mix — after Mary had been unable to care for it. Desma and Jimmy were still living together but they started leading separate lives; Desma spent half of her time at Camp Atterbury, and Jimmy spent many weeks on the road.

That summer, while Desma did her two-week trainings in June and July, the girls stayed with their grandparents in Spurgeon and Josh stayed with his father in Gentryville. After each training session, Desma picked the children up and they all returned to Rockport. With the mandatory trainings taking her away so much, however, she found it hard to care for her children in a consistent fashion, and she did not want to disrupt the children's schooling by having them switch institutions in the middle of the year. Beginning in August 2007, she sent the children to live with the relatives she had chosen to parent them while she was gone, even though she would not go on active duty status for another four months. "You know, let's not uproot them in the middle of the school year," she said later. "Let's do it at the beginning and start off fresh." She did not make too much of the transition. "I'll see you on Friday," she told the girls casually before turning them over to their grandmother. Same with Josh. "See you at the weekend."

Josh established himself at his father's house quickly. He had lived there before, and already had friends in the area. But the girls entered a household that was about to be thrown into turmoil. Their grandmother had been experiencing health problems, and within weeks, Paula got a routine scan and unexpectedly learned she had cancer. The girls gleaned that their grandmother was ill after the house filled with worry and they were brought on rushed visits to doctors. In September, while Desma was at Camp Atterbury again, her mother-in-law was briefly hospitalized. Not until the following month, however, shortly before Desma began another two-week training session, did Paula share word of her illness with Desma. She barely had a chance to assimilate the news. The 113th Support Battalion was not being deployed as a coherent entity — instead, individuals from the battalion were being distributed across the rest of the 76th Infantry Brigade, wherever there were empty slots that needed filling — and she had just been told to report for a two-week training session with the 293rd, a previously all-male infantry regiment. She would serve in Iraq alongside a group of men she had never known.

Desma buried herself in Harry Potter. She reread every book in the series, working her way up to the *Deathly Hallows,* which came out that summer. She also started spending a lot of time with a woman named Charity Elliott. Charity had drilled with Desma in Bedford for years, but had been left behind when the rest of the 113th Support Battalion had gone to Afghanistan. She had volunteered to go so that she could rejoin her own unit, but instead had been sent to Iraq with a National Guard battalion out of Pennsylvania. When the 113th had returned from Kabul, Charity had still been in Ramadi. While in Iraq, Charity had been walking back to the post with a group of soldiers when a car bomb had exploded nearby. Half of the group had just turned a corner, but the other half had been exposed. In her civilian life, Charity worked as an emergency medical technician, and she immediately ran back to do triage. She tried but failed to save the life of a major whom she respected. It had been hard for Charity to settle back into civilian life, and she was eager to deploy again. "Once is never enough," Desma would later say, commenting on Charity's appetite for war service. "Once is never enough."

Between deployments, Charity had been assigned to work in retention with Debbie. They had a bumpy relationship. Charity went to a retention training class and returned with a bunch of recruitment posters that said, ARMY OF ONE (a slogan that did not last long). Then she pronounced the trailer a mess. Debbie had viewed the hot dog truck as a place to get away, but by the time Charity had finished straightening up, it looked like a regular recruitment office. "Debbie was fit to be tied, because this was supposed to be a place to relax and hang out, and now it's all army," Desma would recall. "Charity was taking over, and Debbie wasn't used to having somebody else managing her space."

At about the same time, Stacy Glory — the single mother Desma carpooled with — had begun working in retention, too. Desma had been spending a lot of time in the hot dog truck, because of her close ties to Stacy and Debbie, and in the process she got to know Charity better. Charity struck her as funny, warm, kind, and competent. "She had all her ducks in a row," Desma would say later. Charity had been assigned to 3rd Battalion, 139th Field Artillery Regiment, another formerly all-male part of the brigade that trained in Evansville. Rockport was not far away, and Desma invited Charity to stay over during one of her training sessions. Charity had a girlfriend, and at first the relationship with Desma remained platonic. Charity's sexual orientation was an open secret. The military's Don't Ask, Don't Tell policy prohibited discrimination against closeted gays or lesbians, but barred openly gay or lesbian members from serving their country — and so Charity did not declare she was a lesbian publicly but did confide the truth to Desma. "I got to hanging out in there [in retention]," Desma later explained. "And she and I just got to talking. And we went out and had a few drinks, and went out another time, and had a few more drinks. And then there was the drunk 'wish you were here' text. She and her girlfriend were going through a nasty time. The girlfriend had pulled a knife on her because she thought that Charity was sleeping with me. And at the time, we weren't. It was really close, but we hadn't. And then we did."

Charity possessed an allure for Desma because she was knowledgeable, easy to talk to, and their physical relationship proved satisfying. "Great sex!" Desma would say. She also made Desma feel more comfortable with the idea of going to Iraq, since she had been there already and had made it back in one piece. Desma didn't discuss her new relationship with many people, however, because talking about it publicly could have gotten her kicked out of the military. And she said nothing to Jimmy. "Jimmy had already pretty much told me to piss off. If I was going to Iraq, he wasn't waiting on me, and there was nothing we had in common anymore." She introduced Charity to her children — they took Paige and Alexis out to dinner in Jasper one evening, and stayed over at a hotel that had a pool — although she never explained that they were having a romantic relationship. It seemed like a lot to get into right on the eve of her departure.

Desma started training with the infantry regiment's 293rd Alpha Company in October 2007. The 293rd was based in Fort Wayne, Indiana, way up north at the opposite end of the state from where she lived, and she did not know the soldiers in that regiment. The men who served in the 293rd were also National Guard, and also belonged to the 76th Brigade, but they were infantrymen. They dismissed soldiers who served in support positions and never left the safety of the military post as "Fobbits," from the acronym for forward operating base, or FOB. ("A Fobbit never leaves the wire," the saying went — it was a play on the line "A hobbit never leaves the shire.") They were better, they thought. The soldiers in the 293rd trained harder than other Guard units; they took special classes in hand-to-hand combat and martial arts. They had been to Iraq once already, four years earlier, when they had become the first Army National Guard battalion to see combat since the Korean War.

Most of the men who were serving in the 293rd had never served alongside women. Recent changes in policy allowed female soldiers to be transferred into formerly all-male regiments such as theirs, if the regiments were being deployed in a noncombat role (in this case, the 293rd was providing security to supply convoys). In October, during the first training session that she completed with the 293rd, Desma traveled to Camp Grayling, in Michigan, where she found herself part of Alpha Company, a group that consisted of about one hundred men and only a couple of women. Similar ratios prevailed in the regiment's other companies. The men made it abundantly clear that they had preferred being an all-male group. "There was a lot of animosity," Desma would say later. "They wanted to push the women out, because women meant nothing but trouble."

A few leaders in the 293rd treated her in a friendly fashion — among them a meticulous, thoughtful noncommissioned officer named Roy Dishner, who served as Desma's squad leader — but the rank-and-file soldiers were unwelcoming. Male soldiers kept a wide berth around Desma in the chow line and would not sit with her during meals. Her close friend Stacy Glory had also been attached to the 293rd, but was serving in a different company; when possible, Desma ate with Stacy. Desma had been told she would work in supply. The sergeant in charge of supply sent her down to the range. Desma was fluent on the military's complicated logistical software, she was a whiz with radios, and nobody in the 113th would have thought working at the range was a good use of Desma's talents, but she spent her days making sure the infantrymen had enough ammunition and could qualify safely with their weapons.

One day, after they boarded a truck to ride back to the barracks, Desma asked the other soldiers if they had gathered up the targets they had shot. Nobody answered. She turned to a male specialist and said, "Ask them if they gathered up the targets." He repeated the question, and the men said they had. Desma was being shunned. Later she learned that the soldiers had been instructed to keep their distance from the female soldiers. They are not your friends, their squad leaders had supposedly told them. Don't talk to them, don't socialize with them.

Desma rode in silence from the range to the barracks. When her squad leader ordered the soldiers to shower and report back in two hours, Desma started walking the wrong way.

"Brooks, showers," ordered the squad leader.

"Bullshit," she responded.

Desma stalked over to the command post. "Who is in charge of this motherfucker?" she asked.

"Feathers are ruffled," remarked one of the company's leaders.

"Hey, I'm supposed to be working in supply, but you got me doing range control. And I'm working with a bunch of people who won't speak to me," Desma announced. "How about we have a discussion about how big of an EO complaint I have? And how I'm going to call the IG as soon as I walk out of this room?"

"It's for your safety and for the safety of my Joes," responded one of the brass.

Nobody appeared concerned that she was

accusing the 293rd of violating the army's equal opportunity standards and threatening to report them to the inspector general's office, according to Desma. She did not actually call the inspector general — she decided to wait and see if things got better — but things got worse. Everybody in the 293rd had to pass a weapons qualification test. Desma went to the range as ordered and fired at the targets in front of her, and afterward she was told that she had not qualified. Desma had never gotten a perfect score at the range, but she had never failed to qualify. Desma had already endured a yearlong assignment overseas — which was more than some of the younger guys in the 293rd could say. Failing to qualify wounded her pride. Thinking maybe she was rusty, she returned to the range a second time, and again she was told that she had failed. Four times Desma tried to qualify, and four times she was rejected. Desma felt pretty certain that her supposed failures were a lie.

The October training left Desma feeling more like a second-class citizen than any other experience in her life. After it was done, she rode on a bus back to Indiana with other soldiers from the 293rd. The bus dropped soldiers off at their respective armories. From Bedford, Desma drove to Mary's apartment in Indianapolis, where she spent the night. Mary had also been told she was going to

Iraq. She was the one friend who had been through everything with Desma — the false deployment, Afghanistan, and this. Desma told Mary that she hated the 293rd.

The following morning Desma tried to call her children, but nobody answered the phone at their grandparents' house. She called the fire department and found the girls there with Dennis. She heard her ex-husband tell their children that they should go to Aunt Jo's house. Joanne was his sister; Desma wondered why the girls had to go there. Later that day, Desma got a phone call from Joanne's husband, Gary, who let her know that Paula had just died.

"The girls don't know yet," he said. "When will you be home?"

"I'll be home today, as a matter of fact," Desma told him.

At the funeral, her father-in-law asked Desma to let the girls stay with him, as planned. That's what Paula would have wanted, he said. Desma wondered if it was a good idea — she thought maybe she should move the girls to her cousin's. But it would mean one more upheaval, and her cousin was already overwhelmed, and the girls had suffered a shock at losing their grandmother. This loss was their first experience with death, and it had come just as Desma was getting ready to leave for Iraq. Uprooting them now would be disorienting. Maybe it would be all right to let the girls stay with their grandfather. "Worst mistake I ever made," Desma would say later. "I should have sent them back to my cousin's, but I let them stay with him."

Several weeks later, Desma reported for drill at the 293rd's regular location, the National Guard armory in Warsaw, Indiana. Warsaw lay at the far northern end of the state, close to Fort Wayne, and it took her five and a half hours to get there. While she was there, Desma obtained a copy of her weapons qualification results. Every time Desma had fired a bullet, a computer had recorded her name and her lane and whether that bullet had hit the target. "I qualified four times," she would say later. "And they were trying to tell me I didn't qualify at all. I qualified more than my fair share." It made her livid to discover her true results. Before she left Warsaw, Desma printed out every score she had earned. She was going to need proof of her worth; it was going to be that kind of a deployment.

Desma went on active duty status on December 10, 2007. Her mobilization orders stated that her tour was part of Operation Iraqi Freedom and would not exceed 392 days. Meanwhile, Desma had just gotten a series of text messages from Mary Bell, who had recently acquired a new boyfriend — an infantry soldier in the 293rd. Mary had texted four different photographs of four different pee sticks from four different test kits, and every one said pregnant. "What am I going to do?" Mary asked Desma. Desma wrote back, "Looks like you're going to have a baby." Both Desma and Mary showed up at Camp Atterbury as ordered, but after reporting the pregnancy Mary was sent home the following day. Missing her best friend, miserable about being assigned to the 293rd, and far from her family, Desma turned to Charity Elliott for solace. She decided that Charity was the love of her life.

As it happened, Debbie Helton — who had started going by the name of Debbie Deckard after she got married — had just joined Charity in the 139th Field Artillery. It was some kind of crazy snafu. At drill, the first sergeant had called her name when he read out the stay-back list. In 2004 she had wanted desperately to go with everyone to Afghanistan but she did not mind staying back in 2008, when her battalion was being broken up. All the soldiers who were being sent to Iraq had gotten their new assignments, and because they were being separated, the mood was grim. When she got home from drill that evening, however, Debbie's phone rang. Jeff looked at the caller ID.

"It says Indiana Department of Military," he told Debbie. "Don't answer it."

"I have to answer it," Debbie said.

"They're going to tell you that you're going," Jeff predicted.

"They can't tell me I'm going," Debbie told him. "They just told me today that I was on stay-back."

The phone stopped ringing. Debbie called back. The soldier on the other end asked if she was Specialist Helton. No, Debbie said. She was Specialist Deckard. She had gotten married. The soldier checked her Social Security number and said it matched the number on his list. She needed to report to the armory in Crawfordsville, because she was being deployed to Iraq with the 139th.

"No, I don't think so," Debbie told him. "I was just at drill today. And I wasn't on any of the lists. There's no way. They already told me I'm on stay-back."

The soldier said her name had just come across two hours earlier. He told her to report to the Crawfordsville armory the following day at 7:00 a.m. She would go from there to Camp Atterbury.

"First off, I can't be there at seven," Debbie told him. "I run a salon, and I have a payroll due in the morning. I have people that have to get paid. There's no way I can be there at seven."

The soldier said she didn't have a choice.

Debbie said she could be there by noon.

He said if she would absolutely promise to be there by noon, it would be all right. He would make a note that said, "Did contact, will show up at noon."

"I promise you I will be there," Debbie said. "I have never been AWOL. I have never missed drill. I'll be there."

There was some sort of mistake, Debbie told Jeff — she would sort it out. At Camp Atterbury, Debbie crossed paths with a superior from the 113th, and he asked with confusion what she was doing there. She told him that apparently she was going to Iraq. "I put you down for stay-back," he told her. "Why are they sending you?" Debbie wondered out loud if it could be due to the fact that she had changed her name. "I bet you anything it is your name change," he said. Apparently the army had decided that Debbie Helton and Debbie Deckard were two different people, and although Debbie Deckard had been told that she would remain at home, Debbie Helton was being sent overseas. Debbie tried to explain to her new colleagues that she was not Debbie Helton anymore, but nobody in the 139th knew her history, and they would not listen.

Michelle Fischer was going to graduate from college that December, and she was in the middle of finishing the final exams of her senior year when Debbie called to say what was happening. Debbie and Jeff had promised to host a graduation party for Michelle at the end of that month, and Debbie began apologizing that there would be no party. "Stop apologizing, Debbie," Michelle said. "Seriously! The party doesn't matter. I'm a little bit more concerned with the fact that you're going to Iraq."

Debbie was staying in a female barracks on the other side of Camp Atterbury from Desma. Charity lived there, too. When they finished their training exercises at the end of the day, Charity would walk across the post to visit Desma, or Desma would walk over to see Charity. Charity and Debbie told Desma they felt the 139th was a pretty good place to land. Even though the field artillery regiment had previously been all-male, neither Charity nor Debbie was being hazed. Debbie thought the guys had taken a wait-and-see attitude about her. She was optimistic about how things would turn out because she could see that the 139th had accepted Charity.

Starting on December 23, 2007, the soldiers were given ten days off so they could spend the holiday season with their families. Desma returned to Rockport and tried to create a festive air. She was still shopping on Christmas Eve, but she stayed up late to wrap each gift. They celebrated Paige's birthday, which fell on New Year's Eve. Mary Bell and her boyfriend got married on New Year's Day, and Desma was the maid of honor. At the wedding Mary's mother said, "How could you let this happen?" Desma said, "I tried to talk her out of it." Nobody thought the union would bring Mary happiness. The groom was due to leave for an Iraq deployment in two days, and the couple had not been given enough time to build a strong relationship. Mary was upset that she was not going to Iraq with her husband and her maid of honor. All the people she cared about were going, and she knew they were going to come back altered in ways that would make it impossible to be close to them unless you had been there, too.

And then it was time to go. On January 3, 2008, the Indiana National Guard threw an enormous send-off for the 76th Infantry Brigade in the old RCA Dome in Indianapolis. Three thousand four hundred uniformed soldiers from the 76th as well as fifteen thousand family members filled the stadium. The soldiers hailed from ninety of Indiana's ninety-two counties and represented Indiana's largest single deployment since World War II. During the coming year, Indiana would have more members of its National Guard deployed than any other state in the Union. By this point, the war in Iraq had been grinding along for five long years; after a slew of quick victories, and that optimistic moment when it seemed as though the war might end in a matter of months, things had bogged down. Every year had brought a steady rise in the number of violent incidents.

The removal of Saddam Hussein had created a power vacuum, the elections had not solved the leadership issue, and the insurgency had blossomed into such a powerful force that some people were calling what was happening a full-scale civil war. The previous year had been the worst yet, in terms of the number of attacks on infrastructure, the number of homemade bombs, and the number of ambushes involving snipers, grenades, mortars, rockets, and surface-to-air missile attacks. The average number of attacks per month had climbed to more than five thousand. General David Petraeus had been named commander of all US troops in Iraq and had spent previous months implementing counterinsurgency strategies. Infantry soldiers who had been trained to kill the enemy were being asked to protect the friendly segments of the Iraqi population instead. The counterinsurgency doctrine was proving labor-intensive, time-intensive, and extremely costly, however; President Bush had responded to the latest uptick in sectarian violence by calling for a "New Way Forward," in the form of a surge in troops. He had just sent 20,000 more soldiers to Iraq, bringing the total number of troops stationed there to 157,000.

As the two wars had ground along, the US military had been drawing heavily from all parts of the military, including the National

Guard, and multiple deployments had become routine. For most of the soldiers under the dome, this was their second or third deployment; if they had not already been to Iraq, then they had been to Afghanistan or to Bosnia. Politicians including Governor Mitch Daniels and Senator Richard Lugar delivered speeches to the troops. "Our roles today are backwards," then Congressman Mike Pence told the crowd (he would later be elected governor of the state). "It is I and all of us on this stage who should be sitting in your seats, and you before the microphone. It is one thing to speak of courage; it is quite another to be courageous." Pence said it was a significant moment in Operation Iraqi Freedom, a moment of "widening American success," and asserted that the surge was working. Desma did not know whether that was true; she just knew that she was tired. As the soldiers waited to board buses back to Atterbury, Desma lay down on the floor of the stadium. "I took a nap on the same floor the Colts had spit on," she would later recall. "You know? I slept on the ground in December, in the cold, waiting for a bus so that I could go to God only knows where and God only knows whether or not I was coming back alive."

The soldiers from Indiana spent the next three months training full-time at Fort Stewart. Forty miles southwest of Savannah,

Georgia, Fort Stewart was the largest active duty military base east of the Mississippi, and it was home to twenty thousand soldiers and thirty thousand family members; the Department of Defense operated three elementary schools on the post. On one side of the base, Charity and Debbie shared an enormous tent with other women who were training with the 139th, while Desma lived about fifteen miles away, in a female barracks in the post's cantonment area. Charity and Debbie were learning how to provide security to supply convoys. Charity had been given the job of truck commander and was working with a crew of two young men, a driver and a gunner. Her job involved being constantly on the radio, listening to people back at headquarters, relaying information to the rest of the convoy.

Debbie was assigned to drive a truck with a different crew. Her truck commander, Sergeant Craig Selby, was in his early twenties, and her gunner, Tucker Boone, was only nineteen. They were polite, serious, scared. They appeared surprised to be working with a woman in her midfifties; hardly anybody in the regiment was older than thirty. "They were a little skeptical," Debbie would say later. "It was like, What are *you* doing here? You don't really belong." A little standoffish at first, Selby warmed to Debbie over time. He struck her as conscientious, determined to do a good job. He had different ideas than Debbie was used to, however; he wanted the crew to spend every waking minute together, and instructed the others to meet him for breakfast. "Well, I don't really eat breakfast," Debbie said. "Can I just meet you where we are supposed to start our training?" Selby said, "No." He eased up later when he realized that she would always be where she was needed. As Debbie would say, "He didn't act as crazy about having to eat breakfast together." It was Selby's first deployment, and Boone's, too.

They spent most of their time inside a Humvee. It was Debbie at the wheel, Selby on the radio, and Boone up in the turret. Debbie practiced driving out on country roads, mud roads, dirt roads, roads full of potholes. The official name for the exercise was lanes training, although the route never resembled a lane; Debbie had to concentrate fiercely to keep the Humvee on the twisting, sloppy byways. As she drove, they were fired upon, and had to decide whether to forge through the hail of fake bullets, or stop and shoot back. They came upon bombs. They learned to scrutinize everything: an empty Coke can with wires running out of it, a trash bag left by the side of the road, a dead animal with explosives stuffed into its guts, a plain wire drawn across the road. The ordnance was not live but sounded real. They also learned to read routes by mapping out proposed paths on tables covered with sand, moving miniature trucks along pretend roads of colored yarn. Debbie could see it was going to be critical that she not make a wrong turn. You did not want to get lost in Iraq.

On the other side of Fort Stewart, Desma kept distributing supplies to the male soldiers she was supposed to be training with in the 293rd — although from her perspective, it seemed like the men were getting all the training. They ran lanes, she did not. They did tables, she did not. They identified roadside bombs, she did not. As time passed, Desma began to grow concerned that she was not being adequately prepared. "I didn't come here to not get any training, but I wasn't getting any," Desma would say. "I wasn't allowed. I was the bullheaded female. And I say female with a nasty tone because that's what they did. I didn't go out in the lanes, I didn't do any tables, I didn't go on any convoys. I didn't shoot anything, other than my personal weapon. I ran a supply area. I handled equipment. I gave 'em how much ammo they needed to go out and do their range, and when they come back I picked up their brass. I set up ammo and I took brass, I set up ammo and I took brass. Never once did I go out on a lane. Never once did I have positive identification of a roadside bomb. Never once."

Desma did not see Debbie at all during the three months they spent at Fort Stewart. Only rarely — perhaps three times — did she manage to contrive a face-to-face meeting with Charity, although they stayed in touch by text and by phone. Desma was struck by the difference in their experiences; Charity sounded engaged by her work and happy with her unit, and there was energy in her voice as she regaled Desma with stories about running lanes. Desma made friends with the other women who also had been attached to the 293rd and found them each to be as miserable as she was. It was just a lousy unit to be in if you were a woman, Desma concluded.

The women had been warned not to walk around the post on their own because it wasn't safe, and because there were so few of them in the 293rd they were constantly playing the role of battle buddy for each other. Perhaps Desma's closest friend at Fort Stewart was a female soldier named Bridget Palmer, who was also attached to the 293rd. Palmer was from Evansville — she had gone to high school with Michelle Fischer, had sat right behind her in math class. One evening Desma wrote in a small notebook:

Palmer!

Hey Babe! In the shower. Please will

you be my battle to go to the coffee shop + PX?

Love you!

Desma

Palmer wrote back:

You only love me when you want somethin'.

Desma never filed a formal complaint about how women were being treated, but she believed that another female soldier did, because while they were in Georgia the regiment received an unexpected visit from the inspector general's office. At one point Desma was standing in the back of a truck, tossing out boxes of ammo, when her first sergeant offered to help; then a two-star general walked up and climbed into the truck. The first sergeant stood beside Desma, listening to everything they said. The general wanted to know how things were going. Were there real issues of discrimination?

"Sir, I've not been one to complain about getting my hands dirty," Desma replied. "And I can tell you, I've worked with the infantry on several occasions, but I've never been treated so badly."

The first sergeant shot her a sharp look.

"You know that's right," Desma told him. "You were part of the problem when you told them they couldn't talk to me."

She turned back to the general. "Sir, it's getting better," she said. "The cohesion has got to have time to build."

But the cohesion did not build. Instead, after she was allowed to participate in more of the training exercises, there was sexual tension. At one point, while a group of soldiers were practicing hand-to-hand combat moves, a staff sergeant kept telling Desma that she was doing a move wrong. He said, "Here, lay down." He sat on top of Desma, as she had been sitting on top of the other woman, straddling Desma in a chokehold position. "Shouldn't I be on top?" Desma asked. She was not even trying to make a joke, but the staff sergeant's face reddened. "Because right then and there, he envisioned me on top," Desma would say afterward. "And it wasn't meant to be sexual, but he totally took it there."

Desma's hair became an issue. Per regulations, she tried to keep her hair in a bun, but throughout the course of the day, her hair had a tendency to work its way loose. At one point Desma took her hair down for a moment so that she could put it back up again — but the sight of a woman with loose hair enraged her company commander. "You!" he bellowed. "Put your fucking hair up! I don't ever want to see that shit again!" Loose hair had transformed her in his mind, apparently

— from a soldier into an object of desire. "There was that sexual tension, flat out," Desma would say later. "He found himself attracted to me when I had my hair down." Desma and Charity got a four-day pass and took a trip to Savannah, Georgia, where Desma found a salon and cut her hair short like a boy. "And the repercussions from that were crazy," she recalled. The company commander wanted to know who had given her authorization to cut her hair. No pleasing him, Desma decided.

Yet often Desma knew more about how to get things done in the military than her younger colleagues. The men in the 293rd wanted to believe they were better than her — and some of them had seen combat, and knew more than she did about war — but the young guys in supply did not seem to understand paperwork, filing, or accountability. As the 293rd started shipping equipment to Kuwait, Desma argued with colleagues about how best to ensure that the equipment would actually arrive where they wanted it to go. She got a reputation for being difficult, but simultaneously won the admiration of the first sergeant; she could be undiplomatic but she was often correct about how best to get things done.

Nevertheless, Desma decided that she wanted out of the 293rd. The idea to transfer came about one night, while Desma was talking on the phone to Charity. She wondered out loud if there was any way to get out of the 293rd, and Charity said, "I would give anything for you to be with me." They decided Desma should request a transfer into the 139th. Desma tried to file a formal request, but after she filled out all of the paperwork a platoon sergeant in the 293rd said the request would never go through and put the paperwork into a shredder. Then she and Charity began talking to everybody they knew, lobbying to get Desma switched into the 139th. "That was the only unit that I knew of that I could go to and be treated fairly," Desma said later. Plus, she could be with her lover. Desma called everybody she had ever worked for. "Get me out of here," she said. "These people are going to get me killed."

But the days kept slipping by. February drew to a close and still Desma remained in the 293rd. In March they flew to Kuwait. "Starbucks and Subway," as Desma said later. "It's like America East." In Kuwait, Desma got to see Charity every day, because they lived much closer together. While they were there, Desma heard that Mary's new husband had just gotten terrible news: Mary had lost the baby. When she called, her friend was a wreck; Desma tried to lift her spirits but it felt futile. Desma also heard from Michelle Fischer, who had just moved to Denver,

Colorado. Michelle had found an apartment in Denver's Capitol Hill neighborhood, where Billy, who had refused to sign a lease with her, nevertheless spent almost every night. Michelle had just started working for AmeriCorps. She had made a batch of pot brownies and tried mailing them to Georgia, but Desma had already left by the time the package arrived. Shortly after Desma arrived in Kuwait, Michelle sent her an email.

Hi Des!

How's it going over there? Just wondering where you are . . . if you've made it to Kuwait yet. . . . I miss seeing you daily, even if it was in a shitty situation.

Did you get the brownies? Were they any good??? I was worried, it was my first batch. . . . Baking is different in high altitudes. No, really. You have to add more water or some shit. . . .

I am working damn near for free ($10,908 annually before taxes) since I am in AmeriCorps. Did you know that when you swear in to AmeriCorps, you have to say the EXACT same oath as when you swear into the military??? No shit. I raised my right hand and was like, I feel like I've said this before. Then I realized I am working for the fucking government again. . . .

Ya, speaking of work . . . I should do some.

I miss you tons. Keep in touch or else.

Love,
Michelle

Desma never wrote back. She had a hard time staying in touch with friends over long distances; it was all she could do to maintain contact with her children. Josh turned fifteen on March 16, 2008, and Desma called to say happy birthday. She had already sent him a gift card. She told him that Kuwait looked a lot like Indiana — all the same chain stores.

"When can you come home?" he asked.

"Bub, you know I gotta do this," Desma told him. "Pay attention in school, listen to your stepmother, don't give your dad any trouble."

She heard from her daughters the following day. Each of the girls wrote a short note inside an email sent by her father-in-law, and he wrote a quick line to Desma at the bottom.

Date: Mon, 17 Mar 2008
Subject: Letters from home

DEAR MOMMY

I MISS YOU. I LOVE YOU! I'M DOING OK. HOW ARE YOU? I'M STILL

DOING OK IN SCHOOL!

LOVE, LEXI

DEAR MOMMY,

HIYA DOIN'?.!I LOVEYOU. GRANDpA'S LETTING US USE HIS COMPUTER?!. I"M A GEEK. LOL, HA HA T.T.Y.L

PAIGIE POOH

I told the girls they could do this regularly so they could stay in touch.

Be Careful out there

The weeks in Kuwait slipped by quickly. After Desma complained that she was not getting as much training as her male colleagues, the first sergeant sent her out in the field for four days with two platoons of infantrymen. They shared the same tent. "Asshole to elbow, I'm telling you," Desma would say later. "Everybody was nut to butt, except for this one square in the corner that was mine, and it was marked off by chairs." She was the only soldier to be given a cot; the infantrymen were sleeping on the ground. Desma took the cot, and folded it up, and chucked it out the door. She got the chairs, stacked them up, and put them in the corner. "I was like, 'Look, fuckers. We have to live together for the next year. You're going to have to pull your heads out of your asses.' " Desma tried to earn the respect of the other soldiers by sleeping on the ground, too, but it made no difference. The following day, she could not find another soldier who would accompany her when she had to go to the bathroom, although they had been forbidden to go by themselves. "It was me and two platoons, boys," Desma would recall. "And nobody wanted to walk the girl to the bathroom." Finally a squad leader took pity on Desma and escorted her to a secluded area. He told her not to tell anyone.

At the last minute, just before they left the safety of Kuwait for Iraq, the brigade's leadership shuffled a series of people around, trying to make certain that every soldier had been given the right job. Desma was outside smoking a cigarette when Lieutenant Colonel Joseph Agron approached her, along with a sergeant major. The sergeant major asked if she was Specialist Brooks.

"Yes, sir," Desma said.

"Specialist Brooks, I have an offer for you."

"What is it, Sergeant Major?"

"Do you still want that transfer?"

"More than anything on God's green earth!" Desma said. "Please, I want out of here."

The lieutenant colonel told Desma that if she agreed to take the job, she would serve with the 139th. That group was doing convoy security, and she would probably become a truck driver.

"I've not done any of the lanes training, sir," Desma said.

Colonel Agron looked furious. He made certain that Desma spent the remaining time in Kuwait getting caught up. As she was transferring out of the 293rd, Desma's first sergeant buttonholed her to express his dismay.

"What is going on?" he asked.

"I told you I couldn't be here," Desma replied. "I told you I had no business being in this infantry company because I wasn't going to be able to advance my career and I wasn't taken seriously as a soldier and I wasn't getting any training and to be honest it was because I didn't have a penis. I know that's hard for some people to hear, and they tell me to watch my mouth, but that's what it was, to be honest."

"What can I do to get you to stay?" he asked. "I promise you, things will be different."

"No, First Sergeant, they won't be."

The exact nature of her job became more clear in the days that followed. She would report to Charity Elliott, who would serve as her truck commander. They would be toward the front of a supply convoy, and their mission would be to get the trucks safely down Iraq's highways without hitting any bombs.

Desma figured she would learn on the job.

By coincidence, right before Desma Brooks transferred into the 139th, Debbie Deckard had transferred out of that regiment. The more time Debbie had spent training with Selby and Boone, the more anxious she had grown about being a truck driver. She had completed all the training, and her scores had been fine. But she worried about being responsible for some kind of catastrophe. Three days before they flew to Iraq, Debbie met with Colonel Agron. He asked how she was feeling about her job.

"Well, if this is the job I have to do, I will do it," Debbie told him. "But I feel a little uncomfortable. I'm not sure I get all this driving stuff."

Agron was surprised, because Debbie had scored well in the training exercises. "But you did a fine job the other day," he told her. "I already rode with you. You reacted exactly as you were supposed to."

"Well, I understand that," Debbie said. "But no, I'm not really comfortable with the position."

Colonel Agron had an idea: there was a young man assigned to the brigade's headquarters in Mosul. The job involved interacting with everybody who needed permission to come on and off the base regularly. "He's a very gung ho kid," the colonel said. "He's a good kid. But he cannot sit still for anything in the world, and I don't think that he's mature enough. Didn't you work with people before you came here?"

"Yes," Debbie said. "I was a manager."

Agron said he thought the two of them should switch positions.

Debbie was relieved to accept the desk job. She had not wanted to bear responsibility for the lives of everyone in her truck out on the highways of Iraq. Coincidentally, Desma and Debbie changed jobs at almost exactly the same time, and Desma happened to take exactly the same job that Debbie had given up, although with a different crew. Later, when they discussed those last-minute moves that had taken place right before they left Kuwait, Desma told Debbie that asking for the change had been the right thing to do.

"I'm so glad they found you a different job," Desma told Debbie. "You had no business driving with all that gear on for sixteen, eighteen hours at a time."

"I know," Debbie said with chagrin. "I'd have done it, though, if I would have absolutely had to."

"I know you would have," Desma told her. "But, Debbie — dadgummit. You ain't got no business doing that shit."

Because it was a hard job, being truck driver.

2
Hooker

Iraq: dust, heat, unremitting loneliness. The soldiers who belonged to the 113th Support Battalion had been sundered from one another and were now living far apart on different bases. At least Desma and Charity had each other — that was what Desma thought in the beginning. The two of them lived inside a containerized housing unit called a CHU — basically, half a conex shipping container — at Al Qayyarah Airfield West. The CHU was eight feet wide and forty feet long, and they had twenty feet of its length. A wall separated Desma and Charity from the two male soldiers who inhabited the other end of the same shipping container. The result was something like a trailer without indoor plumbing. The immense, sprawling airfield lay in central Iraq, near the city of Al Qayyarah (a conglomeration of industrial facilities, markets, and residences), 180 miles north of Baghdad, in the vast alluvial valley formed by the Tigris River. What Desma saw when she looked at the surrounding landscape was a lot of sand, some scrubby shrubs, and a few trees. There were no rolling dunes. It was flat, flat, flat.

The former Iraqi Air Force "superbase" had been built in the 1970s and had served as a launching site for Iraqi Mirage fighter jets and MiG-25s during the war with Iran. It was later bombed heavily during the Persian Gulf War and again during the early part of Operation Iraqi Freedom — in the blistering air strikes that Desma had watched on television while at Camp Atterbury back in 2003, during her false deployment. When American-led ground forces took the air base, the soldiers had found weapons storage igloos, aboveground aircraft hangars made of concrete reinforced with steel plates, and subterranean aircraft hangars equipped with hydraulic lifts that had been constructed to withstand a direct hit by a nuclear bomb. An engineering battalion out of Fort Bragg had repaired the damage to the runways, which were riddled with craters, and the air base had reopened as a major entry and exit point for US troops. Officially the post was known as Al Qayyarah Airfield West, but the soldiers who poured into the base started calling it Q-West, and after that, Key West. The base was famous for its unforgiving vistas, remote location, unreliable Internet access, limited phone service, and infrequent outgoing mail deliveries.

Desma and Charity pushed Desma's twin bed under the window, at one end of the shipping container. They pushed Charity's twin bed against one of the other walls so that the two beds made an L. They had also been given two wall lockers and two nightstands. That was it. If they wanted to pee, or brush their teeth, or take a shower, Desma and Charity walked to the communal women's bathroom. They were supposed to make sure they had a buddy. Desma ignored that rule if Charity was not around, for she felt safe enough going to the showers by herself, but after an active duty unit moved into a nearby compound, she started carrying a knife at all times. They had air-conditioning in the CHU — when they had power. It was already hot, and getting hotter. Desma described the CHU briefly in an email that she wrote to Mary on April 1, 2008. "Nice, but small," said Desma. "Would you send my robe & junk when you can?? I really wish you were here."

They did not hang anything on the walls of the CHU. Inside her wall locker, though, Desma taped several pictures of her children. One showed Alexis and Paige playing on a swing set at the park; another showed Paige lying down with a large plastic car on her belly, as if she had gotten run over by the toy; then there was Alexis with a close friend, and Josh's eighth-grade school picture. Desma knew that when she opened the locker she would see the children, and yet it still knocked her sideways to see their faces. She did not carry any pictures with her when she left the post, because looking at images of her children when she was on a mission made her feel physically sick.

As she had during her year in Afghanistan, Desma made certain to speak to the children at least once a week, never on the same day of the week, never at the same time of day. She tried as best she could to do the things a mother would do, albeit long distance. On April 8, 2008, Josh wrote to Desma:

> hey my phone doesn't work anymore because the charger piece broke in it, but other than that im doin good. THIS IS JOSH BY THE WAY. do you think you could help me pay for it to get it fixed? Hows work going? I LOVE YOU and ill talk to you later bye

Desma wrote back:

> I will send you a new phone. I will have it sent from WalMart. That way you can keep your number and all your time. . . . I will set it so you can pick up the phone at the store if I can. I LOVE YOU TOO!!! Mom

But it was easier to do her job as a soldier if she walled off the part of herself that was a mother. She could no longer mix the two roles easily, because the separate halves of her identity were no longer coherent. So she let a certain amount of distance creep between herself and her children, to insulate herself from the pain of the separation. "It was easier to continue what I was doing with being overseas and what have you if I wasn't wound up in what was going on at home," Desma would say later. "Maybe it was the wrong approach to take, but otherwise I might have actually just left. Ta-da, good-bye."

They lived about a mile from the dining facility. Desma and Charity bought a pair of mountain bikes at the PX — one was blue and the other was red — and used them to ride to and from meals. For some reason, the bicycles would not hold air in their tires for very long, but they were good enough for a ride to the PX or the chow hall or the post office. Then Desma saw a flyer that said, "MOVING SALE, EVERYTHING MUST GO." Some guys in the 101st Airborne Division were heading home. For twenty bucks she and Charity bought a nineteen-inch Magnavox TV, two blue canvas lawn chairs, and a coffeepot. Later Desma found a Sony PlayStation for sale at the PX, and they started competing to see who could make it past the devil on Guitar Hero, or else they watched movies on the American Forces Network.

What they saw around them was white CHU after white CHU after white CHU, in a sea of gray gravel. Boxy metal islands in a stony ocean. Outside their CHU, Charity and Desma set up a little area where they liked to hang out as long as the *shamal* winds were not blowing. After the rainy season, the shamal winds sprang up, beginning in May and intensifying through June and July. The strong windstorms could blow for days, carrying vast clouds of dust that sometimes towered fifteen thousand feet in the air. The dust was fine and silty and crept everywhere. It had the consistency of baby powder. Puffs of it rose every time Desma took a step; she made a little cloud just by walking. But between the dust storms, they enjoyed any breeze they could find, sitting outside in the blue lawn chairs. They placed a can for cigarette butts in what they came to think of as their front yard, and put a wooden step by the front door, as well as a rock on which they wrote, "Elliott and Brooks live here." Then they found magnetic letters at the PX and stuck them onto the metal door of the shipping container, so that they could leave messages for each other. AT THE PX, Desma wrote to Charity. And Charity wrote back, WENT TO LUNCH.

In time, Desma and Charity grew fond of some of the guys in the 139th, particularly

Josh Stonebraker, who served as the gunner in one of the scout trucks that led their convoys. He was a big, burly guy who worked as a guard in a women's prison near Terre Haute, Indiana. Everybody called him Stoney. He was a 100 percent devoted family man, and although they saw each other nearly every day in a place where there were hardly any women, he never tried to take advantage of his friendship with Desma. Stoney was a joker. He and Desma began a series of pranks executed on the down days. Usually they ran a mission one day, had a down day the next. They spent the down days cleaning trucks or conducting preventive maintenance checks on their vehicles. The lengthy maintenance checks had once annoyed Desma, but she no longer questioned the practice — a working vehicle had become her lifeline.

Stoney shared a nearby CHU with the driver of his truck, Dustin Ford, while their truck commander, Jeff Stacey, lived about two shipping containers farther away, in a CHU that he shared with the platoon sergeant. The guys from the lead scout truck were a tight group, ran around as a crowd, and Stoney was the magnet that held them together. Once Desma put Vaseline all over the door handle to Stoney's CHU — "so, like, when he grabbed it, his hand would slip off, and he'd be gooey." As it happened, a dust storm blew in, and the Vaseline became a muddy slop. Stoney liked that experience so much that when Desma and Charity left to go and take showers, he rearranged their yard. They returned to find their two mountain bikes, the two blue canvas lawn chairs, the wooden step, the rock, and the butt can all perfectly arranged in their usual configuration, up on their roof. Stoney laughed his ass off at their dumbfounded expressions.

One night Desma heard scuffling, muffled laughter, and the noise that duct tape makes as it is unrolled. She figured maybe Stoney was ducttaping them inside the CHU. Actually he was duct-taping a can of shaving cream to the outside of the conex, and a string to the doorknob so that when she opened the door she would get covered in shaving cream. Desma opened the door a sliver, saw about eight people, and tried to slam the door closed, but the guys shoved it open and shot white foam everywhere. Stoney dropped by often, and when Desma and Charity were not home, he made sure they knew he had been there. They would come back and find STONEY IS A GOD or HEY BITCHES written across the side of their CHU.

Talking over the radio from their separate vehicles during missions that could last for twelve, fourteen, even sixteen hours, they dropped into the habit of referring to each other by nicknames they found out there in the Iraqi desert. Charity became Mojo Mama, or just plain Mama. Stoney became Papa. They called Desma Brooksy or Hooker, a term of endearment. Stoney's truck commander, Jeff Stacey, had buckteeth, and somebody nicknamed him Beaver. He also had a temper, and eventually Desma started calling him Angry Beaver, after a character in a cartoon that her kids liked to watch. The names became who they were — back in Kuwait, they had been Desma and Charity; now they were Mama and Hooker.

It was always the guys out front, in the lead scout position. If Stoney's team was working, then Ford was at the wheel, while Angry Beaver was on the radio, commanding that truck, and Stoney was up in the gun turret. His job was to catch any anomaly the other guys did not see, shoot things that he thought had to be shot, and present a visual threat. The second vehicle was the assistant scout truck, known as ass scout for short, or just plain ass. Running ass meant backing Stoney up, spotting any potential bombs he failed to notice, and being ready to fire if there was an ambush. The two scout trucks ran ahead of the rest of the supply convoy, hunting for wires, for boxes, for mounds of trash, for dead animals, for anything that could signify the possibility of death.

Charity and Desma typically rode in the convoy's third vehicle, right after the two scout trucks. They were the navigation team. Desma drove while Charity, who was in charge of the vehicle, sat beside her manning the radio, and up in their gun turret was usually a guy they called Peaches. Every once in a while they got Brandon Hall instead — they called him BB or B-Boy. The navigation team followed at a slight distance, but maintained communication with the two scout trucks at all times, even if they could no longer see them. No matter what happened to the scout trucks, it was navigation's job to lead the civilian trucks following behind to the correct destination, along the route that had been assigned by the convoy commander. Desma had been blessed with an excellent sense of direction and a good memory for physical landmarks, and she excelled at the job of driving the navigation truck. Charity aided her by tracking their progress on the specialized military GPS system, called a Blue Force Tracking device. The Blue Force tracker showed the position of every vehicle in their convoy, as well as any other convoy within a certain range, and through the device they could also send secure text messages to the other trucks or to the home station back at Q-West.

After them snaked the rest of the convoy. On one mission that spring, they were followed by thirty civilian trucks, then two military vehicles, another thirty civilian trucks, one military vehicle, thirty civilian trucks, another military vehicle, the wrecker, and the rear gun. The military vehicles were constant, but the number of civilian trucks varied every time they went out. Sometimes there were as few as ten or twelve civilian trucks in the intervals between the military vehicles, sometimes many more. Sometimes their convoy ran back-to-back with another convoy until they had several hundred vehicles in a row. The wrecker rode at the back so that any truck that might need help would be ahead of it when it broke down or blew up. The wrecker did not have any outside weapons, however, and it needed the protection of the rear gun truck. The job of rear gun was to cover the backside of the convoy. That vehicle was usually a Humvee, with no armor on the bottom, and the soldiers inside it were more vulnerable than those inside more heavily armored vehicles, but it was almost always the lead trucks that got hit.

The hardest part about Desma's job, at least in the beginning, was getting used to an unfamiliar vehicle. The scout teams and the navigation team drove armored security vehicles. Only eight feet wide, the ASVs were highly maneuverable, but they weighed fifteen tons and had a heavily protected hull, as well as enormous nubbed tires that came to Desma's hips. Over time she grew adept at climbing onto the huge tires to reach the small hatches on the upper part of the truck. There were four panes of extra-thick glass across the front and sides of the vehicle, which gave the soldiers a panoramic view of their surroundings. The ASV had been designed specifically to survive IED explosions; its hull was more heavily armored than a Humvee, and the sides of the vehicle angled outward in a V shape, to divert the force of any blast away from its occupants. The armor that covered the outside of the vehicle had been made of ceramic composite, and in case that armor was pierced, the vehicle also had a spall lining — the inside of the truck had been coated in composite material, too, with the hope of slowing any metal particles that might come flying through the hull. The ASV also had more firepower than a Humvee, as each vehicle came equipped with two machine guns and a grenade launcher. Armored security vehicles were expensive — a Humvee cost $140,000, whereas an ASV cost $800,000 — but they kept more people alive. Plus the ASV could do seventy miles an hour on the highway, could ford rivers that were up to five feet deep, and the crew compartment was fully air-conditioned.

Desma had never driven an ASV before. When they first arrived in Iraq, at the end of March 2008, all she did for several weeks was practice driving the unfamiliar vehicle. It still felt new to her even after she and Charity started running missions, in April 2008. Desma told Charity that she was scared of doing something dumb, like mistaking the turn signal for the headlights or rolling the vehicle, but Charity assured her she was a good driver. Charity kept praising her skills, kept telling her she could do it, kept making her think it would be all right. They spent so many hours inside the vehicle that after one month had elapsed, Desma felt as though she knew every inch of the ASV.

At first they always ran navigation, but after they had been in Iraq for a month or two, Desma and Charity started running assistant scout sometimes. Then it would be Stoney, the Angry Beaver, and Ford in the lead, with Desma, Charity, and Peaches right behind them. Or maybe a different crew would be in the first truck — there were two other teams in their platoon that ran as lead scout, too. "We liked running up front," Desma would say later. "It was just something to do. We were hanging out with them. We could talk to the guys, you know. I got to drive off the road, check culverts and things."

Maybe every third or fourth mission, they would run ass. Otherwise they ran nav. Desma and Charity never took the lead position, which was the most dangerous slot. "Put the boys out front," Desma would say later. "I don't know — it always fell that we were the second or third truck in the convoy. I didn't really want to be out front." No matter what position they took in the convoy, inside the vehicle they stuck to the same roles — Charity on the radio, calling the shots, Desma at the wheel, and Peaches with his head poking out of the gun turret — although once Charity served as gunner when they got stuck at the back of the convoy in the rear gun truck. Bush was still saying women were not in combat, but what else would you call being a gunner on a highway in Iraq in the spring of 2008? It was combat as far as Desma was concerned. She never took the role of gunner, but she would have if someone had asked. "Would I have hesitated to pull the trigger? No."

During April and May, most of their missions involved driving up to Zakho, one of the northernmost cities in Iraq, on the country's border with Turkey, and escorting civilian supply trucks from Zakho down to Al Qayyarah. They were protecting one of the army's main supply routes. The United States–led coalition had established several routes by which to funnel food, water, fuel, weapons, and ammunition into the war theater, including one coming up from Kuwait — but soldiers in other regiments worried about protecting the convoys that were bringing goods up from the south. The 139th Field Artillery was in charge of securing the northernmost supply chain, the one that flowed in the opposite direction, down out of Turkey, from Zakho through Dahuk and Mosul, along a highway that ran roughly parallel to the course of the Tigris River. Their platoon's missions stopped at Al Qayyarah. The same highway continued south to Baiji and Tikrit, but that wasn't their run. Drivers belonging to another platoon in the 139th escorted the supply trucks during that leg of their journey, which was the more dangerous stretch of highway. The farther north they were, the less likely they were to chance upon a bomb. Up past Dahuk, they were in Kurdish territory, in a part of Iraq the soldiers called the green zone. Far fewer incidents occurred there.

And initially they ran only night missions, which also reduced the risk. "Traffic was a lot less at night," Desma would say later. "The incidents were a lot less at night, under the cover of darkness. It's not like you can sneak five hundred vehicles through a town at any point. But incidents were a lot less at night." On a typical mission that April, Desma and Charity started getting ready at four in the afternoon: they loaded ammo into the ASV's weapons, drove out to the range and tested the guns, drove back, and attended a briefing. The convoy commander described the route they were going to take, told them how fast to go, and listed the military trucks by number. After that they lined up every truck and checked every fuel gauge. Tires with visible damage came off; four or five soldiers hustled over to help change the damaged tires as quickly as possible. They got on the road by 8:00 p.m. As they traveled north, they gradually climbed in elevation, leaving behind the flat plain of the Tigris River valley. The river remained mysteriously always out of sight and Desma never saw that silver ribbon. By the time they reached the mountains, it was ten degrees cooler. On the outskirts of Dahuk, before they began the steepest part of the winding climb into the mountains, they stopped to pee because it was safe to get out of the trucks at that point. Then the soldiers got back in their vehicles and negotiated the steep switchbacks of the final climb. This was Desma's favorite part of the drive — it was the most scenic and the least boring. It was 3:00 a.m. by the time they reached Zakho.

They spent the night in a place that everybody called "the hotel," an office building with a couple dozen cots set up in a wide-open area. Desma grabbed an empty cot and curled up to get a few hours of sleep. The following day they met the supply trucks that had come down out of Turkey, turned around, and escorted the trucks back to Al Qayyarah, dropping in elevation as they moved south. They had daylight all the way to Mosul. It was all right to drive in daylight up in northern Iraq, but after Mosul, it was better to drive in the dark. It took them about ten hours to get from Zakho back to Al Qayyarah; they could have gone faster, but they spent the second half of the trip nosing along at thirty miles per hour, looking for shit that might blow up. The following day, another platoon from the same regiment escorted the convoy from Al Qayyarah down to Tikrit. After Tikrit, soldiers who were stationed at Balad took over the job of getting the goods where they were going. It was mind-numbing to drive for ten or twelve or fourteen hours at a stretch while scouring the shoulders for a stray wire or the wrong sort of trash, but Desma enjoyed leaving the post, and the work made her feel more like a real soldier than anything else she had done in her life.

Nobody ever said what was inside the trucks. Food, mail, ammo, weapons, fuel — it could be anything required by the military. Often, after they ran a mission, they would suddenly find fresh milk again in the chow hall, or chips on the shelves at the PX. Once, when they were in the middle of a run, the entire convoy took a bumpy detour — a bomb had blown apart a stretch of highway, and the convoy jounced along some decrepit side roads before turning back onto the main road again — and a civilian driver called for the convoy to halt so he could tend to his cargo. The convoy commander said over the radio that he did not want to stop. The driver said he needed to resecure his load *now,* or they were going to have a problem, because he was carrying Hellfire missiles. "We were like, 'Holy shit!' " Desma said later. "We had no clue there were Hellfires on that truck."

During the time that Desma spent in Iraq, the total number of IEDs placed along the highways began to decline, compared with the year before (the most violent year of the entire war). In 2007, the number of IEDs found each month had peaked in June at 2,588. Since Desma had arrived, however, the number of IEDs kept dropping: soldiers found 1,161 IEDs across Iraq in April 2008, 901 in May 2008, and 602 in June. Most of those were discovered south of Desma's run. Nobody in the 139th had hit as many IEDs as Mancil Smith, another soldier in their regiment who often ran in the lead scout truck. During an earlier deployment, he had been involved in five different explosions, and he hit several more IEDs that year. The bombs had given Mancil a lazy eye. Desma had seen photographs of him that were taken before the war, and his eyes had looked different.

They had it easier. The only time Desma really screwed up during two months of runs to Zakho was the night when she and Charity misread a sign and let the scout trucks ahead of them make a wrong turn. They wound up driving down the main thoroughfare of Dahuk, past all kinds of storefronts. They got their gun turret hung up on some power lines and had to stop. An Iraqi man with a well-trimmed beard who was wearing a plaid shirt and khakis came over with a broom to get them disentangled. In broken English he urged them to leave. "No go here!" he exclaimed. "No military!" He gave the confused navigation team excellent directions, and they got out of there as quickly as possible.

They loved Zakho. A city of two hundred thousand on the banks of the Little Khabur, a tributary of the Tigris, Zakho had been a trading center for centuries. It was known for its rice, oil, lentils, and fruit. Stoney wanted to walk across the Delal Bridge, a local landmark made of ancient stones, possibly of Roman construction. If they made it across, they would be in Turkey, and Stoney wanted to steal a big Turkish flag that they could see from their side of the river, but the customs guys would not let them onto the bridge. They often ate dinner in one of Zakho's restaurants. "They would bring two soups, a salad, beans, all these vegetables," Desma later recalled. "And then the meat. Lamb, beef. They had this purple — I don't know what it was — some sort of pickling they put on onions and other vegetables. And you'd eat that with the naan, the flat bread. Really amazing food." Eating inside the restaurants also brought Desma into contact with local traditions. "Us, as women, we had to stay in the front of the restaurant, by the window, which was a little unnerving. But they didn't want us near the prayer areas. In every restaurant, you'll find an alcove facing the east. Strictly for prayer. Women don't belong in those areas. It was not so much that I was one, a sinner; two, an American; and three, an infidel. You know, it's just, women don't belong in those areas."

Desma and Charity spotted more potential problems than the guys. Stoney liked that the two women were more cautious. "They were very diligent," he remembered. "It definitely helped to have them rotate up front. We were used to seeing lots of stuff and we would just drive by. Having a fresh set of eyes was better." Sometimes, though, he teased them about their wariness. During one particularly long mission, when they were on their way back down from the Turkish border, and had gotten as far as Mosul, and it was maybe a few hours after midnight, Desma and Charity called a halt to the convoy because they had spotted something suspicious. "Did you guys see that?" one of the women asked over the radio. "That could be a wire." Stoney took a look; he thought the object that lay across the road was a water pipe. It was hard to tell in the dark, though, and he figured it was better to be safe. They called EOD and sat around waiting for the explosives guys to arrive — an extra two hours. In the end, the object turned out to be a water pipe. Stoney did not let Mama and Hooker forget. "Did you guys see that?" he chortled over the radio at random intervals. "That could be a wire!" It became one of his favorite refrains, a chorus to their convoys.

One day they were driving south from Zakho with some supply trucks, and had just left the green zone. Stoney, Ford, and Angry Beaver were out front as lead scout. Desma and Charity were two trucks behind, running navigation. They had already descended out of the steep part of the mountains and were surrounded by beautiful, flowing hills. Desma watched Stoney's truck disappear behind one hill, and then a few minutes later, she saw a big cloud of dust. They felt the vibration first, and then they heard the explosion. Desma could not move or reason. Were the guys dead? And then, over the radio, she heard the sound of Stoney's voice, alive and pissed off: "Missed me, motherfucker!" The back part of his truck was speckled with shrapnel, but everybody inside was fine. It was Ford who found the second bomb waiting nearby. They had to sit there while a team from Explosive Ordnance Disposal drove out to meet them, and the second bomb made a huge white flash when it was detonated. The rest of that trip was quiet, none of the usual chatter.

Otherwise, the missions were hot, boring, and interminable. By the time she returned to Q-West, Desma had little energy to put into corresponding with friends who were living comfortable lives back home. Michelle had been sending long, chatty emails to Desma for weeks, but Desma did not respond until May 3, 2008. She kept it short and sweet. She just said:

> I do miss you so very much. Things here have been very crazy and getting to the MWR to get a computer is nearly impossible. I am having a satellite set up in the morning so that I can use my Internet from the house. That will make things so much easier. So, how are things with you? Billy doing alright? Still loving your job? Well, got to go, try to catch you tomorrow. Love Des

Michelle knew from experience that it was difficult to communicate with people back home while living in a war zone. She mailed Desma a box of cupcakes. Then she wrote back:

> It's okay, just glad to hear that you're alright. . . . Things are good with me. I love my job, and I'm getting to meet some really awesome people. Billy and I are doing — okay — not great. He is doing his

> thing and I am doing mine and they aren't really similar. . . .
>
> I miss you tons, Des. I hope you're getting along okay and things aren't too bad. What do they have you doing there? Is Charity nearby??
>
> Love and hugs
>
> Michelle

Desma did not reply — they had missions to run. Mama and Papa and Peaches had become her new family, and Michelle lived back in a place where people did not scan the sides of the road, and had never heard the jubilation of a soldier who had ducked flying shrapnel. Michelle wrote again one week later; she had just gotten some bad news. A friend's husband had been killed in another part of Iraq when a truck rolled over and crushed him. In an email dated May 13, 2008, Michelle wrote to Desma, Debbie, and Patrick Miller, the three people she had been closest to in the 113th Support Battalion, all of whom were now serving in various parts of Iraq:

> I am filled with so many emotions about it, especially since the last time I saw him was their wedding in June. I feel bad but the biggest relief was that the news wasn't about one of you three.
>
> It's going to be such a long fucking year. I know this isn't much comfort but I

wanted to let you all know that a) I love you very much; b) I keep you in my thoughts; and c) I will never take for granted the things you have given me in life. It's a lot; a big part of who I am comes from my experiences and friendships with you.

I know you are all busy and it's hard to keep in touch with everyone. I hope you're safe and that your days are going by swiftly.

Much love, I miss you.

The soldier who died had been in the 152nd, another infantry regiment that was part of their brigade. Desma had not known him well, but it was all too easy to imagine herself at the wheel and Peaches up in the turret. This was more than she could put into an email. Michelle wrote long, heartfelt missives, but Desma kept most of her responses to three or four sentences. They did not match up as closely by email as they had in person, sharing a tent surrounded by pink flamingos. It was Patrick Miller who responded to Michelle. He was stationed at a base in Tikrit, to the south of Al Qayyarah. He did not mention the recent death — people back home needed to be reassured. On May 19, 2008, Patrick wrote:

Hey Doll,

Hope you're doing alright. Things here

ain't bad. Just getting by and waiting to come home. Hope things work out for the best between Billy and you. You know I got a shoulder ANYTIME you need it. Lord knows you've been there for me more than once.

We got Internet now in our rooms finally. Not the greatest but it works. I don't know how to use any of those messenger things except Yahoo, but if you're ever on, look me up. Love to talk to you some.

Miss you Doll.

Patrick

It was not what Michelle would have predicted, that Patrick Miller would become her most faithful correspondent, during the year when everybody she knew in the National Guard had to do a second deployment. "I have been working on a paper letter for you for about a week now, I'll probably finish it up and mail it soon," she wrote in her next email. "I need some beers with you bad. Who knew that was what was keeping me sane all these years?" In the same email, she sounded almost wistful about the time she had spent in the military. "I did some backcountry camping this weekend, it was awesome. I really miss some things about the army, like being forced to camp, and getting free gear. I'd kill to have back my army sleeping bag. Actually I guess I shouldn't use that phrase, if it were true I'd just reenlist. . . . Someone stop me it actually sounds like I miss the army. It's probably just because I miss you. Hope you're well over there. Write back."

Patrick wrote back regularly. Once or twice that summer he even surprised her with a telephone call. "Things have been hectic here," he said in another email. "Long hours, stupid people, you know the deal." Michelle replied by saying that she had a care package for him sitting on her table, but didn't have enough money for postage — yeah, she was that broke. "I hope you're well and have no soldier as bad as me under your command," Michelle wrote. "I'd like to keep that title if I may."

To her surprise, Patrick replied:

> I wish I could say that you were the worst soldier I have ever had, but after this one . . . You are far, far away from that. I'd trade four or five of them for one Specialist Fischer in a heartbeat. . . .
>
> I miss you a lot doll. I give just about anything to have a beer and a dance with you (to Willie Nelson's Angel Flying Too Close to the Ground of course) about now.

In her next email, Michelle suggested to Patrick that they plan a reunion after he and Debbie and Desma returned home. Maybe she could rent a cabin for them to share. Michelle told Patrick that Akbar Khan had gotten a visa that would allow him to live in the United States, and had written to say he was thinking of moving there — maybe Akbar could join them. She was sorry to hear that Patrick was dealing with dumbasses, but that was the army. "Debbie is doing okay, checking locals into the FOB or something," she told Patrick. "Security crap. I haven't heard from Des in a while but I'm sure she's doing fine as well. I am busy working and saving the world. It should be in tip-top shape by the time you get back."

Michelle was surrounded by civilians who seemed to have forgotten that the two wars continued at all, and simultaneously in contact with half a dozen soldiers who were presently serving in both of them. That year, James Cooper surprised her at unpredictable intervals by calling from Kandahar, and Akbar Khan continued to write regularly from Kabul; meanwhile, she had Debbie, Desma, and Patrick spread up and down the Tigris River valley. She showered them all with letters, emails, and care packages, whether or not they found time to reply. Debbie wrote to her faithfully. In her frequent emails, Debbie maintained her habitual cheerfulness, but reading between the lines, Michelle thought her friend sounded forlorn.

Earlier that spring, Debbie Deckard had arrived at Forward Operating Base Diamondback in the city of Mosul to learn that she was the only woman from the National Guard working on the headquarters side of the post. A young woman named Kathleen, who was serving fulltime in the army, also worked in the same office, but Kathleen was in her twenties and was having a not-so-secret affair with an unmarried lieutenant, which kept her rather busy. Debbie had gotten to live in a CHU by herself, which she considered a great luxury, but she made no real friends. Her male colleagues outranked her significantly, and they only socialized with each other. Captain Mark Buchanan mentored her kindly when she struggled to master unfamiliar computer software, but he never spent time with Debbie outside of working hours. The only people eager to talk to her were the foreign national workers who cooked, cleaned, and did construction work on the post. In all her life, Debbie had never been so isolated. She tried to put a positive spin on the experience. "It wasn't the worst time in my life," she would say later. "Probably the best part about all of that was I got my own CHU. I mean, that would be the highlight. I had it all alone, and that was fine. I didn't mind being by myself. I mean, it was hard because I didn't have anyone to talk to. But the Turkish guys were really nice. I met a lot of really neat Turkish guys there."

Debbie assuaged her sense of solitude by

writing to people at home frequently. On March 30, 2008, right after she arrived, she sent a long email describing her circumstances to about a dozen close friends and relatives, including Michelle.

> hi everyone.
>
> well I have finally arrived to my destination here in iraq. . . . its been a long road coming here with all the training in georgia that we went through. much more difficult than when we were going to afghanistan.
>
> i have been actually feeling my age imagine that!
>
> i started out going to be a convoy security driver. and that is what i trained to do, but it was extremely stressfull for me, i said if it had been 10 years ago maybe i would of been a bit more hooah. . . .
>
> my job here is very simple im at a help desk directing people to the right people and places. . . . we do hear the mortars and the guns shooting, we do carry our weapons and ammo. we are close enough that they send little or rather big presents our way. the alarm goes off but so far its been ok.
>
> i got to meet the combat stress dog, he is a black lab and he lavished me with all kinds of slobbers, so it certainly made my

day. i guess we can go and visit whenever we want to so i will probably do that often. . . .

its not like when i was in afghan where i had Will with me this is all new people that im still getting use to.

god bless

love to all
debbie

At work, Debbie recorded the passport number of any individual who was granted regular access to the base — foreign national workers who did janitorial work, Iraqi landlords who owned the buildings they were renting, soldiers from other countries who were collaborating with the American forces — then issued them the proper badge. Debbie received many indications that people valued her warmth and courtesy. Within a short time, various Turkish men were bringing Debbie small gifts — fruit, candy, flowers, snacks. A major told Debbie that he was pleased with her work; before she came, he said, they had gotten a lot of complaints about how people had been treated.

Debbie worked second shift, from twelve noon until 10:00 p.m. Being a night owl, the hours suited her. After work she often stayed up late watching movies, sometimes until 5:00 a.m. or 6:00 a.m. Then she slept until 10:00 a.m., and returned to work at noon.

She also staffed a weekly meeting of the top brass every Monday morning. The post functioned like a small city, and the meetings resembled the work of a city council; the men who handled fire, safety, traffic, and morale took turns delivering reports. Before Iraq, Debbie had never used PowerPoint, but Captain Buchanan taught her how to put the slides into slide show presentations. As the officers spoke she pushed the buttons on the laptop to change the slides. Sometimes Captain Buchanan used the private time when they drove to and from the meetings to express his frustration with certain leaders, but Debbie knew better than to reciprocate.

Debbie had constant access to a computer and began writing to Michelle right after she got to Mosul. She rarely complained. Instead she asked Michelle about her life, or shared the latest news about her granddaughter. In April, Debbie wrote:

> Jaylen will be three on the 28th this month. Hard to believe it was only three years ago we were in Afghanistan. She is quite the pistol. A funny story she was riding with her other grandparents and she was a bit fussy so her grandpa said to her grandma she must be T I R E D only he spelled it to her. Jaylen a few minutes later yelled from the backseat I am not tired. . . .
>
> She does know all her letters and colors,

numbers not bad for three.

EA has done a good job with her.

Michelle wrote back the same day:

> Things are good out here. I am working with Mile High Youth Corps, a nonprofit that works with at risk youth in Denver doing education and community service. We have energy and water conservation programs, trail building programs, and low income housing construction programs. We help kids get their GEDs and scholarships for college etc. . . .
>
> How are things going there with you? I hope you're making some good friends, that is so important to having a sane and healthy year. Did Desma get sent somewhere else? She [doesn't] respond to my emails so I worry for her. . . . I miss everyone a lot; we will have to get together when you guys get back. . . . Life goes by so fast, you really have to grab time with people.

After Debbie had been working on the base for several months, one of the younger Turkish workers began making a point of dropping by to see her. He had an Arabic-sounding name but Debbie just called him Smiley. She figured he was perhaps twenty-two. Debbie was fifty-five. Smiley started coming to see Debbie most evenings, ostensibly to get the key to a soccer field on the post. One evening, however, he asked how late Debbie was working. Probably until 11:00 p.m., she said. Smiley asked if he could talk to her after she got off. "Why?" Debbie asked. "I just want to talk to you," he said. They sat outside, in an area in front of the building where there were some trees, and chatted for about an hour. Technically, Debbie wasn't supposed to fraternize with the foreign nationals, but she figured an innocent conversation would not cause a problem.

Smiley wanted to know if Debbie was married.

"Yes, I am," she said.

"But are you happy?" he asked.

"Yes, I'm happy," Debbie said. "Why are you asking me these questions?"

"I really like you," Smiley told her. "I just want to get to know you a little bit."

"Well, you mean, get to know me as a friend?"

"Yes," he said. "I want to be your friend — I want to learn about the United States."

They talked about Indiana. Smiley returned the following night, and the night after that. Eventually he confessed that he hated working on the post, and he missed the company of women. "You know, you've just got to tell your husband that you're going to run away with a Turkish man!" he declared. "Honey, I'm too old for you," Debbie said. Smiley insisted Debbie was not too old. "Yeah, I am," Debbie replied. "I'm really way too old." This went on for a while. In the end, Debbie had to tell Smiley firmly that they could only meet again if he could accept that the relationship would remain platonic. Friendship was enough for the young man for several weeks — but then he announced that he was in love. "I really, really, really do love you," he told Debbie. "I really would like to be with you."

She said, "Honey, you're just too young. I'm very flattered, but I cannot do that."

Smiley announced dramatically that his heart was broken.

"There's plenty of young women in the world," Debbie told him.

"But you're always so nice," Smiley told her.

Debbie told Jeff about her suitor. "Well, I guess I've got an Iraqi boyfriend," she said during one of their phone calls. Jeff started laughing when she told him the story of the smitten twenty-two-year-old construction worker. Before they said good-bye, however, he turned serious. "Honey, I know you have to be nice to people," Jeff said. "But you do walk home by yourself at night. And it is dark when you leave. Will you please just be careful?"

"Well, what do you think I've got a gun for?" Debbie told him. "I'll just shoot him if he gives me trouble."

Jeff started laughing again. "Okay," he said. "But just be careful."

Later, Debbie went to take a shower by herself one evening late at night. She had been warned never to walk around the post alone when it was dark, but she did not want to bother anyone else, and routinely went by herself to shower at midnight or even 1:00 a.m. That night, she encountered another woman she knew in the women's bathroom. The other female soldier also worked second shift, and also took showers at night. "If you ever come in here by yourself at night you may want to lock that door," the woman told Debbie. "I had somebody come in here and assault me." Debbie did not press for details, but assumed the other woman had been raped. She knew that rapes occurred on a disturbingly regular basis across the post, because the information was included in the statistics that came through her office, and the senior officers who worked there had warned her about the phenomenon.

In the end, though, the hazards that Debbie faced in Iraq were simply not those kinds of dangers. No man ever jumped her at night, and she never found herself presented with any physical threat. Rather the difficulty of Iraq, for Debbie, was entirely emotional. She never left the post, she never met anybody like Akbar Khan, and she did not share a rich communal life with people she had known for years. During her first deployment, she had forged some of the deepest friendships of her life and done work that struck her as meaningful. In Iraq she had a desk job and had been hit on by a besotted twenty-two-year-old, and that was perhaps the most meaningful interaction she had with another human being.

Everybody from the 113th Support Battalion was finding the deployment to Iraq far more difficult than the deployment to Afghanistan, both because the wars had taken an ugly turn and because they were separated from each other. Desma had Charity, but they had jumped into an intimate relationship hastily, and after two months of constant contact, their closeness had started to fray. Desma was living with, working with, and reporting to her lover while surrounded by other people she had only known for a short time. When the new relationship began to founder, Desma found she had nowhere to turn.

During the grinding slog of missions, maintenance, missions, and more maintenance, Desma had grown disenchanted with Charity's leadership and her lack of emotional accessibility. Out on the highways of Iraq, Desma decided that Charity was a lax truck commander. It bothered Desma that Charity did not require their gunner to wear his body armor, as he was supposed to. Of course, they all hated the gear. With every passing day, the temperature climbed another notch or two, and the gear was hot, heavy, and irritating. They wore flight suits made of flame-resistant material, ballistic vests with heavy ceramic plates, Kevlar helmets, and angel wings (ballistic shields they strapped around their arms). "Well, after you've sat in a truck for so long, it doesn't matter what you do, that stuff is just not feasible to move in," Desma would say later. But she wore it, as she was told. Peaches took his off, however, and Charity did not reprimand him. Nor did she require Peaches to shower as often as Desma would have liked. The rank odor of the gunner's body filled the truck; it smelled as though he put on the same filthy, sweat-stained clothes over and over, without washing them. They had little to distract them during the interminable hours they spent inside the ASV, and sometimes Desma fixated on the stink, sometimes on Charity's failure to remedy it. Inside their CHU, Desma found that she and Charity had less and less to say to each other. Charity was not forthcoming, and although their physical relationship remained satisfying, Desma did not feel as close to her as she did to Mary, Stacy, or Michelle. There was one other person at Q-West who had served with them in the 113th, but Charity got mean every time he showed up. Jealous, Desma figured. In her own way, Desma felt almost as isolated as Debbie.

Desma poured her heart out to Mary in an email with the subject line "Rough Week."

Mary,

This is going to be the longest deployment of my life. I hate 90% of these people. . . . I really have no one to talk to. Yes, Charity is here, but I truly cannot talk to her. . . . I hate to bitch when I write; I just need to get it out. I miss having you around. I hope that I have never taken you for granted. I really do feel alone here. I feel trapped, caged, under siege. Like I am drowning and there is no one to call out to. I would give anything to hear your voice. . . . I just wish I had someone else to talk to. Sorry for being such a downer. Thanks for listening.

Love Des.

Mary wrote back:

Desma,

Well you know how deployments can be. Being with someone so much can either make you love them, or hate them. It's definitely not the same as having a relationship here in the states. Over there, you can't get a break or say that you are busy on Friday. They know you're not busy. :) I'm really sorry it's not working. . . .

Keep a journal, listen to music, scream into your pillow, whatever you have to. . . .

I'm kinda worried about when you guys get back. You know how it is when people come back from deployment and they are all buddy buddy. . . . I don't want to be a damn deployment outcast. I wish I was over there so bad. I would give ANYTHING to be there. Augh!

Anyway . . . I love you girl and I miss you really bad. And you can tell me anything, you never have to feel bad about it.

Mary

In June, after two months of night missions up to Zakho, Desma and Charity's platoon traded roles with a platoon that had been doing day missions in the opposite direction. Once they switched roles, they started staging at around 3:00 a.m., and by the time the sun was up, they were checking the fuel levels in the trucks, and looking at all the tires. They got on the road by about 8:00 a.m. and generally reached their destination by 2:00 p.m. Sometimes they still went north to Zakho, or maybe just up to Mosul for fuel, but more often they escorted the trucks that had come down out of Turkey on the next leg of the supply run, south to Tikrit — along the route that saw all the action.

The most dangerous moment came about two-thirds of the way to Tikrit, around the city of Baiji. Located on the same highway that continued south to Baghdad, Baiji was a major center of industry. It was home to Iraq's largest oil refinery, and the site of several major weapons and chemical plants. It also occupied one corner of the Sunni Triangle, a densely populated area of Sunni Muslims who had proved loyal to Saddam Hussein and hostile to the American-led military coalition and their Shiite allies. As Iraq had become consumed by sectarian violence, Baiji had become known for the large number of attacks mounted in that vicinity. Sometimes the insurgents hit the oil refinery or its pipelines; sometimes they hit the supply trucks that constantly passed through the area. Soldiers in the 139th were warned never to drive through the city itself but always to pass around it. The bypass could get congested, however, and frequently they found themselves stuck in heavy traffic as they tried to skirt disaster.

Their final destination was Forward Operating Base Speicher, a military base on the outskirts of Tikrit. When she went to the PX at Speicher for the first time, Desma saw fresh vegetables, frozen meat — ribs, steaks, hamburgers, all imported from Germany. The

PX at Q-West had nothing like it. "I'm going to cook!" Desma told Charity. They bought frozen T-bones, corn, and a hibachi. The following day, they invited the guys from the lead scout truck over for steaks how you like 'em. They gnawed at the T-bones while holding them in their hands because they had no utensils but the steaks tasted like home. After that, they grilled about once a week. Usually Stoney and his crew would join them, sometimes other guys, too. They grilled ribs, steaks, chops, sausages; they tried everything that was sold at Speicher. The guys were grateful. It made one day seem less like every other.

On another run to Speicher, Desma spotted a friend from the 113th Support Battalion who said supposedly Patrick Miller was running a motor pool on the other side of the base. Desma got directions and drove over in her ASV. Miller stormed out of his shop with a tight expression on his face, looking like who the hell are you? when Desma stuck her head out of the hatch. "I'll be damned," Miller said. He showed her around his shop and walked her over to a designated smoking area. After that, she dropped by regularly. Patrick wrote to Michelle, "I see Des every now and then, they got her driving an ASV, with Charity being her truck commander. She stops by my shop when she is on our base. I guess Charity is driving her nuts. Starting to get a jealous streak when she talks to men. I don't know. Better go, time for me to get ready for work."

By July it had ceased to rain entirely, and the shamal winds had picked up. The dust storms were monstrous, and temperatures rose into the 120s. They celebrated Independence Day with another barbecue — hamburgers and hot dogs. At this stage, the men in the unit had accepted Desma and Charity so completely that they no longer viewed the two female soldiers as women who had transferred into the formerly all-male regiment — they were just part of the team. The turning point, as far as gunner Brandon Hall was concerned, came one day that month, after tempers had begun to unravel because of the harsh routine and the heat. Some of the guys started to argue over something stupid in a way that turned personal, and Charity and Desma got up and left. "Mama and Brooksy went back to their CHU and got this big old dildo," Hall recounted. "They came back and slammed that thing down on the table. 'Mine's bigger than all of yours, so shut the fuck up.' " Hall marveled at the tool; he had never seen anything like it. Brooks and Elliott were as good as any of the guys, in his view — he had grown to love them each. "Both of those women are more of a man than I'll ever be," he said.

A few days later, Desma and Charity went

on a night run to Zakho. They figured it would be a breeze — less traffic, less chance of getting ambushed. But a particularly severe dust storm reduced visibility to nothing and their departure was delayed. As they waited to get on the road, Desma visited a Porta-John, knowing that once she got behind the wheel, she wouldn't have a chance to go until they reached Dahuk. While she was inside the plastic enclosure, the ground rumbled beneath her feet. Five miles to the north, in a culvert that the convoy should have been driving over about then, hundreds of pounds of explosives had blown apart the road. When she drove past the crater, she estimated it to be forty feet across. The dust storm had saved their lives, she believed.

Meanwhile, Charity had begun behaving suspiciously. She quickly closed her laptop whenever Desma walked into the CHU. They went out on a mission, and Brandon Hall told Charity that he had looked her up on MySpace. "Shows what you know," Desma told BB. "She doesn't have a MySpace account." Charity turned to Desma and said, "I have one now." Desma was taken aback. Why would Charity have opened a MySpace account and not told her? Later Desma found Charity's page on MySpace and asked for permission to connect; she tried to be patient but days went by and still Charity had not welcomed her. "I know it shouldn't be a big deal," Desma wrote to Michelle. "But I don't understand why she feels the need to hide it from me. It makes all kinds of crazy assumptions come up. I wouldn't hide anything from her like that. Maybe she is hiding me from the majority of her friends back home, well, how is that gonna work out if we are supposed to be living together then too? I don't understand!!!!"

Michelle wrote back that she and Billy had recently weathered a similar situation.

> I've had the same shit in my relationship (I did something bad) and yes we are recovering, but take it from someone that's done wrong . . . if she ACTS like she's hiding something, it's because she IS.
>
> Maybe she's flirting with other girls online, maybe there's a resurfaced ex you don't know about, whatever the case may be, myspace opens up communication with people that you normally would cut out of your life. (How else can I check up on Pete and see which movie set he is working on?) . . . Take my advice with a grain of salt, since I don't know shit about your relationship except what you just emailed me. Listen to your gut, it's usually right.
>
> I love you Des.

Desma and Charity never actually resolved

the issue. Instead they all switched over to Facebook, and Desma felt better after Charity accepted her request to be friends on that site. Later that same month, Josh sent an email saying that Desma would not be able to reach him on his cell phone because his stepmother had taken it away. Josh confessed that he had gotten in trouble:

> You have to call my house phone because im grounded i got caught driving someone car in rockport a couple weeks ago im sorry that i did that and im going to see the probation officer on monday to find out if i can get my licence before im 18 or not. i love you and call the house phone. . . . i love you and ill talk to you when i can bye

What was her second yearlong absence doing to her son? Would Josh have been getting into that kind of trouble if she was at home? Desma wanted to safeguard her children, but they were far apart from each other and the distance complicated everything. That same week, Paige and Alexis told Desma that they had not received a pair of gift cards she had sent. The gift cards were supposed to enable the girls to buy clothes and supplies for the coming school year, and they were the second set to go astray. On July 20, 2008, Desma wrote to her father-in-law to ask if he had seen the missing gift cards, but he had not. Tired of sending cards that did not reach her daughters, and concerned in case someone had been stealing them, Desma mailed the next set to her sister. She mentioned her fears to the girls. Her sister then received a furious phone message from her ex-husband's sister Joanne. In an email with the subject line "Drama that I don't have time for," Desma wrote an exasperated email to her father-in-law:

> Not exactly sure what is going on. I sent gift cards to my sister's house so that she could take the girls shopping. . . . Apparently Joann left my sister a crazy voicemail, yelling about how she is raising the girls, and how little my sister comes to visit. I only sent the cards to my sister because I had sent $300 in cards to your mailbox and they haven't been tracked down yet. When my sister got the cards, I activated them and asked her to take the girls shopping for school clothes. I didn't think it was such a big deal. If it is too much for Joann, we need to figure out what needs to be done. I will be home in a few months. I plan on the girls finishing the school year there. With another deployment to Afghanistan looming for 2010, I want to be sure that I am not going to turn them upside down again.

Honestly, I know its a lot to take care of the girls. If other arrangements need to be made, please let me know.

Love Desma

Her father-in-law, a steady man, sent a low-key reply:

I think we have the issue addressed. Apparently the girls had said that the cards were sent there because they were stolen here. I told Jo that there was probably a difference between what was said and what was relayed by the girls. . . . I don't see any additional problems. We will keep it under control here. You just be careful there.

Love
Dad

A few days later, Desma heard from Jimmy. Her lease had come to an end, the rent checks she had left were gone, and he had decided to move out. He wrote:

Desma,
Writing to let you know that your stuff is in storage, I will keep the unit paid every month so you won't loose your stuff, the unit number is 17 and the code is 5860. I havn't seen the dog I don't know what happen to it. I put the last

check on the electric bill you owed. If your tax check comes in I will put it in the bank. If you'll send a address . . . I will mail the keys to you. I want to get on with my life and you to get on with yours.

Jimmy

Then Jimmy emailed a series of photographs of belongings that he had not deemed worthy of putting into storage and that he had hauled into the backyard and lit on fire. "He sent me a slide presentation as to how all my shit went up in smoke," Desma would say later. For June and July, that was her life — constant missions to Tikrit, occasional barbecues, confusing signals from Charity, drama at home. At the end of July, Desma and Charity did another fuel run up to Mosul. It was a relief — a quick trip in the middle of the day, as opposed to a twelve-hour ordeal. The main military post, Forward Operating Base Marez, stood beside a highway, directly across from Forward Operating Base Diamondback. Desma knew that Debbie was stationed at Diamondback, and had once driven around looking for her, but had never found her. This time Charity said she knew where Debbie was working. They walked through the front doorway of the office building wearing their flame-retardant flight suits — Desma's was tan, Charity's olive-green — and saw Debbie sitting by herself behind a panel of bulletproof glass. She looked stricken. "She had just gotten off the phone with Jeff," Desma would remember later. "Maxx had died. And she was hysterical, almost."

During the lonely months in Mosul, Debbie had missed Maxx terribly. Back in April, she had discovered the therapy dog, a black Lab named Budge, and she had been visiting the dog once a week ever since. She had written in her diary:

> It's a little lonely here at times. I don't have a close friend. . . . No one is mean just not overly friendly. . . . I'm somewhat depressed but it comes with the territory. So you just move on. I need to get on Budge's schedule a dog always helps. That's what was great about Diamond she helped so much to pass the time.

But what she really wanted was Maxx. Or a friend like Will Hargreaves — although he did not have as much space in his life for Debbie anymore. That summer Will had written to let Debbie know that he was going to get married. On Sunday, July 13, 2008, two days after she turned fifty-six, Debbie wrote in her diary:

> Will bought Linda a ring and told me he would wait till I got home to get married. He

went ahead and did it July 9th. I am mad but happy too. I hope it works out okay.

Well I had my b-day pretty uneventful.

One week later, Jeff had opened the door to the garage and called for Maxx but the dog had not come. He found Maxx lying on the concrete, already stiff and cold. Debbie was so upset by the news that she stayed up all night crying. After she reported for work on Monday morning, ready to prepare the slides for the officers' weekly meeting, her colleague Kathleen took one look at her puffy face and asked what was wrong. Everybody Debbie worked with knew about Maxx; she talked about her dog all the time.

"Have you slept at all?" Captain Buchanan asked her.

"No, sir," Debbie answered. "But I'm fine. I've got to get the slides ready."

"I'll do them," Captain Buchanan said. "You don't have to go to the meeting."

"No, I'll go," Debbie said. "It's my job."

"You know what? It's not your job today," Captain Buchanan told her. "I want you to go back to your CHU, and I want you to try to get some sleep. I will do the presentations today."

Debbie was immensely relieved. Sleep still eluded her, so she took out her journal.

I lost my best friend (Maxx) yesterday. . . .

He probably felt so alone with me not there to pet him + talk to him. I hope he went without pain. He really was my best dog ever. . . . He always snuck in to sleep with me in the mornings after Jeff left for work. . . .

It was so good when I came back the last time to have him home + this time will be very sad. . . . He won't be in the way on the kitchen floor while I'm trying to cook or be laying in the bathroom after my shower. . . .

I'm so afraid Dad is next.

Jeff said in a phone call that he and Will had buried Maxx in the woods across the street. Debbie fretted about the location — it was not where she would have buried her dog. "I don't know why he thought that was better," she wrote. "Jeff said it was under some trees for shade. I still would rather he be in my yard." She ordered a marble headstone for the grave, and did not phone Jeff again for several days. "I'm afraid of saying something to him + be sorry later," she wrote in her diary. "I feel like he didn't pay Maxx enough attention + put him in the garage too often when he probably wanted in. I know he wasn't his dog but Maxx loved him too, but I know Jeff thought he was a nuisance." She wanted a drink badly, and at the same time voiced a concern about her own drinking.

I have to get a happy face on I've got several months to go yet. People are not use to me being sad + neither am I. But I don't want to be happy. I might have to put his pictures away I can't say that's my dog anymore. Because now it's that was my dog.

I wish there was some place to go + sit + enjoy a cocktail or 2 + it be legal. . . . I wasn't suppose[d] to be on this deployment I was afraid someone would die again just like last time. I need to find another form of release.

It was the following day when the 139th came to Mosul. After Desma and Charity walked into the building in their mismatched flight suits, hot and sweaty from the road, Debbie jumped up and hugged them both hard, hanging on to Desma for a little longer. "What are you doing here?" she asked. "We had to pick up fuel," Desma said. "The trucks are getting filled right now." Debbie had not seen a true friend in months and hurried to find out how they were doing. Fifteen minutes later, Desma said it was time for them to get back on the road.

The following week, Debbie wrote to Michelle Fischer and told her about Maxx's death. As soon as she heard, Michelle wrote to Desma, thinking that she might not know. "Deb's dog died, if you see her hug her for me," Michelle said. "Love you babe." Desma wrote back that she had just seen Debbie. "I hugged her for all of us," Desma said. "She is looking super thin. Scares me a bit. Love you much, gotta get up early." And then Michelle wrote to Debbie:

> I'm so sorry to hear about Maxx Deb! I do know how much he meant to you, and I'm sorry you weren't with him. . . . [J]ust remember that he had a long, great life, and it was because of you. . . .
>
> I love you! I hear you are looking thin these days — go eat something =)

After Maxx died, Debbie stopped writing in her diary for several weeks. She forgave Jeff, of course — it wasn't his fault, the dog had been thirteen. And it was really herself she felt angry with: she thought Maxx might have died because she was gone. But it helped tremendously seeing Desma, even for fifteen minutes. She knew it was Desma who had told Michelle that she was looking thin. It felt as though they were all connected once more, an unexpected by-product of Maxx's passing. Debbie did not see Desma again while they were in Iraq. She heard about any major incident that took place out on the highways, however; Colonel Agron always made a point of coming to her with news if there had been another explosion. They kept track of all those statistics.

3
Anger Management

By August they were coming undone. None of them had taken a leave that year. Patrick Miller gave his time away to a young soldier who would not otherwise have been able to take a break. Debbie was saving her leave until she got home, so that she did not have to return to work immediately. She had planned a weekend getaway to Qatar but ferocious dust storms kept delaying her departure. Neither Desma nor Charity took a break at all. They had been in-country for five months and they had been running a lot of missions and they had to wear a lot of gear and it had been hot for a long time. The heat did strange things to their bodies, made their blood run like water. Stoney cut his hand on his weapon and it bled for more than an hour. Later they returned from a twelve-hour mission, and Desma emerged with her flight suit stained dark red from the middle of her back down to her ankles. The maintenance crews took one look inside her truck and decided to change out the driver's seat, saying it looked like a crime scene. Desma had always had a heavy menstrual flow, but she had never experienced anything like this. The medics said it was the heat — it was thinning her blood.

Due to the heat, and the missions, and the relentlessness of the deployment, and the drama at home, Desma grew irritable. She did not realize the extent to which the deployment had worn her down until she began to snap. One morning Desma went down to the motor pool to pick up a vehicle and saw the same truck she had already checked back in line to be serviced again. The previous day, she had done every required end-of-mission maintenance task, but somebody else had spotted sand inside the vehicle and decided it needed to go through the whole routine again. Desma had not had a cup of coffee yet — it was hard to find coffee without walking all the way over to the chow hall — and when she saw her vehicle back in line, her face turned thunderous.

"You're looking pissy," said the first sergeant.

"The chow hall doesn't open for an hour, and I need coffee," snapped Desma.

"I have an extra cup in my office," he said. "Let's go have a talk."

The first sergeant had an office they called the Crow's Nest because it sat on top of the building. He liked to invite soldiers to join him for coffee so that he could find out what was going on. Desma felt at liberty to be frank, and her supervisor was grateful to get some straight answers.

A couple of days later, when Desma returned to the motor pool, the first sergeant said, "Would you like to have coffee in the morning?"

"Sure, I'll be there," Desma said.

Mike Quigley belonged to another platoon in the same company. "Wow, openly fucking the first sergeant," he volunteered.

Desma swung the Kevlar helmet she was holding as hard as she could and hit Mike Quigley on the side of his face. The helmet thwacked against his skull and Quigley went down. Desma stood over him and asked, "Should I do it again? Do you want to keep running your mouth?"

"You!" the first sergeant bellowed, pointing at Desma. "Anger management! Now!"

Anger is an emotion, said the therapist who worked in anger management. People can't make you angry. Situations don't make you angry. Your inability to control your emotions makes you angry.

"If Mike Quigley wasn't an asshole, I wouldn't have hit him in the face with my Kevlar," Desma said.

The therapist told her to watch a PowerPoint presentation about controlling her emotions. Afterward Desma was waiting at a bus stop to catch a ride back to her CHU when an active duty kid told her he wanted to lick her all over like a lollipop. She told him to shut up. Then he said he would like to drag her behind some Dumpsters and got a little graphic. "I just left anger management because I smashed a guy in the face with my Kevlar for doing this very same thing — being an ass," Desma told the kid. She wanted to hit him, too, but instead she restrained herself and responded by reporting the verbal harassment. Then she wound up in the equal opportunity office with her first sergeant and his first sergeant and a lot of people asking if she wanted to file a formal complaint. Desma said she did not want to file a complaint, she just wanted someone to teach the kid how not to be a complete turd. The kid's first sergeant made him write Desma a two-page letter of apology including how he should treat women in the future.

A week later, Desma loaned her truck to another member of her platoon. That soldier tore up the tires driving on a bad road, and her truck wound up in the shop. As a result, Desma had to borrow a different truck that belonged to somebody else. Drivers were responsible for their own vehicles, and his was full of trash. Desma told the other soldier to get his Honey Bun wrappers and Rip It energy drink cans out of the truck. He refused and started to walk away. "Worthless motherfucker!" Desma said, and hurled her Kevlar helmet at the guy. Back to anger management again; different therapist, same PowerPoint.

"Would you like to come back again next week?" the therapist offered.

"I got a job to do, I'm not here to go to anger management," Desma said.

The following day, while Desma was out on a mission in the borrowed truck, a discarded lithium ion battery that had been pulled off a radio started rolling around on the floor. Desma could hear something thunking around but didn't know what it was. When she went around a ninety-degree curve, the battery got caught in her steering linkage and locked her steering wheel in the turn position. Desma found herself about to roll the truck into a ditch. She couldn't get the wheel straight, couldn't get the wheel straight, couldn't get the wheel straight, and finally yanked the wheel as hard as she could and the battery popped in half. She found it down there, still intertwined in the linkage, after the mission was over. If the soldier who had left that in his truck had been standing in front of her she would have done more than just throw her Kevlar at him.

About one week later, Desma and Charity had left the coffee shop at Q-West and were walking over to pick up their laundry when they heard one single shot. It sounded close; the range was more than a mile away. It was a guy from another unit alone in his hooch. His girlfriend had taken his kid and his money, and had begun sleeping with somebody else — too many deployments, too much time apart. Two other soldiers found him and tried to stop the bleeding but his chest was a wide-open cavity and his heart was in smithereens.

Desma realized that her daughters had moved in with their father when she started having to call the girls at Dennis's house. They just migrated there, as best she could figure out. She knew right then she was going to have trouble when she got home, because Dennis did not know how to discipline the children properly, in her opinion. They just ran wild, according to Desma. (Dennis said he thought Desma was too harsh with the girls.) Her exhusband was doing his best, however, and she heard from him regularly. Knowing that she missed her children terribly, Dennis emailed Desma a photograph of Paige looking a lot like her mother, hugging a blond-haired, blue-eyed girl Desma had never seen. Dennis wrote:

THIS IS PAIGE'S FRIEND CHRISTIAN, THEY HANG OUT A LOT TOGETHER.

BE CAREFUL AND TAKE CARE, GIRLS SAID HI AND THEY LOVE YOU, THEY

COULD NOT THINK OF ANYTHING TO WRITE.

Alexis turned nine years old that September. Desma sent Dennis $100 and asked him to take the girls to see *High School Musical 3.* Dennis emailed short updates about the girls' lives, and allowed the girls to keep in touch with their mother using his email account. On September 12, 2008, they wrote: "hey it's paige if you have internet get on poptropica.com and you can use my password. . . . I love you very much!" "Hi, it's Burgerbutt. I only had 1 F in grammar but that's because I didn't study. Are spelling words are e-a-s-y. LOVE, ALEXIS." Dennis wrote again to clarify that actually Alexis was earning good grades; her report card had been all As and Bs, and the F she had mentioned was for one paper, not her overall grade. Paige was not doing quite as well. Dennis wrote:

> Paige has 3 d's 3c's and 2 b's and 1 F. . . . The papers she brings home all have 95%–100% on them so I don't know why her midterms are the way they are.

By the end of September, the girls were counting down the days until Christmas, because that was when their mother was supposed to be home. Alexis and Paige sent Desma their Christmas lists on September

27, 2008.

Hi, mommy! I have got As and bs on my medterm's, but two people in my class has a F in behavior and their names are Aniyah and Alex. Do you want are chrismas list if you do heare it is.

1. Hanna Monntana best of both worlds
2. you
3. the movie High School Musical 3 movies
4. you
5. to go back to Rockport
6. you

Love,
bugerbutt/lexi

hey its me i have my list

1 that seventys show season 1
2 dell cool bean

ok luv ya
paige

Desma was already thinking about Christmas, too. In the small green notebook that she carried on her missions — it was filled with notes about the briefings from their convoy commander — Desma had jotted down thoughts about the gifts she wanted to order for her children. She was planning to buy Alexis pajamas, a video game, and a Build-A-Bear. She was planning to buy Paige pajamas, an MP3 player, and a Build-A-Bear. And for Josh, five T-shirts and a video camera.

On October 19, 2008, Desma and Charity left Q-West on another mission to Tikrit. It was daytime and they were running ass, right after Stoney and his crew. Brandon Hall was their gunner that day, which was a relief; Desma was glad to have gotten rid of Peaches. They joked around with BB the whole way. It was as good a day as they got in Iraq, Desma thought. When they reached the Baiji bypass, at about 10:00 a.m., they saw oil everywhere, however, black liquid sinking into the white sand. The pipeline had been sabotaged again, it seemed. They still had radio communication with the rest of the convoy, but they could no longer see the trucks behind them. Stoney saw a box by the side of the four-lane highway. Part of the box was covered in bright silver tape, the same kind that they used on their own post — it glinted in the searing sun. Some asshole dropped a box, thought Desma. Another convoy in front of them had reported sighting the box but had decided not to check it out. She had heard someone else say, "Leave it, it's nothing." Stoney wanted to make sure. "Hold up," he said. "We need to look at this box."

His truck slowed down and Stoney leaned way out of the turret.

"Mama, I can't see in that box," Stoney said over the radio. "Can you get closer?"

"I got this," Charity told him.

Desma slowed to a crawl and turned the wheel of the ASV so that the right front tire lipped the shoulder. The box was maybe four feet away, but BB still could not see inside. Charity told her they needed to get a better angle. Desma inched forward. Then the truck thrust heavenward and Desma saw blue sky for a moment and abruptly everything went black. She could hear an awful high-pitched squeal. Ages passed. It dawned on Desma that the noise was the sound of a radio that had been disconnected. When she reached up to turn off her headphones, she found that somebody had shoved her helmet down over her eyes, which was why she could not see. She took her helmet off. The vehicle was filled with smoke.

"Are you okay?" Charity was saying.

Charity was lying on the floor of the vehicle, over on the passenger side.

"What the fuck just happened?" Desma said.

"Are you okay?" Charity repeated.

Desma looked out of the front windows and saw Angry Beaver standing on the hood of her truck. He looked more furious than she had ever seen him.

"Get out of the truck!" he was screaming. "Get out of the fucking truck!"

"Okay, okay. Hold on a minute," Desma said. "I can't get my seat belt off."

Desma was stuck between the steering wheel and her seat, which she had elevated so that she could see out of the windows. Somehow her angel wings had gotten caught in her seat belt — and she could not reach the lever to lower her seat back down. Charity undid Desma's seat belt. They were both covered in hydraulic fluid. BB was sprawled out in the back of the truck, trying to sit up. Charity told BB to stay put, they would get him out in a second. Then she climbed out of the hatch. Desma followed, but the drop was not right. She hit the ground too soon, which was how she realized that the truck was damaged. The last thing Desma had seen before everything went black was Stoney, peering out of the top of the lead scout truck, watching her get close. Was he dead? No, there he was, picking pieces of her tire assembly out of his gun turret. They opened the back hatch and got BB out. He started wandering around with his flight suit halfway off, no bulletproof vest, no helmet. "You got to put your vest on," Desma told him. "You can't walk around like that." BB had a big welt on his forehead. He had taken his helmet off because his scalp had been itching and he had thought maybe he could see better without the helmet. Then they had gone up in the sky and he had bounced his head off the .50-caliber. He seemed dazed and not himself.

The medic put his hands all over Desma's body, way up under her vest, while staring into her eyes at the same time. Was it sexual? She wanted him to stop touching her. "I'm fine," Desma told the medic. "Make sure BB's okay." He ignored her. He said he had to give her a MACE test — it stood for Military Acute Concussion Evaluation. "Elbow, apple, carpet, saddle, bubble," said the medic. "Repeat those words back to me." Desma could not get past apple. They tried again. She could not get past carpet. Charity was directing traffic into the other lane, but the drivers must have feared getting shot, because instead they started heading off into the desert. Then a big tour bus came along. Desma could see women and children looking out of the windows. The driver looked fearful; Charity had her finger on the trigger of her M-4. Just then another military truck from their convoy pulled up between Charity and the bus. Desma looked up at the gunner, a guy named Talbot. "Get that bus out of here before she hurts somebody," Desma told him. "Rog-er," drawled Talbot.

Desma walked over to look at her truck. It listed by the side of the road, one wheel missing entirely, the rest of the tires blown flat.

Hatches and headlights lay strewn across the highway. Mechanics had recently added an extra layer of metal to the truck's armor, and that outer hull was scoured by deep grooves. Desma put her thumb into one of them. It fit inside the groove all the way up to the meaty part of the joint. What had made that mark — ball bearings? Big ones. Without the extra layer of armor, who knows what would have happened. She walked around, found fragments of wires, a cell phone battery, and pieces of a tap light that had scorch marks. A homemade pressure plate.

The translator who had been riding in Stoney's truck was freaking out.

"I just got hit by a bomb!" he told Desma. "They tried to kill me!"

"Tag, you're it," Desma said in a weary voice. "Do you need a water?"

Then the wrecker showed up.

"We're going to change the back tires and drag it," the driver told Desma. "I need you to climb in there and turn off all the electronics."

"You want me to go back in there?" Desma said.

"Yep. Turn that shit off."

Inside the truck, everything was a little bit wrong. It smelled like dirt and hydraulic fluid and she could hear the radio still squealing. Weirdly, Desma could not recall the proper steps to power down the Blue Force Tracking device. She used to teach other people how to use the complicated military GPS system, but all that information had been erased from her mind. She just turned it off without following the prescribed procedure. When she reached up to turn off the radio, something popped when she lifted her arm, and a jolt of pain shot through her shoulder. She climbed out of that vehicle and got into the lead scout truck with Stoney and his crew. The medic came over.

"Let me see your weapon," he said.

She handed it to him out of the truck's window. He dropped the magazine, unchambered a round, put it on safe.

"You got this now?" he asked. "You had one in the chamber, Desma."

It had all happened so fast. Sky, smoke, dirt, getting felt up by the medic, trying not to shoot up a tour bus. She could have shot herself by accident on the ride home. Or someone else. When the convoy got back on the road, Stoney resumed his place in the turret. He had been maybe ten yards from the blast, and must have gotten rattled around, but he resumed his job as the lead scout's gunner. When they reached Speicher, everybody from the two scout trucks went to the hospital. Stoney and his team had concussions, but the doctors let them go after several hours. Desma, Charity, and Brandon Hall they kept for most of the night. Desma was wearing a neck brace and Charity was wearing a neck brace and there was a television set playing something stupid. Desma wanted a cigarette badly, but the nurse said she was not allowed to go outside. The doctor who had examined them conferred with a doctor in Balad by telephone — and then a doctor in Germany. BB had hit his head pretty hard on the .50-caliber, and Desma and Charity appeared to have hit their heads on the roof of the ASV. Desma had also wrenched her right shoulder, after her arm had gotten stuck inside the steering wheel. The bomb had been a big one, and they had been right on top of the blast — maybe ten feet away, according to the doctor's note. All three of them kept failing the MACE test. The concussions they had were severe and the doctor considered whether to evacuate the three soldiers out, but finally he let them go at 2:00 a.m.

Stoney, Ford, and Angry Beaver had stayed at Speicher to find out what happened, and they drove everyone back to Q-West the following day. The medics at Q-West gave Desma shots of a synthetic opioid pain reliever called Tramadol, as well as a migraine medication called Imitrex. When the Tramadol and the Imitrex wore off the pain in her head was astounding. Desma started working at the motor pool, sending trucks with broken air-conditioning out for repair, tracking where the vehicles went on the military's vehicle maintenance software. Or she took naps, watched TV, sold her shit, packed. The silver box was her last mission. The medics were having trouble suppressing the blinding headaches that she, Charity, and BB were experiencing, and nobody thought it was a good idea for them to go back out in an ASV. It felt like a demotion, and Desma missed hanging out with Stoney. At the same time, whenever she got behind the wheel of a vehicle — even just to drive across the post — she fought a boiling anxiety. Desma felt ashamed about not running more missions, but then a convoy returned after hitting another bomb, and she heard Mancil Smith slurring his speech as though he had suffered a stroke. It was the ninth IED blast Mancil had experienced — his fourth during this tour. One bomb had been enough for her. She was ready to go home.

Stoney was back out on the road, like all the guys from the lead scout truck. On the drive back to Q-West, he had given Desma a hard time.

"You ran that shit over," Stoney said. "Why the hell did you do that?"

"I didn't do it on purpose," said Desma. "It was there. We got close. We got closer."

"Horseshoes and hand grenades," said Stoney.

It was the name of a song they both liked by Green Day.

"Roadside bombs," answered Desma. She shrugged at him.

To the end, Desma maintained that sort of attitude — casual, no exterior sign of distress. It was how you were supposed to behave if you were a soldier. In truth, she had been terrified that she might have killed him. She did not admit this out loud, but she thought Stoney was right — she had run that shit over. When a bomb had tried to get Stoney, he had dodged it, and she had heard the triumph in his voice when he had yelled, "Missed me, motherfucker!" But she had not dodged her bomb, and she had not gotten to yell that the enemy had missed. "And it was my fault," Desma would say later. "I hit it. I hit that bomb. I didn't try to hit that bomb, but I was driving. And I was the one who ran over it." She harbored a smothering sense of culpability.

Earlier that summer, Colonel Agron had come to find Debbie Deckard. He knew that she had trained with a crew that was doing convoy security with the 139th, and he had just heard some bad news. A bomb had gone off in Mosul. It wasn't the biggest improvised explosive device that the 139th had encountered, but it had detonated less than one hundred feet away from the truck that contained the two young men Debbie had trained with back in Georgia — Selby and Boone — as well as the young man whose job she had taken — Sam Caulfield. Selby, Boone, and Caulfield had been in a convoy along with another soldier in the 139th, and the other soldier had seen the initial charge go off. "IED! IED!" he had yelled frantically over the radio. "Where?" Selby had asked. Then there was a rumbling boom. Everybody in the 139th had laughed about that exchange, back at Q-West: IED! Where? Boom. It was like a joke with the perfect punch line, they told each other. You had to laugh or you would fall apart.

The three soldiers had all gotten concussions. "They got rattled around," Colonel Agron said to Debbie. "The young kid whose job you took, he was driving. It knocked their heads around a little bit. But they are going to be okay."

Later, the three young men had stopped by to see Debbie. They just wanted to see her, they said. Just wanted to drop by, just wanted to say hello. Yeah, they had gotten hit; no, it wasn't a big deal, they were all fine. They had been given three weeks off, before they had to go back out in a convoy. They were back on the road now.

Then Colonel Agron came to find Debbie again. A big bomb had gone off down around Baiji, he said. Brooks and Elliott had been hit. Of course they were going to have some time off for evaluation, but they were all right. He thought she would want to know.

And she did. She did want to know. For the rest of the time that she spent in Iraq, however, Debbie frequently reflected about the fact that Sam Caulfield had been driving a truck while she was sitting in the chair that had once been his, safely behind bulletproof glass. She was supposed to have been inside that truck, and instead he had taken the thump of the IED. Later she would say that when she had gotten the news about those two IED blasts, involving two sets of people she had known, she had felt cheated. "I mean, that sounds like a weird thing to say, but not really cheated in a bad way, just cheated like maybe I should have been there," she would say. "Maybe I could have controlled it and I didn't. You know, he is young. Or maybe I could have shared that with them. So not cheated in a bad way, but, you know, I wasn't part of that. I mean, there's nobody in the world that wants to be in a vehicle that's hit by an IED. But you feel, well, I would have been there." And what she meant was she *should* have been there. It would chew Debbie up for years, the idea that Caulfield had taken a blast that was meant for her. The bomb had had her name on it, and there had been some awful mistake, and the wrong person had gotten blown up in her stead. She felt that way all over again as soon as Agron told her about Desma.

▪ ▪ ▪ ▪

V
Colorado and Indiana, 2009–2013

▪ ▪ ▪ ▪

1
Huge Billy Clubs

After she moved to Denver, Colorado, in February 2008, Michelle waited impatiently for her battalion to return from Iraq and watched her new home get turned upside down by politics. In August 2008, Denver was hosting the Democratic National Convention. The Democrats had chosen to hold their convention in Colorado for strategic reasons, as the general election looked as though it would swing on what transpired in a few states, and Colorado had gained prominence as one of them. Tickets to hear Senator Barack Obama speak were so coveted that his handlers moved his speech to the Broncos' football stadium to accommodate a larger crowd. Vehicles full of law enforcement officers patrolled the city in droves to quash any disruptions. On August 24, 2008, Michelle wrote in an email to Debbie Deckard:

> Hope everything is going well for you. It's DNC time here in Denver, it's gonna

> get crazy! Police everywhere, with HUGE billy clubs. Ready to crush protestors for exercising their First Amendment Rights! Holy cow, I've never seen anything like this. I'm hoping the anarchists take over the city . . . well . . . kind of.

Since Michelle had left Afghanistan, Akbar Khan had continued to work as a translator for the US military. Akbar had gone ahead and married his first cousin, and they now had a child. Afghanistan still did not have a viable economy, however, and Akbar hoped to parlay his military connections into a better life. That September, Michelle received an email from Akbar saying he had made it safely to the United States. He was staying with a friend in Lexington, South Carolina, and had just applied for a Social Security card. He wanted to find a job and save some money. Akbar had left his wife and son back in Afghanistan and was planning to send for them after he got established. He hoped to see Michelle soon. On September 17, 2008, in an email with the subject line "BEST DAY EVER!" Michelle broadcast the news to Debbie, Desma, Patrick, and George Quintana, saying, "Akbar is in the States! WHOOOO!!!!!!!!!" She wondered if they might be able to pool their money and pay for Akbar to travel to Indiana to celebrate Christmas. Everybody who was serving in

Iraq would be home by then, and Michelle wanted them all to be together. GQ had just gotten word of another deployment, however, and replied morosely, "What LUCK, He's in NC [*sic*] and I'm leaving back to Asscrackistan."

Several days later, Michelle turned twenty-six. In lieu of a gift, Desma contributed $100 to a nonprofit that provided mentoring to at-risk youth. "Holy cow, Desma, thank you so much!" Michelle wrote. On her birthday, Michelle and Billy rented a pair of scooters and rode up the scenic back roads around Long's Peak, one of the best-known fourteen-thousand-foot mountains in the Rockies. "It was so exhilarating and beautiful — I'd love to have some land up there someday," Michelle wrote to Desma. "We headed back towards Boulder after that, stopping in Lyons for some yard sale-ing and a gigantic lunch at Oskar Blues Brewery, home of Dale's Pale Ale, one of my favorite beers." While they were checking out the yard sales, Michelle heard her cell phone ring but she let the call go to voice mail. Michelle cried when she listened to the message — it was Debbie, calling from Qatar. She had remembered Michelle's birthday in the middle of a deployment.

Debbie had flown to Qatar for a long weekend. The dust storms had been terrible, and her departure had been delayed repeatedly because of high winds and bad visibility. Shortly before she had left, a contractor for the Department of Defense had asked her out for coffee. They had talked until 5:30 a.m. He was married but they were both lonely. Nothing physical happened; it was just remarkable to find someone with whom she could have a real conversation. Right after that, another Turkish young man had attached himself to Debbie. "These young Turkey boys must like older women," Debbie wrote in her diary. "It's flattering. At 56 I just see nothing very attractive when I look in the mirror." With only a few more months to go, Debbie was wondering about the meaning of the year she had spent in Iraq. "I would have liked to have done something more significant," she wrote. "But just being here is probably enough. . . . If it helps at all for my grandkids future then my small part will be worth it."

In Qatar she noticed all the ways in which Camp As Sayliyah had changed during the three years since she had last been there. At the Top It Off Club, the proprietors had added a karaoke machine and bowling lanes. Regulations governing the use of alcohol were just as strict as before, though: only three drinks a night. Soldiers desperate to guzzle more were paying cash to anybody with unused drink tickets, and by the end of the night it was a seller's market. "People were charging $20 to buy a $5 beer," Debbie wrote in her diary. "I would of given mine away if I wasn't a lush."

The soldiers who belonged to the 113th Support Battalion had been told only that their deployment would conclude sometime at the end of November. Michelle had identified several cabins in a state park in Brown County that would be large enough to hold the whole group — Patrick and his wife, Desma and Charity, Debbie and Jeff, Will and Linda, herself and Billy, and maybe Akbar Khan. Throughout October and November she sent a flurry of emails about the cabins to Debbie and to Patrick's wife, Beth. Separately, Michelle and Debbie exchanged other emails in which they worried about Akbar, who was having trouble finding work. Debbie wrote to him from Iraq:

> Hi Kiddo
>
> Michelle says things are going a little rough. I'm sure you knew it would be a little difficult, but I know you are a strong person so don't give up. . . . Sometimes things just take a little longer than we want but that doesn't mean that it won't work. I know between me and Will you have a place to stay at least in Indiana. Michelle is good at finding info so with her help we will figure out something.
>
> Try not to get to discouraged and give

yourself some time. You have all of us that love you lots and want to help as much as we can.

Hopefully we will all be together in December when [we] return.

Love ya
Mama Debbie

Once again, Michelle decided to eschew both major party choices in the upcoming presidential election. "Hi my wonderful friends that are coming home soon!" she wrote to Desma, Patrick, and Debbie on October 16, 2008. "I realize that you have been missing all of the political action while you are serving, and are probably being subjected to mass amounts of propaganda that holds no truth whatsoever." Michelle set them straight. "The American People have been tricked into thinking we must choose between two candidates: both of which stand with corporate interests and have no balls to do what is right for the people of this country. So I thought I'd let you know that Ralph Nader is running again, and I'm voting for him. Come on, you know I'm not stupid. I know he's not going to win. But here's why I'm voting third party: if any candidate receives 5% of the popular vote in a presidential election, they are entitled to public election funding in the next race."

Michelle also asked her friends if they could

commit to renting a cabin in Brown County. Debbie wrote back that same day, saying she would love to do that. Michelle replied that she would book a cabin as soon as she heard from Desma. She never heard from her, though — Desma was so unreliable, Michelle thought, when it came to email. After Desma's silence stretched on past the point when they needed to make a decision, Beth went ahead and booked the Cozy Bear cabin in Brown County for December 26 and 27. With the military discount, each couple would owe $206.77, said Beth.

Michelle wondered in an email to Debbie if Patrick and Beth would smoke pot; she figured they probably would not partake, but she hoped they wouldn't be offended if everybody else got high. Michelle planned to bring food to grill and asked Debbie to stock up on wine. They worried that Akbar might find them debauched, but then Michelle told Debbie that Akbar had recently said, "I am not the boy you remember, that blushes every time he is around a woman." She wanted them to recapture some of the joy they had found in each other's company when they had served alongside each other in Afghanistan:

> To tell you the truth Deb the thought of all of us being together again without a care in the world for a few days kinda

> chokes me up. It has been so long, our lives so different. . . . I'm not sure if Des will come, but I wanted to make sure she knew she was invited. I hope she does make it. I've never really met Charity.

And still Desma did not write. Michelle did not hear from her during the second half of October, nor in November. Debbie said nothing about the IED blast to Michelle. You did not worry people back home unless it was absolutely necessary, because the distance and the lack of control could make them hysterical, and then they would plague an exhausted, stressed-out soldier with emotional emails and phone calls, seeking reassurance. Meanwhile, Will wrote to say he wasn't sure if he and Linda would join them at the cabin. Debbie had missed his company terribly while she was in Iraq; her wish that Will could be there, too, had become a repeating refrain in her diary. ("I think it's different because here I don't have Will around," she had written in September. "I'm by myself so much.") Debbie called him to find out what was wrong and Will confessed that his new wife did not want to spend the night with the rest of the group. The amount he drank had become an issue, Will told Debbie — particularly the amount that he drank when he was around his friends from the Guard. "He said they would come during the day and stay into the evening," Debbie wrote in an email to Jeff. "I don't see why they just don't stay. . . . I can't believe she won't let him enjoy his friends. He said he would not come without her." Even though Linda was now Will's wife, Debbie was shocked that he would choose Linda over the armament team.

Akbar still had not found work. He was too proud to accept help with airfare, and it seemed unlikely that he would join them at the cabin. Over the next several weeks, Debbie wrote to Akbar often. She said she would help him shop for warmer clothes; she wondered how the job search was going; she asked if he had tasted alcohol yet. "Michelle says you told her you were not the same shy boy you used to be," Debbie told Akbar. She worried about his frame of mind. The stature Akbar had possessed in Afghanistan had not followed him to the United States; in South Carolina, his brown skin and his foreign accent led other people to treat him as though he lacked intelligence. Debbie fretted that Akbar seemed dejected. She wrote to Michelle, "He didn't sound as happy as I would of liked when he emailed me."

By this point, James Cooper had almost completed his deployment in Afghanistan, too. Throughout that year, Cooper had been in regular contact: Michelle would pick up the phone and hear his voice from halfway around the globe. It would be nighttime in Afghanistan and morning in Colorado, or the other way around, and Michelle would put all the warmth she knew how to muster into her voice, hoping to span the awful gap between them. Cooper told her all about where he was. The city of Kandahar was the second largest in Afghanistan, and the area was known for pomegranates, grapes, and wool. Michelle told him to read *The Kite Runner;* maybe he could see Afghanistan through her eyes. To her surprise, Cooper proved a willing pupil; he avidly consumed the books she suggested, and when he called, she could hear the sound of marvel in his voice. After a while, Cooper began to tell her stories of his colleagues, and how he had to police them so they didn't run amok. The other soldiers had a hard time thinking of Afghans as fellow human beings, he said. Michelle started to think of Cooper as the conscience of his unit, the one who would prevent an atrocity. They found themselves in agreement about all kinds of things — the wonders of Afghanistan, the shittiness of deployments, the obliviousness of civilians. Michelle felt as though Afghanistan were working on Cooper, transforming him. Sharing a deployment to the same place, albeit four years apart in time, united them.

Michelle wanted James Cooper to have her kind of deployment — the kind where you never had to fire your weapon — but she knew it wasn't like that in Kandahar. Not by this point. The Taliban had established a strong presence in southern Afghanistan in the years since Karzai had been elected, and US soldiers stationed there were squarely at the center of the ongoing conflict. Insurgents were placing more and more IEDs by the sides of the roads, making bigger and bigger explosions, and when Michelle didn't hear from Cooper for a few weeks, she began to worry. She started checking in with him whenever she could, even if it was just a sentence or two on Facebook. One day she wrote, "where are you? was hoping to catch you online today. hope all is well in kandahar." Sometimes he would write back immediately but sometimes it took days.

In the fall, their communication lapsed briefly. On October 9, 2008, however, Cooper surprised Michelle by calling on her cell phone while she was at work. She dropped what she was doing and excitedly began asking questions, but then her boss walked into Michelle's office. She sent him a note on Facebook, apologizing for ending the call abruptly. On October 29, 2008, Michelle sent Cooper a short note. "Hi," she wrote. "Miss you. Hope you're doing well." Cooper wrote back on November 1, 2008, sounding dispirited; he had been in Afghanistan for almost a full year. "I am doing alright," he said. "I miss you. Blah."

A few weeks later, Michelle's cell phone rang. She heard Cooper's familiar voice on the other end of the line — but then he said, "I'm at Walter Reed." "Oh, my God!" she cried. "What happened?" He had been on a mission just outside the city of Kandahar, Cooper told her, and they had gotten into a firefight in the middle of a vast field. There had been rows and rows of grapes. Then heavy gunfire. His buddies had run back for him, and carried him the length of six football fields before they had reached a place where it was safe for a helicopter to land. In Germany the military doctors had made sure he would live. Six days later he went into surgery at Walter Reed, to see what the doctors could do about his legs. A single round from an AK-47 had gone through both of his thighs.

As soon as she heard the term "AK-47," Michelle thought it was a miracle James Cooper had not bled to death. She knew how big those rounds were. Then she asked herself: Had she worked on that gun? Had she checked its sights, or replaced its trigger mech? And even if she had not worked on that gun, what about all the AK-47s that the armament team had repaired? How many people had been shot by those weapons since she had written down their serial numbers? Twenty thousand assault rifles, multiplied by four years of warfare, plus however many times they had been fired. Michelle could not stop crying. Cooper just listened to her, a little perplexed. It was horrible; everything was backward — she should have been comforting him. He was the one stuck at Walter Reed; he was the one who had been shot. But instead Cooper kept telling her that he was going to be okay, everything was going to be all right. The phone call opened a dam Michelle had not known she had constructed, and the guilt that came pouring out had been stored in some high place for a long time. She was awash for days.

In the weeks that followed, Michelle spoke to Cooper frequently. He called to say that he had stood up and taken a couple of shuffling steps. He thought he would be in the hospital for a short time. When the doctors at Walter Reed learned the full extent of the nerve damage in his legs, however, they told him it might take a while longer. They did surgery after surgery, and somehow the weeks turned into months. Cooper would stay at Walter Reed from November 2008 until March 2009. During the four months he spent in the hospital, Michelle called regularly. Sometimes he was in surgery and could not answer; sometimes she caught him while the nurses were changing the bedding, or in the middle of physical therapy. But at least once a week, she found him sitting around, watching television or reading a book, bored out of his mind. He was relentlessly upbeat. He worked at physical therapy with furious diligence. They distracted themselves from the tedium of his recuperation by talking about politics and books. She told him to read *A People's History of the United States* by Howard Zinn, and he did. They still did not agree on essential matters but they had constructed a common language. Cooper could walk again by the time he went back home. The ordeal was not over — he would return to the hospital with various setbacks in the years to come — but a person who saw him on the street would not have known he had been to war.

Debbie, Desma, and Patrick Miller came home at the end of November 2008, right in the middle of Cooper's early flurry of phone calls from Walter Reed. Desma told Michelle about the IED explosion in their first phone call. Michelle was furious and hurt that she had not been told. "The soldier in me understands, but the friend in me is really upset," Michelle would say later. In December Michelle flew back to Indiana to spend Christmas with her family in Evansville, then drove north to the rolling hills of Brown County. No other county in the state had more square miles of untouched forest. The parks had always brought Michelle a sense of peace, and she hoped it would be a restful place for the others, a chance to unwind.

They gave the master suite to Patrick and Beth, while Debbie and Jeff took one of the smaller bedrooms. Billy had decided not to join them, and instead Michelle had brought her mother, who spent the weekend reading cheap crime novels. There was a large fireplace, a wooden carving of a black bear, a front porch with a swing, and an outdoor fire pit. They made tacos for dinner, then built a fire outside and got drunk. The temperature dropped into the low twenties, but they huddled close to the flames and stayed warm. Michelle had brought craft beer and the rest of them teased her about being highfalutin. Patrick was drinking Bud Light and Debbie was drinking sweet white wine. When she was halfway plastered Michelle remembered all over again that she had little in common with the kind of people who were drawn to the National Guard, and even less in common with their spouses. She liked Beth, but she didn't like Beth. They would never have been friends if Beth had not been married to Patrick, and Patrick had not served with her in Afghanistan. Beth was obsessed with Kenny Chesney, and that twangy kind of music drove Michelle crazy. They battled over the CD player. They also battled over the subject of peace. At one point Michelle started talking about Iraq Veterans Against the War, and somehow that led to pacifism in general and the particular stance taken against Vietnam by John Lennon. Beth said John Lennon was the scum of the earth. Michelle was just sober enough to realize there would be no profit in conducting a drunken argument with Patrick's wife. It was always more of a stretch to meet her fellow soldiers' partners. They did not share a deployment, they did not have that glue. Michelle and Patrick stayed up late playing pool, which had been one of the things they had always done at Shorty's.

The following day, Michelle nursed a hangover and worked on a scarf she was knitting. She was still learning how to knit. As the hours slipped by, the large ball of blue- and fuchsia-colored yarn slowly shrank and the scarf grew longer and Michelle got a better sense of what the last year had been like for Patrick and for Debbie. At first Michelle had been elated — the armament team was back together, her friends had made it home alive. She had thought that would mean she could stop worrying, yet the more time she spent with Patrick and Debbie, the greater grew her disquiet. Debbie was drinking so much that Michelle could hardly believe what she was seeing — was it really possible for one person to consume so much wine and remain standing? — and Patrick Miller was swigging Bud Light pretty fast, too.

Michelle had expected her friends to remain constant, but they had proved mutable in unexpected ways. Patrick had always been a diehard fan of country music but now he wanted to listen to reggae. When Michelle asked what was going on with him and Bob Marley, Patrick said Beth had become afraid of him because he was so angry, and had asked if he would listen to reggae music to calm down. The more Patrick drank, the more he talked: he did not know why he had been sent to Iraq, he did not know what they had accomplished, he had not been able to direct his soldiers properly because he could not understand the purpose of their missions. Patrick said this tour had been bullshit.

To hear Patrick sound so disenchanted alarmed Michelle — Patrick never used to talk like that. He was 100 percent promilitary when he was himself. All his buddies had been sent elsewhere, Patrick said, none of them had been with people they trusted. Now one of his close friends had just checked into a mental clinic after attempting suicide. And another guy Patrick knew had succeeded in killing himself. That was Ken Martinson, who had been Angela Peterson's fiancé. Angela and Michelle had not been close for a while but Michelle would always remember doing push-ups with her in the hotel in Louisville. Now the other Alpha girls were saying that Angela was falling apart in slow motion. Iraq had been far worse than anything she had imagined, Michelle began to realize.

Will and Linda showed up on Saturday afternoon. They were friendly and everything seemed fine but they left after only a few hours. Then Desma arrived, as the sun was getting low, in a red Chrysler Pacifica that she did not own. She had just begun picking up the pieces of her old life and was in the middle of everything. She was in the middle of buying a used car (the dealer had allowed her to borrow the Pacifica for twenty-four hours) and she was in the middle of training a new puppy (another pug and beagle mix named Princess) and she was in the middle of remembering how to care for her children. They were still living with other relatives, although the two girls were going to move in with Desma at the end of the school year. All three children were staying with her temporarily over the winter break. They were in the car, and the dog was in the car, too. Charity was not in the car. Once more Desma was looking to Charity to make her feel secure in the midst of upheaval, but Charity had been pulling away.

It was shocking for the others to see Desma. She was shattered, not herself, could not focus long enough to have a coherent conversation. Right in the middle of telling a story, Desma turned around, leaned over a fence, and threw up on the ground. She said she did not know if she had caught a stomach bug or if she was throwing up because of her head injury. "I have this unbelievable headache," she said. "I have this headache that is just out of control." Desma threw up again fifteen minutes later, while Michelle held her hair away from her face and Debbie ran inside for a towel. Desma said she had been seeing doctors at the VA hospital in Indianapolis, but they had not yet been able to find a medicine she could tolerate that was strong enough to subdue the pain.

After only an hour Desma said she had to go, and by then Michelle wanted to start weeping. She spent the rest of the day knitting intently, trying to stitch herself back together, but she was so jangled that she knit the yarn too tightly, and that part of the scarf did not match the rest, so she had to undo her work and stitch it together all over again. She finished the scarf, but it was stuck on the knitting needles, and if she pulled it off it would unravel. Debbie tried to help Michelle figure out how to cast off but they were both wasted and neither could determine how to resolve the final stitches. They puzzled over this dilemma and tried things that didn't work and laughed about what half-assed knitters they were. Finally Michelle pulled out her laptop and found a YouTube video that showed how to cast off. They watched the video four times before Michelle got the scarf off the needles. "That was when I realized that something was pretty wrong," Michelle would say later. "My friends were different, and not in a good way. And I felt a lot of guilt around Debbie, because she shouldn't have gone. Who sends a fifty-five-year-old woman to Iraq? I mean, we're sending our grandmothers to war. Twice. That's how hard up we are. I felt a lot of guilt about all of it, because I was out in Colorado, starting my new life, and they were going through that for no reason. A lot of guilt and a lot of — I was just really worried and afraid for them."

2
HAPPY BOMB DAY

Coming home again — becoming a civilian again — proved harder the second time around. After Debbie had returned from Afghanistan, she had been part of a close-knit team, and she had stayed in touch with the rest of armament. Just picking up the phone and speaking to Will or Michelle had made a difference. This time, however, nobody she knew had served with her in Iraq. She did not feel as comfortable calling Will now that he was married to Linda — and then Will made it clear that she should not call at all. It happened after a raucous Fourth of July party that took place in Jeff's mother's yard. Debbie and Jeff brought deerburgers, hot dogs, pepper slaw, beer, and wine. Jeff put on a fireworks display of professional quality, using firing tubes he had constructed to launch glowing whirligigs into the night.

Everybody came away with conflicting versions of what took place next, but Michelle heard that Debbie drank too much wine and threw her arms around Will and gave him an embrace that to Linda had looked romantic. Afterward Will ceased all contact with Debbie. And Michelle now lived in Colorado. Besides, neither of them had been to Iraq. This time around, Debbie was on her own.

Some mornings she woke up with the sensation of being enveloped in Saran Wrap. Debbie called it being inside the bubble. It was a feeling of profound alienation, but it manifested itself as an almost physical sensation, as though there were literally a transparent barrier cutting her off from the rest of the world. If she did not have to go to work, she had a hard time getting out of bed. A day without appointments or obligations terrified her; she wanted someone to tell her where to go and what to do. The appalling endlessness of the empty hours stretching before her suggested that her life had no meaning. And the problems with her memory worsened.

When Debbie went to the VA clinic in Bloomington for medical appointments, her doctor asked how she was doing psychologically. At first Debbie maintained a cheerful front and said she was great. Later, when she revealed that she was having difficulty going to sleep at night and getting out of bed in the morning, the doctor recommended that she speak to a therapist. "Oh, no, I'm fine," Debbie said. She hewed to the belief that mental issues were things a person should settle on her own. Surely there were other soldiers who needed the sessions more than she did. "Why should I take something if I wasn't really injured?" she would say later. "I didn't lose a leg. I didn't get blown up."

During Debbie's childhood, her mother had experienced two nervous breakdowns, and had required medication to pull herself back together; Debbie did not want to be so weak. Her dad would have pulled himself together, she was sure, if he had gone to war. Over the next several months, however, Jeff pointed out that Debbie was having crying jags, and Michelle said she had grown concerned because she could not get Debbie on the telephone, as she was now screening calls, and had started to isolate herself. Debbie did not leave the house; she did not answer the phone; she did not seek out friends. Once the most gregarious person in the entire battalion, Debbie now shied away from human contact. People who had known Debbie for years said she was not herself.

One day, when Michelle flew back to Indiana to visit family, Debbie picked her up at the airport, and Michelle saw that she was drinking alcohol out of a coffee mug while she drove, smack in the middle of the day. Red-flag behavior, Michelle thought. To Michelle, it seemed as though the Debbie she knew was slowly vanishing.

Michelle spoke to Desma about her worries, but felt shy about confronting Debbie, who was thirty years her senior. The older woman was an authority figure — it was like confronting a parent. Eventually, however, Michelle and Desma told Debbie they feared that she might be drinking too much. "They do [worry]," Debbie would acknowledge later. "And I know they do. And probably it's somewhat accurate, in a sense, that they worry. For me, having that whole year [in Iraq] kind of to myself, there was something about being alone like that — you can find solace in things that maybe you shouldn't. Being the oldest one, I probably take what they say with a grain of salt and go on my way. Not that that's the right approach, necessarily. But it's just stuff that I have to work through myself. I always feel if you are able to pay your bills, and take care of other people, and keep a job, then what's wrong, as long as you are not hurting anybody else?"

And Debbie could still hold a job, and pay her bills, and take care of other people. Soon after she returned from Iraq, she resumed caring for everybody in her family. As her mother's health deteriorated, Debbie spent increasing amounts of time accompanying her mother to doctors' offices. Debbie's parents turned to her for help with basic household chores such as grocery shopping. Then Debbie's daughter ran into marital problems and subsequently lost her job.

Debbie tried to help by caring for Jaylen, sometimes overnight. Often she invited Jeff's granddaughter Mallori to sleep over, too. The two girls shared no blood, but they had the common bond of knowing Jeff and Debbie as their grandparents. On the weekends, Jeff built big fires outside, and they roasted marshmallows as the sparks flew upward into the dark.

Debbie gave and gave and gave. She did not know how to receive support, though, except from Jeff, who had a quiet way of providing help without fuss. Most of her peers had retired from the National Guard, and Debbie found she had fewer friends at drill. She turned fifty-seven in the summer of 2009, and there was talk of another deployment coming the following year, when she would turn fifty-eight. She could see sixty approaching; Debbie did not think she had another deployment in her. She retired in 2010. Belonging to the National Guard had been an essential part of her identity for almost a quarter century, and severing her membership in the group left a large void. She found herself still automatically checking the calendar to see when her next drill weekend might be, even though for her there would be no more drill weekends.

During this same period, Debbie found she could not extricate herself from a stubborn depression, and finally realized she needed help. She started seeing a therapist who worked at the VA clinic in Bloomington. Delia McGlocklin was a veteran herself — she had been in the air force — as well as a licensed clinical social worker. She was in her thirties, served as the president of her homeowners association, had a husband and children, and had an impressive collection of fashionable shoes. McGlocklin helped Debbie acquire a prescription for antidepressants. And when Debbie told the social worker about the sensation of being trapped inside Saran Wrap, McGlocklin said it was normal to have such feelings after a deployment. Debbie wanted to hug the woman, because she had thought she was losing her mind.

Desma Brooks was now living with Charity Elliott in a small town outside of Bedford, Indiana, in the central part of the state, but she drove down to southern Indiana almost every week, ferrying her children back and forth between different households. Desma often stopped in Bloomington to see Debbie on her way to or from southern Indiana. It was good to get out of the car and stretch her legs. And it was good to see someone else who had been through the same two deployments and the same two attempts to make it back home. But Desma could see that everybody else relied on Debbie, and she didn't want to add to Debbie's burdens, so she kept things light and rarely disclosed her struggles. At one point, however, Desma happened to mention that she was seeing a therapist at the VA hospital.

Debbie said, “So am I.”

“Really?” Desma said. “Who are you seeing?”

“Delia McGlocklin,” said Debbie.

“Me, too!” Desma said.

It was an immense relief for Debbie to learn that she was not alone in seeking help. At least with Michelle and Desma, maybe she did not have to hide her problems so scrupulously. “There’s no judgment there,” Debbie would say later. Debbie and Desma gossiped about Delia McGlocklin — Desma marveled at how many pairs of shoes the social worker owned, and Debbie described introducing Delia to her favorite doughnuts. They asked each other if the therapy sessions helped. Yes, they concluded — although Desma was locked in a battle of wills with the therapist over how far back into her past they should dig.

For months, McGlocklin had been trying to get Desma to talk about her childhood. What had happened when she was in middle school? Why had she been put into foster care? The therapist suspected that the answer to some of Desma’s current problems lay in unresolved issues from the past. Psychologists had been puzzling over the question of why some soldiers returned with post-traumatic stress disorder and others did not, even when they had been exposed to similar kinds of shock. Two million soldiers had been sent to Iraq and Afghanistan, and hundreds of thousands had returned with PTSD, but there was not a direct correlation between the severity of the soldiers' wartime experiences and their psychological responses. One theory held that soldiers who had experienced traumas earlier in life might be more vulnerable to PTSD. Delia McGlocklin believed that something had happened to Desma in her youth that was sudden, unexpected, and out of her control — some other silver box had gone off. Perhaps Desma's experiences in Iraq were even more disturbing than they would otherwise have been because they were compounded by that earlier disaster.

When McGlocklin asked about the incident that had led to her removal from her mother's care, however, Desma told her it was of no consequence. It had nothing to do with today. There was no point in bringing up stuff she had left behind so long ago. As far as Desma was concerned, the therapist's inclination to probe into the past only added to her stress. "Patient reported that since our last session she has been thinking about her avoidance to talk about the bad stuff," McGlocklin wrote in one of her many progress notes that became part of Desma's lengthy VA file.

"Patient reports that when she started to think about it, it started to flood her with emotion." But the only emotion Desma could name was anger — anger with McGlocklin for making her return to matters she wanted to keep at a distance. McGlocklin suggested that Desma attend a women's group therapy session. Desma said, "I don't want to sit in a circle and hold hands and talk about our problems, I really don't."

Desma had been dealing with a difficult constellation of symptoms ever since she had arrived home at the end of 2008. During those first days at home, Desma had not even told her children that she was back in Indiana, because she did not feel well enough to care for them. She went to sleep with a headache and she woke up with a headache — her head hurt all the time. On some days she was sensitive to light and on others she had vertigo. Noise magnified the headache. She could not remember things properly. And Desma was angry, all the time, every day. It was a snarly, pissy kind of rage, her primary souvenir from Iraq. She did not think she would be a good mother in that condition.

Also, the kind of homecoming that the military had organized was not the way she wanted to greet her children. Some vast hoopla inside an airplane hangar — that's what Desma and Charity had walked into, right off the plane. Then, after perhaps an hour or two of socializing, the soldiers had separated from the crowd and boarded buses to Camp Atterbury for demobilization. Why drag the kids to some circus act, tell them she was back, and then tell them she was leaving again? It had been easier not to tell them she was home at all. "I needed to start to adjust on my own before I brought my kids into that," Desma would say later. "And I don't like crowds, so when you come off the plane into this big hangar and they release you, it is a nightmare. We are all happy to see our families — we are ecstatic to see our families. But doing it in a dog and pony show . . . let's parade the soldiers in, and then put us back on a bus, and send us to Atterbury for five days. Let's just be traumatizing to our families again. I'm sure they would have loved to be there and greet me, but I did not want to have to tell them, I can't come home, I got to go to Atterbury. You drove up here to Indianapolis and missed a day of school for a crappy cookie and watered-down Kool-Aid."

In the first weeks back, Desma spent most of her time reading. She worked her way through the entire *Inheritance Cycle,* by Christopher Paolini, a four-book series about a sixteen-year-old boy who receives a terrible battle wound and is magically healed by dragons. The books offered a complete escape from reality, and she buried herself in their pages. She called the children to wish them a Happy Thanksgiving but did not go see them over the holiday. Briefly, she tried taking online courses at the University of Phoenix, thinking she could complete the bachelor's degree that she had begun before the deployment, but she found it impossible to concentrate. She stopped taking the courses and started seeing Delia McGlocklin. Eventually, over the course of two years' worth of therapy, McGlocklin would come to define Desma's core psychological issues as the avoidance of thoughts or feelings associated with trauma, anger management problems, and hypervigilance, but it took some time for McGlocklin to assess her new client. When they first met, McGlocklin simply asked how she had been spending her days. Desma said, "I'm just staying home and relaxing and reading a lot."

It was all she could manage at the beginning. Then in December 2008, the girls mentioned that they were performing in a Christmas pageant, and Desma promised to be there. She picked up Josh first, then drove over to see her daughters. "It's about time," said Alexis. They went to the pageant, drove up to central Indiana to spend the weekend together at Charity's place, and then Desma drove the children back to their respective guardians. Josh was sticking with his plan to live with his surrogate father through the end of high school. And Desma had decided it would be better for the two girls to remain with their father for the duration of the school year.

It was hard to pull a family back together again after a yearlong absence, as Desma learned in ways both big and small. While she was in southern Indiana, Desma found her dog Goldie at a neighbor's house. Jimmy had let the animal loose, and a young girl who lived up the street had adopted the stray. When Desma said she wanted Goldie, the girl said Desma was stealing her dog. "But in reality, it was the dog I left when I went to Iraq," Desma said afterward. "And I wanted my dog back. I had the dog in my arms and I climbed in the car and I felt like such a shit bag for taking this kid's dog, but it was really my dog." The problem was Goldie did not know she was Desma's dog anymore. After the dog started whining, Desma let go of Goldie, and watched the animal run back to the girl. She cried and cried about that, alone in her car, as she drove away. It was still her dog as far as she was concerned, even if nobody else understood.

Then she visited the elementary school where the two girls were enrolled and had a confusing conversation with the woman in the front office. Desma brought up the subject of how Paige was doing in fifth grade.

"She's in fourth grade," said the woman behind the counter.

"What do you mean?" Desma asked. "She did fourth grade last year."

"But she didn't successfully complete the fourth grade," the woman said.

"Excuse me?" said Desma.

She could not fathom how one of her daughters could have failed a year of elementary school and nobody thought to tell her. It would not have happened if she had been in Indiana, she was certain — Desma believed that Paige was repeating the fourth grade because her mother had been in Iraq, and her father had not known how to make her do her homework. When Desma asked Paige what had happened, Paige said that she had been told everything would be fine if she went to summer school. Desma could not help herself — she snapped at the child, saying apparently that hadn't gone so well, either. Paige's failure seemed commingled with her own choices, and she found it hard to separate herself from Paige enough to parent her well.

Two weeks later, all three children came to spend the Christmas holiday. They did not do much — Desma did not even try to make fudge or chocolate-covered pretzels, which she usually did at that time of year — mostly watched a lot of movies and ran a few errands. Desma took the children along with her when she went to buy a new car. At the dealership, she asked for something used, with all-wheel drive, and a third row of seats. Her head hurt and it was hard to make decisions. The salesman brought her a new Ford with two-wheel drive. Desma told him, "Don't yank my chain, I said something used with all-wheel drive." He said he had this one vehicle. Her kids were inside the Pacifica before Desma could get a good look at the car. "Mom, it's got a DVD player!" Paige announced. "Mom, it's got leather seats!" cried Alexis. Josh took a look at the sticker on the window and said, "Mom, you can't afford this."

Desma checked out the car: it was three years old and had thirty thousand miles on the odometer. She could haul three kids and still have room for friends. Both her mom and her mom's oxygen tank would fit inside. But Josh was right; it was more than she should spend. She hesitated. Then she told the car salesman that he had probably bought the car at an auction for no more than $2,000, so there was no need to toy with her on the price, and by the way, she had just gotten back from Iraq and she understood he gave discounts to people who served in the military. The car had been priced at $21,000 but the salesman offered it to her for $11,000. He let her drive the car out to Brown County and back again. She bought the Pacifica the following day. Perhaps only Desma's closest friends, like Stacy Glory or Mary Bell or Michelle Fischer, could see how heroic it was, that she had managed to buy a car while caring for her children at the same time. Desma could barely function.

Driving freaked her out. The roads were wide open, and she felt frighteningly unprotected. Trusting civilians barreled along without scanning the roadsides, and hers was the only moving dot on the GPS. She missed the rest of her convoy. Desma was driving the Pacifica through Bedford, with a marked police car on her tail, when she spotted several small black plastic bags of trash in the middle of the road. She locked the brakes and swerved. The cop almost rear-ended her. Desma could not see properly, could not breathe, could not think. The cop pulled up behind her, lights flashing.

"I'm so sorry!" Desma told the officer. "I didn't mean to freak out, but you don't understand."

"Well, help me understand," he said.

"I just got back," Desma said. "I've been home all of a few weeks and somebody's put all this trash in the road!"

"Just got back from where?"

"Iraq."

The cop said they should get out of the road and talk. They both pulled into the parking lot in front of a pizza place. Desma sat on the curb and the cop sat down beside her. He asked her what had happened. She had hit a roadside bomb, Desma said. It had just looked like a box. Now there were bags of trash in the road — people should pick up their shit! Her hands were still shaking. The cop told her that she needed to get less panicky, or maybe she should not drive.

But Desma spent many hours on the road. Charity lived in central Indiana, while her children lived seventy-five miles to the south. On the weekends, Desma drove down to pick up the girls and Josh, back up so they could spend the weekend in central Indiana with Charity, down again to bring the children back to their guardians, and up again to get herself back home. On the highway, she hugged the bumper of the car in front of her, driving as close as she could, because that's what you did in a convoy — you did not leave room for the enemy. The other drivers did not know they were in a convoy, however, and they sped up to put distance between themselves and Desma. So she sped up, too. She got pulled over for speeding so many times that she lost track of the number of tickets. Maybe it was thirteen traffic violations? Two for disregarding stop signs, two for reckless driving in a construction zone, nine for speeding — something like that. At one point, driving too fast out on a country road, Desma topped a hill and saw trash strewn across the road. She spun out.

It struck her friends as a little bit crazy how

much time she spent behind the wheel — a little too much like being assigned to run convoy security — but Desma resisted any suggestion that she was purposefully repeating the past. "I feel like all my time is spent in the car," Desma told her therapist. Delia McGlocklin advised Desma to spend less time on the road, given that she had hit a roadside bomb, and driving was clearly stressful. Desma snapped that she did not have a choice. She could not imagine rearranging her life so that she did not always have to drive — she lived with Charity, and her children lived seventy-five miles away. That was the way it was. Beginning in February 2009, she also started commuting to a new job at Camp Atterbury that required her to drive an hour and twenty minutes each way. Driving to work, sometimes Desma would go into the mindless trance she knew from Iraq — that stupor she used to enter, ten or eleven hours into a mission, when she would just follow the vehicle in front of her without thinking. One day Desma snapped back into the present moment and saw a sign by the side of the highway that said GREENWOOD. What the hell was she doing up there? She had driven forty minutes past the exit for Camp Atterbury. But she did not have an unconscious desire to relive the hours she had spent as a truck driver in Iraq, she said — it was just the way things were.

Desma had told the group home for troubled youth that she could not return to work there shortly after she got back. She did not trust herself to be around kids in the foster care system. "After being hit with an IED — I am a much angrier person," she would say later. "I had to go and tell them that, you know, with the headaches and the anger and the issues I was having after my last tour, I was unable to come back to work. And they were distraught. I still get emails saying I really wish you were here from the staff." The job at Camp Atterbury paid $40,000 a year, approximately double what she had been making at the group home. She considered herself lucky — the salary transformed her finances. She had to reenlist to get the job, however, because it was known as a dual status position, meaning that it could only be filled by a soldier currently serving in some branch of the military. Desma reenlisted for one year. If she wanted to keep the job at Atterbury, she would have to sign up again the following year.

At Camp Atterbury, Desma did the same type of work she had done at Camp Phoenix, in Afghanistan — she tracked maintenance on military vehicles and equipment. The job was familiar and Camp Atterbury was familiar. What was unfamiliar was how the new job put her inside the military environment fulltime. Her deployment had ended, but she still wore a uniform, addressed her superiors by rank, and took orders. On the one hand, she was surrounded by constant reminders of what had happened in Iraq, and on the other hand, she was also surrounded by people who understood what she was living through. One day in March 2009, another soldier who worked in the motor pool plugged in a carbon monoxide detector to see if it worked. The carbon monoxide detector emitted a high-pitched squeal. Desma was back in the vehicle, surrounded by darkness, listening to that sound. She could smell the smoke, she could taste the dirt.

"I got to go," she told the other soldier, and stumbled outside.

He came out, too, sat down beside her. "I'm so sorry," he said.

He had been in Iraq — she didn't have to explain.

Later a battalion that was about to deploy set up an IED simulation right outside the motor pool. There was .50-caliber fire and M4 fire and the thump of roadside bombs. None of it was live, but it all sounded real. Desma was not the only person in the motor pool who hit the ground. At home, Desma started hollering in the night. "I'm never going to get any sleep if you don't shut the hell up," Charity told her. When Josh spent the weekend, he said, "Mom, what's wrong with you?" After Desma woke up, however, she remembered nothing. "Denies nightmares but significant other reports that she screams out for help in her sleep," wrote Delia McGlocklin in her notes.

Meanwhile, at a routine health assessment that had taken place during the same month when she had started working at Camp Atterbury, Desma had gotten labeled a problem. Medical staff on contract with the military had been checking soldiers' hearing, vision, physical strength, and mental health. At every station, Desma had been forced to sit and wait. Toward the end of the process, she found herself sitting next to a guy who had just been told to repeat the entire process all over again; she knew he had already gone through every station, because she had waited with him at each juncture, but somehow the staff had neglected to check off his progress on the required list. As far as the army was concerned, he hadn't done the exercise at all. The whole experience was aggravating — the stupidity of the assessment, the idiocy of the guy being told to go through it twice, the way the exercise was consuming valuable hours. Her head was screaming. The doctor who conducted her mental health screening bragged that he was going down to Haiti to provide assistance after the earthquake. He sounded pretty pleased with himself.

"That's awesome," said Desma. "Can we just get this done?"

"Are you irritated?" the doctor wanted to know.

"I'm extremely irritated," said Desma. "I just want to go home."

"Do you want to hurt yourself or anyone else?"

"I have no desire whatsoever to hurt myself, but there are a couple of people I could hold underwater until they quit kicking," Desma said.

You should not carry a weapon, nor live in an austere environment, Desma was instructed. Soldiers who had their weapons taken away did not usually advance in their careers — they had been given a "profile," in military lingo, and were labeled as damaged goods. Desma believed she would have said something similar at any point in her life if faced with someone as self-satisfied as the doctor, when a series of other people had already vexed her. But once you got a profile it was hard to undo. She had hit an IED, and then she had made a stupid remark to the wrong person; now she had become one of those scary veterans, a possible shooter. After the evaluation, Desma was given a 30 percent disability rating — 10 percent for the continuing headache, 10 percent for her shoulder injury, and 10 percent for stress fractures in her legs. She was told she had a 0 rating for post-traumatic stress disorder. As a result of her partial disability rating, Desma was given an extra $315 per month as compensation.

Initially, having her weapon taken away did not affect Desma professionally, because she was still attached to the 139th. The guys she had served with in Iraq considered her someone they trusted, no matter what her profile. Desma was promoted that same month, making her an E5. The specialists had to call her Sergeant Brooks. The main issue she ran into at her job was that she could not get her brain to work properly. Once she had been able to master any software or technical device, and she still had an aptitude for that kind of work, but when her boss gave her a list and explained what the items meant, five minutes later she could not recall what he had said. She would look at the piece of paper and not be able to decipher its meaning.

Shortly after Desma began working at Camp Atterbury, she started seeing a medical doctor at the VA named Douglas Mottley. He suspected that she had traumatic brain injury, although she had not been given that diagnosis and was not being compensated for that disability. He also believed that she had PTSD, according to his notes in her VA file, even though she was not being compensated for that, either. In an extensive evaluation that he conducted, Dr. Mottley noted that Desma had constant headaches, moderately slowed thinking, episodes of vertigo, severe sensitivity to noise, severe concentration issues, severe forgetfulness, severe difficulty making decisions, and very severe irritability. "Since restarting work, she has had difficulty remembering instructions that she has been told, difficulty with organization, difficulty remembering appointments, days of the week, forgetting where she places her keys," noted Dr. Mottley. He concluded that these findings were consistent with a diagnosis of traumatic brain injury — the signature injury of the current wars. Pentagon officials estimated that more than three hundred thousand soldiers had come back from Afghanistan and Iraq with invisible head wounds due to the tremendous explosions that had been detonating in both theaters. The armor on their bodies and their vehicles had kept them alive, but the blasts had sometimes caused winds in excess of three hundred miles per hour, and many of the soldiers had been knocked around so badly that their brains had sheared inside their skulls.

Dr. Mottley recommended that Desma see speech pathologists for help with memory and organization and that she see doctors in neurology about her headaches. He also ordered an MRI. Over the next six months, Dr. Mottley and the neurologists prescribed various medications, but nothing blocked Desma's headache. "Will also put her on a gradual Neurontin taper to see if it decreases the headache intensity," wrote Dr. Mottley at the end of April. Desma took the medicine for three days and could not function. Finally, in September 2009, the doctors in neurology decided to try Topamax, an anticonvulsant more often used to treat epilepsy. After Desma started taking the Topamax, her headache became bearable; the medicine reduced the pain to an almost imperceptible level. When she failed to take the pills, however, the headache came roaring back. She took the Topamax daily.

After the doctors looked at the MRI, they determined that she did have TBI — they deemed it a mild case of the disorder, which did not mean the symptoms were easy to live with but only that they had seen worse — and Desma also began to receive compensation for that condition. "America's grateful to you for your service," said the letter she received about her latest disability rating. "Please safeguard this important document."

Over the same period of time, Desma saw several different speech pathologists who taught her coping strategies they had developed for veterans with cognitive problems. "She reported that her main concern was her difficulty remembering how to do her job, which required several steps to be able to complete," wrote Kathleen Krueger in a summary of the consultation she did in April 2009. "Her supervisor has done things to assist her like writing down steps of tasks, but she reports he sometimes gets agitated." Desma was having similar problems at home, too. "She reported, 'My kids think I'm crazy because I can't remember what I told them,' " wrote Krueger. "She reported that she failed to take them on some trips that she promised to because she forgot. She also loses cash."

The speech pathologists taught Desma to use email and Post-it notes and calendar entries to remind herself of critical matters that she had once kept in her head. She could no longer form reliable short-term memories, so she had to provide herself with prompts. If she needed to remember something, she sent herself an email or stuck a note on the refrigerator. Desma created an elaborate color-coded system of sticky notes at work. Yellow was for everyday stuff, because that was the color of normal sticky notes; blue meant something she had to pay attention to personally; red indicated something she had to bring to the attention of someone else. For the most part the system worked, although sometimes it caused Desma frustration, because she would look at a note she had written and she would not have any idea what it meant. It made her furious, being so disabled. "She has used many organization strategies that work but gets mad that she has to use them," observed Susan McGarvey Toler, another speech pathologist who worked with Desma.

The speech pathology staff at the VA wanted to give Desma a BlackBerry or an iPhone or an iPad. They had all this free technology, but they were not offering to pay the monthly bills on the devices. Desma already had a phone, and it had a much cheaper service plan. She declined. McGarvey Toler wanted Desma to relax; she coached Desma to add daily reminders on her phone's calendar, telling herself to breathe. The only problem was that when Desma got home and looked at the phone's calendar, she saw that every single day that month had turned red. Usually she only entered one or two things per week, and the only days that lit up red were birthdays or days when she had an appointment at the VA. Desma could not stand looking at the all-red calendar and took out the breathing reminders.

The speech pathologists also suggested that Desma might want to take medicine for attention deficit disorder. She said she didn't think she needed another prescription. She already had a shoebox full of pills, and it contained so many bottles that she joked about lining them up "in formation." The list of medicines that Desma had been prescribed included Topamax for her headache, as well as both Trazodone and Ambien for sleep, and the anti-inflammatory drugs Naproxen and Diclofenac for the pain in her shoulder. Then she had Metoclopramide for nausea, Zomig for migraines (which she took on days when the Topamax was not enough), a variety of muscle relaxers to reduce the tension in her body that contributed to the severity of her headaches, and Wellbutrin to combat anxiety.

One of the main things making her anxious was her love life. Over the previous six months, Desma's relationship with Charity had been slowly deteriorating. Charity was going to school to become a paramedic, and had returned to her job as an emergency medical technician. Maybe Charity wanted to return to other aspects of her former life, too. In the spring of 2009, Desma had found a letter that Charity was in the middle of writing to her ex-girlfriend, in which Charity said she wished she could have the other woman back in her life. As a friend? A lover? The letter did not specify. Desma worried that maybe Charity had only agreed to live together so that Desma could help pay the bills. Charity did not offer much affection; she had grown distant. Desma moved into a separate bedroom to sort out her feelings. In one of her therapy sessions, Desma told Delia McGlocklin that she was still in love, but she believed that her partner no longer reciprocated her feelings.

At the beginning of June 2009, right before Desma's daughters were supposed to come live with them, Charity told Desma she was not happy and did not want to do this anymore. Desma tried to look for a new place to live but could not find a decent home in a good school district that she could afford. She called her therapist in a state of near hysteria. "Patient reported that she had a full panic attack," Delia McGlocklin wrote in her notes. "Patient reported that last week her partner stated she wanted to end the relationship, and patient reports she is in pain with the loss. She also reported that her children are due to move in with her in the next two and a half weeks." Desma felt overwhelmed at the idea of becoming a full-time mom again. "She reported at times she finds it easier not to have to worry about mom duties," wrote McGlocklin.

Paige and Alexis were supposed to resume living with Desma at the beginning of July 2009, but did not actually move in until that August. Josh had stuck to his plan and was continuing to live with his surrogate father. Charity told Desma that she and the girls could stay at her place until Desma got on her feet. It was important to Desma that the children not have to change schools twice; she wanted to get the girls settled, and then look for a new place within the same school district.

It was after the children moved back in to live with Desma that things started to fray. When they had come for the weekend, they had been happy to see her, but now they said appalling things. The girls had been eight and ten when she left; now they were nine and eleven. Nine and eleven and sullen, obstinate, rude. "Why don't you just go back to Iraq?" Alexis said at one point. "That's where Dad says you prefer to be." Desma blamed Dennis for the change in their behavior. "It's come around that he told the kids that I left because I would rather go overseas than be with my children," she would say later. "There was a lot of disrespect when I come home. They weren't made to pick up after themselves while I was gone. He didn't take care of them the way I did. He didn't discipline them the way I did. And when I come home, they hated me." Once again, Dennis remembered things differently — he said that when Desma came home from Iraq, she argued with everyone constantly and was impossible to get along with.

Desma did not feel as though she deserved ungrateful children. Sometimes she forgot to show them love. Her kids told Desma she was the one who had changed — and the person who had come home from Iraq was not even the same person as the one who had come back from Afghanistan. "It's different every time you come home," Alexis told her. Living with Charity became more fraught after the girls moved in, and although Desma looked, she could not find alternative housing. She told Delia McGlocklin that she was contemplating living out of her car.

Desma went into a tailspin. The therapist tried reminding Desma of her many attributes. Earlier, McGlocklin had written up an evaluation of her client's strengths and weaknesses. In the plus column she noted that Desma had "hope, resiliency, positive attitude, expressing desire for change, motivation for change, adequate housing, has a job, transportation." On the negative side, however, McGlocklin observed that Desma had "limited social supports." She had few family members to rely upon — only her cousin and her sister. Otherwise she was trying to rely on Charity, who did not want to be relied on anymore. The therapist reminded Desma that she had other friends: Mary, Stacy, Michelle, Debbie.

That fall, Desma began calling Michelle regularly. The phone calls were agonizing from Michelle's perspective — she was listening to Desma hang on to a deployment relationship long after the deployment had ended. Michelle answered the phone every time, however; she could not imagine having endured Camp Phoenix without the pink flamingos and the vibrators and Desma's colorful insouciance. Anytime Desma wanted to talk, that was fine with Michelle. Their friendship deepened.

On October 19, 2009, Desma went to the VA hospital for a follow-up appointment with

Dr. Mottley. She told him, "Happy Bomb Day."

He asked what she meant by the comment.

"She says that today is the one-year anniversary of the IED blast," wrote Dr. Mottley in his notes. "So she feels a little more anxious than usual."

At the same time, Desma reported with relief that ever since she had started taking Topamax, her headache had remained under control.

That November, Desma received another promotion and her annual pay increased by $10,000. Around the same time, Dennis also began paying Desma child support of $44 a week, after their arrangement changed and she took sole custody of their children. Because of the raise, the child support payments, and the additional money that came about as a result of her increased disability rating, Desma was able to afford to move out of Charity's house. She found a trailer half a mile away, which she rented for $550 per month. The girls would not have to change schools. Desma hoped to move in December 1, but her landlord had a hard time evicting the prior tenant, and she did not get the keys until Christmas.

By then, Desma had started seeing someone new. Earlier that year she had run into Roy Dishner at a workshop run by the National Guard in Bloomington. Dishner had been

Desma's squad leader during the time she had spent in the 293rd, before she had transferred out of that unit. He was one of the few men who had been warm, when others had refused to speak to her at all. In October, Dishner had come to Lafayette to see Desma during her drill weekend. Because Desma had become a noncommissioned officer, too, the rules governing interactions between them had changed; previously they had been forbidden to fraternize, but now it was permitted. They had gone out to dinner and talked for hours. After that, Dishner had started calling frequently and they had seen each other a few more times. On the day after Christmas, when Desma pulled up at the trailer, carting a load of moving boxes in her red Pacifica, she found Roy parked in her driveway.

"I brought you some plates," he said.

She wasn't sure what she wanted, but she liked that he was kind.

3
Numb

Healing took years. In some regards, they never fully returned to the people they had been before. There was no going home, in the sense of going back to the way things had been earlier — there was only going forward. Maybe, out of them all, the person who changed the most was Akbar Khan. He came to visit that Christmas, just as Desma was moving. He had spent the better part of the previous year working at a Home Depot in Bayonne, New Jersey, operating a forklift for $11.75 an hour. He had moved to Oregon after failing to find work in North Carolina, and then to New Jersey, where he was sharing a small apartment with a friend from Afghanistan. He arrived bearing gifts. He brought Debbie a heart-shaped necklace, and Michelle a diamond ring. Akbar told Michelle that he could not really propose, because he was already married, but she was his soul mate. The implication was that if he had been allowed to make the choice, he would have picked Michelle to be his wife.

Michelle accepted the ring because of the high regard she had for Akbar and because he had saved $1,000 to buy it by operating a forklift at Home Depot, but when Michelle told Billy that she had accepted an engagement ring from another man, he got terribly angry. She loved Billy, so she did not bring the ring home — she left it with Desma. Desma kept the ring in her closet, along with the sky blue burka that Akbar had helped her find in Afghanistan. One day, while they were still at Camp Phoenix, she had put the burka on inside the B-Hut. Michelle had walked right past her, thinking she was an Afghan woman. "I was a blue lampshade," Desma would say later. Alexis and Paige had marveled over the burka when Desma had shown it to them. She let them dress up in it and show it off to their friends, who all wanted a turn looking out at the world from behind the blue mesh window.

Michelle and Akbar were that way for a long time: psychologically entwined, physically far apart, never able to muster a proper romance, never able to keep things truly platonic. They were like the two countries to which they belonged, unable to extricate themselves, yet unable to forge a real partnership. Then Akbar heard that a company called Mission Essential Personnel was paying linguists unusually high salaries. Akbar moved back to Afghanistan and began working inside the detention facility at Bagram Airfield. He earned $184,000 a year translating during interviews with detainees and during legal proceedings — the pay was so good because there were very few people who could do the work. It was an awful job, though. After he started spending his days at the prison, Akbar began to wilt into a darker person. He grew sarcastic and bitter, an entirely different person from the young man Michelle had tried to shield from Mountain Dew. It was not safe for him to let his family know where he was working; it was not safe for him to visit his wife or son; there was the question of whether it would ever be safe for him to work anywhere else in Afghanistan, after so many members of the Taliban had seen his face.

At the same time, he earned so much money that he bought a new house for his family, set his brothers up in business, purchased costly digital cameras for himself, and showered friends with gifts. He had to return to the United States every year to renew his visa, and during one of his visits, Akbar was hanging out with Debbie one day when he announced he was going out for cigarettes. He returned instead with a flatscreen television set, which he insisted on giving to Debbie, despite her vehement protests. Later he gave Debbie and Desma each an iPad, and Michelle an iPod Touch. Then he sent Michelle a pair of fancy sunglasses that had probably cost several hundred dollars. They had white plastic frames and gold-tinted lenses and made her look like a movie star.

Michelle left her position at AmeriCorps, began working at Colorado Brownfields Foundation, and then got a job at a nonprofit called Veterans Green Jobs, which sought to reduce dependence on oil. Her car died, and Akbar tried to buy her a new one, but she told him she could not accept a vehicle from him — it would not be fair to Billy. They were trying to make things work. Michelle was twenty-eight years old, and half her friends had gotten married. She wanted more than anything else in the world to have children. Billy felt their relationship had some negative aspects, however, and he was not sure they could fix what was wrong.

After Michelle started working at Veterans Green Jobs, she became close friends with her colleague Garett Reppenhagen, the son of a Vietnam War veteran and the grandson of two World War II veterans, who had worked as a sniper in Iraq. While there, he had started writing an antiwar blog and later had become the first active duty member of Iraq Veterans Against the War. Reppenhagen introduced Michelle to Denver's progressive veterans community. The Veterans of Foreign Wars had been established in Denver in 1899 by veterans returning from the Spanish-American War, and Michelle started hanging around with some of the other veterans she met at VFW Post 1, the oldest VFW post in existence. Izzy Abbass, a forward-thinking veteran of the Gulf War, was in the middle of transforming the post. He had stopped serving alcohol, had started holding meetings in the Rooster and Moon coffee shop, and was organizing a lot of outdoor activities. He was also trying to make the organization friendly to women.

For the first time, Michelle found a group of people who shared both her personal history and her political orientation. Michelle stopped hiding her past and talked openly about her deployment. It was a relief. She began to see that it had been somewhat haphazard, who had experienced an easier deployment, and who had experienced a harder one; who had escaped physically untouched, and whose bodies had been changed forever. At one point Michelle went snowshoeing in Rocky Mountain National Park with a group of veterans from Colorado. Michelle and a nurse who was in her sixties were the only two women in the group. They talked about how much the role of women in the military had changed during their lifetimes; when the nurse had enlisted, that job had been the only option available, but by the time Michelle had enlisted, women could become truck drivers or weapons mechanics. Now people in Washington were discussing the possibility of allowing women to serve in combat positions.

Coincidentally, every individual in the group had chosen to wear their combat boots. Michelle had not been able to find anything better than her well-worn Gore-Tex boots, in terms of waterproofing and warmth; apparently the other vets all felt the same way. They had so much in common and yet they were so different. "I was making jokes about being able to get pedicures at Bagram," Michelle would say afterward. "Because I did — every time I went to Bagram I would get a pedicure. But I was joking with some of these ex-marines, and I was speaking to someone who was in Fallujah. Jordan, who was with us, he got hit with an RPG, and it almost killed him. He was a marine. So, you know, me saying stuff like that to those guys, it makes my experience seem so trivial. And they look at it that way, too. I mean, they were like, Oh, my God, we were sleeping on cardboard boxes. So then it's like, why do I have any feelings that are negative about my experience at all? Because it was very easy, compared to that. But these wars are different for everybody, and they're different every day, in terms of easy, difficult, painful, fun. At any given moment, something could happen to you that will change the rest of your life. That's the thing about living in a combat zone. You could live through a whole year and escape unscathed, where the worst scar that you have is your smallpox vaccination, but it depends on where you're standing and in what moment. Everything is so random that you never know."

Jordan had gotten hit, and Michelle had not, but she remembered the sound that the RPGs had made when they had fallen around her. She joked about getting pedicures, and she could not compare her experience to that of a marine who had been to Fallujah, but she also knew that she could have hit an old land mine or a new IED. While spending time with other members of Colorado's progressive veteran community, Michelle heard the term "economic draft" for the first time, which was another moment of epiphany — yes, she thought, that's what George W. Bush had done. He had used money to draft the same poor people over and over again to fight his fight, and he had left his own class virtually untouched. Most of the veterans she befriended were men, and sometimes they made Billy feel uncomfortable. "I would like to meet one other female veteran who has a successful relationship with a civilian man," Michelle would say later. "The gender stuff is really wacky. Because it is really important for me to be in the veteran community, which is also 85 percent male. And I had a very masculine job. You know, it gives me a very colorful past, and I think when I first met him he was fascinated by it, but now I feel it's just some sort of a liability. I don't know, it's so hard for me to reconcile being with him and being a veteran. He's really antimilitary. Anytime he talks about my experience he paints me like a victim. And I don't think I see myself like that. But he's really important to me. He's a really amazing man. Good men are hard to find."

Meanwhile, Desma kept speeding. On March 29, 2010, she was pulled over for doing eighty-four in a seventy-mile-per-hour speed zone. She had been trying to make it to Indianapolis for an appointment at the VA. "Case manager spoke with patient by phone," wrote a staff person at the VA hospital. "Patient . . . is being detained by state police. . . . Case manager could hear the police in the background during phone conversation. Patient asked that message be relayed to Dr. Mottley. Patient did not foresee that she could make the appointment on time."

That same month, Desma heard that the military was going to evaluate veterans for PTSD according to different measures. She called the VA hospital and said she wanted her disability rating to be reconsidered. "Veteran would like to appeal her rating," noted a staff person. "Veteran believes she should be rated for PTSD." After that phone call, the VA staff added a progress note to Desma's VA file saying that she had tested positive for PTSD. The note enumerated the symptoms Desma had described in the phone call. Did she have nightmares or difficult thoughts about a traumatic experience? Yes. Was she constantly on guard, or easily startled? Yes. Did she feel numb or detached from others? Yes. From her surroundings? Yes. Along with the earlier diagnosis of TBI, the PTSD diagnosis boosted her overall disability rating to 50 percent. This increased the financial compensation she received for her disabilities to $1,150 a month.

Desma had been dating Roy Dishner since Christmas, even though they lived 130 miles apart. The trailer where she lived was outside Bedford, while his house was close to Hagerstown, two and a half hours to the north. Roy courted her with old-fashioned industry. They talked on the phone frequently, and about once a month he came to spend the weekend. Roy lived by himself in a large, two-story house, and he had the air of a person who had been lonely for a long time. He was also reliable, punctual, polite, and scrupulously honest; Desma found his trustworthiness comforting. He was careful and precise, a mechanic who always kept track of his tools. Locked in the basement of his house was his extensive gun collection, and he liked to fix old tractors for fun. When he was not wearing his uniform, he often wore a gray T-shirt that said ARMY, and in his free time he watched movies on the Military Channel about soldiers doing heroic things.

At first Michelle viewed the relationship with skepticism, but then she learned that Roy believed in saving energy as passionately as she did. After he had returned from his deployment to Iraq, he had decided the best way to avoid future bloodshed would be to transform his home into a model of energy conservation: he had insulated the walls, weather-stripped every door, replaced all the windows, and put in a geothermal heating system. Michelle approved of Desma's new romance.

In May 2010, Michelle persuaded Desma and Debbie to meet her in Washington, DC, to support the work of Veterans Green Jobs. A clean energy bill known as the American Power Act had been introduced by Senator John Kerry and Senator Joseph Lieberman. One month earlier, an oil rig had exploded in the Gulf of Mexico, and it was spilling crude oil into the water at the rate of one thousand barrels a day; people in Washington thought the disaster might boost support for the bill. Veterans Green Jobs was arranging conversations between veterans from swing states who believed in clean energy and staffers on

Capitol Hill. Michelle asked Desma to recruit other soldiers, too, so Desma called Roy and said, "Hey, you want to go to DC for the weekend?" Roy wanted to know how much that was going to cost. "Apparently it's all-expenses-paid, you just have to have business attire," Desma said. She helped Roy buy his first suit, and the guys at the armory taught him how to make a knot in his tie.

When they met with the young, middle-class staffers who worked for members of Congress, few of whom had volunteered, Desma stole the show. She told the staffers about driving the gun truck, about running ass, about what had happened when the bomb had gone off. It was the first time Michelle had heard her speak in detail about the IED. Desma made all the connections — how the supplies that she had been escorting were going to military bases to feed soldiers who were guarding an oil pipeline.

Now that Michelle lived in Colorado, it was rare for the three of them to have two days together, and the trip felt like a reunion. Desma had never been to Washington before, and they walked around sightseeing until their feet hurt. They saw the Lincoln Memorial and the Washington Monument and the White House. They were standing on a corner when a motorcade passed by. As the car slowed to make a turn, someone inside started to roll up a window. Before the mirrored glass obscured her view, Desma glanced inside and found herself looking at the familiar face of President Hamid Karzai.

"Look, there's Karzai," she told Roy.

"Who's that?" Roy asked.

"He's the current president of Afghanistan," Desma said.

"Really?" Roy asked skeptically.

"Yeah," Desma asserted. "He's a crook."

Karzai had come to speak with President Barack Obama about his plans to withdraw troops. Obama had already begun withdrawing troops from Iraq, and had announced that he intended to start pulling soldiers out of Afghanistan in the middle of the following year. Since they had left that country, Desma had heard a lot about corruption there. It had tarnished the once shiny sense of pride she had taken in being part of a military force that had helped bring about Afghanistan's first democratic election. A lot had happened since that woman with the black scarf had knelt down before her in the middle of Camp Phoenix and said thank you.

That evening they went out to a Japanese restaurant. Desma ordered a margarita and they gave her Patrón on ice; everybody else drank too much sake. They sang karaoke: Sir Mix-a-Lot's "Baby Got Back" and then "Nobody" by Sylvia. At some point they moved on to a pool hall, where at last call Desma ordered not one but two drinks. It was a mad scramble to catch the early flight home the next morning and at first Roy could not rouse Desma. He went for reinforcements. "Come help me get her dressed," Roy begged Debbie and Michelle. "What's everybody doing here?" Desma asked when they finally got her conscious. Debbie and Michelle were fast friends with Roy after that.

In the summer of 2010, Desma moved in to live with Roy. "Patient reports that since her last appointment she has started to try to 'let new people in my life,' " wrote Delia McGlocklin. At about the same time, the therapist informed Desma that she would be leaving the clinic at the VA. McGlocklin would be able to see Desma for only a few more months. "Started to process with patient the writer's transition out of clinic," noted McGlocklin. That fall, Paige and Alexis started over at new schools in Hagerstown, Indiana. Alexis began fifth grade and Paige began sixth grade. The problems Desma had been having with her daughters had not gone away; Alexis seemed perpetually angry and talked back a lot, while Paige grew quiet and started cutting herself. Desma covered Roy's refrigerator with notes to remind herself of the meetings she had with their teachers, but it was still a struggle to show up. She had never been that way before. Desma had always made certain to be the kind of mother who remembered commitments, because her own mother had not. The girls were disappointed in her and she was disappointed in herself.

Roy had no children of his own, and he met Desma's when they were half grown. They were not small, not adorable — he had missed all that. They were surly preteens going through what they would almost certainly look back on as a difficult period in their lives. Roy tried to muster the requisite patience but in some ways he was rigid. He fretted if Desma hung pictures in places where he would not have hung them; he asked Desma not to wash his clothes because he liked to fold his laundry in a certain fashion. The children were messy and they did not obey orders. He had to tell himself they were not part of a squad that was under his command. Put your dishes in the dishwasher, he said more gently. Don't speak to your mother like that. He was trying but there was friction.

Roy lived to the northeast of Camp Atterbury. Desma's commute to work was virtually the same as before, but the drive down to southern Indiana was more than twice as long. Her ex-husband started meeting her halfway so she didn't have to do all the driving. Nevertheless, that November Desma was pulled over for speeding yet again. This time the police officer said she was a "habitual offender" and threw her into the county jail for the weekend. Desma shrugged off the episode. When asked later if she had been driving too fast, she would reply, "That's what he said. I coulda gone faster." Michelle felt as though she were watching a statistic play out. "You know how veterans come home with dramatically increased risk behaviors?" she would ask. "Well, Desma was speeding to the point where they arrest you. She never had that behavior before."

Roy saw that Desma was spending $1,200 a month to fill the tank of the red Pacifica. In December 2010 he cosigned on a loan so that she could buy a blue Prius. Desma lined up a series of five stickers on the rear bumper of the new car, her own little joke about the last decade. The bumper stickers said AFGHANISTAN, SNAFU, WHISKEY TANGO FOXTROT, BOHICA, IRAQ. (Translated into civilian, that was, "Afghanistan, Situation Normal All Fucked Up, What the Fuck, Bend Over Here It Comes Again, Iraq.") Desma kept driving long distances, but she did slow down. She also discovered books on tape, and listened to *The Help* and Walter Isaacson's biography of Steve Jobs, which made the hours on the road less boring.

Even as Desma was pulling her personal life together, she fell out of favor at work. The people who had served with Desma in Iraq had known why she was angry, and had not judged her when her weapon had been taken away. As long as she worked alongside soldiers who had also deployed with the 139th, Desma had been understood. Her first NCO evaluations had been glowing. "Extraordinary initiative," a supervisor in the 139th had written back in May 2009, just a few months after Desma had become an NCO. "Dedicated hardworking individual who shows her responsibility. . . . Exacting approach to work ethic; pays attention to detail. . . . Possesses the leadership skills necessary to lead any company on the battlefield."

At the end of that year, however, Desma had been forced to transfer out of the 139th because it was a field artillery regiment and technically not open to female soldiers. She could be transferred into that regiment during a deployment when the soldiers in it were acting in a supportive role, such as providing convoy security, but she could not belong to it at home. After leaving the 139th, Desma had transferred into a unit she had never belonged to before that was part of the 638th Support Battalion. Her next evaluation, written in January 2010, had remained positive. A supervisor had written, "Constantly sought ways to learn, grow, and improve. . . . Projected confidence and authority. . . . Always a team player." But one year later there was a stark shift in how Desma was described. "Struggles with following up with tasks," wrote another supervisor from the 638th in

February 2011. "Lacks desire to improve overall physical fitness. . . . Needs to realize importance of tact when questioning orders."

Desma received the critical assessment shortly after getting crosswise with her company commander. Desma had wanted to attend a Warrior Leader Course — the first leadership course that noncommissioned officers were supposed to fulfill to qualify for promotions. She enrolled in a class that was being taught in Utah. But her supervisor told her that she could not go because of her profile, which stated that she could not carry a weapon, and canceled her flight. Desma asked that the company commander write a memo stating that she was the victim of a combat injury, so that she would be deemed eligible to attend the class. "All he had to do was write a one-page memorandum saying that my profile was the result of a combat injury and that I was fully capable of going to school," Desma would say later. "He would not do it." According to Desma, the commander expressed doubt about Desma's claim to have been injured. Injudiciously, Desma lashed out with fury in her voice, telling the commander that he had no idea what soldiers went through.

Her commander said he knew what it was like to be in a combat zone.

"I know what it's like to be in a combat

zone as well, sir," Desma told him. "I've been there."

"Well, how are you injured?" he wanted to know.

The commander did not appear to be aware that she had spent a year driving a gun truck at the front of a supply convoy or that she had hit an IED, according to Desma. Even after she described the bombing, he seemed unconvinced that she had suffered a real injury. Desma must have looked fine to him; perhaps he thought that because he could see no sign of her medical challenges, she was manufacturing everything. All over the country, soldiers with traumatic brain injury were running into similar problems. Within the medical community, it was widely known that damage to the frontal lobe could cause memory issues, irritability, poor impulse control, and increased risk-taking due to a compromised ability to regulate behavior. But the public, including many in the military, did not know that traumatic brain injury caused these issues. Soldiers with TBI often just looked like difficult people. Medical personnel were calling traumatic brain injury "the silent epidemic" because they were seeing so many people with TBI and because it was so hard for others to grasp the extent of their liabilities.

Desma hated working for that particular commander, but she could not find another job that would pay as well. She reenlisted with the National Guard for an additional six years — her new official end of service date fell in 2016 — so that she could keep her job. As time went by, her standing did not improve. "Life is easier in a combat zone," Desma declared at one point. All she meant was that in many ways, her life had been simpler at Q-West, when other people had done her laundry, fixed her meals, and planned her day. Her supervisors appeared to view the comment as a sign of instability, however, as someone added a note to her military file that said, "Process for fit for duty." If a commander considered a soldier unable to perform a job, for physical or mental reasons, the commander could ask the army's Medical Evaluation Board to determine whether the soldier was fit for duty. If the soldier was deemed unfit, the finding could result in involuntary retirement. Desma went to her next therapy appointment and said she believed she was being pushed out of the Guard. "Patient reports that since her last appointment she had discovered that she may be being medically-boarded from the service due to her PTSD," wrote McGlocklin.

The idea of being forced out unnerved Desma because she could only hold on to her well-paying job as long as she remained in the military. When she spoke to the company commander, he said he had no intention of forcing her out of the service. She did not fully trust him, however, and upon reflection she thought perhaps the best way out of the unhappy situation was to seek a medical retirement voluntarily. If she could not take leadership courses, and could not advance in her career, she might as well find another way to make a living, Desma figured. She spent several months amassing the documents she would need — she had to prove that she had done two tours of active duty, had been in an IED blast, had sustained traumatic brain injury, had PTSD, and could no longer perform capably as a soldier. If she could demonstrate all of the above, the medical board might allow her to retire early with a partial pension, perhaps 50 to 70 percent of her active duty salary — which would be $1,700 a month. Desma sent off her documents and waited. It would take more than a year to hear back, the Medical Evaluation Board told her.

The ten-year anniversary of the airplane hijackings that had started the two wars fell on September 11, 2011. All US combat troops had pulled out of Iraq by then, and the drawdown of US troops from Afghanistan had just begun. That fall, however, as the war in Afghanistan persisted, it surpassed Vietnam to become the longest war in US history. Michelle was thinking of returning to graduate school to become a physical therapist or an occupational therapist — she wanted to work with veterans who were returning with traumatic brain injury. She had just learned that she could use the GI Bill to defray part of the cost of the tuition. Meanwhile, Debbie had been speaking with Delia McGlocklin about how she might fill the void that retirement had created, and with the encouragement of her therapist Debbie had started studying welding at Ivy Tech, the tuition subsidized by her benefits. Everybody else in her welding classes wanted to work at one of Indiana's factories, but Debbie wanted to make sculptures. She completed most of her course work by the spring of 2012. To celebrate, Jeff took Debbie to Mexico for what was meant to be a second honeymoon, but while they were partying in Puerto Vallarta, Debbie got the news that her mother had been hospitalized for complications having to do with pneumonia and heart disease. Debbie wanted to cut the trip short. Everybody at home said her mother seemed to be improving, however, and urged her to stay in Mexico. Unexpectedly, Debbie's mother died several hours before Debbie's plane landed in Indianapolis. After years of caretaking, Debbie did not get the chance to say good-bye — anytime she left the country, it seemed, somebody important passed away.

As luck would have it, when this occurred,

Akbar Khan had just returned for another visit to the United States. Michelle, Desma, and Akbar knew that Debbie was going to have a terrible time forgiving herself for being on vacation when her mother died. Akbar was already planning to fly to Indiana; Michelle jumped on a plane and flew there, too. One week after Debbie's mother's funeral, they drove to Bloomington and picked up Debbie, then drove to Roy's house. By this point Desma owned three dogs: a fast German shepherd named Ginger, a tiny Chihuahua named Tori, and a roly-poly black Labrador mix named Sammy. Sammy had just given birth to a litter of ten, and the newborn puppies were crowded around their dam, all trying to nurse at the same time. When they woke the next morning, Desma discovered that one of the puppies had died in the night. Michelle and Akbar volunteered to bury the one dead puppy, and told Debbie her job was to get an eyedropper and feed the nine puppies that were still alive.

Michelle turned thirty years old in September 2012. After seven years together, she and Billy had recently ended their relationship. In the weeks that had followed, Michelle had turned fragile and weepy, and one night she drank too much and got a DUI. Now she was driving around Colorado with a Breathalyzer attached to her steering wheel. It seemed important to move on, however; Michelle was not getting any younger. That fall, she was out on a date with a man she had met recently when Akbar called her cell phone. She did not answer. He sent a text message. She did not write back. He sent another text demanding that she call. Then Desma sent a text saying Akbar was trying to reach her. Michelle wrote back: I'm having a sleepover tonight and he needs to back off. Desma replied: Got it!

When Michelle finally returned Akbar's calls, she learned that he had been trying to reach her because he had been shattered by witnessing a horrific attack. He had been at Bagram, standing with a group of colleagues, when an RPG had blown up several of the soldiers. Akbar had been covered in blood and gore. He could not eat, he could not sleep, he could not keep track of his keys or his phone. Doctors had prescribed psychotropic medication and he had to take the pills to calm down. Meat reminded him of what he had just seen, and he could put only fruit or vegetables into his mouth. He tried to quit his job at the prison, but Mission Essential Personnel said he had to finish out the remainder of his contract. Meanwhile, Akbar's wife had been diagnosed with cancer, and shortly after the RPG attack Akbar learned that she might need to seek treatment in Dubai. It would be very expensive. He decided to keep working at the prison.

That same fall, when Desma went to one of her regular drill weekends, she was instructed to participate in another mandatory health screening. Desma stood in line for hours, got fed up, and blew off the screening. She walked into a building and down a flight of stairs, and there he was, Josh Stonebraker. She had not seen Stoney since they had gone through demobilization. Four years had elapsed.

"Papa!" Desma cried.

Stoney said warmly, "Hey, Hooker!"

He wrapped her in a bear hug. They created their own little island, let other soldiers wash around them. Stoney wanted to know how she was doing. Desma told him they would not let her carry a weapon anymore, her career had stuttered to a halt, and she was seeking a medical retirement.

"I'm sorry," Stoney said.

"For what?" Desma asked.

"I'm sorry I led you to it," he said. "I was the one directing you in. I'm sorry."

"I was just trying to get a little closer," Desma said. "I wasn't trying to hit it."

"You didn't hit the box," said Stoney. "The box went PFFFFFFT, turned into confetti. I watched it vanish. You never hit the box."

"I know I didn't hit the box," said Desma.

"I gave you shit for it afterward," said Stoney, rueful.

"Because that's what we do, man," said Desma.

She went home thinking about that little scrap of conversation. Hearing that Stoney shared some piece of her yawning sense of being at fault — it meant that she was not alone. The conversation did not erase her sense of accountability, but it made her realize that she was not carrying that weight because she was female, or not as good as Stoney, or inadequate in some other fashion — all those things she had accused herself of when she had searched for the why of it. Why had she hit a bomb? Why had her truck gone nose up in the air? Why had she not been able to yell, "Missed me, motherfucker!"? She kept telling herself it was her fault. But if Stoney carried the same burden, then maybe they had just been in the wrong place at the wrong time.

In the two years since Desma and her daughters had moved to Hagerstown, the problems Desma had been having with Paige had escalated. One day, Paige had called 911 while Desma was out shopping. Paige said afterward that she had called the ambulance because her mouth had gone dry and her heart had started racing and she had felt dizzy. Desma had little sympathy, however, because she got a bill for $3,000. Why hadn't her daughter just picked up the phone and called her? Paige maintained that after she left school she went straight to the Boys' and Girls' Club and stayed there all afternoon, but the staff told Desma that her daughter vanished for long stretches. Paige also created an alter ego for herself on Facebook, a supposed friend named "Haiydan." On more than one occasion, "Haiydan" wrote emails to Desma asking if Paige could spend the weekend down in Spurgeon. Alexis stayed on the honor roll, but Paige was put on academic probation. Her seventh-grade report cards were littered with Ds and her eighth-grade report cards were not much better. Paige swung around like a weather vane that did not know which way to point; half of her still longed for the comfort of childish things, while the other half of her spun toward grown-up declarations of pain. At one point, she taped a sign to her bedroom door. It was a list of things she wanted to get:

1. Gauged ears
2. Lip piercing
3. Good grades
4. Abs!
5. Orbies!
6. Ceiling stars
7. Neon colored eyeliner

When Desma determined that Paige had been lying about remaining at the Boys' and Girls' Club, she took away her daughter's electronic devices. In response, Paige said that she found living with Desma to be intolerable, and demanded to live with her father. With a mixture of sadness and relief, Desma let her go — although a few months later, Paige asked to return to Hagerstown. Desma welcomed her back, but the trouble continued. They tried counseling, to no avail. "Those little people have been really hard to live with these past six months," Desma told Michelle in one of their phone calls.

In the end, though, it was Josh who broke her heart. He had graduated from high school at age eighteen in the spring of 2011. The following summer he had gotten arrested for possession of alcohol as a minor and spent one night in jail. That fall, Josh had asked if he could move in with Desma and Roy, saying he needed a new start. Desma had fixed up a bedroom for him and bought him a black 1998 Neon and gotten him a job working part-time at UPS. Josh had failed to show up regularly, however, and after a while he had been fired. Then Josh had moved back in with his surrogate father and started working at a plastics factory, but he lost that job after fighting with a colleague. Afterward he was arrested for possession of marijuana. He moved back in with Desma and Roy again. Desma never expected her son to be lazy, but Josh seemed to have a sense of entitlement, an idea that good things should simply come his way. He spoke of enrolling in community college but never filled out the forms. He spoke of finding another job but never did that, either. At night he had insomnia and during the day he seemed only half awake.

One day Roy came home to find his stereo missing and his tools gone. There was no sign of forced entry, and he suspected it was Josh. Desma did not want to believe that her son would steal from Roy, but she feared that maybe he had. Those tools meant the world to Roy and he was so angry that he asked Desma to give him back the key to his house. In the evening, she had to wait in the driveway until he got home before she could enter. Josh went to live with his surrogate father again, and Desma told him to straighten out or else he was going to wind up in jail. But Josh had acquired the wrong kind of friends and the wrong kind of habits. In February 2013, Josh was arrested for breaking and entering a home in Richmond, Indiana. The police said Josh had beaten up an elderly man and stolen prescription medication, cash, and credit cards. According to court documents, Josh faced charges of burglary, burglary resulting in bodily injury, armed robbery, battery, battery resulting in bodily injury, theft, and resisting law enforcement. He was put in jail to await trial. Desma went to see him but it was awful: they had to talk on a phone, separated by glass, and she was asked to leave after only fifteen minutes. His lawyer told Desma to expect the worst, and so she was not entirely surprised when Josh was sentenced to twenty years. Maybe he could get out in eight, for good behavior, the lawyer said.

Desma asked herself: Would this have happened anyway? Would Josh have turned to crime if she had stayed home? Or was he in jail because she had gone to Afghanistan and Iraq? Should she have skipped one of the deployments? Both? Then in the late spring of 2013, Desma learned that Paige had failed eighth grade. "Over the last five years since I have been home, I have tried very hard to show my kids how much they mean to me," Desma wrote shortly afterward in an email. "I just can't seem to help Paige with whatever she is going through." Repeating eighth grade would put Paige two years behind her peers, in the same classes as her younger sister, Alexis. Desma did not think she could handle Paige anymore. She considered sending Paige to a therapy-driven boarding school, but ultimately decided to allow Paige to live with her cousin Lesley instead. Desma recognized that she was prone to fly off the handle and that she and Paige had developed a conflict-ridden dynamic; she hoped that her cousin could do a better job parenting her daughter than she could herself. "I really wish raising kids was easier," Desma wrote wearily. Again, she asked herself: Would this have occurred if she had stayed home? Was Paige in trouble because of the two deployments?

At the point when Desma learned that Paige would not move on to high school with her peers, it had been almost five years since Desma had hit the IED. She had recently started seeing a new therapist, a psychologist named Dr. Heidi Knock. The psychologist did not believe it was important for Desma to recount painful memories of her own middle school years, and what had happened right before she was placed into foster care. She focused instead on modifying Desma's present-day behavior in small, concrete ways. Dr. Knock asked Desma to go to a movie and sit in the middle of the theater. "I wouldn't sit in the middle of the room before the Batman shooting, there's no way I want to sit there now," Desma objected. "There's no way to get out, in case of a fire, if you do that." Dr. Knock pointed out that this was an example of hypervigilance. Desma argued this was common sense. Dr. Knock gave her a different assignment. She told Desma to go to a restaurant and sit with her back to the door. Desma went to an IHOP and tried to do as instructed, but the sound of unseen people coming up behind her made her half crazed. Dr. Knock asked her to keep practicing until she could sit through the experience without discomfort. She also asked Desma not to switch lanes so often on the highway, and to adjust her speed to the flow of traffic. If she felt impatient, she was supposed to breathe deeply and try to relax.

In the summer of 2013, after they had been working together for several months, Dr. Knock asked Desma to make a series of voice recordings in which Desma would describe the explosion in detail. She was then supposed to listen to the recordings daily, and discuss them with the therapist every week. Rather than avoid her frightening memories, the psychologist wanted Desma to wring them dry of emotion. The bomb blast was accidentally stuck in the present moment, the therapist observed; every time Desma thought about it, it was as though the incident were happening all over again. Dr. Knock wanted to help her get it safely into the photo album of history, where it would carry less valence.

In the first recording, Desma recounted everything she could recall about that day. She was inside the truck, and had just taken off her helmet. She could see Jeff Stacey standing on the hood of the vehicle, yelling to get the fuck out. But she could not reach her angel wings.

"And what's going on with you, Desma?" asked Dr. Knock.

"I can't hardly move," Desma said.

"So you feel stuck in there?"

"Yeah, I'm stuck," Desma said, and laughed

her belly laugh.

"Why do you laugh?"

"Because it's funny."

Desma listed the reasons she could not get out of the truck.

"And what's going on with you emotionally?"

"Nothing. Just do what you gotta do. Get out of the truck."

Desma described how Charity undid her constraints. She described climbing up out of the truck's hatch, watching Charity pull security, and seeing the huge tour bus come barreling toward them.

"What's it like, standing outside your vehicle after just getting hit, with all these people passing by you?" asked Dr. Knock.

"It's another day in Iraq," Desma said.

The therapist told her to continue. Desma described walking over to the bomb-battered armored security vehicle she had been driving and inspecting the destruction.

"What's it like to see the vehicle so damaged, and know you were in it?"

"Awe-inspiring. Holy shit, check this shit out!" Desma said. "It works, the V bottom. It deflected the blast."

She described the deep grooves in the side of the metal-plated truck. Without the extra armor, she said, they might have all been killed.

"What's that like, when you realize that?"

asked Dr. Knock.

"Makes me hate people," Desma said. "Who sets bombs by the side of the road to get a random person?"

And that was the only emotion that Desma could name, at any point in the fifty minutes they spent discussing the incident: anger.

"You have a hard time identifying your emotions," Dr. Knock pointed out. "You're so numb, Desma. But your face is red, and your breathing is elevated."

Desma said once she saw a picture of a marine giving the finger to a map of Iraq. She said that was exactly how she felt. Fuck them all.

"Anger is part of it," the psychologist acknowledged. "I'm not asking you not to be angry. But what drives your anger? How about the fear of knowing that you almost died?"

Desma said the idea that she might have died that day had not occurred to her until later.

The therapist reminded Desma to listen to the recording every day. After a few weeks, they made a second recording. This time Desma's voice grew fragile. At a certain point she stopped, saying she could go no farther, and began crying silently, with her knees up to her chest and her arms wrapped around them, curled into a ball. She still could not name her emotions, but the therapist had brought her to a far more vulnerable place. Desma said she felt nauseated. She objected that what they were doing was bringing back her former difficulties — once again she found herself tailgating, speeding, and overreacting to trash. The psychologist assured her this was normal. Her symptoms would spike temporarily, but if they continued with the work, they might be able to liberate her from the incident forever. They pressed on. Dr. Knock asked Desma over and over again to say what she might have done differently, if she could rewind time and live that day over again, knowing only what she knew at the time. Desma said maybe she could have driven past the box. When Knock asked what would have happened in that case, Desma conceded that most likely other people would have gotten killed — someone else would have triggered the blast, and they might not have been protected by an uparmored ASV. And hadn't Desma been ordered to get closer? Yes, Desma acknowledged. She had been told to get closer.

"Who's really to blame?" the psychologist asked.

"The bastard who put it there," Desma said.

But her voice lacked conviction. She wanted to assign the blame to the bomber, but in her heart she still blamed herself. She had torn up an $800,000 truck, she had almost gotten everyone inside of it killed. That was where the bomb had thrown her, and where she still remained.

At the same time, the therapy had some mysterious effect. Alexis and Paige both started eighth grade in the fall of 2013 — Alexis living in Hagerstown, and Paige back in Petersburg. Meanwhile, Desma let her hair grow long and put on a few extra pounds. One day in the kitchen, she announced in front of Roy that being in a relationship had made her fat, and he rolled his eyes, as if to say, And this is *my* fault? Desma encouraged Alexis to join the band even though it cost a lot of money and then she went to every one of Alexis's performances. To make a few extra bucks, Desma started selling sex toys at house parties and at bars. ASK ME ABOUT A QUICKIE! said the button she put on before she set out her wares.

In October 2013, Republican legislators shut down the federal government, trying to defund Obamacare, putting Desma out of work. Desma borrowed Roy's chain saw and started cutting up dead trees on the property to keep herself busy. She amassed a pile of logs as tall as her chin; she called it "chain saw therapy." One day that month, when the sun was shining and the leaves had turned burnt orange and the air was crisp enough to make her face glow, she was out there with the saw buzzing, cutting a huge tree limb into pieces, chips of wood flying everywhere, when her cell phone vibrated. She took it out and saw she had a text message from Charity. "Happy Bomb Day," Charity wrote. The date was October 19, 2013 — it was the five-year anniversary of the silver box. She stood there, startled, holding the chain saw in her hand, with the smell of freshly cut wood in the air, looking at the words on her phone. Every other year, she had counted down the days anxiously, getting more tense as the date had approached. How weird, how wonderful to have forgotten to notice!

When Desma thought about that explosion, what it had done to her personally, and what the two yearlong deployments had done to Josh and to Paige and Alexis, she realized they would all be counting, possibly for the rest of their lives, what the last decade had cost. What it had cost the people who had gone away and the people they had left behind. Sometimes, when Debbie and Desma and Michelle got together, they tried to reckon the final tab. Economists were saying that the wars were going to cost upward of $3 trillion, when all was said and done, and more than six thousand service members had been killed during the two conflicts. Returning soldiers were also reporting record rates of alcoholism and depression, especially those who had endured multiple deployments. And soldiers who had served in the two wars had been committing suicide at the rate of roughly one per day.

Or sometimes they hurt other people. Michelle could hardly believe it when she heard that Aaron Schaffer had shot and killed a man during an argument. Schaff had a bunch of children, one of them was just a baby. She had such fond memories of him. He was the soldier to whom she had once passed along a bottle of Southern Comfort, after Pete had mailed it to her for Valentine's Day, back when they were in Afghanistan. When he confessed to the homicide, Schaffer told police that he had shot the man in the way he had been trained by the military; after the man had threatened to shoot him (although he would turn out to have been unarmed), Schaffer had simply emptied his gun, firing until he had no bullets left. That's what you were supposed to do, he said, to make sure you didn't get killed. He also told police that he had shot an unarmed civilian while he was deployed — most likely in Iraq, Michelle figured. Schaffer said he had thought the civilian was reaching for a weapon, only to learn afterward that the man had been reaching for a piece of paper on which someone had written the words "Thank you." Had that been chewing him up? Was that what had made him unravel? She wondered if he would spend the rest of his life in jail. And she had liked him so much, back when he had joined the armament team every once in a while to work alongside her and Debbie, fixing those broken AK-47s. She could have sworn he was one of the good guys.

What had been accomplished? What had been lost, and what had they gained? They asked themselves these things, Debbie racked with guilt because she had not hit a bomb, Desma because she had, and Michelle because she had had it easier than both of her friends. Even Debbie sometimes questioned what purpose the two wars had achieved, although she deliberately turned her thoughts to positive accomplishments. One night, while hanging out with Michelle, Debbie pointed out that when they had first arrived in Afghanistan, the hillsides around them had been dark, but by the time they were packing up to go, they had been able to see lights go on in the evening, little pinpricks of electricity, spread out like the stars above. That was something tangible, that was a real improvement. And Desma still wanted to believe that they had changed the situation of women in Afghanistan for the better.

Michelle, who felt quite certain that the entire decade had been one long, terrible mistake, simultaneously thought with gratitude of all she had learned and what abiding friends she had made. If given the choice, she would not take back the year she had spent in Afghanistan. When she filled out her applications for graduate school, she wrote that she wanted to become an occupational therapist because of the moment in an Afghan village when she had held a nine-month-old child in her arms as medics had treated the child's mother. That was when she had first glimpsed what she now understood to be her life's calling: to help fix what was broken in the world, to alleviate suffering. As long as she could be guaranteed the exact same deployment — one in which she never fired her weapon, never took a bullet, got to see Akbar Khan fly that kite, and got to comfort that child — she would do it all over again. Life would unfold this way sometimes, she came to understand, a curse and a blessing, both at once. It had been wrong, the war in which she had served, of that she had no doubt, but it had been a thing of immense proportions and she had been part of it and it had been hugely consequential to her personally. As wrong as they were, those days of sand and sun and bleached friendships and whistling rockets, they were sacred to her.

Even Desma could not bring herself to say that she wished she had never gone to Iraq. Because it had gotten under her skin, once she had been sent to a war zone, the desire to prove her worth in that arena. The desire to match someone like Stoney, to be just as capable, just as nonchalant. What Desma said, when she looked backward, was that she just wished she had gotten the same training as everybody else. She wished she had gotten to run lanes, she wished she had been taught to identify roadside bombs. When Michelle considered the tally of what Desma had paid, however, and added onto that what the two deployments had cost Desma's children, the total seemed simply too high. Earlier that year Obama's secretary of defense, Leon Panetta, had announced that the military was going to lift its ban on women serving in combat positions. The three women had divided in their response to the news. Debbie felt a pang of regret, for she had missed her chance — secretly, she had always wanted to be a sniper. Michelle opposed the change. "Women have more important things to do," she said. "They're mothers. Society should prioritize mothers over soldiers." Desma shrugged at the announcement. "Women are already in combat," she said. As far as she was concerned this was making official something that was already a reality. Maybe now, she thought, they'll train women right.

Yet they only made such reckonings every once in a while. Mostly, when they got together or they talked on the phone, they spoke of their hopes for the future. Michelle wanted a healthy relationship. In the years since Afghanistan, she had put on some weight, and after she and Billy split up, she started exercising more, then went on date after date, slogging through a series of prospects she found online. One day she told Debbie and Desma about a labor organizer who was smart and funny and believed all the same things she did. He owned a copy of *The Activist's Handbook,* too. He might be the one, she said. Debbie let her thick, dark hair grow long, which made her look younger, even as white strands started appearing in the midst of her brown curls. Her father's health began to fail, and she helped him move into a nursing home. Then Debbie started volunteering at the VFW as a bartender. She worked a double shift once a week, drinking alongside the World War II vets and the Vietnam vets, making their dark evenings brighter with her constant affirmation. Desma visited Josh in jail regularly and welcomed Paige back home again after Lesley said Paige was more than she could handle.

In the ten years that they had known one another, they had survived two wars, two deployments, two homecomings, a dozen men, one lesbian affair, a lot of heartache, and many questions about the well-being of the three children who had gotten caught up in the evolving question of what role women should play in war. Ten years of comings and goings, ten years of upheaval and disruption and having to start over. And through it all ran the constant guideline of their friendships, their attempts to love one another enough, the way life kept taking each of them apart and the way they kept turning toward one another to make themselves whole again. What Debbie would say, when she tried to describe what they had experienced, was that after so many years, she and Michelle and Desma had become so interlaced, they were even more like a family than their "real" families. What they shared was not war, exactly, it was their cumulative responses to the events of the past decade — the opposite of war, in a sense. That was what they had in common, what they shared, and what they valued. The ways in which they had stood through it all together.

ACKNOWLEDGMENTS

I am tremendously grateful to the MacDowell Colony for the chance to have several glorious, rainy weeks of uninterrupted work time in June 2013, when I was struggling to finish this book. I loved writing the end of this story in Kirby studio, to the sound of rain on the roof, with my manuscript spread out across the top of a grand piano, and everything I had left to do mapped out on a memory board. I did about three months' worth of work in three weeks' time and it was an extraordinary experience.

The three women featured in this book patiently sat through multiple years of lengthy interviews, showed me around Indiana, answered endless follow-up questions, and turned over personal correspondence, email, diaries, photographs, military records, medical records, and therapists' notes. Their primary motivation has always been to help other people understand what veterans live through, and to help other veterans know they are not alone in their struggle to put their lives back together after a deployment. A story like this can only be told when people are so brave and honest.

All gratitude to my agent, Denise Shannon, for believing in this idea at the outset. Thanks also to Denise for introducing me to Colin Harrison, the editor at Scribner with whom I have been so lucky to work with for the past ten years. Colin, thank you for encouraging me to pursue this idea, for talking to me about my progress every single month, for reading every chapter as the words were being written, and for telling me to keep going even though the early pages you saw were a mess. From start to finish, I felt I had a friend and guide who believed in this book even more than I did.

At the beginning of this project, I was inspired to talk with veterans about their experiences in Iraq and Afghanistan after hearing a speech given by Steve Price, a social worker with the Veterans Administration in Fort Collins, Colorado. Joe Rice, a former state legislator and an Iraq War veteran, spent many lunch hours discussing this subject with me, as did Pam Staves from the Veterans Administration. Linda Lidov introduced me to one of the three women who became the subjects of this book. Veterans Jordan Schupbach, Izzy Abbass, Eryth Zecher, Krystal Florquist, Jaclyn Scott, Jason Crow, and Garett

Reppenhagen all took time out of their busy lives to help me understand this subject better. Later I had the great joy of getting to know the wonderful Ed Wood, a fellow writer and a veteran of World War II, who read this manuscript in draft form and provided terrific feedback. Nate Matlock at Regis University's Center for the Study of War Experience generously advised me, read an early draft, and provided interns who helped with research. Interns Michael DeGregori, Stephanie Farnsworth-Edwards, Patrick Ross, and Steven Ferrel from Regis transcribed interviews, researched the history of the National Guard, summarized the history of women in the military, and compiled a timeline of the wars in Iraq and Afghanistan. I am deeply grateful to all of these individuals for their time, generosity, and patience.

While trying to comprehend the wars in Iraq and Afghanistan, I found the following books invaluable: *The Forever War,* by Dexter Filkins; *Yellow Birds,* by Kevin Powers; *Love My Rifle More than You,* by Kayla Williams; *Redeployment,* by Phil Klay; *You Know When the Men Are Gone,* by Siobhan Fallon; *In the Graveyard of Empires,* by Seth G. Jones; *Fiasco: The American Military Adventure in Iraq,* by Thomas E. Ricks; *Cobra II: The Inside Story of the Invasion and Occupation of Iraq,* by Michael R. Gordon and General Bernard E.

Trainor; *The Gun,* by C. J. Chivers; and *The Good Soldiers* and *Thank You for Your Service,* both by David Finkel. Many thanks also to David Finkel for his words of encouragement and his generous advice.

John Hickenlooper and I separated during the writing of this book but helped each other through that transition in all kinds of ways. John, thank you for believing in this project, for supporting me while I wrote this book, and for the way we have remained a family. Teddy Hickenlooper: Remember when our plane got stuck in New York and the iPad broke and we ran out of books to read and I told you this entire story from start to finish? You said, Mom, it's cool the way the stories you write are about really hard things but they still have happy endings. You are the greatest joy of my life, a wonderful travel companion, and a keen observer.

Toward the very end of this project, I developed a confusing shoulder problem and thought I might not be able to write anymore. Pete Emerson helped me heal. Thank you, Pete. My good friends Jane Cahn and Eleanor Wright listened to me talk for hours about this book; I am deeply grateful for their support. I am thankful for the prayers and the kindness of the amazing Deborah Fisch. My close friends Gillian Silverman, Mary Caulkins, Belle Zars, Liza Prall, Peter Heller, Lisa Jones, and Rebecca Rowe have been constant sources of love and strength, and each of them read early drafts or talked me through this journey. Pete, thank you especially for the moral support, for your astute comments on my first draft, and for putting all those exclamation points in the margin! To Vicki Novak, Jeremy Snyder, Lydia Ballantine, Rachel Ballantine, and Valerie Beck: Teddy and I are eternally grateful to you for being there for us in all kinds of ways. Last but not least, I want to thank my parents, Marie and Larry Thorpe, as well as my siblings, Lorna and Brian Thorpe, and their spouses, Marcus Sueiro and Donna Marie Thorpe. I feel incredibly lucky to be going through life with such a warm and loving clan.

ABOUT THE AUTHOR

Helen Thorpe is a writer who lives in Denver, Colorado. She has been a staff writer for the *New York Observer, The New Yorker,* and *Texas Monthly.* She has also written freelance stories for *The New York Times Magazine, Slate, Harper's Bazaar,* and other publications. *Soldier Girls* is her second book.

The employees of Thorndike Press hope you have enjoyed this Large Print book. All our Thorndike, Wheeler, and Kennebec Large Print titles are designed for easy reading, and all our books are made to last. Other Thorndike Press Large Print books are available at your library, through selected bookstores, or directly from us.

For information about titles, please call:
(800) 223-1244

or visit our Web site at:
http://gale.cengage.com/thorndike

To share your comments, please write:
Publisher
Thorndike Press
10 Water St., Suite 310
Waterville, ME 04901